The Lonely Mind of GOD

An Acosmist Answers the Primordial Existential Question by Solving the Omniscience Riddle

Sherman O'Brien

Phrase Bound Publications
Woodland, California, USA

Publisher's Cataloging-in-Publication Data

Names: O'Brien, Sherman, author.
Title: The lonely mind of god : an acosmist answers the primordial existential question by solving the omniscience riddle / Sherman O'Brien ; edited by Robert Craig.
Description: First edition. | Woodland, California : Phrase Bound Publications, 2021. | Includes index.
Identifiers: LCCN 2020921187 | ISBN 978-0-9963075-5-0 (paperback) ; ISBN 978-0-9963075-9-8 (hardcover) ; ISBN 978-0-9963075-6-7 (EPUB) ; ISBN 978-0-9963075-7-4 (Kindle) ; ISBN 978-0-9963075-8-1 (audiobook).
Subjects: LCSH: Metaphysics. | Ontology. | Hidden God. | Idealism. | Reality. | Illusion (Philosophy). | Epistemology. | BISAC: PHI013000 (PHILOSOPHY / Metaphysics) ; PHI004000 (PHILOSOPHY / Epistemology).
Classification: LCC BD111.O375 2021 | DDC 110–dc23.

First Edition 2021
3 5 7 9 10 8 6 4

Contents

Part I: Principles of Acosmism

Introduction

*In a black-and-white world, it is
subversive to think in color.*

Seeking the answer to one of the most profound questions ever considered must begin with an understanding of the concepts involved and what constitutes success in answering it.

The fundamental question that is the focus here concerns the concept of "existence," and more specifically, why what now exists manifested itself, if indeed it has; one may also ask why it could not have been otherwise or, indeed, why anything at all had to manifest. Early pre-Socratic Greek philosopher Parmenides of Elea (ca. 515–480 BCE) asks, "How could [what is] have come to be? [For i]f it somehow came [into being, then] it is Not[, n]or is it, if ever it is going to be in the future."[1] The frustration in Parmenides's statement with which he seems to be struggling is the idea of how existence *per se*, which he saw as eternal and unchanging, could somehow transition from a state of non-being to one accessible to human perception. Roman poet and philosopher Lucretius (ca. 99–55 BCE) is more assertive when he declares that "nothing can be made from nothing."[2] This notion of "*ex nihilo nihil fit*" (Latin for "out of nothing, nothing comes," often abbreviated *ex nihilo*[3]) seems to undermine the very concept of a physical creation. If nothing can be brought into a state of existence, then nothing could ever have been created; what appears to exist, then, either always existed or else is an illusion in that it does not or cannot actually exist.

German rationalist philosopher Gottfried Leibniz (1646–1716) phrases the question in a way that to some resonates better in the modern ear: "Why is there something rather than nothing?"[4] Inherent in this question, as phrased, is the idea that there could have been, as the starting point of the Universe, nothing. Moreover, a few even interpret in the phrasing of Leibniz's question that he considers it possible that nothing, or rather, nothingness, might affirmatively have been the default condition preceding existence and that some overtly creative action would thus be required to move the default circumstances from this void state to or toward the something which we now experience, via our senses and awareness.[5]

It falls to modern German philosopher of science Adolf Grünbaum (1923–2018) mockingly to dub "this query as the Primordial Existential Question and […] use the acronym PEQ to denote it."[6] His derision arises over how ill-conceived he considers the PEQ to be.[7] He arrives at this conclusion because, regardless of whether nothingness is even a possible state, he can find no empirical basis for it being the default state—a state that a creator must counteract by actually creating something contingent or unnecessary that would otherwise not exist on its own—and since cosmology depends on empirical evidence, the PEQ, in his view, is rendered meaningless. This conclusion, however, hinges on subtly equating contingency with existence, as in the assertion that if nothing contingent exists, then nothing exists; yet, whether or not anything contingent also exists, if something necessary and absolute exists, as most agree it does, it would certainly be a mistake then to infer that, oblivious to absolute necessity, somehow nothing existed.

Since the PEQ is not ill-conceived, we are altogether right both to pose it and to attempt to answer it. Such an answer may prove to be knowable and within the reach of human intellect, for if the human mind can frame the question, it should be able to conceive an answer, even though humans likely experience only a fraction of the totality of reality, no matter how it is defined. Using Leibniz's formulation of the PEQ that asks why there is something rather than nothing, clearly the answer to the question cannot be obvious or straightforward, because if it were, the great minds of history who have unsuccessfully applied themselves to resolve it would have already reached a consensus. Thus, if it turns out an answer to this most vexing of questions is available to us, we must prepare ourselves for such an answer to be unexpectedly peculiar. Furthermore, we must commit to using logic and the law of parsimony in order to choose among any available options and to ensure that the chosen answer is no more bizarre than is necessary to obtain a reasonable resolution.

To the extent the general pursuit of truth has any utility, the PEQ matters because it is vitally important to that pursuit in terms of providing the foundational premise for all truths. Admittedly, examining an artifact without regard to its origin is possible, although such an approach would be tantamount to archeological malpractice; likewise, one can live a life oblivious to any inkling of its purpose. But a PEQ answer provides perspective and thereby puts everything in context. It symbolizes the certitude on which other knowledge can be built. While human nature compels us to want a complete picture, knowledge is rarely comprehensive, making it necessary for us to use belief to fill in the gaps. If a belief is a placeholder for an eventual truth, though, it ought to be malleable in conforming to new facts as they become known; the natural human tendency, however, is to hold fast to long-held beliefs and vigorously to defend them, even in the face of overwhelming contrary evidence. This is what makes a PEQ answer relevant, because we are much more apt to fare better when we lay a foundation based on what is categorically true than when we unthinkingly adhere to beliefs that might later prove to be false.

To be acceptable, a PEQ answer must represent a state of affairs that is possible, complete, and plausible. An impossible answer is not only easy to dismiss; it should be dismissed as unworthy of consideration. An incomplete answer will likewise not furnish the groundwork on which sturdily to base other philosophical judgments. Finally, only a plausible answer can compete with other possible and complete answers, since we are apt to use plausibility as part of the criteria we use for evaluating such answers and selecting the most reasonable ones.

A study of existence should begin with the well-founded assertion that something exists. We must, however, examine precisely how we know this to be true. Moreover, we must be able to describe that something, or else we will be unable to draw any conclusions about it or relate it to other philo-sophical concepts. Philosophers, who are lovers of truth, and scientists, who dedicate themselves to testing it, use entirely different methods, yet presumably, they share a common goal of seeking to discover whatever truth or wisdom lies within the reach of humanity.

While we are naturally bound by the Lucretian ontological maxim that nothing can be made from nothing, which we can rephrase a bit more positively as "something cannot come from nothing," the vast, physical universe does appear to have had some kind of cosmological birth, and we conscious beings do experience it, not only through our senses but mentally, as a real-ity that consists of raw yet seemingly ordered information. This orderliness is constantly being given a tiny shuffle by quantum randomness. Even space and time, which form the very frame-work of our reality, have strange, illusory qualities; they at least seem to organize how we experience reality and remain firmly embedded in reality through a kind of operational consistency.

The physical universe as a whole, however, carries none of the attributes of existence, which is why we must distinguish existence (i.e., actuality or manifestation) on the one hand and reality (i.e., experience) on the other. Using this distinction, the fact that we merely experience the physical universe as presented to us means we must consider the possibility that the Universe is simply a compelling and consistent illusion. Existence is instead reserved for something else; here, one is compelled to choose a word and attach a label, strictly as a reference, for "that which exists" that is both the most apt (i.e., no better word) and the least apt (i.e., too many contrary connotations)—God. Such a position, namely, that only God actually exists while the physical universe is an illusion, is generally called "acosmism," and it challenges us to reconcile what we have distinguished.

As more formally defined, acosmism is "a theory that denies that the universe [...] has any existence apart from God."[8] This vague definition needs further refinement. Under this philosophical system, the physical universe is not thought of as being attached to God as a kind of *subsidiary* existence, like an ornament hung on a tree, as though it were an accessory merely dependent on the divine. Rather, acosmism affirmatively refutes altogether the existence of the cosmos, hence, the etymology of the word, from the Greek, the "*a-*"prefix meaning "without" and "*kosmos*" meaning "world." An acosmist does not contend that nothing exists but merely insists on a more precise definition of existence that precludes it from being applied to a reality based on the phenomenal world of human experience. The concept of containment, in particular, will figure prominently in the refined definition to come, as will the interrelationship between existence and reality.

In Western civilization, the first person whose ideas were later interpreted, perhaps misinterpreted, as acosmism is Dutch rationalist philosopher Benedict de (or Bento *née* Baruch) Spinoza (1632–77). His philosophical system equates Nature with God, and in so alleging, questions whether God could be personal or persuadable by prayer to perform miracles or as generally depicted in holy Scripture, thereby challenging the authority of his synagogue, which, in 1656, when he was twenty-three years old, excommunicates and curses him, forbidding others in their congregation from ever coming within several feet of him or reading any of his writings; his primary work, *Ethics*, published posthumously in 1677, is immediately censured by the States of Holland as a "profane, atheistic, and blasphemous book."[9] Denying the god of Judaism thus amounts to the "evil opinions" and "abominable heresies" stated in the execration and, notwithstanding that God is entirely the focus of his philosophy, leads to his being labeled, or mislabeled, an atheist by the religious authorities of his day.

Less than a century later, however, German rationalist philosopher Ernst Platner (1744–1818) affirms that "[Spinoza] does not actually deny the existence of the deity, but the existence of the world,"[10] rebutting the atheist moniker yet somehow failing to brand Spinoza's philosophical system with the label of acosmism. Litto-Austrian philosopher Salomon Maimon *née* Shlomo ben Joshua (1753–1800) writes some years later that "[i]t is inconceivable how any one [sic] can make out the Spinozistic system to be atheistic, since the two systems are diametrically opposed to one another[, because i]n the latter, the existence of *God* is denied, but in the former the existence of the *world*[, so] Spinoza's [system] ought therefore to be called the *acosmic* system."[11] Maimon is thus the first, in writing, to coin the word "acosmic," although later still, German idealist philosopher Georg Wilhelm Friedrich Hegel (1770–1831) succeeds for a while in popularizing the word "acosmism" in an effort to rescue Spinoza's reputation by clearly distinguishing his God-centered philosophy from the godless atheistic heresy of which he had been accused.[12]

When Spinoza opines that "the force, nevertheless, by which each thing perseveres in its existence follows from the eternal necessity of the nature of God,"[13] he belies that, unlike a true acosmist, he is indeed able to conceive of individual things existing somehow separately from, although still utterly dependent upon, God; in a previous part of the same book, though, he says that "things are nothing but modifications or modes of God's attributes, expressing those attributes in a certain and determinate way,"[14] thereby suggesting that any existence independent of God is inconceivable. He seems to want to adopt the view that Nature is an expression of God, but in speaking of things as they exist—and from his perspective, exist they do—he ultimately shies away from a truly acosmic outlook.

Spinoza is also regarded as "Pantheism['s ...] great prophet"[15] because his identification of Nature in its dynamic form with God supports a pantheistic position that everything is within the essential unity and totality of the divine, which is to say, each particular thing is both in and of God. He has also been associated with panentheism, which is the view that God permeates everything without being identical or interchangeable with it or with any reality we inhabit. So, the rationalist philosopher, condemned by his own community as an atheist, is acclaimed as the first (Western) acosmist, pantheist, panentheist, naturalist, and materialist. His complex logic of substances, attributes, and modes leave him open to strikingly diverse interpretations, which is why, in the end, Spinoza ought to be classified uniquely and simply as a Spinozist.

Millennia earlier, acosmism surfaces in non-Western, religious contexts, as well. The nondual Advaita Vedanta school of

Hinduism's concept of *maya* (Sanskrit for "illusion" or "appearances") expresses the motivating force underlying the acosmic view in concluding that "[t]hen it is all mere delusions (*maya*) / With which the God deceives [H]imself."[16] Similarly, Chabad-Lubavitch Hasidism's monotheistic monism version takes the approach of looking at the world from the transcendent perspective of an unchanging deity, where the materialism inherent in motion becomes a distraction or misdirection to consciousness, although the notion of a divine immanence that "*permeates* all the upper and lower worlds"[17] is more aligned with the vocabulary of panentheism than of pure acosmism. In trying to fit the square peg of acosmism into the round hole of religious faith, these efforts to form a theistic basis for acosmism tend to fail, as they are often aligned with the doctrines of a specific creed instead of allowing the dictates of reason and logic to reach the conclusions toward which a philosophically based acosmism is naturally inclined.

The most widely accepted PEQ answer emerges out of the theistic worldview, namely, that the physical universe is created *ex nihilo* by a supernatural being, as an act of divine will, presumably for the creator's own amusement. Aside from the way it clearly anthropomorphizes the issue, theism ultimately falters on the criterion of possibility, since, despite theists' insistence to the contrary, *ex nihilo* creation is not logically feasible. No one has ever observed, nor has an experiment ever been successfully devised to show, something coming wholly and independently into existence out of nothing. Indeed, large particle accelerators only "produce" short-lived, subatomic particles by momentarily converting the energy of particle collisions; these reactions do not create matter out of a vacuum, which, even at the quantum level, has a minimum stable amount of convertible-to-mass energy.[18] A phenomenon that has never been empirically observed has no believable, explanatory basis.

Another—or perhaps one should say, the other—worldview that offers a PEQ answer is diametrically opposed to theism: atheism, which ironically is based on the same, flawed premise of *ex nihilo* creation as theism. The difference is that the atheistic or scientific position is that the physical universe appeared out of nothing spontaneously in an act of self-creation. Such an impossible event is no more practicable as an explanation than theism.

The reasonable mind is forced to retreat at the prospect that these worldviews, theism and atheism, represent the only PEQ answers available to us. A choice between impossibilities is no choice at all. A logical intellect, confronted with these nonchoices, might be forced tongue-in-cheek to profess, "I think I'm an agnostic, but I'm not sure." There must be another approach that will yield a better, or at least more sensible, outcome.

Unsatisfactory answers naturally invite inquiry. Literally anyone is qualified to write about the subject at hand who, as a human being, has been rendered inquisitive by the shortcomings of the available answers to the essential question of existence. This book represents one person's response to this most vexing of all questions, based on the wisdom acquired during a lifetime of study and reflection; any failure to persuade would be redeemed if even a single reader is inspired to spend some of an all-too-brief life's precious moments contemplating a different, better, or more compelling answer than the one presented here.

By way of disclaimer, this book may *not* be for you, however, if you are inclined to believe in any of the Abrahamic religions, past life reincarnation, aura emanations, astral projection, anti-science bias, superstition, the Devil, demons, angels, faith healing, occultism, extrasensory perception, the law of attraction or manifestation, or the logic-defying claims of new-age spiritualism.

One must begin by returning to the concept of "that which exists," or God. For the acosmist, He is all that exists, so when He thinks, or rather, when a thought occurs or has occurred to Him, to speak of the "lonely mind" of God is altogether appropriate, for He has a mind and is starkly alone. This is close to the concept of *maya*, but the real insight is how the Omniscience Riddle, as formulated here, exploits what might be called a flaw in the very nature of knowledge, suggesting that it (knowledge) is necessarily self-limiting. The Riddle's solution helps indirectly to provide an answer to the PEQ by framing the issue as an epistemological dilemma rather than an ontological one. Using our experience as finite beings in acquiring knowledge, we will be compelled to recognize that, inescapably, there is something that an omniscient being does not know, and on that basis, thereby summons the world to appear.

As we shall see, this acosmic PEQ answer is possible, complete, and altogether plausible. Furthermore, it has clear implications for issues like faith, consciousness, death, free will, morality, and the purpose of life: Faith becomes unnecessary, once the object of belief is thoroughly known and understood by logic and reason; consciousness is the currency of existence and represents how we participate in the divine; death is the absence or cessation of life, and without a mechanism for memory or identity to persist, there can be no afterlife; a person behaves according to, and in perfect alignment with, his or her personal genetics, experiences, and education (in short, what goes into a personality), so we cannot truly be free agents operating within the predetermined machinery of the Universe; all morality is based on the Golden Rule, since only through feeling empathy toward others can we ultimately survive, both collectively and as individuals; and the purpose of life is, quite simply, to live, and we cannot help but fulfill this purpose, no matter how we think or behave—all are purely God's acosmic avatars.

Chapter 1:

Something Exists aka "Aseity," or The Axiom of Existence

*[A]ll the rest of existence is not life, but
merely time. —Seneca[1]*

Though he barely ever physically exceeded five feet (1.52 meters) in height,[2] German idealist philosopher Immanuel Kant (1724–1804) is nonetheless a towering figure in the history of philosophy because he not only produced unique philosophical ideas in an effort to mediate between or reconcile the rationalist and empiricist schools of thought, but he established a framework for how we must approach the nature of experience and its limitations. He is one of the first philosophers to recognize the ability of science to generate genuine knowledge based exclusively on empirical data, but he insists that experience itself is always subjective and must be put into a larger context and grounded in, or subjected to, reason.[3]

With Kant's admonition in mind, philosophers have long understood human knowledge to be founded on two distinct forms of cognition: experience and reason. Some might see education as an additional basis, but inasmuch as it consists merely of imparting the experiences of an authority, typically a trained professional in the field, it ultimately falls under the rubric of experience, albeit a shared one.

In what ways, though, are these two pillars on which all knowledge rests different? An important distinction between experience and reason is that the former is always acquired from an external source whereas the latter would be said to be known innately or internally and therefore in some sense, if true, necessarily true. This distinction is helpful in another way because, given that we often judge credibility on a source's reliability—e.g., "seeing is believing" or as a reputable and trustworthy expert reports—how something is known may be as significant a determinant of its truth as the fact itself. To introduce a little terminology, a "proposition that is knowable *a posteriori* is [said to be] known on the basis of experience,"[4] while knowledge that is innate or that precedes experience is referred to as *a priori*.[5]

So, the two pillars of human knowledge—experience and reason—are distinguishable based on their sources. Are both genuine, in the sense that they actually inform our understanding? Or are they merely theoretical? A pure empiricist denies that anything can originate exclusively in the mind and, by asserting that "reason alone does not give us any knowledge,"[6] effectively declares that our sensory experiences, or those of others who educate us, are the sole reliable foundation of apprehension. In contrast, a rationalist asserts that, for example, mathematics or the laws of the physical universe are true and thus represent knowledge, whether or not they manifest themselves in a way that can be experienced[7]; in this view, one can always and unerringly know *a priori*—i.e., apart from experience—that two plus two is four, even in a universe that somehow consisted of only three countable objects.

In any case, when we ask how we know what we think we know, we should begin with examining whether the source of the knowledge is empirical or intuitive and whether the asserted fact is genuinely known or merely assumed to be true. A special case that does not lend itself to such an approach is when a mental state is itself the experience, because then the intrinsic nature of the event is in conflict with it being an objective observation, and yet it is not entirely subjective, particularly when the mind involved is not one's own.

Nevertheless, how do we know that something, or anything, exists? "Whatever is referred to must exist," American analytic philosopher of mind and language John Searle (1932–) asserts, inviting us to call this "the axiom of existence."[8] Some identify a problem with Searle's axiom when applied to fiction,[9] noting that it loses its meaning when fictional characters or entities must be granted enough existence for reference purposes yet denied actual existence. The confusion arises because we refer to an idea or concept, which itself either corresponds to something that exists or is simply the product of someone's imagination. Kant observes that "[*b*]*eing* is obviously [or evidently] not a real predicate [but] merely the copula of a judgment,"[10] by which he means that existence is not some kind of pin-the-tail-on-the-donkey attribute that can be ascribed to something but rather a statement about something, namely, that it appears or manifests itself in the world.

Russo-American objectivist Ayn Rand (1905–82) states it directly, that "logic rests on the axiom that existence exists."[11] Many deride this version of the axiom as a mere tautology from which nothing can be learned[12]; tautologies are of no use in attaining the goal of philosophical inquiry, namely, inductively to elevate or perhaps transcend our individual experiences into a higher, generalized realm of universal truth. Moreover, a tautology is often presented as a conclusion, which obscures a clear understanding of what is being asserted. For example, what does it mean to exist? And to what does the initial (noun) word "existence" refer? Presumably, she is referring to an objective world, independent of any observer, but if so, how could she consider axiomatic or self-evident or indubitable that such a world must exist? And by "to exist," does she mean "is always there" whenever someone interacts with it? If so, then that world would hardly be independent objectively if it perpetually relies on subjective validation.

French rationalist philosopher René Descartes (1596–1650) makes the argument, *"Je pense, donc je suis"*[13] (French for "I think, therefore I am," later rendered in Latin as *"Cogito, ergo sum"*[14]), which serves as an effective *a posteriori* proof that something exists. Rather than asserting the occurrence of a thought as evidence that something exists, he rashly identifies his own mind as the source of the thought, even in the midst of doubting any idea not conceived clearly or distinctly. He challenges his own certainty by envisioning an evil genius (or demon)[15] actively deceiving him about the external world through a carefully crafted illusion, and yet, Descartes feels reassured that the all-perfect god he insists must exist—on account of the idea of a deity somehow being innately in his mind—could neither be this deceiver nor allow one to exist because "fraud and deception necessarily proceed from some defect."[16] It does not seem to have occurred to Descartes that the god he envisions could legitimately for some benign purpose have been deceiving itself.

In formulating a Theory of Mind,[17] philosophers consider it a sign of metaphysical maturity to accept that other minds than one's own exist.[18] This view is mistaken: Multiplicity of perspectives is not proof of a multiplicity of existences. Seeing a well-edited motion picture that uses various camera angles while orchestrated by a single director, for example, proves just the opposite, that multiple perspectives do not demonstrate multiple observers or their minds. There may be other grounds for rejecting solipsism, but the apparent existence of unique perspectives is not one of them. As a quote commonly misattributed to Roman Emperor Marcus Aurelius (121–80) states, "Everything we hear is not fact but opinion, and everything we see is not truth but perspective."[19]

When English utilitarian economist John Stuart Mill (1806–73) says, "I conclude that other human beings have feelings like me, because […] they have bodies like me […],"[20] he likely thinks it a refutation of solipsism: If other minds were an illusion, why would one imagine them with bodies, and in particular, with bodies like one's own? But physical bodies are the result of well-defined, evolutionary processes. In arranging organic chemicals for life generally, and allowing specifically for human life to develop, both body and mind, the concept of other humans includes that they have similar manifestations—i.e., that the apparent bodies or minds of others follow a genetic pattern. A solipsist could dismiss Mill's conclusion by contending that the idea of evolution, starting with mindless single-celled animals and ending with mind-endowed mammals, is part of the mechanics of the delusion, and in no way does the appearance of like-bodied characters make it any less of a delusion.

The self-refuting fallacy of the "stolen concept" pronounces that we cannot argue against our own existence, though, as doing so tacitly requires our existence as a premise.[21] Yet, we may be deceived as to who we really are. The *prima facie* observation that thought exists is a scientific *a posteriori* "brute" fact—it is how we tap Zen-like into the eternal.

But, really, the conclusion we can draw from the foregoing is that thought exists, which perforce leads us to conclude that a thinker must then exist. *Cogitandi requirit aliquis qui cogitat* (Latin for "Thinking requires someone who thinks"). Like a child, we must repeatedly ask "Why?" in order to elicit more about this "thinker," being careful not to assume, as Descartes does, that we are necessarily the author of our own thoughts. We should not rashly suppose, as Mill does, that the appearance of others or their perspectives necessarily means more than one "thinker." Furthermore, we must not fail to realize that thought may be no more than a symptom and, as such, should not necessarily be equated with or causally connected to its apparent source.

In addition to being an *a posteriori* "brute" fact, existence is also an *a priori* truth. An idea that cannot be expressed without contradiction is a false idea: "Nothing exists" is an oxymoron and therefore false; hence, something exists.

Is truth what we innately sense to be true, though, or is it instead a conclusion at which we arrive when we apply some oft-used, reliable truth-seeking method? While our instincts may lead us astray, we may also find ourselves rejecting a conclusion as absurd, regardless of how proven the method is that led to it. In the end, we can only consider as true what we are willing and prepared personally to accept, consensus and objectivity be damned.

Our inability to use language accurately to describe concepts is its most obvious limitation. Poetry demonstrates the power of language to evoke thoughts and feelings beyond its literal meaning. Saying "something exists" is unavoidably inaccurate. Some interpret it to allow for a diversity, because they can imagine exchanging one referent "something" for another; for others, it declares instead a singularity out of which no multiplicity can be drawn. Existence cannot be sliced and diced: once something is said to exist, it cannot impart its existence to something else, since such an action would invite us to treat existence improperly as an attribute, or worse, a vessel. Pure existence, however, simply is. While the physical universe is undeniably a manifestation of such an existence, we only contend that it possesses a reality independent of its underlying foundation through the bias of our sensory perceptions. One cannot be sure, but one hopes that the sentence "something exists" evokes in the hearer or reader an idea that transcends its literal and admittedly imprecise or contentious meaning.

Chapter 2:

The Necessary Properties of What Exists

It is better to fail in originality than to
succeed in imitation. —Herman Melville[1]

Having established that something exists, now comes the task of trying to describe it. One must ask whether it, whatever it may be, even possesses properties we are capable of describing.

One guidepost that might assist in this is Leibniz's "Principle of Sufficient Reason" (PSR), which states that every event or condition is logically traceable to a prior cause or reason for being.[2] Reasoning might be likened to a solvent, assaying the truth, under the premise that what is true must accordingly conform to our notion of common sense. The universal validity or usefulness of the Principle is controversial and has long been debated by philosophers.[3] It turns out to be more of an appeal to psychology than metaphysics.[4] If the PSR were always true, as a law of the Universe would be, it fails to guarantee that the cause or reason be known or even knowable; its real effect would be simply to banish any arbitrariness in the way events occur. Applied to reality, the PSR seems to suggest that existence depends on the apperception of a reasoning mind, because in the absence of a witness, what exists would somehow go unnoticed.

Moreover, humans tend to impose causality on stochastic events, especially at reality's most fundamental level, the quantum level, which is driven instead by probability (or regression toward a mean) and where quantum entanglement can misorder the very idea of causality.[5] The PSR may apply, if it does at all, only to the world as currently constituted. Of the world prior to, or as part of, its creation, however, the very concept of causality, and hence, the rationale for the PSR, may lose its meaning altogether.

Spinoza understands that what exists ("all that exists") must be infinite, because, to be finite, it would have to be limited, restricted, or circumscribed by something else, which is impossible, since it is all that exists.[6] By infinite, one means that which cannot be exceeded. Moreover, he reasons that what is infinite cannot be divided, since the parts that result from such a division could neither be infinite, since an infinite part would rival the whole, nor could the parts all be finite, since then the act of dividing would have thereby annihilated the infinitude of the whole.[7]

Spinoza's insight here is actually more about composition or extent than divisibility or cardinality. On account of parts composing a whole, he can conclude that what is infinite must indeed be indivisible, because no one part (of potentially multiple parts) could ever equal the whole, which would be the case if any part were itself infinite, and in addition, there could never be enough finite parts to make the whole infinite.

Proto-empiricist Greek philosopher Aristotle (384–322 BCE) mentions an earlier fellow Greek philosopher, Zeno of Elea (ca. 490–430 BCE), and his paradox about how fast-running Achilles can never overtake a slow tortoise in a race because whenever Achilles reaches a point the tortoise has been, the tortoise will have then advanced to a further position to maintain its lead.[8] Zeno's contention about the impossibility of motion is based on the idea that a finite object supposedly cannot traverse an infinite number of interstitial gaps or intervals into which one can conceivably divide any given segment of space. Although the resolution ultimately involves making a distinction between dimensionless points and objects of extension, the paradox illustrates that just because a finite space can be bisected an infinite number of times does not make it indivisible or incapable of being traversed. In contrast, attempting to dismantle what is infinite is, again, about composition rather than divisibility. Using numbers as representations simply reintroduces the paradox.

Furthermore, such logic about infinitude does not apply to sets. For example, the set of all numbers is clearly infinite, yet the proper subset of rational numbers is also infinite.[9] A set is deemed "infinite" if it can be put into "a one-to-one correspondence with a proper subset of itself."[10] Division of an infinite substance is hypothetically arbitrary and not according to a definitional rule, such as how set membership is established for rational numbers. An infinite "part" of an infinite whole would be a separate entity rather than a divisional product,[11] and unlike sets, which maintain their relative cardinality when transformed, the futility of having two infinite entities renders such a division impossible.

Infinity, however, is more than being merely limitless or without bound. It represents an immensity so large as to be beyond definition or comprehension. We reach what might be called the border of human understanding and then contemplate something further. In a puzzling way, what is infinite cannot materially manifest itself through the mode of extension because to do so would shatter the reality required to experience it. The substance to which Spinoza refers is thus infinite in nonextensible ways and along dimensions that transcend the phenomenal world.

In his *Metaphysics*, Aristotle introduces the aptly named "Law of Non-contradiction" (LNC) by stating that "opposite assertions cannot [both] be true at the same time."[12] His attempts to prove the Law appear feeble, if not outright circular. To deny the truth of the LNC is to accept an absurdity, and so we are instead compelled to accept the Law as stated. One Christian apologist concludes that a person "may as well try to describe a one-ended stick as to deny the law of noncontradiction."[13] The problem is that the LNC reads more like an axiom than an incontrovertible law. Rather than simply assert that the LNC is manifestly true, perhaps a better approach would be to incorporate it in our definition of objective truth: We can only regard a proposition as objectively true if it conforms to the LNC. Non-conforming statements are thus either false or else their truth value cannot be determined. So long as our goal is to ascertain the truth, we use the LNC like a candle in the dark to navigate among competing theories of reality.

Some wonder how a single substance with no discernible features—infinite and indivisible, though it may be—would be indistinguishable from nothingness, even going so far as to call this singular state incoherent,[14] perhaps even unknowable; but, it is not necessarily featureless, in that what exists may have a mind, not in the sense of a human brain, yet something akin to self-awareness or a consciousness. After all, thought must have a thinker, and that is a feature which nothingness could never possess. The nature of such a mind would noumenally transcend all phenomenal understanding and experience.

In the pursuit of truth, the Scientific Method is a bottom-up approach: It consists of gathering observable facts to develop an hypothesis that both explains those facts and has some predictive power that can be tested; scientific theories never transcend the facts on which they are based or can feasibly forecast. In contrast, Philosophy is a top-down endeavor: General principles are identified that lead to logical conclusions about the mundane; the danger in such an approach is that it may "miss" reality entirely, because the principles it begins with might never manifest factually. While perspectives may vary, truth itself should remain unwaveringly consistent and the same for everyone, even if scientists, focused on empirical observation, and philosophers, driven by reason, approach it via diverse methods.

Science concerns how or by what laws processes occur, whereas philosophers ask why they occur. Moreover, because science can take us only so far in terms of the phenomena that manifest themselves in our experiences, we must rely on reason to take us the "rest of the way." A useful analogy is that of a movie theater: Those who focus on the mechanics of the film projector—such as the lighting, electricity, the reel sprocket, the twenty-four frames-per-second rate, etc.—are scientists, while those who concentrate on what the film being shown is about—such as its content, whether the images are symbolic or real, how the cast and settings were directed, etc.—are philosophers. The analogy suggests that, given the varying focuses in approach, some truths may indeed be beyond science, not because science falls short but rather what its aims concede.

Philosophy's reliance on reason, though, is not the so-called "god of the gaps" argument[15] in which science's current inability to explain a phenomenon is fallaciously taken as proof of a nonscientific explanation, typically a theological alternative. (It is "so-called" because it is more of an objection to unscientific claims than itself an argument.) Also, the emphasis is on the word "current," exposing the view that rests on the principle that science will eventually explain everything and that anything science cannot "currently" explain is either false or involves something that does not exist. This view is what American naturalist philosopher Alex Rosenberg (1946–) terms "scientism," namely, that "science is the only [reliable] path to the truth."[16]

With its ever-expanding ability to explain initially mysterious phenomena, science has been almost unerringly successful over the last four hundred years. To the extent we benefit from the technology it produces, both as consumers and technical workers, all humans participate at some level in the often-revolutionary progress of science and its triumph over ignorance and superstition.

Nonetheless, examples of unscientific claims that science cannot now, but may eventually be able to, explain still abound. For instance, about 90 percent of humans are right-handed, despite there being no biological or genetic basis for such a preference.[17] Fully 95 percent of the Universe is thought to consist of dark matter and dark energy,[18] both of which are undetectable by any scientific (or nonscientific, for that matter) instrumentation presently available; since dark matter would be 80 percent of all mass, while dark energy would be 70 percent of all the content of the Universe,[19] the hope is that someday scientists will be working with and basing their theories on more than the measly 5 percent that comprises the detectable universe we presently know. Surprisingly, the temperature of our sun's corona is actually higher than the surface[20] above which it hovers like an aura; no known astronomical phenomenon explains this counterintuitive situation. As for a fundamental aspect of reality, despite the symmetry of almost every physical phenomenon, the "Arrow of Time" always only moves in one direction: forward[21]; despite some speculation about time flow being related to thermodynamic entropy,[22] why, out of all dimensions, time is the exception to a natural symmetry remains a mystery to science. In the Standard Model of physics, there should be an equal amount of antimatter in the Universe as matter, and yet mysteriously, all that scientists have detected is an overabundance of matter[23]; the nature and whereabouts of the missing antimatter remains an unanswered question and a gaping hole in our understanding of the fundamental character of physical existence. As a final example, because the post-Big Bang inflation expanded space faster than the speed of light, the visible light from one of the Universe's edges, over forty billion light-years away, might still not have reached us,[24] so the size of the Universe—possibly (although not logically) infinite—is ultimately unknown; moreover, the rate at which the Universe is expanding continues to accelerate,[25] at what some have called its own "escape velocity,"[26] meaning that eventually, when, at its heat death, the expansion reaches the speed of light (i.e., the limit on the rate of the transfer of information), the exogalactic universe and its edges—what might be called the bounds of being—will cease forever to be visible to us. The prospect of never being able to detect, measure, or explain these wildly elusive phenomena ought at least to dim some of the optimism of the advocates of scientism.

The unavoidable consequence of scientism is the conclusion that the Universe consists exclusively of elementary fundamental subatomic particles like fermions and bosons, moving about aimlessly and without any discernible purpose. To imbue a pattern or trend onto random events is logically erroneous, while it is likewise a blunder to deny intendment where it is present simply to support a view that cannot be proven scientifically and that is based entirely on the axiomatic premise that the Universe is purely phenomenal. While excising purpose from the World, the advocates of scientism ostensibly impose the requirement that the Universe be thoroughly logical and consistent, which it may be operationally, yet it may also otherwise be altogether scientifically inexplicable. The greatest weakness of scientism is its failure to acknowledge the unfathomable. As English sociologist and naturalist Sir Herbert Spencer (1820–1903) concludes, the "most certain of all facts [is] that the Power which the Universe manifests to us is utterly inscrutable."[27]

The rejection of scientism should not be taken as embracing an anti-science agenda, because, of course, the limits of reason attenuate its own reach, as well. Logic cannot explain randomness or, generally, exceptions to the rules (i.e., anomalies). Are science's laws so generalized as to make anomalies inevitable? Does the establishment of a rule already contain its own exceptions as a necessity? Should the goal of science be to minimize exceptions, thereby making the rules more general? Or should it be to make specific rules while conceding that anomalies are unavoidable? This boundary of logic ensures there will likely always be specific questions that science cannot adequately answer, even as it addresses more general concepts.

Belief directly confronts this inexplicable realm and is often deliberately beyond science in that even the purported phenomenon itself (e.g., an afterlife) is dubitable and perhaps unobserved or undetectable. In something akin to a defense mechanism, science has established criteria for claims about observable facts: The phenomenon must be measurable; the observations, as well as conclusions about them, must be true everywhere, always, and for everyone; an effort must be made, through blind testing, to minimize both outcome error and any preexisting bias or prejudgment; the parameters and goals of experimentation must be stated in advance to avoid cherry-picking or data mining; the hypothesis being tested must be falsifiable (and not, in fact, falsified); and the conditions and results of testing must be independently reproducible (i.e., possible to replicate).[28]

A problem with this framework is that "historical truths are by nature non-repeatable."[29] If the physical universe is viewed as the laboratory, then what is being tested by science can only be those principles that collectively govern unique events, not what makes those events unique, for that is beyond science. If "empirical science leads only to more empirical science,"[30] then truth may indeed lie "*outside* the visible universe,"[31] out of the reach of the probing instruments of science but still within the purview of human reason.

Kant makes the philosophical distinction between observable facts (what he calls "phenomena"), which are only apparently true, and transcendent truths (or "noumena"), which are truly true. In this view, human knowledge is cabined by what is perceptibly accessible to us. We know the world of appearances by the qualities of objects we encounter, yet the true nature of these "things-in-themselves"[32] remains forever inaccessible and unknowable, including whether they even exist at all. In addition to asserting that an underlying noumenal world exists, Kant may be suggesting that this unreachable world nonetheless has a perceptible "face" which we experience as phenomena. Through the characteristic of being unknowable, anything is possible in the noumenal world, although some consider that the very concept of "possibility" only makes sense in the world of phenomena.[33]

The philosophical questions that address the noumenal world are different in kind than the scientific ones about the phenomenal world. Kant makes a further distinction that our intuitions evoked by our senses are not the same as the purely mental concepts that form our ideas, which are independent of, if not entirely uncorrelated with, reality, as Kant defines it.[34]

In describing reality, Kant refers to the categories of thought he identifies, which he says "cannot be circumvented to get at a mind-independent world [but] are necessary for experience of spatio-temporal objects."[35] Spanning all conceivable classes of concepts—quantity (one/many/all), quality (real/unreal/limited), relation (property/cause/reciprocity), and modality (possibility/existence/necessity)—the categories prepare the mind for, and thereby make possible, experience; they do so by rendering inaccessible (i.e., deceiving the mind about) the supersensible realm, which cannot be directly experienced.

In portraying the mind's structure for making experience possible, Kant distinguishes between truths that are analytic (self-evidently and necessarily true) as opposed to synthetic (contingently or only accidentally true).[36] He also differentiates truths according to the ancient distinction between what is known "*a priori*" and "*a posteriori*," the former exemplified by mathematics, while the latter, almost by definition, represents science. The resulting two-by-two matrix allows for a narrowed analysis: Although all analytic statements are known *a priori* and never *a posteriori*, and all synthetic *a posteriori* statements are at least theoretically discoverable scientifically, synthetic *a priori* statements or judgments are contingently yet inevitably true independently of experience.

Kant says the categories—as well as space and time—are not mere figments of the imagination, despite the mind of the knower making the *a priori* contribution to experiencing them, because science allows us to know objects in precisely the way they appear to us.[37] We are incapable of experiencing objects that are not in space and time, even though space and time themselves cannot be perceived directly. He blames this incapacity on the fact that we neither have nor are a purely intuitive consciousness, an essence or quality Kant reserves exclusively for God, and yet, he insists he must presuppose something permanent outside of himself—from which he is able to distinguish himself—so that he can be aware of his own existence.[38] Such a conclusion sidesteps the situation in which a solitary entity might deceive itself by thinking a separate existence is even possible. Kant's "transcendental enquiry" is not, and never was, about worldly knowledge (science), after all, but transcendently about knowledge itself (epistemology).

Science would counter Kant's view by claiming that space and time are not imaginary, simply because they form the bases for an observer to experience objects situated within the space-time continuum. They might be imaginary, however, if what truly exists is wholly independent of the spatio-temporal framework that our consciousness imposes onto the world to make the process of experiencing it achievable.

That subset of reason that sits altogether apart from perception is what Kant defines as "pure" reason, and his critique of it centers on the concern that reason alone cannot tell us anything about things-in-themselves.[39] He nonetheless grants that, while all learning is empirical, we can infer necessary and universal truths from our experiences.[40] Proponents of the logical positivism movement have gone further by asserting that empirical proof is the only possible basis for meaning[41]; the problem with this assertion is that it cannot itself be empirically proven. The truths of mathematics, which are pedagogically held out as examples of synthetic *a priori* propositions, are entirely conceptual rather than empirical, even if they are conceived so as to have empirical application in the same manner that language represents rather than embodies the truths to which it refers.

Kant claims that *a priori* knowledge is merely a precondition of experience and cannot be used to extrapolate the existence of a noumenal being outside the phenomenal world of representational appearances.[42] While he concurs with the rationalists that the mind is not a "blank slate" at birth, he asserts that the existence of a mind-independent world cannot be based on pure, *a priori* knowledge, since it would no longer be subject to the conditions of experience and would lead to conceptual contradictions. Such contradictions Kant labels "antinomies," which involve creation, composition, causation, and contingency.[43] For example, the thesis that the space-time continuum has a boundary is supported by the argument that, were it limitless, each point on the continuum would be the conclusion of a never-ending or infinite series, which is impossible; likewise, the antithesis or contrary thesis that the space-time continuum is indeed limitless can be demonstrated because, were it finite, there would conceivably be a point outside the all-encompassing continuum, which is also impossible. If the space-time continuum is neither finite nor infinite, then one must conclude that it is a contradiction or paradox. Of course, the way that English cosmologist Stephen Hawking (1942–2018) explains the Big Bang Theory[44], modern cosmological thinking embraces the continuum's finitude by accepting that space and time physically came into being, relegating any noncontinuum point to a status as imaginary as the mathematical square root of a negative number, useful as a concept but not correlated with any phenomenon found in reality.

Eschewing a mind-independent world based on *a priori* knowledge, Kant concludes that no metaphysics can be based strictly on pure reason, that is, unconnected to experience.[45] The mind, he argues, actively participates in establishing the contours of experience and operates exclusively in the empirical dimensions of space and time.[46] As a result, knowledge seems to be constrained to the realms of mathematics and the sciences of the natural or empirical world; as such, knowledge cannot be extended to the supersensible realm of speculative metaphysics. Kant is cautious to warn that relying on pure reason can mistakenly lead us into denying the very existence of things-in-themselves, which he considers vital to reality.[47]

Moreover, when taken out of context, observable facts can be misleading. Imagine attending a magic show. You invite a Nobel Prize–winning physicist to accompany you. At the show, the two of you watch rapturously as the magician appears to levitate a volunteer from the audience several feet in the air; the conjurer passes steel hoops around the floating individual to demonstrate that no strings or harness lines are being used for suspension. Your physicist companion is certain that what the two of you are witnessing is an illusion, and perhaps even the magician admits a trick is being performed, but merely knowing so fails in any way to break the deception. Like impressionable children rapt in awe, you are "locked in" and, in the absence of knowing the precise mechanics of the trick, if the magician ever deigned to reveal them, you simply cannot escape the ruse.

An observer might mistakenly conclude that humans had mastered the power of levitation, which demonstrates that observable facts, taken out of context, can be utterly misleading. The scientific approach of starting with observable facts must acknowledge the necessity to first put such facts into context before they can be used to extrapolate to a higher truth. If the phenomena we observe are inherently indirect and subjective, we cannot then use our observations of the illusion itself to gain an external perspective. Or, using Kant's terminology, we must realize that we cannot use our observations of the "phenomenal" illusion somehow to gain a "noumenal" perspective of the context in which the trickery is occurring. As Austro-American mathematician Kurt Gödel (1906–78) proves, at least mathematically, any axiom-based system is necessarily either incomplete or inconsistent. We cannot extrapolate from our involvement in delusional phenomenon to the noumenal reality of the things-in-themselves.

As to the origin, theism posits an eternal deity suddenly creating a physical universe, while atheism is content with the presumption that the physical universe came into existence spontaneously in an act of self-creation. Both of these views attempt to establish a causal chain in which the Universe as we find it is an ultimate effect and that has an initiating event, arising from an uncaused or self-caused source. Conceiving of existence as being somehow brought forth out of nonexistence belies a misunderstanding of what the nature of being truly is: We can instead imagine an entity that is neither created nor self-created but rather uncreated or simply existing. This then is the concept of "aseity" (Latin for "of oneself"),[48] which can be defined as an entity that exists independently of, or autonomously from, all space, time, or any possible causal chain. Basically, it just exists.[49]

Some attack the concept of aseity by claiming its definition is circular.[50] For them, the word is as much a tautology as the objectivist phrase "existence exists." What saves aseity from circularity is that it is merely foundational. It refers to existence itself, and if anything exists, which we know to be true as purely a brute fact, then "that which exists" cannot logically be denied to exist. Ergo, the principle of aseity establishes that, since nothingness cannot obtain or prevail, something necessarily exists.

What word, though, can we, or ought we to, attach to this something, to "that which exists?" Perhaps the acronym TWE, representing the initial letter in each word of the phrase in English, would suffice. While one could justifiably invent a contrived, never-before-seen word, doing so obviates the purpose of words, and language generally, which is effectively to communicate; therein lies the problem with coining new terms, because if a made-up word obstructs the conveyance of the concept that the word represents, then it has utterly failed. Consequently, we must choose an existing word, with the acknowledgement that it may not be entirely apt, thereby detracting from its true meaning, and, in some ways, it may even be the worst and most inapt, fraught with self-conflicting and contradictory connotations, like a symbolic train locomotive, pulling railcars weighed down with intellectual baggage and unsuitable meaning. Yet, overall, the word that comes closest to epitomizing the phrase "that which exists" happens to be an utterance that is universally understood across all human societies and cultures. The one word is: "God." (Although this word is strictly gender-neutral, by convention and for the sake of convenience, it will hereafter be used as though it were masculine.) When God is taken as "that which exists," His existence is undeniable and no longer subject to debate; a definition removes all the frustrating ambiguity and divisiveness.

But God's aseity does not serve to reintroduce theism's role for Him as creator, because, by necessarily existing outside all space, all time, and whatever causal chain may or may not have led to the physical universe we now experience, He can have no existential connection to it. In fact, to the extent He is "that which exists," or existence itself, He is all that exists; there can be nothing else. While it will become clear that the Universe is a product of the "mind" of God, He is alone, and thus His mind may symbolically be described as lonely. Aseity compels it.

As one website so eloquently states, "God is not [...] a being among beings, but Being [...] itself."[51] No matter how this well-defined statement succeeds in capturing the essence of aseity, some critics of the so-called Doctrine of Divine Simplicity (DDS) insist that equating God with what would normally be considered one of His "properties" denies Him both the personhood their religion requires and the status of having all other truths dependent on Him.[52] These criticisms fail to acknowledge the acosmic truth that nothing except God actually exists, so no nondivine entity's supposed or imagined being could ever somehow bootstrap itself into making an inequitable attribute out of God's unshared existence.

Somewhat at odds with the concept of aseity is the possibility of a creative force[53] rather than an existing entity being involved in the initial conjuring of a universe. When Spinoza asserts that all things and events in the Universe are in—albeit not necessarily solely within—the infinite mind of God,[54] whose existence he considers to be ethically or axiologically necessary, he is speaking of an energy or power, even if a purely immanent one, that is capable of constructive feats. Similarly, Teuto-American optimalist philosopher Nicholas Rescher (1928–) envisions a neo-Platonistic, value-based, creative vitality or dynamism that he calls "axiogenesis"—quite apart from, although not inconsistent with, any theistic entity—that mysteriously navigates the contours of complexity to ensure intelligence emerges without overwhelming it.[55] Unfortunately, axiogenesis suffers from the same logical irregularity as does theism or atheism, namely, by claiming that physical creation of a universe out of nothing is possible, which, moreover, can never be as simple as an immanent aseity.

The pessimists lament that we cannot "[d]educe the existence of something without using any existential premises;"[56] were that true, the PEQ would be unanswerable. Optimistically, though, we can indeed conclude absolutely that something exists because, in delineating the quality or nature of aseity, we find we are dealing, not with something that contingently may or may not exist but, with existence itself.[57]

On the surface, atheism's *causa sui* stance appears to suggest that the concept of aseity could just as easily apply to the physical universe as to God. If the acosmist can contend that God is "just there," uncreated, then surely the atheist feels entitled to make nearly the same claim about the Universe spontaneously coming into existence uncreated and "just there." The difference in these seemingly equivalent claims, though, is the role played by the dimension or element of time. Aseity requires an existence outside of time and temporally driven causal chains; the god equated with "that which exists" is independent of time, whereas the physical universe is utterly reliant on time as a relativistic measure, and its state is entirely a function of time. True aseity is timeless, so in that sense, the atheist's universe cannot be "just there" but must be the product of some process, event, or creative entity.

Thus, God's aseity attends to neither theism nor atheism, the former by not being part of the causal chain of any potential physical creation and the latter by being fully atemporal in the face of a physical universe inexorably imbued with, if not defined by, time-driven events. Likewise, aseity exposes the indefensible position of self-contradicting, pre-creation conditions; for example, despite the undeniable wisdom of the ancient Hindu scholars, the Rigveda's Creation Myth[58] envisions that, prior to creation, there was neither existence nor nonexistence—nonexistence cannot ever obtain or prevail, while aseity assures that existence always does.

Chapter 3:

Reality Consists of Multiple Things That Appear to Exist

There is a cult of ignorance in the United States[, … and] anti-intellectualism has been a constant thread, nurtured by the false notion that democracy means that 'my ignorance is just as good as your knowledge.' —Isaac Asimov[1]

English astronomer and mathematician Sir Fred Hoyle (1915–2001) is the foremost proponent of the steady-state theory of creation,[2] which asserts that new matter continuously appears to replace older matter as it recedes from view,[3] so it is with some irony that a rival view he sarcastically dubs the "Big Bang" theory has become the basis of all modern cosmology.[4] The cosmic microwave background (CMB), discovered in 1964, has settled the competition in favor of the Big Bang theory, the only one of the two theories consistent with the nonpolarized nature of CMB radiation.[5] Nonetheless, the recognition that the Universe had a beginning, potentially establishing an absolute origin coordinate of the space-time continuum, is fraught with enormous philosophical ramifications.

Of course, an eternal universe has its own difficulties, including the so-called "infinite regress" problem. Had anything existed

35

forever already, it would never have reached what we might call arbitrarily-but-distinctly "the present." Some wrongly claim that causality breaks down in the midst of an infinite series or sequence of events,[6] but as British analytic logician Bertrand Russell (1872–1970) points out, such a claim commits the fallacy of composition, in the same way as the fallacious argument he cites for comparison: Every human has a mother, so the human race as a whole must have one.[7] There can be a "local" causality within an infinite series with no definable starting point. The quandary surrounding infinite time, though, is that the events which form the basis of time elapsing are themselves finite, so, inasmuch as an infinite substance cannot be composed of finite parts (i.e., never enough to make the whole infinite), no quantity of finite-elapsing events can ever span an infinite period of time.

The Universe appears to have had a beginning with the Big Bang, and Hawking is something of a champion for the theory, as he argues that, since time itself began as part of the event, there was no time preceding it in which a creator could exist.[8] The laws of physics, and the mathematical equations that express them, seem on their own somehow to compel the Universe into existence, with enough negative energy "borrowed" to create all the matter in the detectible universe. Collectively, these ideas are not only consistent with but indeed require that the Universe have a beginning. Contemporary scientific thinking does not nor cannot support the notion of a universe having already existed for eternity.

There is an obstacle, however, perhaps even an insurmountable one, which both philosophy and science alike encounter when, as their respective views on creation require, they contend that something can in any way emerge from nothing. The admonition of Lucretius that "*ex nihilo nihil fit*" (Latin for "out of nothing, nothing comes") is a long-standing truism, as relevant to cosmology as the incontrovertible law of the conservation of matter and energy has been in physics. The debate has shifted recently to trying simply to redefine the word "nothing" in order to circumvent the rule; if the imperative is that "something" cannot come from "nothing," and "nothing" is somehow made out to be "something," then "something" coming from "something" (originally, "nothing") is not such a tall order. This ploy allows creation advocates to focus almost entirely on explaining the process of transforming an initial not-nothing state into the something that became our universe.

When scientists refer to the low-energy field of a so-called quantum vacuum,[9] devoid of matter, the transformation involves the well-known process of converting energy into matter, per the famous equation, $E = mc^2$, of Teuto-American theoretical physicist Albert Einstein (1879–1955).[10] This redefinition of what constitutes nothing, right in the midst of the inquiry, goes against how the Scientific Method is properly or at least commonly conducted. Knowing in advance that energy and matter are interchangeable, positing the initial state of an energy field presupposes the potential for matter, thereby sidestepping the impossibility of something coming from nothing. The "free lunch" hypothesis that the energy involved in the quantum vacuum state may be balanced against the negative energy of gravitation[11] fails to account for the fact that gravity has long been associated exclusively with the presence of matter. By containing anything at all—even a low-level, matterless energy field—the quantum vacuum is not nothing, and anything that emerges from it is not the result of an *ex nihilo* act of creation.

Alternatively, some scientists speculate that a universe could appear from nothing through a process of quantum tunneling,[12] but it too relies on redefining the word "nothing" to include a kind of "space-time foam" to provide a framework for the tunneling to occur.[13] Moreover, the tunneling process relies on the quantum wave function representation of an existing particle or entity crossing an otherwise-insurmountable barrier,[14] so the phenomenon involves a thing that must exist at the outset, not a true void out of which something materializes. According to other scientists, the occurrence is impossible to confirm[15] and remains highly speculative, anyway.

Contrasting the concept of *ex nihilo* creation as an event with any attempted explanation as to how the event may have actually occurred is an important distinction. Either such a creation happened or it did not; perhaps in the end, it could not. Even though, strictly under laboratory conditions, certain types of particles have been detected to appear spontaneously as the result of atomic reactions in a supercollider,[16] scientists have never observed the creation of matter—that is, the total amount of matter and/or energy together increasing within a closed system—as a natural phenomenon.[17] As we witness star formation at the ignition of stellar fusion, the collision of galaxies, supernova explosions, and evidence of stellar collapse into black holes, *ex nihilo* creation has never been seen, either naturally or recreated artificially. Treating it as a reasonable assumption, presumed to have occurred at the inception of the Universe, is an unworthy and unscientific conjecture. Furthermore, were the process reversible, one might expect an event to occur somewhere across the Universe occasionally in which something truly and utterly disappears into nothing, not matter to energy or energy to matter,[18] and yet, likewise, no such event has ever been observed. Part of the problem is the inherent contradiction in imagining nothingness being present alongside existence.

The theist confidently insists that the physical universe was created out of nothing by a supernatural being, presumably for the creator's own amusement, while the atheist is certain that the physical universe was self-created out of nothing and without purpose. Any reasonable analysis would conclude that both these views are wrong, ironically for the assertion on which they agree, namely, that a physical universe could be created out of nothing. The acosmist considers that, instead of being created at all, a universe is only imagined to exist. To a denizen of such a universe, all three explanations—God-created, self-created, or imagined (as an illusion or delusion)—involve subjective perspectives, material objects, and interactions that are indistinguishable from one another. And yet, only acosmism avoids the problem of *ex nihilo* creation; in addition, because the concept of causality applies only to physical events rather than to mental ones, an imagined universe needs neither a cause nor a context in which to exist.[19]

In reconciling the two current world views, one cannot but allow that each is also wrong in different but equivalent ways. It is as though atheism or agnosticism had said that two and two make five, while theism had asserted the same sum were a billion—both are ultimately wrong in their respective conclusions, but the latter is decidedly of a fundamentally different kind of mistake. The rounding-error of atheism is harmless and has little or no negative effect on human thought or behavior, while theism's blunder can and has ruined lives and misled most of humanity on fundamental and life-defining matters. The atheist is in a position merely to nod at the prospect that he or she operates in an imagined yet godless world, while theists, feeling initially vindicated by acosmism's assertion that a divinity truly exists, must face the prospect that all of their speculation about such a divinity and their personal relationship with it has been a monumental and irredeemable misstep.

One guidepost is the "anthropic" observational selection principle, also known simply as the anthropic principle, which constrains what is possible based on what actually came to be (or to be imagined). It refutes the specific claim that terrestrial conditions were tailored or fine-tuned to support human life; an application of the anthropic principle would observe that human life can only arise under favorable, or at least adaptable, conditions, so no fine-tuning is required and to make a contrary claim is to commit the fallacy of *post hoc ergo propter hoc* (Latin for "after this, therefore because of this"). The anthropic principle guarantees that the Cosmological Constant, calculated to be 10^{-120}, is not zero, because were it zero, the Universe immediately would collapse or else quickly expand to near-vacuum status; since the Universe has neither collapsed nor attenuated, the Cosmological Constant cannot be zero. The realizations gleaned from the anthropic principle do not preclude that the laws of physics in some sense precede (by allowing for) the Universe's existence. Time then becomes the issue.

The distinction between "emptiness" on the one hand and "nothingness" on the other is an important one. By empty, one means devoid of objects, in particular those particles or fields that make up matter and energy; by nothing, one means the very framework in which one would situate objects—i.e., the space-time continuum—is missing or has been removed. Those whose reality unwittingly consists of illusion, and specifically the delusion of diversity and multiple objects, are bound to be "counters" for whom counting down to zero is easy, reaching an empty state that they mistakenly call nothing. In actuality, nothingness is an impossibility, whereas emptiness connotes a container, albeit one with no objects in it, which remains something, even as the last object is theoretically eliminated. The word "nothing" refers to a denial of our spacetime-bound experiences, and that is not a true "nothingness," which is really a nonexistence. Ironically, virtually all of the matter with which we interact consists almost entirely of empty space, so even materialists must acknowledge their view lacks what might genuinely be called substance.

Kant reasons that, if something exists "absolutely necessarily, [… then] it exists because the opposite cannot be thought at all."[20] This nearly prefigures Rand because, to the extent its opposite cannot be conceived—that is, nonexistence cannot exist or be thought of as existing—one must declare: Existence exists. Hegel, the inventor of the dialectic approach—thesis, antithesis, and synthesis[21]—and the concept of "absolute idealism" or "absolute mind," would likely agree, since the nonexistence of nothingness compels its antithesis, existence, to exist, achieving an absolute truth out of a synthesis of these potential states of being.

When, in 1927, German theoretical physicist Werner Heisenberg (1901–76) establishes his "uncertainty principle," it represents a metaphysical constraint on how precisely any observer can ever measure a particle's complementary properties.[22] As a result, quantum mechanical systems, including vacuums, have a minimum energy level below which they tend not to fall. As noted, the lowest possible minimum energy level is called the zero-point or ground state energy. In the vacuum of outer space, however, and across the Universe, scientists detect a fundamental energy level operating in the background called the vacuum energy density.[23] There is no reason the smaller of the two, the observed vacuum energy density of 10^{-9} j/m^3, should be significantly, by orders of magnitude, different from the theoretically calculated zero-point energy value of 10^{-113} j/m^3, and in fact, the discrepancy is one of science's many unsolved mysteries known as the vacuum catastrophe,[24] although this might be partially explained by the energy stored in the curvature of empty space to a degree consistent with the flat universe required for the current cosmological inflation theory.[25] Contrary to the current thinking among scientists, the exact value of "zero" in terms of a vacuum uniquely would not violate Heisenberg's uncertainty principle because no measurement of it is necessary, and hence, neither accuracy nor precision are implicated. Moreover, since negative values are impossible as it relates to matter, uncertainty as a "fudge" factor cannot preclude zero values; disallowing a true zero value would violate Heisenberg's uncertainty principle, because without negatives, we would have to know the actual value twice as accurately, unless zero itself is permitted.

Furthermore, when the temperatures of substances are lowered to near absolute zero, where all molecular motion is expected to cease, there remains nonzero vibration energy due to quantum field fluctuations.[26] The quanta of these fields manifest themselves as wavelike particles, depending on the nature of the field: matter fields, such as fermions like quarks and leptons, or force fields, such as bosons like photons and gluons.[27] The conclusion is that empty space is not really empty but that subatomic particles used for detection such as electrons or photons quite simply do not interact with the vacuum. Even in the sparsest regions of outer space—the vast, unoccupied areas between the galaxies that collectively represent the majority of the physical volume of the Universe—are host to, at least on average, a single hydrogen atom per cubic meter.[28] The Universe's vastness, especially as its expansion continues to accelerate, dooms the presence of matter to a rarified state that is not unlike at the subatomic level, where the nucleus and its electron account for less than a trillionth of 1 percent of an atom's volume.[29] The objects we encounter thus consist of almost entirely empty space; their solidity is a well-known illusion created by unseen electrostatic forces.[30] If the entirety of the physical universe is similarly attenuated, then, absent an invisible force or presence and despite its expanse, it too is close to being nothing and thus nearer to an illusion than an actuality.

The concept of "existence exists" is not a tautology in that it makes a genuine assertion, namely, that nothingness neither obtains nor prevails. Moreover, it does not make existence some kind of onto-logical attribute, because it applies only to a single "thing," which is existence itself. Spinoza's conclusion that existence consists of a single, infinite, indivisible substance forces us to concentrate on the whole of existence when referring to anything that might exist.

And yet, there appears to be more than one thing here. Reality presents itself as being expressed in multiple things, a diversity of eminently finite and downright divisible, heterogeneous objects, awash in an endless sea of space, jockeying one another for position. Limits, such as the Planck scale[31] of 1.6×10^{-35} meters in length or 5.39×10^{-44} seconds in measured time, define values below which objects become not so much immeasurable as no longer meaningfully significant to reality.[32]

Objectivism asserts that "God" cannot be a spirit (i.e., a consciousness) without a body, because there cannot be a consciousness without both a means of being conscious and an identity. Acosmism recognizes, however, that a body is an actualized form of potential existence that is itself merely a conception under mental aseity, wherein thinking is thought, in the same manner as "existence exists." Those who subscribe to the tenet that spirituality somehow does not require a brain[33] should note that beheading tends severely to reduce one's capacity for thought. Every phenomenon, however, is mental, both as perceived and as experienced. As such, the very notion of a body is a mental concept that we are prone to attach as a foundation for consciousness, simply because that is how we have observed it, both through our own mental processes and emerging from a physical, biological configuration of cells. The mind of God conceives a material manifestation without actually creating it, and within the boundaries of that conception, the concept—not the actual existence—of an individual mind emerges; if we fail to recognize that God's mind precedes all, then we will find ourselves mistakenly locked into the mechanics of the illusion rather than seeing its purely immanent underpinnings.

An analogy might be an actor who needs a script to speak dialogue, yet, well in advance of the performance, the author is the one who conceives the play. No one observes our actor speaking without a script, perhaps never knowing of an author, who formed the script wholly in his or her mind. The physical brains we need for our minds to function are just like these scripts. We as actors speak from the script, while God is our scriptless improviser and, sans body or brain, He is the author of our universe. God thus need not be a brain-based mental entity, such as a person, nor is He an immaterial spirit: He is existence itself and, utterly alone, through His bodiless mind, He conceives this world from a vantage point altogether outside all of space, time, and matter.

Chapter 4:

The Nature of Illusion or Delusion

*Eternity is long... especially towards the
end.*[1]

The chaos of contradiction will not, must not, and cannot prevail in any version of reality. Inconsistency is a signal of deception, since an illusion must mirror some truth in order to be believable. Stated differently, a compelling delusion must mimic perfectly what it purports to represent. To those whose main objection to acosmism is "but it [the physical universe] *seems* to exist," the acosmist's response is: Precisely!

The materialist contends that our ability to measure, and reliably remeasure, things in reality somehow refutes idealism, as if imaginary objects are blurry, have fuzzy edges, and only suggest extension rather than fulfilling it. That a well-executed illusion demands consistency in order to be plausibly sustained disproves this contention. The fact that some illusions are less detail-oriented than others in no way unseats the power of a divine imagination to deliver a sufficiently intricate idea to fool us.

Another respect in which an illusion's need for consistency manifests is that it leads to the apparent inviolableness of the physical laws or other rules governing it. Any anomaly can shatter the illusion. Both consistency and the experiential framework are constraints that ensure not everything is possible within this conception. While some decry an adherence to a "foolish consistency,"[2] such a conformity is the bedrock of a compelling illusion. A miracle, which is the arbitrary violation of physical laws, is ironically seen as divine when, in reality, divinity is at work exactly in seeming to enforce an unerring compliance to regularity. Conversely, an illusion where essentially anything goes, unexplained anomalies abound, or miracles routinely occur ultimately lacks the requisite consistency to make itself convincing as an illusion.

Although a good illusion or delusion is founded on being both compelling and consistent, knowing that what is presented is indeed an illusion does not dispel its power to deceive. Recall the Nobel Prize–winning physicist who might have accompanied you to a magic show being unable to dissuade you about what the two of you are seeing: You see what you are meant to see. While existence is actuality, experience—actual or imagined—is reality. One may call "real" what one experiences, irrespective of whether the circumstances surrounding it actually exist.

The word "ontic" is used as superficially equivalent to a particular noumenon but qualified as though somehow a reality beyond the phenomenal world could serve as an anchor for meaning or morality. This Kantian division, however, obscures the distinction acosmism would make, namely, between an actual noumenal existence and an experienced phenomenal reality. To the extent that any reality can be perceived, no meta-reality is possible then but rather an existence that cannot be directly experienced; a phenomenal reality mediates between that existence and the world we experience.

In light of acosmism's assertion that phenomenal reality is an illusion, though, the distinction between actuality and experience becomes even more salient. The illusion assertion must not be misused to alienate human beings from their own lives in the context of reality. The compelling illusion that is the phenomenal world can neither be dismissed nor overcome, so we must behave as though it exists: Such is the ontological premise on which it is based.

One can logically extrapolate from a magic show to the large-scale illusion that is the entire physical universe because the operative part of the delusion, the deception of the observer based on sensory perception, is the same or functionally similar in both cases. If one can be compelled to witness something defy gravity by being levitated at the illusionist's hands, then one may likewise be deceived in seeing the same something fall to Earth due to an unexplained force that is always operating and does so at vast distances across the known universe.

The circumstances are not unlike a house of mirrors in that those who are stuck in one must accommodate their perceptions and alter their behavior to conform to the twisted reality in which they find themselves. You might liken it to using your hand while your arm is submerged in a tank of water: The liquid diffracts any light passing through it, so your hand appears skewed along angles that you know do not correspond with the underlying actual hand; if you must pick up an object at the bottom of the tank, you alter the motion of your hand in accordance to how it appears, not how you think it actually must be. We who are trapped in an imagined world must likewise fashion our actions and behavior to how that universe appears to operate rather than how we, as acosmists, know it actually is. We have no choice but to work within the illusion and its rules.

Early Vedic philosophers of the Hindu religion in the *Upanishads* posit God as the only true reality, relegating the concepts of diversity, time, and cause-and-effect as mere aspects of an illusion called "*maya*" that obscures a fundamental, underlying unity beneath a world of sensory, perceptual experience.[3]

In Sanskrit, the root of the word *maya*[4] refers to measurability, limitation, and formation,[5] and attempting to apply in this sense any of these attributes to the world as it truly is results in the delusion. Once freed from the cloaking power of *maya*, however, the truth of an immeasurable, infinite, and unified god is supposedly revealed as a single, supreme consciousness in the form of the "atman," or true self.[6]

An eerie correspondence can be drawn between Hinduism's concept of *maya* and Kantian Transcendental Idealism, with its nearly identical distinction between the worlds of phenomena and noumena. One of Kant's most ardent devotees, German pessimist philosopher Arthur Schopenhauer (1788–1860), says, characterizing Spinoza's view on knowledge of the mind, "[W]e do not know either ourselves or things as they are in themselves, but merely as they appear."[7] Indeed, Schopenhauer openly embraces Eastern religious thought while curtly declaring the "world is my representation,"[8] although he feels this world to be, in contrast to Leibniz, the worst possible, only barely good or functional enough to exist, with life's satisfactions always remaining tantalizingly out-of-reach.[9] He reasons that, since diversity or multiplicity is so essential to all phenomena, the Kantian "things-in-themselves" or noumena can only be collectively a single, homogeneous whole, experienced by observers through its manifestation in them as individual will.[10] He makes this driving force of will his overarching philosophical theme and, recognizing when it exhibits itself as human desire, contends that it precedes both our philosophizing about it and even existence itself.[11]

Sir Herbert Spencer observes that the human mind by nature is limited to the world of phenomena, undergirded by what he calls "the absolute" basis of reality, a realm forever out of our reach, which he earlier dubbed "utterly inscrutable."[12] That we are even aware of this realm, according to Spencer, is because "all things known to us are manifestations of the 'Unknowable.'"[13]

Fitch's "paradox of knowability"[14] suggests astonishingly that all knowable truths are already known, but it mistakes being knowable for being known: Every true proposition may eventually be known (i.e., is knowable), even if not yet currently known. Fitch's paradox, as stated, hinges on a contradiction from which we supposedly conclude that we cannot know that something is unknown, but something presently being unknown that will someday be known (i.e., learned) is not a contradiction. Of course, things are learned through time and occasion, and the absence of any time limit ensures that anything that can be known will always have at least the opportunity to be known sometime in the future. The questions are whether there exists anything unknowable, and if so, what implications that may have for an entity (if any exists) who is omniscient, as commonly defined.

That lack of knowledge makes something unknown is a straightforward concession, but what would make it unknowable? The physical limits to knowledge that we have discovered play a role. For example, Heisenberg's uncertainty principle represents a limit on our knowledge about a particle's complementary properties. Even though the mechanics of, say, tumbling dice are scientifically well understood, the ever-present elements of probability and chaos ensure that humans will never have the complete knowledge of circumstances necessary to predict the future or prove the occurrence of a past, unrecorded event. The past, by definition, is neither truly repeatable nor replicable in any practical way, in defiance of a requirement for scientific testability or verification, so history as a process, particularly when not observed, is not capable of being scientifically interrogated. Scientists are loathe to declare anything as forever out of their reach, since it seems to undermine the Scientific Method as a reliable avenue to the truth.[15] We know only, however, what we can perceive, remember, or predict, and given our capacity and incomplete knowledge, some events are, for us, unpredictable. Therefore, again, strictly for us, some things in the Universe must be unknowable or beyond our ability to comprehend. Such an unknowable universe functions like a consistent and compelling illusion. Since a world that wrenches itself into actual existence is not functionally different from an illusory one that is somehow only imagined to exist, then regarding it as simply nonexistent, a delusion whose complexities dissolve in its own effervescence, is philosophically less complicated.

Some, like Austrian physicist Anton Zeilinger (1945–), try to quantize reality by saying it is based on or can be equated with data or information,[16] the smallest unit of which is the quantum-level qubit.[17] Of course, quantum mechanics views the world as probabilistic, the electron being reduced mathematically to a mere "probability cloud" rather than truly a fixed particle.[18] Heisenberg himself admits that "quantum theory deal[s] no longer with the particles themselves but with our knowledge of [them]."[19] As a result, precision effectively does not exist as a feature of reality, although the evolutions of systems over time can exhibit measurable trends. Moreover, quantum mechanics shows the futility of claiming that science deals with an objective reality which is ultimately governed by odds and ambiguity.[20] A reality based on an imprecise spatio-temporal framework does not suddenly become objective simply as a result of the introduction of individual perspectives; the experience of a shared delusion, made personal through the uniqueness and layering of such perspectives, nonetheless remains both illusory and, as a mental projection, stubbornly subjective.

We ought then to focus our attention on our direct experiences of the phenomenal world rather than on the empirical methods used to examine it. The randomness on the quantum level that intrudes into experience is less a complement of information than its converse: Information expresses existence, while randomness obscures it, like a blotter pressed on the ink of reality. Thus, reality can be thought of as information plus quantum randomness, but again, acosmism sidesteps the problem by concentrating on potentiality instead of manifestation.

As Aristotle formulates it, his "Law of Non-contradiction" (LNC) specifically exempts time, in that opposite assertions can indeed both be true, provided they concern objects or events observed at different times. To question the sole exception to an otherwise-inviolable rule is altogether appropriate, particularly a rule that operates as unfailingly as the LNC does across the expanse of the known universe. The LNC would truly be sacrosanct, notably, were time an illusion representing relationships instead of itself being an independent manifestation.

The Kantian categorical framework through which experience can occur invites us to view time as somehow implanted at the outset in our own sentience or consciousness.[21] Despite the inevitable heat-death of the Universe, everything would seem possible in the span that encompasses the full measure of time, and yet time is an empirical limitation because it requires an unerring consistency while serving as a categorical basis for all phenomena and our experiences of them.

One of the Cartesian god's essential roles is to provide the persistent attention and creative support in order serviceably to maintain the Universe's continued and ongoing existence.[22] If the Universe were merely an idea, however, and the concept of temporal continuation is embedded one way or another in the idea itself, like batter is baked into a cake, then time would appear to unfold for such a timeless idea, ending before it had begun.

When Hawking contends that time cannot precede the Universe,[23] he is acknowledging that time is part of the Universe, having been created with it, which means that true existence is independent of time, no longer tethered to its limitations or temporal requirements.

The illusion of time, though, does require, as all illusions do, an infallible sense of consistency, at least when it comes to how it appears to operate. Time is one of the dimensions of the space-time continuum, yet unlike the spatial dimensions, it can only flow forward so as to avoid the inconsistencies of time travel; the LNC exception must itself be further constrained in an asymmetrical way in order to prevent self-contradiction. There must be sufficient, eventful activity involving innumerably many objects to make the pacing of time give the impression of continuity and connectedness rather than a discrete stuttering that would expose the illusion.

Truth emerges from timelessness. Apotheoses are nearly always snapshots: the dew-dappled rose, the symphonic crescendo, or the emotive awe at dusk. Such sublime moments of ineffable beauty, frozen in time and thus eternal, are those for which humans perpetually strive.

Most humans and nearly all mammals are endowed at birth with the five senses.[24] Some nonhuman animals can also sense the presence and strength of magnetic or electrical fields, while others perceive a spectrum which is wider than the one visible to humans and that includes infrared or ultraviolet ranges.[25] In terms of brain functioning in humans, a large part, the occipital lobe, is devoted to processing visual cues involving shapes, motion, color, and orientation[26]; the superior temporal gyrus handles sounds but also monitors the inner-ear sensations for balance control[27]; the olfactory bulb in the bottom forward part of the brain allows us to differentiate among, augment specific, or filter out some odors[28]; taste receptors on the tongue reach the lateral sulcus between the temporal and frontal lobes, providing survival-promoting cues related to salt (good for humans to retain water necessary for blood flow), sour (alerting us to the presence of harmful bacteria in overripe fruit or spoiled meat), bitter (typically in poisons), and sweet (signaling high-caloric carbohydrates, whose energy can be stored to stave off potential famine)[29]; and the lateral postcentral gyrus, a prominent structure in the parietal lobe, manages touch sensations involving temperature, pressure, shape, and texture.[30] Additional systems govern other, related sensations, such as vestibular (eye movement), proprioception (muscle and/or joint movements), and interoception or organ-based sensations (hunger, thirst, and air).[31]

The organisms that emerged out of the primordial or prebiotic organic soup[32] initially develop a responsiveness in moving toward or away from chemicals that were either beneficial or harmful to them, their survival, and the survival of their progeny.[33] Although chemico-tactile receptiveness is the earlier advancement, the mutated photosensitivity of skin or membrane cells, a precursor to sight, is the more significant.[34] These photosensitive skin cells evolve over a long period of time into separate, symmetrical organs; the organs, later populated with rod and cone receptors, are now recognized as "eyes," which have become the principal means of sensory awareness in primates and humans.[35] Later still, vibrations in the air stimulate the tiny hair cilia of the ear, leading to auditory sensations.[36]

The purpose of these evolutionary strides, to the extent one can educe a purpose in a process driven almost entirely by random events (genetic mutations assayed according to environmental adaptability), is to empower hosts in finding food and evading predators.[37] But for this aim, the development of the eye from photosensitive skin cells seems mostly accidental. And even with this survival objective as the developmental goal, and with constantly adapting to, and improving for, an ever-changing environment, biologically based sense perceptions are notoriously fallible and unreliable.[38] Appealing to our fallible senses demonstrates rather than disproves the chimeric quality of reality; a dream is precisely what fools our perception without being rooted in actuality. Never a consideration, nor an inevitable aftereffect, is the creation of a sensory portal to an objective reality of a physical universe. So, anyone who claims that everything humans see is an accurate picture of things as they truly are has failed to understand the mechanics and, perhaps more importantly, the history of sensory perception in an adapting world. A bat using echolocation sonar or a snake sensing heat through infrared detection would likely deem such a human-centric picture at best incomplete.

Unwavering belief in the credibility of sensory perceptions may also have arisen historically because it serves an evolutionary purpose. The ability to detect light proves beneficial to a species' continued existence, and accordingly, the skin cells eventually evolve into a focused and vision-oriented eye. As the sensitivity becomes more focused and acute, this burgeoning sense of vision further promotes survival and endurance in the capturing of prey, foraging for food, and avoiding becoming preyed upon. We use the same eye today to behold the beauty of a sunset or appreciate the artistic crafting of a sculpture, and likewise, we use the same ear to exult in the emotive sounds of a symphony. Our sense organs arise through a gradual evolutionary process and are only reliable to the extent they advance the adaptation of our species. We have no reason to boast that our sensory perceptions are at all accurate discernments of reality, any more than believing an x-ray could somehow photograph a "soul." Sense modalities evolved strictly for physical survival, not as gauges of ultimate reality nor as instrumentalities of existence.

Moreover, the mechanics of sight in mammals is complicated. The eye is used to detect light reflecting off of objects and then signal the visual areas of the brain via electrochemical transmitters.[39] The eye's lens, protected by corneal and aqueous layers, in conjunction with the iris aperture, focuses the collected light onto the retina, with its light-sensitive rods and cones, which stimulates the fibers in the optic nerve leading to the brain.[40] The ocular signal to the brain is based on contrast—i.e., changes in the light's intensity—rather than on light itself.[41] When the brain receives the sensory-input messages, it creates an inverted mental image of the original object being perceived[42]; the host "sees" that mental image as a representation. The perception is therefore indirect, although the brain adjusts its representations based on subsequent input that forms a predictive confirmation.[43] In rare cases, the brain's representations can persist, even without sensory input, as in Anton–Babinski syndrome, variously termed Anton's blindness or visual anosognosia, where those afflicted consciously deny their stroke-induced blindness.[44] Since our representation of the world is already a mental experience, however, the idea that the stimulus itself—Kant's thing-in-itself—may likewise be a purely mental phenomenon is hardly far-fetched. Existence no more inheres in what we experience than a poem or a painting or a symphony contains the emotions they evoke.

Kant calls space and time mere "constructs of the [human] imagination."[45] All events collectively occur in unison and altogether in one place. In an effort to make sense of such a mishmash of events, humans mentally impose a spatial and temporal order to the chaos and impute a cause-and-effect sequence where none really exists. We must remember that the dimensions themselves of this imposed, imaginary order neither actually nor independently exist.

Space and time are thus meaningful methods by which an observer arranges, not simply events but, the objects involved in events. Rather than genuine properties attached to objects, the connection between the spatio-temporal methods and the objects to which they apply is merely an association and is no more objective than if we mentally arranged things alphabetically, according to the arbitrary words our language assigns them. In fact, speakers of different languages would make the alphabetical arrangement differently involving the selfsame objects, and the framework of space and time as an arrangement is no less arbitrary.

Scientists are aware of this problem and have devised the "spacetime interval" as a way to deal with it relativistically.[46] The interval takes as inputs any net changes in position and time; it is computed as the difference between the square of the change in position and the product of the square of the change in time with the speed of light. Squaring guarantees that positive changes and negative changes are treated as mathematically equivalent. Adopting the interval as a convention of the physics governing space and time ensures that causality remains the same for all observers, regardless of where they may be situated.

A convention, however, is not reality, and convenience is hardly a firm foundation for truth. Moreover, the very concept of space-time has long been plagued with inconsistencies.

As far back as Ancient Greece, Parmenides observes that the motion of an object over a finite distance requires an infinite number of fractional steps, which he considers impossible, and concludes that, since the action of motion is thus impossible, time itself must be a delusion.[47] Eternalism's static block theory[48] of the universe has time as an additional spatial coordinate, making the passage of time, rather than time itself, the illusion. English physicist Julian Barbour (1937–) has championed the notion that the apparent flow of time stitches together seamlessly an eternal sequence of spatial configurations involving matter, sometimes described as "richly detailed snapshots" of reality, that do not communicate with one another and that are "deduced" after the fact as atemporal "slices" of space,[49] achieving an illusory reality. The attempt to reconcile relativity with quantum mechanics results in the Wheeler-DeWitt equation, and the absence of time as a variable in this fundamental equation suggests we can describe reality altogether with purely "timeless" numbers; if time is dispensable mathematically, then space, as a dimensional component of the framework of the space-time continuum, must be too.

Indeed, similar problems arise concerning space, particularly empty space and the supposed void of outer space. As noted, even taking the average of one hydrogen atom per cubic meter of intergalactic space, and the overwhelming percentage of atomic volume that is devoid of matter or energy, outer space is (very nearly) empty. And when scientists say "empty space," they claim to mean truly "nothing." So, under the scientific view—aside from a thin layer of atmosphere, orbiting satellites, space debris, solar wind radiation, and stray wisps of gas and dust—there is nothing between the earth and its moon; one may ask whether it is the same "nothing" that separates objects adjacent to each other. Descartes observes that "two bodies must touch each other when there is nothing between them."[50] In an analogous way, ancient Greek philosopher Melissus of Samos (ca. 470–430 BCE), when considering an empty flask and how the absence of anything in it is deemed a vacuum, proclaims it must yet be something, since, in speaking, he is able to refer to it[51]; he would like to conclude that no vacuum exists, but in determining that no shape of jostling atoms permeating all space avoids an interstitial vacua, he has no choice other than to declare that empty space must exist.[52]

Truth could be defined as merely an accurate judgment about or account of what happened in the past. Events constitute what happens when objects interact; the occurrence of events, as well as the existence of their related objects, can extend into an indeterminate, perhaps eternal, history. Space is a relationship between objects as measured by referencing a comparative, such as a ruler; time is a relationship comprised of, and measured as, events that involves objects in space and their motion.

Time must be either continuous or discrete. Broken down to the smallest subatomic components, the maximum number of objects, taken to be the fundamental elementary particles of fermions and bosons, in all of the Universe has been estimated at 10^{80} objects,[53] an unimaginably large number but hardly infinite; also, were there somehow an infinite number of objects, gravity would immediately collapse the Universe, which instead appears to be expanding at an ever-increasing rate.[54] To be continuous, time would require an infinite number of events, which is to say, between any two given events, there would always have to be a third, intervening event—yet, there cannot be an infinite number of events or relationships in a universe with a finite number of participating objects, so time must be discrete. Furthermore, because, as noted, Planck length represents the smallest measurable distance (10^{-35} meters), and given the known and constant speed of light, the measurement of time has a minimum value, earlier identified as Planck time (10^{-43} seconds), which renders the dimension of time effectively discrete to the accuracy of this reckonable minimum.

Any interval of time below the detectable quantum threshold of Planck time is, as noted earlier, utterly meaningless. As a consequence, we seem to perceive ourselves measuring time, what might be termed "clock-watching," rather than experiencing time itself. We have encountered before, however, the problem with characterizing time as discrete, since there remains a need for time to be thought of as continuous in order to achieve an operationally consistent reality. Moreover, a discrete temporal dimension suggests the presence of "islands" of time when events occur, separated by "pockets" of no-time, when the clock ticks through an interval until it becomes measurable; the notion of islands and pockets only serves to highlight the ultimately illusory quality of time.

According to eternalism's static block view of the universe, the future has already occurred, coexisting with the foregone past and with a present inexorably on path to overlay it. In a sense, an individual observer is equal to that arc of spacetime, from birth to death, for which he or she is present to witness events.[55] The anti-absolutist asks, "Where exactly is space, and when exactly is time?" The same infinite-regress problem besetting the cosmology of the Universe likewise afflicts the nature of time.

Spacetime is just a framework which, contrary to substantivalism, does not exist independently; its localized curvature under general relativity is merely a mathematical description of how gravity works. As the "hole argument" demonstrates, by observation and predictive power, along with Leibniz Equivalence that only distinct systems are transformatively unrelated, spacetime cannot be a physical manifestation but merely a covariant set of four-dimensional relationships.[56] The framework's dependence on matter—such as, the sun "warps local spacetime by approximately four seconds of arc per century"[57]—is such that, if all the matter in the Universe were removed, spacetime would altogether disappear.

To the extent spacetime is entirely separate from what it contains or that for which it provides coordination, it thereby does fail to manifest itself in reality. As a framework in Kantian fashion, it serves as an *a priori* precondition for the experience of reality, even one represented by a non-Euclidean or Riemannian finite-but-unbounded gravitational geometry. Any attempt to define space and time, either scientifically or philosophically, demonstrates how they fall short of being an essential part of our conception of reality and ultimately of what exists.

British idealist John McTaggart (1866–1925) argues more directly, and from a metaphysical perspective, more persuasively, that time cannot be real.[58] He identifies that time requires change and order or precedence, and yet no comprehensive view of how time operates can ever deliver both. If time necessarily involves change, it cannot consist either of atemporal tenseless relations among events (what he calls the "B-series") or of a monadic tensed flow of events that contradictorily are part of every timeline (the "A-series" in his terminology). The tensed A-series would have a proposition be true or false at a specific time, while the truth value of the selfsame proposition would always and perpetually hold in the tenseless B-series. Both series, as well as combinations of the two, are thus an inadequate representation of time. The A-series is contradictory in that an event cannot simultaneously possess pastness, presentness and futurity, where one precludes the other two; similarly, the B-series falls short as a complete description of time in that its changelessness creates what some call a "frozen universe"[59] which denies or otherwise impedes causality and further creates a time-within-time problem. In settling on a C-series of mentally arranged perceptions of events as descriptive of reality, McTaggart exposes his idealism by explaining how the illusion of time operates in an atemporal actuality. While events which have already occurred must, in our minds and of their own accord, mysteriously recede into the past, a seemingly limitless series of new events will insert themselves into the timeline at the present, making the past events appear to retreat in our memory. Not merely the passage of time but time itself is a mental phenomenon, a psychological trick to which we are attuned, like watching a film projected at twenty-four frames-per-second. The sequence of events forming the timeline may suggest causal relationships, yet the events no more manifest causation than that functioning movie projector manifests motion. If time is neither a moving lens whisking across the timeline nor the timeline itself, then, as real as our experiences of time and the ordering of events may be to us, time cannot exist independently and must be an illusion.

Furthermore, one cannot rationally assign a rate at which time passes or seems to pass, as in "one hour per hour," from which one must conclude that the passage of time is also an illusion.[60]

Moreover, apart from time being an illusion, our perception of time spans some temporal duration, so even our innate sense of time is illusory. Here again, Barbour weighs in, stating that he believes "that time does not exist at all, and that motion itself is pure illusion"[61] and that the "here and now arises not from a past, but from the totality of things."[62] Those supporting such arguments, however, may be seen by some as committing fallacies of composition. Working with gases, Austrian physicist Ludwig Boltzmann (1844–1906) identifies heat as the result of molecular motion, noting that the molecules involved in generating heat are themselves neither hot nor cold.[63] This cannot be taken to mean that heat does not exist, so using a similar logic, one can argue that time may emerge from timeless events. Nonetheless, the downward causality necessary for an emergent property would require that altering time ought somehow to influence events, yet time, so far as we know, is unalterable.

At the subatomic level, when an electron, bound in a stationary-state "orbit" around a nucleus, transitions from one discrete energy level to another by emitting or absorbing a photon or other energy packet, it is called a quantum leap.[64] Because the electron is restricted only to specific, discrete energy levels, there can be no intermediate levels; mathematically, the transition is a probability function between the two levels involved, beginning with one-hundred percent at the original level and ending with one-hundred percent at the post-leap level.[65] The leap is the change in the shape of the electron as a wave function rather than a change in spatial position.[66] Even so, the change in the amplitude of that wave, from crest to trough, never crosses intermediate distances but is confined to displacements permissible by quantum theory. It is as if these intermediate distances do not exist, inasmuch as the transition occurs without them, which reinforces the illusory quality of space, whether empty or not. At the astronomical scale, the theoretical presence or creation of wormholes[67] in space, as predicted by general relativity, so-called shortcuts between distant points, further evidences the delusion of space as anything other than a purely relational, mental attribute with no independent existence.

If consciousness actualizes possibilities into events, we should observe consciousness at the outset of life, not at the apex of evolution. The early universe apparently existed without consciousness, and life also formed without it. Consciousness emerges only when brain function is sufficiently complex to generate self-awareness; it is not the precipitating cause of matter. Likewise, quantum theory posits the reifying power of being observed, as though only observed phenomena actually occur, while having very little to say about the act of observing, apart from its effect on the determinacy of measurement. For example, detection, or lack of detection, forces a controlled stream of electrons or photons to behave variously as either particles or waves.[68] Perhaps the observer's brain, as a potentiality, through the very act of observing, becomes itself real enough to actualize the objects it observes.

As noted, by establishing an absolute lower limit on the size of an object as the Planck length, quantum mechanics renders the Universe countable at an estimated 10^{80} possible "things" in the form of elementary particles or their components. This realization inadvertently explains, or at least avoids, Zeno's paradoxes of motion; the solution is that dimensionless points are not adequate stand-ins for any entity of extension, and the Planck length ensures no observable object is without dimension. On the Planck scale, the quantum mechanics branch of physics demonstrates that our macro-level perceptions are merely representations and not themselves manifestations of reality.

Yet, no finite set can be elevated to infinity simply through iteration or generation,[69] the import of which is that the exhaustive set of permutations involving the 10^{80} potential objects in the known universe, while astonishingly large, remains nonetheless decisively finite: Even given an infinite amount of time, presuming the Universe ultimately survives or perpetually oscillates between creation and demise, the configuration of objects at any given time will eventually recur and will do so an infinite number of times. The cycle is inescapable. This has implications on the fecundity of possible worlds in a multiverse or, if the Universe is understood to encompass all of physical existence then, any set of "subverses." Others consider a multiverse to consist of an ensemble of universes wherein each is governed by different physical laws or parameters,[70] yet the permutation limitation would still apply, meaning only large-but-finite configurations could obtain or prevail.

The Universe has no "outer edge" nor is there an "end of space." Some have mistakenly understood this observation to mean that the Universe is somehow infinite,[71] but space is merely a "spatial" relationship between or among objects. Even they must concede that the largest spatial relationship yet conceived, say, the forty plus billion light-year radius of the known universe, is finite but can grow as the relationship may change due to expansion, only limited, however, to a distance where any two existing objects could conceivably establish an association.

As noted earlier, fully 95 percent of the physical universe is currently undetectable by any of our sophisticated scientific instruments. While 68 percent is so-called "dark" energy and 27 percent is "dark" matter—the word "dark" simply means, in addition to nonluminous or not interactive with light, undetectable, or else, likely, subatomic particles that either weakly interact or move randomly with high energy[72]—the totality of everything that humanity has ever conceived in its history to exist may comprise only the remaining 5 percent that is normal matter. The space-time framework may thus have unseen influences that make it impossible to describe or understand as currently conceived.

By rewinding our view of the expanding universe, we arrive potentially at a singularity, where both the curvature of spacetime and material density is infinite: The space it "occupies" is zero, the concept of time is meaningless, and all the laws of physics have broken down by losing their predictive power.[73] The Big Bang event inflates space itself, like the rapid unfolding of a paper road map, and the process occurs so rapidly that it violates the speed-of-light limit which has otherwise governed everything in the Universe ever since.[74] Because the inflation of space is not uniform in any direction, all points are simultaneously the center, and thus the observable universe has no center of gravity.[75] The continued, accelerated expansion of the Universe, as every galaxy is hurtling away from all others, suggests an unseen force or "dark" energy, much as dark matter mysteriously accounts for sufficient matter to set the galaxy's rate of rotation and hold the Universe together.[76] Other theories advocate an initial state other than a singularity and put forward the possibility that the physical universe is eternal, perpetually expanding and contracting, but the contraction "misses" making any crunching collision, allowing the next cycle of expansion through sideway velocities or Bohmian trajectories to occur without a boundary.[77]

As noted earlier, the "Arrow of Time" only ever points in one direction. The past is forever unchangeable, fixed in every dimension, in an almost divine way. The experience of the past resides only in the memory of conscious beings, although certainly the effects of the past—what might be termed "Nature's memory," as are manifested in the evolutionary processes of geology and biology—are written on the face of the environment and in its flora and fauna. Moreover, even if the gravitational force ultimately overcomes whatever is accelerating the expanding universe, any Big Crunch is not expected to reverse the Arrow of Time.[78] While positioning in either direction along a spatial axis from a given point is theoretically achievable, only positive movement temporally seems to be possible. In the same way nonglobal organization does not violate the laws of thermodynamics,[79] associating the Arrow of Time with the direction of increasing entropy should not necessarily preclude localized temporal anomalies. Time flowing backward as an anomaly is different from a temporal stoppage at a black hole's event horizon.[80] Despite allowing for the possibility, nowhere in the known universe is such a phenomenon observed, meaning that time is very likely irreversible. Again, unlike spatial positioning, once an event that has occurred, and because events are how we measure time, every event becomes permanently legacized in time. Perhaps the stubborn persistence of time and its inexorable, unidirectional flow help us avoid the paradox of retrocausality. Either the observer or the entity conceiving the observer projects the space-time framework onto the Universe, affecting how it operates. And yet, space and time as concepts are so fraught with inconsistencies and problems that one cannot but conclude that, in behaving like illusions, they do not and never could exist, except as mental constructs that aid us in organizing the objects and events that we as observers experience. The unmooring of space and time as objective actualities is also an important foundational basis for acosmism.

Chapter 5:

The Discrepancy Between What Must Be True and What Appears to Be True

*I talk to God but the sky is empty. —
Sylvia Plath[1]*

The concern of science is that any proposed hypothesis ought to match actual observation; if the proposal fails to fit existing facts or to predict accurately experimental outcomes, science will duly abandon it. Philosophy, on the other hand, starts by positing universal truths and then looks in the world for manifestations of those principles; if observation fails to live up to what philosophers know to be true, then the perception is deemed false or illusory. For science, observation is the final arbiter and embodiment of truth, whereas for philosophy, that embodiment is the sometimes-flawed expression of a higher, unperceived truth, arrived at through the power of logic and reason. In the face of conflict between tenet and so-called facts, science blindly embraces "facts" as truth, while philosophy tries to impeach the credibility of those selfsame dogma-denying facts in defense of an overarching truth to which science chooses to remain oblivious.

As established under the principle of aseity, "that which exists" (i.e., God) is a single, homogeneous, infinite, indivisible entity. What must exist, as a consequence of the nature of existence itself, is this single thing, which, logically, is the only thing that can exist. Yet, what appears to exist instead are multiple things, diverse in kind and widely distributed; no one thing in the Universe, regardless of how immense in size it may be, such as the light-years-long interstellar gas and dust towers of the Eagle Nebula known as the Pillars of Creation,[2] can ever be considered anything but miniscule alongside the infinite, and only a very few things, such as the fundamental subatomic particles known as fermions like quarks and leptons, are too small that they cannot be further broken down into component parts. Thus, a contradiction arises between what must exist on the one hand and what appears to exist on the other, in cardinality, variety, extension, and divisibility.

Recalling Aristotle's "Law of Non-contradiction" (LNC), that "opposite assertions cannot [both] be true at the same time," at most, only one of two contradictory statements can be true. Either, based on aseity, exactly one thing exists—or rather, the nature of existence does not admit of nor allow for multiplicity—or else the many things objectively presenting themselves to our perception in the physical universe do actually exist. The LNC ensures that both statements cannot be true; the temporal exception that would allow both to be true at different times does not apply, since aseity is outside of space and time. The assertion that only a single thing exists is a proposition that logically must be true, whereas the claim that many things exists concerns an observation which merely appears to be true. A falsity that deceives us or is wrongly perceived by us or is misinterpreted by our senses constitutes the common definition of illusion.[3] A person who willingly accepts an illusory deception internalizes it as a delusion.[4] A universe containing multiple things, potentially up to 10^{80} things, is thus an illusion, and to the extent that we allow ourselves to accept the illusion as true, we suffer from a profound delusion.

The possibility of an actual, physical universe, teeming with particles and force fields, is pushed off the table by the realization that what must exist is a single, pervasive entity which reifies the character of existence. More than that, though, the physical universe carries none of the attributes of existence, such as homogeneity, singularity, infinitude, etc. Oddly, its characteristics are completely the opposite, such as heterogeneity, multiplicity, finitude, etc. This implies the physical universe does not nor cannot actually exist, as acosmism asserts, yet unlike the Ontological Argument that treats existence itself as an attribute, acosmism attempts to prove the nonexistence of the physical universe through the absence of attributes necessarily associated with existence.

The moral of the fable of the blind men and the elephant[5]—each blind person encounters one part of a pachyderm, but collectively, they fail to identify it in its entirety as an elephant—is that context is essential in the search for truth. Saxe's poetic rendition observes that "[t]hough each was partly in the right [...] all were in the wrong!"[6]

Context certainly is important to avoiding erroneous conclusions based on composition, but another type of error occurs when a presumed whole is unsupported by its component parts. Suppose you receive a large crate labeled "Elephant," whose contents, aside from narrow air slits, is hidden by all the wooden sides of the crate. A mammal is stirring inside. You pry open the crate using a crowbar and see a creature that looks nothing at all as the crate's label had led you to expect. It has no trunk, no tusks, no large ears or flat, stomping feet. In fact, it lacks every attribute of being an elephant of which you can think. You ought to disbelieve what is written on the crate, that it was somehow mislabeled, rather than try to redefine the term "elephant" so as to include in the definition the decidedly non-elephantine creature you encountered in the crate.

In the same way, the physical universe is "labeled" as existing, yet it lacks the very attributes of existence, such as singularity, homogeneity, infinitude, and indivisibility. As with the non-elephant in the crate, we should mistrust the label rather than our definition of existence, which is based on the concept of aseity or pure existence and what will prove necessarily to be true.

Not only is time, as measured by events, discrete rather than continuous, but using a similar logic that the number of configurations into which the 10^{80} objects in the known universe could be placed is ultimately finite, there is thus only a finite time span over which these configurations could manifest without recurring. Any non-infinite multiplicity of objects will inevitably encounter a hard limit on what events are possible or can ultimately be realized.

Moreover, the present could never be in the middle of an infinite series of events, since the earlier half of such a series could never "complete" so as to serve as a precursor to the present. Likewise impossible conceptually is the rewinding of an infinite series of events, also known as an infinite regression. From the foregoing, the Universe could not have "always" existed or appeared to exist, although were that possible, it would avoid the *ex nihilo* creation problem. Had the Universe truly always existed, then of the finite number of permutations into which every one of its objects could be configured, each would already have occurred, and will continue to reoccur, an infinite number of times, for no apparent reason or fathomable purpose.

American philosopher Quentin Smith (1952–) outlines the cosmogony of a self-caused universe by suggesting the possibility of an infinite number of simultaneous yet causally connected events.[7] This line of reasoning is invalid, however, because simultaneity, so necessary to avoid the infinite regress problem, is precisely what fails: A finite universe containing a finite number of objects cannot produce presently an infinite number of events.

Some who propose an "always existed" universe suggest one that perpetually oscillates between expansion, contraction, and reexpansion.[8] The problem with this hypothesis is that science knows of no mechanism which could smooth the additional entropy such a universe would bear at each bounce.[9] What is more, a perpetually oscillating universe would require, besides an infinite future, an infinite past, which is an insoluble quandary, given both the precursor and regress issues. Moreover, as noted, the Big Bang singularity represents the absolute onset of time, so there is no previous time in which either a creator or an earlier instance of the physical universe could exist.

In another view, the ekpyrotic universe, also known as the "Big Splat," consists of what results from brane collisions at higher dimensions.[10] Spacetime is envisioned statically as being multi-dimensional in super symmetry, with the normal three spatial dimensions and one temporal dimension bounded by two three-dimensional walls, or branes.[11] One of those three-dimensional walls makes up the space in which we live, another brane is hidden from our perception, and the third brane between the two bounding branes can hit our brane to trigger an inflationless Big Bang through thermal conduction into our universe.[12] This theory may have been invalidated by the recent discovery of so-called "gravitational waves," which are more than mere ripples in spacetime[13]; such waves would not otherwise be measurable using current methods.[14]

Polish astronomer Nicolaus Copernicus (1473–1543) credits as the basis and inspiration for his heliocentric view of the solar system the musings of Greek mathematician and astronomer Aristarchus of Samos (ca. 310–230 BCE).[15] Aristarchus's original hypothesis—that the Sun is the center of the solar system, with the planets, including Earth, revolving around it—conflicts directly with Aristotle's long-accepted geocentric or Earth-centered view.[16] Similarly, in death, Copernicus triggers the posthumous attention of the Inquisition due to his restatement.[17]

The heliocentric view envisions the seemingly rooted Earth orbiting a stationary Sol, now known itself to revolve around the center of the Milky Way galaxy every 225 million years.[18] The eventual adoption of heliocentrism renders meaningless a common question, "Where does the setting sun go?" We now know it is the earth in rotation that daily turns its face and obscures our view of the ever-burning light of the sun. Still, with newly acquired knowledge, we lose the very basis of the questions we once posed while ignorant.

In the same way, with the realization that the physical universe and the space-time framework in which it operates are purely illusions, any questions become moot about where such a universe comes from or why it exists, or presents itself as existing. Moreover, the cosmological issues surrounding origin, causation, and time are collectively only conceivable in the context of an actualized universe. The source of a mentally conjured apparition is none other than the mind that conceived it, and its reason for being lies in the psychological recesses of that same intellect. Religious folk inappropriately look for God beyond the stars; rather, it is God, in looking for something beyond Himself and His own existence, who imagines both the stars and the folk. Understanding the cosmology of the physical universe begins with peering into the lonely mind of God and examining what motivates Him to imagine the world in which we find ourselves.

Chapter 6:

Bridging Existence and Reality, or The World as An Idea in the Mind of God

*[I]n life, there is actually no truth to
be discovered; there is only errors to be
exposed. —H. L. Mencken[1]*

No non-philosopher is apt to make a distinction between existence and reality. The two are commonly equated, so an analogy may serve to make the distinction clear. Imagine you are dreaming something fantastical, such as flying unaided like Superman over a city; accompanying the visual sensation are the whoosh of air rushing passed your ears, the contortions of your muscles as you fitfully try to navigate the unassisted flight, and the impression of buoyancy as you hover above the city's lights. You are thoroughly engrossed. Unfortunately, just as the adventure begins to get interesting, you are jarred awake by your alarm clock.

As you sit up in bed, you pose a simple yes-or-no question: "Did that just happen?" The answer cannot be "yes," since asserting a mere dream actually occurred amounts to lunacy, but nor can the answer be "no," because you not only experienced the flight yet also have a vivid memory of it. Whenever a yes-or-no question cannot be answered "yes" or "no," it becomes a paradox. (Any paradox here disappears once we resolve the ambiguity of the word "that" in the original question: "Did *that* just happen?" Is "that" referring to a genuine event? Without hesitation, we would answer "no." Or, is "that" referring to a dream event? In this case, "yes" is the clear answer. Philosophical inquiries nearly always come down to refining our definitions.)

Nonetheless, this quickly resolved paradox illustrates, or provides an analogy for, the distinction between existence and reality. You did not actually fly through the air unaided, which corresponds to existence or manifestation, but you did experience it, which is analogous to reality. Actuality is existence, while reality—whether "your reality" or "my reality"—is the totality of our experiences, which may or may not be based on what genuinely or actually exists.

To a mind, particularly one whose evolution is founded on mentally processing sensory perceptions, a compelling illusion can create an experience just as authentic as an actuality. The pieces begin to fall into place as we recall that aseity substantiates that only the divine mind of God actually exists and that the illusion of a physical universe furnishes us a reality within which all our experiences seem to transpire.

As another analogy, imagine you are in a darkened movie theater as a heartrending film is being projected. Common sense would confirm that the narrowed focus of the cinematographer's camera obscures that the depicted action takes place on a movie set with fake backdrops and suggestive lighting. The actors recite memorized dialogue but do so in a way that makes it come across as spontaneous. The music swells at the critical moment, on the cue of the film's scorer and composer. You find tears begin to well up in your eyes, and soon, the emotion overwhelms you, and you sit in the dark, gently sobbing. The circumstance the film portrays is phony, albeit using the Hollywood magic that constitutes the modern art of entertainment, yet you cry over an experience that is neither real nor strictly your own. In what way is our experience of the physical universe truly different?

The acosmist position is that we experience the phenomena of the physical universe as the basis of reality, but no underlying existence actually supports it. Conversely, since God is existence, His presence is actual, yet He does not participate in our reality. The distinction between a nonexistent but experienced reality and an unreal existence beyond all experience allows the acosmist to bridge the two in order to find the middle ground where truth so often lies.

English cosmologist John D. Barrow (1952–) notices how the laws governing the Universe are based on symmetry, while life-creating events materialize by breaking these very symmetries—so-called flaws in laws.[2] By looking at patterns, he sees "glitches" that suggest an artificial mind or computer simulation operating as the foundation of reality, echoing an idea originally proposed by Sueco-English philosopher Nick Bostrom (1973–), essentially about potential levels of reality amid the likelihood of human self-extinction.[3] When what is real and what is fiction seamlessly blend so that no clear distinction between them can be made has a name: *hyperreality*.

Austro-Irish physicist Erwin Schrödinger (1887–1961) points out that unobserved states can only be described using probability and represented as a wave function, but once the state has been observed, the wave function collapses into certainty: The observer's role is thus vital to reality.[4] His belief that quantum physics reveals that all is mental results from his devotion to the views of the Advaita Vedanta philosophy, which he expresses in several opinions, including that "multiplicity is only apparent, [and] in truth, there is only one mind," and that "[t]he plurality that we perceive is only an appearance; it is not real."[5] Moreover, when the wave function collapses for one observer while it remains in superposition to others, it creates two conflicting realities which some have interpreted to mean that no genuinely objective reality exists.[6]

In 1801, English physician and physicist (and Egyptologist) Thomas Young (1773–1829) devises an experiment in which sunlight is detected on a photosensitive screen after passing through two metal plates, the first with a single slit aperture opening and the second with two such slits.[7] The interference pattern of illuminated and darkened bands that persistently appears on the screen unquestionably demonstrates the wavelike nature of light. Other experiments like the photoelectric effect, where electrons are liberated from conductive metal by light (but only above a threshold frequency), show light behaving as though it consists of particles (i.e., photons or quanta of light).[8]

These experimental results demonstrate the wave–particle duality of light—that photons may behave variously as either waves or particles, or sometimes both simultaneously—what some mockingly dub as "wavicles."[9] Later versions of the double-slit experiment involving delayed choice and quantum erasers confirm that the wavelike nature corresponds to probability, which "collapses" or decoheres a quantum superposition into a particle-like nature upon being measured or observed.[10] Those who fail to grasp the mathematical underpinnings of quantum mechanics, though, are prone to misinterpret the results of these experiments, pitching what is known as "quantum woo,"[11] by seeing evidence of retrocausality (misordering the precedence of cause and effect) or "spooky action-at-a-distance"[12] in place of predictable phenomena like quantum entanglement. While consciousness is essential to observation, at present, no experimental support or consensus has yet been reached for the claim that, because consciousness is a precondition of experience, it in any way shapes the nature of the physical reality it encounters. Nor does wave–particle duality violate the "Law of Non-contradiction" (LNC), since the phenomenon is never actually both a wave and a particle at the same time to the same observer: Potentially, it is both, but ultimately, an observer detects it as only one or the other. If the physical universe is an illusion, it operates at a higher level than any individual consciousness with which it interacts.

Nonetheless, "experimental verification of the violation of Bell's inequalities" at the quantum level[13] exposes a correlation between phenomena that share neither causal connection nor a common originating causal event. It seems the Universe is better conceived in its entirety, as though it were the product of a single mind or overarching consciousness. Anglo-American physicist and cosmologist Paul Davies (1946–) suggests that a universe can only exist if, at some point in the course of its evolution, it eventually contains a mind or observer.[14] At least two extraordinary ways to explain the life-supporting nature of the universe in which we find ourselves vie for explanatory contention: One is religion's intelligent design of a universe intentionally made for life by a supernatural creator; the other is a multiverse's luck-through-plenitude of a universe that happens to foster life among innumerably many that cannot. Davies is unable to accept either of these explanations and instead envisions a universe in its entirety becoming conscious, a decidedly teleological and idealistic take on the traditional anthropic principle.[15] Our Universe is hardly teeming with life, though, since the only life known to exist is on a single planet, orbiting a less-than-average star in the outer arm of a spiral galaxy among billions of galaxies with a trillion, trillion other planets.[16] As English physicist, astronomer, and mathematician Sir James Jeans (1877–1946) expresses it, "The universe begins to look more like a great thought than like a great machine. Mind no longer appears as an accidental intruder into the realm of matter."[17] Acosmism acknowledges, in a way that science either will not or does so only grudgingly, that there is an undeniably mental aspect to the entirety of reality.

The notion of the Universe as an unactualized idea, even as the foundation of a genuine PEQ answer, might be crossing a line into a realm of eerie absurdity. In reference to the PEQ, though, American analytic philosopher Robert Nozick (1938–2002) declares that "[s]omeone who proposes a non-strange answer shows he didn't understand this question,"[18] while Barrow observes that "[a]ny universe simple enough to be understood is too simple to produce a mind able to understand it."[19] That we, as an evolved species, are even capable of formulating a question like the PEQ, let alone boldly attempting to answer it, is a testament to humanity's intellectual brazenness, if not authentic achievement.

Any viable answer to the PEQ can be neither straightforward nor direct. Were it either, such an answer would already have been discovered. The question itself, and the basis on which a suitable answer might be formulated, has challenged the greatest minds in human history, yielding no consensus or satisfactory conclusion. Hence, any proposed answer that is not utterly bizarre should be regarded with suspicion, as either deceptively simple or as having missed a key requirement. And even among the acceptable solutions that are consistent with both fact and reason, other things being equal, only the least outlandish warrants thoughtful consideration.

Thus, expect the PEQ answer to be bizarre. Sir Arthur Conan Doyle's Holmesian maxim, "[W]hen you have eliminated the impossible, whatever remains, *however improbable*, must be the truth,"[20] squarely applies here. Ultimately, what is possible consists of that thin plane formed when the Inevitable (or, what must be true) and the Impossible (or, what cannot be true) collide.

If we know in advance that the answer to the PEQ will be bizarre, we must ensure it is only so to the extent necessary to resolve the question and no more bizarre than other possible answers. Even a philosophical or religious system taken as true undermines its credibility when it solicits belief that is needlessly fantastical in matters away from its core faith, such as a talking snake, an inextinguishable burning bush, or a claimed recent global flood altogether at odds with the geological record. The beggaring of belief is the hallmark of a system that is less than confident in its truth. Lack of knowledge among the target audience is also fertile ground for sowing the seeds of unreasoned belief. Some appeal to mistaken common sense, like flat-earth models. Others exploit ignorance, such as the extraordinary claim of a "virgin" birth, or spontaneous human parthenogenesis. The double-helix structure of DNA, the genetic blueprint of every living organism, means that the only form of asexual reproduction possible by a single human parent is cloning,[21] which is hardly how the faithful envision the miracle that itself must somehow be all-the-more miraculous than the process of "regular" childbirth. Moreover, while a male-to-female clone could utilize the parent's X chromosome by doubling it, a female-to-male clone would require substantial postcloning genetic engineering to change gender.[22]

Despite the promise of continuing the strides made over the course of history in our understanding of the Universe, we must presume the answer to the PEQ to be presently fathomable to humans, or else it will likely remain forever out of our reach. Since the PEQ itself can be conceived, unless the answer is either hidden or operates at a level inaccessible to the rational mind, that answer cannot unexpectedly be incomprehensible. Purely as a matter of probability, a PEQ answer is unlikely being actively withheld or obscured when nature's other physical secrets like electromagnetism and thermodynamics have surrendered so absolutely to the probing scrutiny of science. Einstein remarks, "The eternal mystery of the world is its comprehensibility[, and t]he fact that it is comprehensible is a miracle."[23]

As an analogy, imagine a group of hikers; to survive an attacking bear encountered in the woods, an individual hiker need not be able to outrun the bear but just has to run faster than at least one other hiker. Likewise, a metaphysical system need not be altogether sensible but must simply be less bizarre or of better explanatory or probative value than all others presently available. Or to state it differently, the chosen PEQ answer must be no more bizarre than other possible answers, which themselves have to have been odd enough even to be considered.

Medieval English Franciscan friar William of Ockham (ca. 1285–1347) formulates a principle of logic known as Occam's Razor that, all things being otherwise equal, the simpler solution to a problem, or the one that requires fewer assumptions, is often better or more correct.[24] Also known as *lex parsimoniae* or the law of parsimony, Occam's Razor is used not only by philosophers but by scientists as well, in some sense being implicitly incorporated into the Scientific Method as a basis for interpreting the results of experiments involving potentially multiple causes, at least as it relates to falsifiability.[25] Part of the logic behind Occam's Razor is that fewer assumptions means fewer ways an hypothesis can be proven wrong, thereby minimizing a disproof's "surface area."

While many may believe that simpler explanations have the advantage of being vindicated more often statistically, the way in which Occam's Razor is applied can be altogether subjective. By characterizing "simplicity" in different ways, Occam's Razor can and has been used to justify any given position, as well as its opposite—e.g., theism and atheism, Newtonian physics and special relativity, wavefunction collapse and the many-worlds interpretation, among many others. An hypothesis whose predictions are more accurate, for example, is always better, whether or not it is truly simpler. Moreover, it may be just as important, not to mention more reasonable, to focus on the quality or type of assumptions rather than merely the quantity—one hypothesis based on many uncontroversial assumptions might be preferable to another that is based on very few yet outlandish or disputed assumptions.

Some systems are built incrementally, where subsystems evolve directly and become components in a larger system whose evolution is indirect. Biology is an example of such a system; as earlier discussed, the mutation of photosensitive skin cells which began an eventual progression into a vision organ like the eye represents a subsystem that could not have evolved directly within a biological system. Occam's Razor tends to fail spectacularly for such systems, because the advocated simplicity ignores the natural evolution of component complex subsystems. It is misapplied when invoked for such incrementally built constructions.

From one perspective, Occam's Razor may be seen as a base appeal to common sense. This is dangerous as it relates to time, space, and matter, because quantum mechanics, now universally accepted by the scientific community, fails as a commonsense solution while seemingly also to violate the call of Occam's Razor for parsimony. Recall that Occam's Razor is merely an heuristic preference, not a form of proof; the solution toward which it may point must still neatly fit all the facts. It serves as a guidepost in the crossroads of competing solutions that are comparable in extent and aptness.

Human nature understandably compels us to desire a complete picture, so we will tend to "fill in" with a belief any missing piece in the jigsaw puzzle that is our current view of the Universe. The problem is that a belief can become a stubborn placeholder for the actual truth, whose revelation tends merely to suppress rather than fully supplant earlier mistaken beliefs. The potential biological benefit of false belief in terms of survival, such as envisioning the outline or pattern of nonexistent faces in the shrubbery of the forest,[26] may explain why humans tend to be so gullible in other respects where belief is actively solicited. We must, therefore, strive to have as few beliefs as possible and always remain open-minded as we perpetually put our beliefs to the test. Italian philosopher and theologian St. Thomas Aquinas (1225–74) invites us to love both right and wrong opinions, as each helps us, albeit in different ways, in our search for the truth.[27]

Nonetheless, the reduction invited by Occam's Razor may likewise confuse categories of evidence. For example, in an effort to dramatize through confrontation and violence, many popular movies and television programs create a false impression in public opinion; they depict that often-unreliable, direct eyewitness testimony is somehow better evidence of a crime or perpetrator's identity than neutral, indirect, circumstantial or forensic evidence. This is rarely the case and may, in fact, often be quite the opposite.[28] Direct and indirect data or facts represent different categories of evidence, and both may play a role independently in determining the truth. The maxim "absence of evidence is not evidence of absence" is hence misapplied, because when an hypothesized phenomenon is expected unfailingly to produce a specific result, the non-appearance of that outcome is indeed some, even if not necessarily conclusive, evidence of the absence of the original condition.

The preference for simplicity may leave some things unexplained, especially in the area of etiology or causation, where accepting that an effect has no cause at all is rarely right. No epistemological system can be constructed if facts are only accidentally or arbitrarily true. While we need not expect a sufficiently rational reason underlying every cause-and-effect situation, we can and should assume that some concrete explanation exists, even if we must abandon simplicity in order to explain adequately an irreducibly complicated state of affairs. The phenomenon of emergence, for example, allows complex properties to materialize unexpectedly out of seemingly unrelated constituent elements, like the wetness of water.[29] The process whereby consciousness emerges from nonconscious material is hardly simple, and yet, it serves to explain how consciousness can unexpectedly appear in biological and artificial systems. It might also show how a "mind" can possibly exist without necessarily requiring something physical (e.g., a brain) as a basis for its existence.

Those who contend that God could only exist in a universe where something exists necessarily,[30] necessity being an alethic modality, thereby ignore the acosmic axioms that existence itself is necessary under the principle of aseity and that God is indeed "that which exists." These same philosophers see perfection and virtue as incompatible on the logic that, to be virtuous, a being must be capable of suffering, which a perfect being is not,[31] yet acosmism reminds us that God is not necessarily the greatest that can be conceived but rather the only thing or entity which actually exists. A malevolent god considered the absolute and sole source of morality would always, and ironically, be right; we should recall that, while the Golden Rule represents morality in the context of reality, for the god of acosmism, frankly, no "others" exist to serve as the objects or targets of any such malevolence.

The science of cosmology is good at describing existence but poor in explaining the causation involved: The Big Bang event initiates time itself when an incredibly dense, subatomic speck of matter that later becomes our universe spontaneously pops into being.[32] Conversely, theism invests its explanatory power in causation but struggles with proving the existence of its foundation: An already existing, infinite, omniscient, and omnipotent being causes a physical universe to materialize out of nothing through a deliberate act of creation. Declaring that the Big Bang singularity is utterly simple, while an infinite deity creator is somehow deemed to be overly complex, may not be enough because the real trade-off, altogether sanctioned by Occam's Razor, is between the supposed loss of simplicity in exchange for the explanatory power of complexity, or in other words, whether unexplained causation simply stated is preferable to a solid cause-and-effect explanation where the very existence of the complicated instigating cause itself becomes a contentious issue. We do not learn about or understand nature, however, when supernatural explanations are invoked; such explanations may even confuse the situation, as we must now turn our inquiry toward questions about how these supernatural forces might work and how they could interact with what is directly observed. While it might be said that "designers are more complicated than the things they design,"[33] a designer's vision is decidedly less complicated than the finished product.

No trade-off is really necessary, though, once we realize that, by combining the inexorableness of aseity with the power of divine imagination, it results in a simplicity that is superior to both principles taken separately. We perceive an artifact but are at a loss to explain or comprehend its originating source. Thus, two distinct types of logical errors can follow from this explanatory shortfall. One type of error is mistaking perception for actuality; acosmism arrests and forces us to realize that, in our discernment, what we are dealing with is only sensory data, not the thing-in-itself certainty. The second type of error is mistaking a supposed link in a causal chain for a mere projection of the mind's eye, where causality is predetermined from the outset of the initial idea.

Although the notion that the Universe is "just there" may be considered simpler than other explanations, especially if the proffered cause is deemed more complicated than the effect, acosmism is simpler still. The idea of something is necessarily simpler than were it to manifest itself in the actuality of existence precisely because an idea of a thing contains its own potentiality, which would be a necessary precursor to its existence.

Moreover, according to Occam's Razor, even were it not simpler, it need not be, provided it has more explanatory power to show either how the simpler explanation fails fully to explain, or how the more complex explanation better explains, the phenomenon. Such greater explanatory power can resolve incongruities, reduce dilemmas, and/or reconcile disparate views. It solves the discrepancy between what-must-be-true existence and what-appears-to-be-true reality. And it eliminates quandaries like an uncaused first-cause and an eternal world in which a universe is paradoxically envisioned to have always existed. Finally, it squares scientific materialism, which we may regard as a true description within the realm of reality, with the metaphysical idealism that is true in an ultimately overarching sense.

A system is considered complex when it consists of many interconnected components, regardless of whether its parts interact efficiently or synergistically.[34] As with Occam's Razor, complexity does not reduce simply to counting rotely the number of parts, because a system with several basic elements might be less complicated than one with fewer, yet more intricate, parts.

Take a natural phenomenon, say, a lightning bolt. The scientific explanation—that lightning is an electrical discharge from a cloud—involves oppositely charged particles, electric currents, and heated air in the atmosphere; though each part individually is well understood, various objects and physical laws contribute to the phenomenon, some in complicated ways. An angry deity like Zeus casting a lightning bolt from above the clouds involves fewer "moving" parts than the scientific explanation, namely, one, and yet, that one part—an unseen Olympian god, wielding great power and motivated by human-like emotions—is far more complicated than the principles of cloud convection and electric differential. Similar reasoning applies to, with the same conclusion reached on, countless other real-world examples.

The explanatory power of scientific understanding seems always to trounce theism's *deus ex machina* account on every issue within the ken of humankind. Nonetheless, both are complicated, not to mention bizarre, in their own ways, as they address how a physical universe appears out of nothing: It spontaneously "pops" into existence to evolve into what we now observe versus it having been deliberately created for a supernatural being's amusement. A third option, though, is both far simpler and considerably less bizarre: A being, whose inevitable presence is equal to existence itself, conceives in His mind a physical universe as if it existed, nevertheless operating, perhaps anthropically, according to the laws of science that we have so far discovered or may yet come to discover, and does so for a specific reason or purpose (to be revealed in the next chapter).

The theistic view, however, presents God as a thing among things. He is pictured as the prime mover, the coordinating master over the "stuff" that comprises our universe, like a conductor, summoning specific sounds harmoniously from the various sections of the cosmic orchestra with a wave of a baton. Extending the metaphor, scientists impassively examine the symphonic sounds with their oscilloscopes. For acosmism, however, God is not a thing among things but rather the only thing that truly exists, or existence itself; He is alone, composing the whole musical score in His mind. One may conclude that acosmism emerges as the most parsimonious, as well as least bizarre, of the PEQ answers vying for broad acceptance.

Although its premises may be valid and the sequence of logic leading to its conclusion impeccably sound, acosmism might prove difficult to accept, even for an open mind; its denial of the existence of the vast physical universe might seem, in the final analysis, perhaps a bit too bizarre. And yet, acosmism is compelling because it is fittingly odd, its statement about our mysterious reality resonates, and there appears, for now, no better alternative on the horizon. To appropriate another movement's famous slogan, acosmism says of the physical universe: It's *not* here, it's queer (that it's not here), get used to it.

Chapter 7:

What Is the "Idea" in the Mind of God?

*All that we see or seem is but a dream
within a dream. —Edgar Allan Poe[1]*

An omniscient being does not acquire knowledge, yet we finite creatures do. Understanding the difference not only resolves the Omniscience Riddle but also helps indirectly answer the PEQ by framing it as an epistemological dilemma rather than an ontological one.

Having selected the word "God" to represent the phrase "that which exists," one must make some effort to identify the ways in which the choice of such an imprecise word might still be unsuitable. Sharing in Einstein's dismissal of religion as "an incarnation of the most childish superstitions"[2] is easy. The pantheist Spinoza equates God wholly with nature when he states that the "eternal and infinite Being we call God or Nature acts by the same necessity from which He exists."[3] While theism is fractured into so many disparate views, a unifying theme seems to be the role assigned to God as the one and only creator of all that is. To deists, that is His only role, while other theists envision God as the ruler of His creation, interacting in real time with human affairs and regulating in every respect the awesome operation of the entire physical universe. Still others see a supreme, omnibenevolent being as the wellspring of moral authority, embodying spiritual or abstract concepts like Justice or Love, who is worthy of a capitulating worship and idealized emulation. He is often depicted anthropomorphized in art, as (the father of) a corporeal person, aged with a white beard, sitting upon a throne, dispensing judgment on the fate and fortunes of individual humans, both during their lives or after their deaths, or on the destiny of nations in the course of human history.

In the acosmism here advocated, God is none of these. He is, as the prime advocate of acosmism, Hegel, describes, "Absolute Thought"[4] or Infinite Mind. Divine thought, however, is not based on physiology, as it is in humans, where mind or consciousness emerges from the physical biology of our brains, which serves to mediate our sensory perceptions into mental representations. Rather, God's thought is both immanent and immediate: It is not representational but is a timeless expression of an actuality that could never be. Even though no instance is known in which any being has demonstrated the activity of thinking in the absence of a physical (neurological) brain or (artificial) computing processor, this may be due merely to the limitation on our experiences and does not establish an indispensable material basis for all thought. As one Christian commentator reflects, "Thinking no more requires a brain than digging a hole requires a shovel."[5] The notion of God thinking is strictly a metaphorical way to describe how the product of His mind, outside space and time, becomes our reality, an illusion we mistake for actuality.

Take the sentence: "God is sitting there thinking." Each and every word of that sentence is wrong; not just imprecise, but horribly and irredeemably false. "God" is not a person; "is" connotes the passing of time, which is part of the illusory framework that undergirds our reality; "sitting" suggests a body, and more specifically, a derriere, which is not something a being whose existence is assured under the principle of aseity possesses; "there" implies a location in space, and yet space is as illusory as time; and "thinking" typically entails a physical brain, which is how we humans gather our thoughts, but it is not so for a being of pure existence. So, this simple phrase—"God is sitting there thinking"—can only be taken metaphorically and is doomed to be hopelessly inaccurate, if not downright misleading and/or untrue.

Metaphor and symbolism are nonetheless necessary to discuss what is inexpressibly beyond human comprehension.[6] Any criticism is invalid that attacks these metaphors and symbols rather than focusing on the underlying truths that they represent. This is more than a linguistic deficiency, in the manner that Austro-English philosopher of language Ludwig Wittgenstein (1889–1951) famously expresses as the "limits of my language mean the limits of my world."[7] And yet, we socially accept many metaphors that are useful, such as speaking of the sunrise or sunset when we know the sun only seems to move due to Earth's rotation. We navigate with maps that present the earth as flat, even when all but a tiny group of Luddites know our planet is roundly oblate. God thinking, an activity we associate with a physical brain or mind, is similarly metaphorical: It is patently untrue but helpful to our understanding about how to resolve the discrepancy between what must exist and what appears to exist. Like an emotion-evoking poem that relies on fantastical imagery to signify mundane affairs, the metaphors and symbols that acosmism uses, especially in denoting God's mind or thought, ought to be taken as transcending their literal and admittedly imprecise meaning. Acosmism is merely a layer of abstraction operating underneath perceived reality. It is no more unfalsifiable than the universe it undergirds and for which it provides a framework. The scaffolding is not less real than the erected structure.

As an additional analogy, the burgeoning universe following the Big Bang is often likened to the inflation of a balloon[8]; to dwell on matters such as the color of the balloon or where the pinch-point is located are criticisms that focus on how the metaphor fails instead of how it succeeds. Without the metaphor, the idea is inexpressible. The hope is that the metaphor will help to evoke the gist of the idea without overtaking it. The image of a giant, bearded deity, seated on a throne, wistfully spending an afternoon conjuring up a daydream of a universe is not only to have taken the metaphor too far, but it actually detracts from its symbolic or allegorical power to inspire a glimmer of the genuine idea.

Epistemology, which is the study of knowledge, allows us to make the insightful observation that we non-omniscient humans can accomplish something no omniscient being can, and that is actually acquiring knowledge. We are able to transition the threshold from a state of not knowing to a very different state, that of knowing. This experience teaches us something important about the nature of knowledge and how it may apply to a being that is reputed to be omniscient.

When asked, every human can likely recall a time, perhaps in early childhood, when he or she did not yet know the answer to the question, "What is two plus two?" What goes through the mind of a child at that point when the question is posed? If the child is not brazen enough to guess a possible answer or enlightened enough spontaneously to deduce the correct answer, he or she will typically respond, "I do not know." Later, the child learns the answer, not by rote or mindless repetition but, by grasping with full comprehension that two pairs make a quartet. Once the sum is learned, barring a memory lapse, that person will always know the answer is "four" and cannot help but think so whenever confronted with the question. The child at such a point truly knows the answer.

Has the child not lost something, though, as part of the process in which the knowledge is acquired? He or she can never again honestly reply "I do not know" when the question is asked. The child has lost access to his or her own previous mental state of not knowing. No histrionic act of pretending to not know will ever be convincing, especially in the child's own mind. The important observation is not about ignorance *per se* but about the mental awareness of ignorance.[9] In a strange and unexpected way, a special kind of knowledge is forever lost, even as other knowledge is acquired.

The Omniscience Riddle may be phrased thusly: "If you were omniscient, which is to say you knew everything (that is, to some, you were God), what is the one thing, by definition, you would not know?" Most, when confronted with this riddle, offer the trivial solution, namely, that there is nothing an omniscient being would not know; they deride the question as not even a riddle, because to suggest a nontrivial solution would seem to invite a contradiction. Yet, as we have seen, knowledge, and specifically, the awareness of ignorance, is lost, even as knowledge is acquired, so something about the very nature of knowledge—call it a flaw, if you will—suggests it is inherently self-limiting. Finite beings lose their awareness of ignorance by acquiring knowledge. Consequently, the PEQ becomes epistemological rather than ontological.

The solution to the Omniscience Riddle is decidedly not trivial. It is solved by considering the implications of the awareness of ignorance itself being the object of knowledge. The one thing, by definition, you would not know if you were omniscient, which is to say you knew everything (that is, to some, you were God), is: what it is like *not* to be omniscient, or *not* to know everything (or *not* to be God).

For the acosmist, God, as the only existing being, is omniscient and His knowledge encompasses everything, except that He cannot know what it is like *not* to be God. Note that this solution to the Omniscience Riddle does not address what cannot ever be known, as that may indeed be nothing, but instead, it concerns what would not, by definition or in the natural course of things, be known. It identifies a loophole in the nature of knowledge: Omniscience does not naturally encompass the experiential awareness of its opposite. Omniscience's lost awareness of ignorance thus describes an entire physical universe, or as the MerlinsScience.com website so aptly and succinctly puts it, "Our knowledge fills libraries, our ignorance a universe."

As an historical aside, philosophers have always been obsessed with establishing definitions, and while some critics have considered this fixation on linguistics or meaning as a form of sidestepping the underlying problems, a consensus about what is meant by a word or phrase can serve not only to clarify the question but ultimately to reveal the answer.

An example is the so-called "Paradox of the Stone," which asks, "Can God create a stone so heavy that even He cannot lift it?" The question supposedly creates a dilemma because the answer seemingly cannot be either yes or no; if yes, then God's inability suggests He is not (or no longer is) omnipotent, or if no, then He never was omnipotent. A yes-or-no question that cannot be answered "yes" or "no" is deemed a paradox.

Heaviness, however, is a result of the gravitational effect of a planet, star, galaxy, or other material body. One ought then to speak of moving a mass rather than of lifting it. Also, it need not be a stone but can be any object. So, a better phrasing of the question would be: "Can God create an object too massive for Him to move?" The dilemma remains, but at least it is phrased with greater scientific accuracy.

The "Paradox of the Stone" is so obviously of ancient origin, because its very phrasing demonstrates an utter lack of understanding about material objects. Other than a black hole, which theoretically follows its own nonstandard laws of physics, the densest object otherwise known to exist is a neutron star—this is a star that has collapsed in a way that has fused all its atoms so that only incredibly dense, uncharged matter remains.[10] A five milliliter teaspoon of neutron star matter theoretically would weigh over five trillion kilograms on Earth.[11] This likely represents a genuine limit on physical density, and hence, how heavy or massive an object can become. This would not prove too unwieldy for a truly omnipotent being to lift or toss about effortlessly.

Although not quite achieving a consensus, as some critics hold to a stricter view, several philosophers like Aquinas and British author C. S. Lewis (1898–1963) settle the dilemma philosophically by defining "omnipotence" to be the ability to do that which can logically be done, in essence, to act within the realm of possibility.[12] It does not detract to say an omnipotent being cannot do the impossible. In chess, the most powerful piece, the queen, has full range legally to move in any direction on the chessboard but has no power or freedom of movement off of it. Aquinas's definition resolves the omnipotence paradox. Similarly, the unknowable is outside the realm of omniscience. Note that acosmism's view would concern God merely thinking of the object, but more importantly, God would not be participating at all in a conception, the main idea of which is imagining the state of affairs in His hypothetical absence; the stone is on its own.

Another dilemma seems to occur in the same-river paradox of ancient Greek philosopher Heraclitus of Ephesus (ca. 500 BCE) when he says, according to later fellow Greek philosopher Plato (ca. 427–347 BCE), that you "could not step twice into the same river."[13] The concept of "flux" recognizes that rivers appear stationary in terms of where they are situated, but different water is constantly flowing through them. A definition removes the dilemma: A river can be defined as all the water that will ever flow in it, regardless of where its identified location may meander. A comparable circumstance would be any site on Earth or any other planet, whose absolute location could not be considered permanently fixed, given that planets rotate, revolve, and move along with their star systems around their galaxies—e.g., our solar system revolves around the Milky Way galaxy, which itself is accelerating away from all other galaxies in the expanding universe. A proper definition is thus the first firm step in the journey toward truth.

The Purpose of the Universe, or the Acosmist's Answer to the Primordial Existential Question

A question with no answer is a barrier that cannot be breached. —Milan Kundera[1]

The solution to the Omniscience Riddle reveals a limitation of knowledge, namely, the tendency to obscure the awareness of ignorance inversely as the realm of understanding expands. If you were omniscient (i.e., knew everything), you would not know by default what it is like *not* to be omniscient (i.e., *not* to know everything); the experiential discernment of something you would not naturally know is tantalizingly beyond your ken. To know something affirmatively is to comprehend it, but to not know something is rarely catalogued as part of anyone's expertise.

So, God, in His omniscience, does not know what it is like not to be God, and it must occur to Him then to wonder what it would be like if He simply did not exist. This specific atheistic pondering is the illusion we have come to call our material universe, which, in support of the delusion of existence, operates altogether and unfailingly according to mechanical rules that govern the concept of matter within an imagined space-time continuum. And because both space and time are themselves elements of the illusion—indeed, time is embedded or baked right into it—the fleeting thought that God is having—namely, "What if I did not exist?"—is altogether over, finished and done, precisely as soon as it has begun. In this way, under the philosophical umbrella of acosmism, theism's assertion of divine aseity is fully reconciled, even if obliquely, with atheism's scientific materialism.

By reflecting on self-nonexistence, an oddly reverse form of solipsism, "that which exists," to which we attach the word "God," is obliged to start entirely from scratch. Additionally, in contemplating what it would be like if He did not exist, God must shroud the beginning in a thick fog of mystery or else risk exposing the impossibility of existence beyond His own aseity. A Big Bang singularity, reifying time itself and initiating the inflation of space, serves as a sufficiently nebulous inauguration of how a godless material universe might begin, amid a quantum chaos tamed into stable order by the regularity of the known physical laws.

To the extent the Big Bang can be thought of as an event, it would occur nowhere and at no time, or more properly, it precedes the manifestation, as we know and understand them, of the dimensions of space and time.[2] In some theories of time, additional spatial and/or temporal dimensions exist beyond the normal ones, such as imaginary time (mathematically, a rotation making its coordinates multiples of the square-root of negative one), which, although not directly detectable or within our scope of experience, may manifest into our reality[3]; Hawking envisions reaching an antipode of a curved continuum, akin to the South Pole of the earth, where further latitudinal or longitudinal progress is no longer possible in two dimensions but a change of altitude along a third dimension is; when referring to the beginning of the Universe in the four dimensions of spacetime as an absolute temporal limit, imaginary time then becomes a launching point in being able to speak of the potentially endless time that might have preceded the Big Bang.[4] Pre-singularity time, which blurs the distinction between past and future, is not real, despite its effects "projecting" into our reality.[5] Additional dimensions might prove a mathematical necessity, however, for any theory of physics that seeks to unify the fundamental forces of the Universe.[6] In the Hartle-Hawking Model, leading up to the initial Planck time of 5.39×10^{-44} seconds, the burgeoning universe's four spatial dimensions slowly morph into three plus a temporal one.[7]

Nonetheless, the Big Bang is neither an event nor a process; were it so, the existence of time would have to straddle it, in that time would have had to have passed both prior to it as well as subsequently. Yet, no time could have preceded the initial singularity that "birthed" time itself.[8] Therefore, no transition occurs, and it cannot have been a temporal process nor a point-in-time event. Furthermore, were God absent, either actually or because He excludes Himself from His own idea, the so-called creation of the Universe without cause would have to at least appear to be plausible, or else the deception, even as a self-deception, would collapse at the very outset.

The view that God imagines what it would be like if He did not exist explains God's seemingly strange absence from the world He is conceiving and His apparent indifference to its ongoing operation. Were you dreaming a scenario in which, say, you attend your own funeral—not an uncommon flight of the imagination—you could play no part other than observer. God's reverie would be no different: He neither does, nor can, play any part, not for lack of interest or benevolence, but because the idea itself, that He be not existent, precludes any participation or interaction. In addition, the act of involvement suggests engagement over time, yet time is an illusion, or rather, time is part of the illusion of nondivine existence; since God's existence is atemporal, He cannot take part in the delusion He has mentally conjured.

Contrast this view with that of the personal deity or deities of religion. A religious deity, operating invisibly, is secreted away from human observation, though affecting the world generally, and humans specifically, in ways that are purportedly undeniable. French mathematician and theologian Blaise Pascal (1623–62) describes his frustration with the concept of the strangely absent creator with the Latin phrase, "*Vere tu es deus absconditus*" (Latin for "Truly Thou are a hidden God"),[9] often referred to simply as the doctrine of *Deus Absconditus*. A number of biblical citations support this doctrine, mostly from the Old Testament, including: "[T]hou art a God that hidest [T]hyself" (Isa. 45:15), which is not intended in the sense of being unknowable but rather being truly hidden; "And the Lord spake unto Moses face to face, as a man speaketh unto his friend" (Exod. 33:11), despite a few sentences later, when God allegedly says, "Thou canst not see [M]y face: for there shall no man see [M]e, and live" (Exod. 33:20); and, in reference to God, "Wherefore hidest [T]hou [T]hy face[?]" (Ps. 44:24).

British evolutionary biologist Richard Dawkins (1941–) appears in a critically panned documentary film in which he is asked, "What if after you died you ran into God[?]," to which he replies, "Bertrand Russell had that point put to him, and he said something like: [S]ir, why did you take such pains to hide yourself?"[10] The actual anecdote concerns a party guest for Russell's ninetieth birthday, asking him, "[W]hat if—uh—when the time comes, you should meet Him [meaning, God]? What will you say?" to which he is reported to have replied "Why, I should say, 'God, you gave us insufficient evidence.'"[11] Christian apologists might insist that God is not hidden whenever He speaks via His creation or through the words of His prophets, but Russell and Dawkins are essentially declaring the obstacle that prevents atheists, agnostics, and other scientifically minded nonbelievers from accepting even the possibility that God exists, namely, that unlike all other natural phenomena in the

Universe, God seems to be hiding or strangely absent. What purpose could that possibly serve?

Moreover, the alleged concealment requires for credence an act of faith, which sets the individual at odds with information, since faith means knowing without evidence. Were this truly a personal god's universe, the proof of both its existence and nature would be everywhere; it would not be lurking clandestine nor allow any finite creation cryptically to obscure or eclipse it. Instead, according to acosmism, God absents Himself precisely as the premise of the Universe, so His non-appearance is ultimately no mystery whatsoever. The obstacle for nonbelievers evaporates, while a sufficient reason forms as to why the ultimate truth is inscrutably different from the facts that otherwise inform our view and understanding of the Universe.

God's lack of participation, or essential inability to take part, in His imagined realm also solves, or to some, sidesteps, the problem of reconciling His presumed omnibenevolence with the apparent wickedness of our world. The irreligious god of acosmism is neither personal nor anthropomorphized with human qualities of goodness, kindness, or empathy. As such, the illusion of the Universe, along with all its elements and related events, unfolds as it would be expected to do if it actually existed on its own and not as the product of a cruel or indifferent divine being. The connection between the inescapable existence of aseity and the uncaring vicissitudes of nature is finally broken: The idea is its own fulfillment.

When we unavoidably create episodes in our lives, we achieve life's basic aim. Our experiences, particularly ones involving emotion, are separate and distinct from the illusory universe in which they occur: They are real, even in the midst of a fantasy. Emotions are powerfully real, because they represent shortcuts in both experience and knowledge[12]; they add another dimension to the spectrum of joy and suffering, which helps explain the religious tendency to identify God, either with the emotion of love or as the personification of anger.

In an overarching sense, whether the Universe itself has a purpose is akin to an abstract painter: The pseudorandom slapping of paint against a canvass can come across as haphazard, but one must never forget that for every painting there was a painter sometime who used art as a form of expression. The spacescape that is the physical universe is like the canvass, and the seemingly random events that transpire are the paint—the purposefulness of the "painting" is that God, the sole thing that truly exists, is contemplating what might happen in His absence: The knowledge of the experiences that follow—in and of itself—is the purpose. It is as though experiences are the food of God's mind, and He is never sated.

In his *Conversations with God* series, American "New Age" (or "New Thought") author Neale Donald Walsch (1943–) claims to identify a desire in God to experience what He is not; he suggests that this yearning motivates God actually to create the physical universe.[13] These particular views come close to acosmism, but what starts as a small difference in ascribing a divine motive becomes a gaping chasm by the time he reaches his conclusion about God's role in His creation.

Ignoring Walsch's ethical stance that allows him apparently to become something of an apologist for Nazi atrocities, his ontological view of what he calls the "Divine Dichotomy" in which God creates "What I Am Not, in order that I might experience What I Am"[14] is remarkably similar to the solution of the Omniscience Riddle and to acosmism's vision of God wondering what it would be like if He did not exist. The two worldviews are distinguishable, however, in that Walsch has God creating a physical universe in which He then participates, whereas acosmism asserts that God need only imagine a universe as if it existed and then very specifically exempts Himself from it. A God wondering what it would be like if He did not exist only needs to imagine, not physically create, a universe. Furthermore, Walsch's spirituality assigns a human-like motivation to God, as though He feels a desire, and has Him splintering His infinite self into human parts; acosmism recognizes the idea as a fleeting thought to which God is already disposed and appreciates that, per Spinoza, an infinite being cannot be divided into or consist of parts.

Italian astronomer and physicist Galileo Galilei (1564–1642) is famous for having said that mathematics "is the language in which God has written the universe"[15] and that the "great book [, by which] I mean the universe [, …] is written in the mathematical language."[16] English theoretical physicist Paul Dirac (1902–84) agrees when he observes, "If there is a God, he's a great mathematician."[17] The geometric patterns in nature and the equations or formulae to which the physical universe dutifully conforms serve to elevate mathematics as more than a mere mental tool: It is evidently the most efficient way to "store" information and, hence, is naturally how the Universe is best conceived, especially as a projection of the direct mathematically oriented thoughts of God.

God's thought in imagining a universe need not be restricted to a single instance. He could be contemplating an infinite number of variations, and this raises the possibility of what has been termed the "multiverse", or equivalently, according to some, the many-worlds or Everett interpretation of quantum mechanics.[18] Each idea would have the quality of a fleeting thought and would represent a permutation of possible outcomes, given the same initial conditions. The notion that any of these imagined universes could interact with one another is unlikely and maybe even contrary to the purpose of the contemplation. Moreover, not all possible universes would necessarily be regulated according to the same mechanics or laws of physics, but the principles that rule our universe are preeminently unique in that those have led to a world that has in some ways manifested, albeit as merely a hauntingly persistent illusion.

One issue is whether, among this infinite set of ideas, some subset, itself perhaps infinite in number, would consist of what might be called "empty" universes. Can we even discern what is not or cannot become manifest? Imagine two such empty universes, each governed by different laws of physics. Despite being unmanifest, both are distinguishable, though, because like mathematics, the laws of physics are anthropically necessary since, were they otherwise, a world might be precluded from existing. In stating his "Principle of the Identity of Indiscernibles,"[19] Leibniz is right in concluding that, notwithstanding such invented distinctions, there can be one and only one empty universe. Leibniz's principle eliminates the possibility of duplicates as well, so the set cannot ultimately be infinite; 10^{80} objects yield ten to the 10^{122} distinct combinations, and thus, there being no duplicates, the number of universes in the entire multiverse likewise cannot be infinite. One estimate puts the number of photons emitted since the Big Bang at 4×10^{84} particles,[20] so only a finite configuration of this number of objects is also possible. This is very much akin to Hegel's dictum that "all cats are grey at midnight."[21] American analytic philosopher Peter van Inwagen (1942–) is apt to agree, observing that, among the infinite possible worlds, a nonempty one is quite simply more likely statistically to obtain or prevail.[22]

Wittgenstein defines an object's properties, or its relationship to other objects, as facts.[23] An empty world is one that is essentially factless. Inasmuch as a factless world would be an oxymoron or logical contradiction, an empty world is therefore impossible.

Yet, if God is conceiving a world without Him, a godless universe becomes perforce a possible world. A consequence is that God's own existence then proves not to be necessary. The saving grace, so to speak, is that God's aseity as "that which exists" does make existence itself a necessity, and purely the functioning of existence is rendered contingent. So, while a godless universe always remains actually impossible, it must be a theoretically plausible world, or else it could not be imagined to exist, even by God.

The core concept of acosmism—that God imagines what it would be like if He did not exist, resulting in the illusion that is our physical universe—has the altogether unintended effect of reconciling the diametrically opposed systems of theism and atheism. This coincidental consensus requires that both systems be identified as being right about some things while wrong about other things. Theism may be right about God's metaphysical existence and atheism is right that no god exists within, or influences the operation of, the physical universe, at least as it appears; both, however, are wrong about something on which, ironically, they do agree, namely, that the physical universe can be created *ex nihilo* out of nothing.

This synthetic consensus or reconciliation is a compromise on which the extremists on both sides will never agree. Militant atheists, those "against all gods," will insist that nothing exists which cannot be detected through sensory perception, perhaps enhanced using the instrumentation of technology; the dogmatic defenders of theism will insist on the possibility and moral necessity of a personal relationship with a supernatural being whom they regard as the author of our existence. Acosmism strikes a balance in recognizing that the perceptions of the senses are illusory and that illusions, especially self-delusions, depend on both the deceived and the deceiver alike. It rejects both the pure materialism of the atheist and the purported divine relationship of the theist. The former cannot be true in the context in which God is all that actually exists, while the latter likewise cannot be true in the context of a godless universe, where a divine relationship is as imaginary as the physical universe itself.[24] Metaphorically speaking, the god of theism plays with the "marble" that signifies the world's affairs, while the god of deism simply once and for all gets the marble rolling; the god of acosmism has an even more limited role: In the manner of "there is no spoon" from the movie "The Matrix,"[25] there is no marble, since it is only imagined to exist.[26]

Another way in which contradictory ideas can be resolved is using the concept of containment. The principle involved is that, if the separateness of the ideas creates the contradiction, then removing the divergence through containment reconciles the conflict. Continuing with the marble metaphor, suppose that you were assigned a task: Taking two differently colored marbles, say red and blue, which can fit in your hand, the task requires you to hold in hand only one of the marbles but also to hold in hand both of them. How might you accomplish this seemingly contradictory task?

Perhaps if you held each marble at different times, you could then say you were holding both but not simultaneously, while satisfying the condition of holding only one of the marbles at a time. Recall that time is the one permitted exception to Aristotle's "Law of Non-contradiction" (LNC). But, no, let us say the task must be performed at a single moment, not across a span of time or at different times.

Perhaps if you held each marble in different hands, such as the red marble in your right hand and the blue marble in your left hand, you could then say that you were holding only one marble in a hand while holding both, albeit in different hands. This would be an attempt to redefine the task in order to make it possible to complete. But, no, let us say the task requiring a marble in hand means one hand only.

Perhaps if you managed to put one of the marbles inside the other, using the concept of containment, you could then place the composite marble in one of your hands and rightly claim you had completed the task as requested. An example of this strategy would be asking whether an egg is white or yellow: While the albumen is white and the yolk yellow, the egg as a whole is assuredly both, precisely due to containment. This concept of containment is an effective, albeit the least obvious, way to reconcile diametrically opposed statements that may yet be independently true.

Using the concept of containment forces us away from the traditional either/or logic and toward more "omnivalent" thinking. Applied to theism and atheism, an acosmist would say that the idea of a physical world is contained wholly within the mind of God, so that both a godless universe and God's sole aseity could both obtain or prevail without contradiction. As "that which exists" on the metaphysical level, God alone exists, in support of a theistic view, while an idea in God's mind, where He imagines what it would be like if He did not exist, is a world that operates as though there were no god, in support of the atheistic or scientific view. Containment synthesizes these at-odds views so that both can be true in their respective realms, even though they cannot separately both be true in a noncontainment context. Furthermore, Kant aptly declares that, because we should not apply speculative propositions to a nonexistent world of appearances, as they relate to such notions as finitude or determinism, we can doctrinally hypothesize that no such limits exist and that a noumenal being might (or might not) have caused the phenomenal world without manifesting itself within that world.[27]

It may be argued that all systems of thought are founded upon axioms, which are assumed to be true, so long as they are noncontradictory and are both consistent and compatible with reality[28]; perhaps they are even self-evidently true if their opposite cannot be true. One can identify four axioms, taken as true but with some compelling justification, upon which acosmism rests. If these axioms were somehow disproven, or shown under any circumstances to be false, it would be hard to see how acosmism could survive such scrutiny. Axioms tend to be chosen precisely because they are nearly impossible to falsify, so other means must be employed with which to evaluate and test them.

Acosmism's first axiom borrows a phrase from objectivism in declaring that "existence exists."[29] In spite of the phrase's construction, this is not a mere tautology, but rather, in fact, a denial of its opposite, namely, that nothingness exists, which cannot obtain or prevail in any nonempty world. Perhaps a better phrasing would be "something exists," which is true for the same axiomatic reason; it also happens to be true as both a reasoned and a brute fact.[30] It becomes purely a matter of convenience, however, and with some regrettable likelihood of confusion, to label "that which exists" as God.

Acosmism's second axiom is that God thinks, or rather, since what exists is situated outside of and does not experience time, God is capable of having a thought. The problem this axiom poses is that it may be far from clear how consciousness, manifested in a mind, can emerge or even occur without the mechanism or physical means of consciousness, such as a brain. We speak metaphorically or perhaps poetically of the so-called "mind of God" by ignoring the logistical challenge it presents. To be sure, humans are only conscious, so far as we know, because we have brains, so if God has no physical brain, how can He be conscious?

With advances in Artificial Intelligence or A. I., we are beginning to discover that thinking is not always an entirely brain-based phenomenon.[31] If actual thought can be made to transpire using nonorganic silicon in place of biological carbon, for example, then we must accept that thought can occur in unexpected ways, including divinely; highly cognitive brains, human or otherwise, might themselves even be thought of as somehow being the indirect recipients of the expression of God's consciousness.

Humans tend to define consciousness as the perceptual awareness of phenomena.[32] Yet, God, being atemporal, neither does nor could perceive anything, as we understand the process. In a Kantian sense, He exists noumenally beyond all phenomena. The act of perception results in mentally separating the subject or perceiver from the object being perceived.[33] For God, though, as all that exists, there can be no such separation, and He becomes what some label "superconscious."[34] Human evolution tracks precisely how we initially came to be capable of perceiving our environment, after which we became aware, not only of our situation but of ourselves, as consciousness emerges like a swarm of bees out of the imprint of our biology.[35] God, out of time, never does evolve and is essentially conscious from the outset as a product of His existence or aseity. Being capable of thought is not to say that God actively thinks, which He cannot, nor that God necessarily could have multiple thoughts, although that would comport with the notion of a multiverse, a "Principle of Fecundity"[36] in which He mentally explores all possibilities. Being capable of thought simply asserts that God has, at least, a single thought, and indeed, that thought is this universe.

The second axiom could also be subsumed under the concept of mental aseity, wherein, akin to existence exists, "thinking is thought." From this perspective, thought represents the possibility of existence: In order for something "to exist, it must be possible beforehand for it to exist."[37] If thought precedes existence, then "that which exists" must be capable of thought.

Acosmism's third axiom is that the illusion that results from God's thought can be and is mistaken for actual existence. By distinguishing existence and reality, we can say that, while the physical universe is undeniably real in the sense that we experience it, nonetheless, it does not exist, at least not in the manner in which God, who is conceiving it, exists. For an illusion to be compelling, it must be persistent, insistent, consistent, and nonexistent. Appropriating Kant's terminology,[38] reality is phenomenal, and existence is noumenal. The axiom affirms that we conscious beings, who are ourselves a part of the selfsame delusion being projected by God's thought, cannot tell the difference between a thing–say, a chair–actually existing and that same thing (that is, the chair) being merely imagined to exist by God. We mistake reality for existence, because we experience what is real and can only infer, errantly, that what we perceive actually exists. If we could encounter the thing-in-itself apart from its perceptible attributes, we could "see" something existing and know it exists, belying the axiom and thereby avoiding the mistake; in truth, though, because existence is not directly observable, we are condemned to mistake reality for existence, precisely because we only know what we perceive or discern.

Acosmism's fourth and final axiom is that the constructs of imagination, including and especially quantum indeterminacy and the mental-only framework of a space-time continuum, facilitate the mechanics of the illusion of a physical universe. This axiom is necessary, because the nature of such an all-encompassing illusion inheres not merely in deceiving the senses of a few short-lived creatures but in erecting an imagined world so subtly deceptive within its presentation of a reality that it can fool the most powerful mind in all of existence. The very character of what passes for real in the context of the delusion must take hold of the mind and reprogram the innate processes it uses to discern objective truth and certainty. Quanta is the pixelation of simulated reality,[39] Heisenberg's uncertainty principle representing the limit on how closely we can examine the apparatus of the ruse, and the Big Bang shrouds in ambiguity the onset of the deception sufficiently to quell any misgivings one may have about the initial circumstances of cosmological causation.

The axioms of acosmism can be summarized as follows: The something that necessarily exists is capable of having a thought about an illusory reality which, through the constructs of imagination, is ineluctably mistaken for actual existence. The impossibility of there being nothing assures us something does indeed exist, call it "God," while the Cartesian *Cogito* guarantees thought itself exists; in order for such a thought to have any content whatsoever, though, it cannot concern what truly exists (i.e., a single, homogenous, indivisible, selfless, atemporal entity), and, in asserting a separable, finite, egocentric mind as the source of the thought, must therefore be an illusion; and for such an illusion of reality to be relentlessly misidentified for existence, the very mechanics of thought, or the constructs of the imagination, must be appropriated, or else the delusion becomes implausible and fails.

Chapter 9:

Critiques of Acosmism

The further a society drifts from the truth, the more it will hate those who speak it. —George Orwell[1]

Descartes categorizes ideas into three distinct types: adventitious, or based on direct sensory perception; factitious, or constructed from other ideas; and innate, or known without experience or instruction.[2] He admits to never having encountered any deity by perception, nor does he believe his idea of God to be an assemblage of other, simpler ideas; he concludes that his knowledge of God and His existence must be innate and therefore, as long as it is clear and distinct, indubitable.[3] With respect to infinity, he asserts that humans can only conceive of a potential infinity, whereas God represents an actual infinity.[4] Descartes fails to recognize, however, that extrapolation is a form of construction, so the notion of a Big Father in the Sky is hardly detached from the ideas we have of earthly fathers, as he suggests in denying the factitious nature of divinity. Had a genetic mutation introduced a beneficial trait of an additional digit on the hand in the evolution of humans, Michelangelo's image of God in the "Creation of Adam" would assuredly be sporting an extra finger.

Some studies show that children are not born with an innate belief specifically in the figure of God,[5] while other studies seem to demonstrate that a general religious propensity, perhaps buoyed by the evolutionary advantage in facilitating tribal cohesion, is not necessarily learned or culturally acquired.[6] The otherwise innocuous use of "fairy tales" for toddlers, for example, can make their minds more susceptible as adults to the inculcation of fantastical religious claims.[7] Of course, if we as humans are biologically prone to being duped, then we must compensate by being skeptical and requiring solid if not irrefutable evidence for non-natural or supernatural beliefs and/or their effects.

When we extrapolate from what we know, every instance of which involves something finite, to an infinite unknown such as God, we run the risk of inventing a figment that is real only in our mind's eye. Dirac admonishes that, "If we are honest—and scientists have to be—we must admit that religion is a jumble of false assertions, with no basis in reality [and that the] very idea of God is a product of the human imagination."[8] Combining the reasonableness of such a caveat with the assertions of acosmism engenders an eerie, Escher-like logic were one to claim to be a figment of the imagination of a Being who is Himself a figment of one's own imagination!

Likewise, little intellectual solace comes in discovering the paradoxes that result from considering whether some profound questions are even answerable. Imagine a sphere that loosely encompasses the entire known universe. Now envision shrinking that sphere just enough that it still contains within it all that is known or thought to exist or to have ever existed. What is outside such a sphere? Given the limits of knowledge, it can be only one thing: the inside of the sphere! No true infinitude could ever be bootstrapped into existence from a finite beginning. So, what exists—truly exists, not merely appears to exist—cannot be bound and must be infinite, due solely to its existence. This realization is the solitary logical escape from the paradoxes of finitude.

Each of the various other philosophical systems or schools of thought handles the question "Why is there something rather than nothing?" differently, either metaphysically or as a matter of morality. While these systems may not seem wholly inadequate in resolving the question, they fall markedly short of the answer that the worldview of acosmism offers.

For example, nihilism replies with its own question: "Why not nothing?" The nihilist considers it metaphysically feasible for a possible world to contain only abstract ideas like numbers or physical laws but no objects; van Inwagen calls it a statistical certainty, however, that a material (or materialistic) universe like ours would manifest itself.[9] What defines nihilism is the pessimistic skepticism that existence is necessarily without any purpose, irrespective of whether a god exists to embody or create it. Seeing a universe devoid of meaning is destructive and causes the nihilist to question if any morality can be found at all to guide or circumscribe human activity specifically and, more generally, the course of nature at large.

Another philosophical system is solipsism, which is relevant because acosmism, in a sense, is a kind of third-party or divine solipsism. Solipsists are skeptical that the external world, including other minds, exists, at least beyond their own contemporary thoughts, perceptions, or feelings.[10] In less metaphysically oriented versions, solipsism may grant a form of existence or "presence" to other objects or minds, but it retains the central tenet that the "self" is the only thing of which anyone can have direct knowledge.[11] The solipsist recognizes his or her own mind or consciousness as the boundary of what can be known as an individual; non-solipsists generally reject, on logical grounds, the solipsist's conclusion that, because of this self-based epistemic limit, the external world therefore does not actually exist.[12] The non-solipsist must advocate for humanity as a whole by asserting that knowledge is not limited to the individual, although the criticism proves invalid that a single perspective is inadequate to explain the Universe: Think of a motion picture director, along with a cinematographer and editor, using multiple cameras, oblique angles, snaking-dolly track shots, and banking drones to display imaginatively a varied story involving a panoply of characters in unique settings and circumstances—no single-perspective issue there.

Of course, solipsism suffers from insurmountable logical inconsistencies. No explanation is offered, nor likely is any explanation possible, as to why the solipsist's mind finds itself somehow midway between complete ignorance and full omniscience; no answer is ever provided as to why, or perhaps ultimately, how, it came to be in, or put into, the midst of its present situation. Solipsism is thus a form of egocentrism, as when children believe all perspectives must be the same as their own.[13] Acosmism's third-party solipsism is valid, however, because in light of there being only a single existence, perspectives become merely different albeit unique views of the same quasi-objective reality.

The primary nonreligious system is metaphysical materialism,[14] called also variously the scientific view, scientism, and, perhaps errantly, physicalism or naturalism or atheism. These latter variants are broader than strict materialism, which asserts that only matter, or what may arise from its interactions, exists; physicalism encompasses nonmaterial forces and energies, while naturalism expands the worldview to declare that reality is the product of natural laws governing natural constituents, natural phenomena, and natural relationships—atheism goes furthest in denying any supernatural or non-natural cause for, or influence on, the physical universe, although some respected scientists claim privately to hold personal theistic convictions.[15] To the materialist, the truth or falsity of a proposition can only be considered if applying the scientific method leads to its potential verification.[16]

Under materialism, the physical universe is self-created, in the sense that it supposedly came into existence spontaneously out of nothing. Some materialists reject the concept of self-creation because in the absence of a "self" earlier in time, the Universe cannot have been its own cause[17]; as noted, however, cosmologists have reached a consensus that time itself emerged from the singularity which spontaneously produced the physical universe, meaning that there was no earlier time in which the matter of a precreated universe could exist. The scientific consensus also precludes the notion of the eternally existing universe envisioned by earlier materialists.[18]

The materialists, in spite of this, want to reformulate the PEQ so they can answer it easily and naturalistically; they claim the PEQ is ill-posed and unanswerable in its standard formulation.[19] English philosopher David Wiggins (1933–) introduces the idea of a "dummy sortal" as a "thing or space-occupier,"[20] a noun that fails to reference any actual substantive instance. Americo-Canadian philosopher of religion Stephen Maitzen (1964–) builds on this definition by declaring that, because the PEQ seems really to be asking why there are contingent, concrete things—a dummy sortal of the first order—the PEQ invites an impermissible bootstrapping: using solely things of a certain kind to justify why there are things at all[21]; he concludes that we can answer a transformed and more specific PEQ which inquires as to the origin of a particular thing, but not all things or things generally. Of course, acosmism asserts that no contingent things, concrete or otherwise, actually exist, so such a PEQ reformulation is unnecessary. But more importantly, a double negation is not a transformation, as is evident by phrasing it in a way even Maitzen would be hard pressed to deny: *Why isn't there nothing rather than something?* No dummy sortal is involved, and the phrasing avoids any need for reformulating the PEQ. We humans tend to base our sense of an object's presence entirely on our perception or detection of it, so the phrase "there is nothing there" does not sound inherently contradictory, but in actuality, "nothing" can neither exist nor obtain or prevail, meaning the PEQ is thoroughly answerable as formulated.

Other materialists assert that we have no evidence of any minds except human minds and that the notion of an "infinite mind" is purely an invention which does not serve to conjure it into being.[22] Mental aseity acknowledges, however, that "thinking is thought" (ala "existence exists") and that, irrespective of a mind, the potentiality of existence means a physical universe can be conceived apart from its creation.

Acosmism is in no way opposed to science, which, being focused on the detectable phenomena of matter in motion, tends to describe processes rather than the purely detached existence or ontology of beings. We may study an illusory reality, realizing that, to be compelling, it must be persistent, insistent, consistent, yet ultimately nonexistent. The details of the mechanics of how the illusion operates is worthy of scientific scrutiny, analysis, and understanding; the fact that the rules seem to break down or prove less predictive at the pixelated plane of the quantum level is *prima facie* evidence that it is indeed an illusion we are studying.

Another way in which acosmism can be an adjunct to materialism is that, foundationally, it too is a go-about-your-business philosophy. Acosmism addresses solely the inception of the Universe—once that universe is conceived to "exist," science can freely describe the mechanisms, according to the laws of nature, by which it unfolds and develops through evolutionary forces, just as if it had emerged into actual existence spontaneously. After the ball is rolling, so to speak, an imagined universe and the one envisioned by the atheist become indistinguishable. Thus, the scientific viewpoint is not displaced, but nor can it lay claim as the simplest cosmological explanation in that it requires the impossible feat of something coming from nothing rather than merely being conceived. Acosmism liberates rather than constrains. Scientists can now freely speculate about how the Universe began, even knowing full well that it never did actually begin. The process is akin to deciphering a dream: The subject may exist outside of reality, yet it follows its own internal rules and unfurls its own unique history and modes of operation. While acosmism addresses the ultimate substratum of existence, its framework does not at all limit the ways in which the subsequent phenomena can be interpreted or explained. Only dimensionless differences and ratios next need to be fine-tuned, and even Kant says the architect of a finely tuned universe cannot be supernatural if strictly subject to the same laws of nature.[23] Only the curious need to know the billionth digit of the transcendental constant π—which happens to be nine—and yet, were that single digit any different, the entire universe itself might suddenly become an impossibility.

In a sense, acosmism is a bridge between consciousness, albeit a divine one, and the materialism that governs the physical universe. Nonetheless, anything less than an infinite number of worlds results in a capricious randomness, and what finally rescues science from such arbitrariness is the anthropic principle, which obviates the fine-tuning requirement through observation. A genuine nothingness would preclude those laws of physics that allow a universe to appear, and yet, it remains possible that, were the known laws of physics any different, no universe could be either conceived or experienced. Similarly, mathematical truths seem to "transcend," or prevail independently of, all possible manifestation, so both numbers and the laws of physics precede existence only anthropically rather than actually.

A sufficiently distinct offshoot of materialism is deism, which resorts to a supernatural creator but, once the proverbial marble is rolling, essentially devolves into a strict naturalism.[24]

According to some analyses,[25] deism is less about the ontology of creation (religious cosmology) than about the epistemology of religious knowledge and how it is acquired: The movement's roots in the Enlightenment steer it into stressing reason over revelation. Deism suffers from the same flaws as materialism when it comes to failing to explain the arbitrary size of the Universe and additionally the timing of precisely when God chose to create it. The deist's impersonal watchmaker-like god exists in time, decides at some point to create a physical universe for no particular reason, and then mysteriously and mutely observes from the celestial sidelines as His creation fitfully writhes into a sustained existence, or eventual heat-death destruction, without His intervention or guidance, albeit perhaps according to His predetermined or foreordained plan. The acosmist interposes the now familiar question: Why would God go to the trouble of physically creating a universe out of nothing, if that were even possible, when He could instead simply imagine it as existing?

Some may be tempted to conclude that, if acosmism is unduly vague, it can easily be discarded; if it cannot help us determine the truth or sort worthy hypotheses from futile conjectures, at least as it relates to questions of cosmology, then it can be dispensed with or otherwise ignored. For example, one indication that the physical universe is an illusion has to do with it being a particular size with a specific finite number of objects in it—the Principle of Sufficient Reason compels us to reject that what really exists would be any arbitrary size, so either something else must exist, which is contrary to the definition of a universe as all that exists, or no universe with a particular size could actually exist. Yet, reducing the physical universe to an idea does not remove the dilemma concerning its apparent size, which the Principle of Sufficient Reason suggests cannot be imagined to be arbitrary. If acosmism does not solve the arbitrary-size quandary, then it might as well be false, and we could return to a universe that somehow physically exists.

Acosmism is redeemed from this criticism because its scope encompasses all possible universes. Although scientific theories abound that concern the notion of multiverses (i.e., multiple universes),[26] they are philosophically unsound and merely an abstract result of applying mathematics to more dimensions than can be perceived by humans. If a universe is "all that exists," then there cannot exist more than one of them. Were matter distributed so that groups of galaxies lie beyond the edge of the known universe, that is an obstacle to our ability to perceive, not evidence that multiple universes somehow exist. Spinoza's proposition regarding indivisibility would be more pertinent the vaster the scope of the Universe extends. In contrast, acosmism would permit God to contemplate all possible universes at once, without any of them being existent, or even most of them being real, in the proper sense. That we find ourselves in one of these possible universes that happens to be a particular size thus does not violate the Principle of Sufficient Reason, so long as all the rest are reified in the mind of God.

Of the possible universes—and given their illusory quality, one might prefer the word "plausible"—the total number, duplicates having been eliminated under Leibniz's Principle of the Identity of Indiscernibles, cannot then be infinite, since each is necessarily comprised of a finite number of objects, and hence, of configurations involving those objects. If physical constants do not vary across the possible universes, the number may be even more limited. Take the gravitational constant, represented by the uppercase G symbol, whose value is 6.67×10^{-11} N-(m/kg)^2. With this value, lower and upper limits on the number of mass-containing objects circumscribe what could be present in a plausible universe. If the number were below the lower threshold, there would not be enough to coalesce to form stars or planets, while if the number were above the upper threshold, the gravitational force would instantly crush such a universe out of existence. So, at its currently known value, the gravitational constant establishes a "habitable zone" for universes in terms of their size. The range is not quite arbitrary, unless only one instance in this zone is favored with existence: In that case, it would run afoul of the Principle of Sufficient Reason. Acosmism permits every single one in the zone to be divinely contemplated, and we only anthropically favor the one in which we happen to live.

Were the gravitational constant not the same value in each universe, it would nonetheless be constrained to a range of values, outside of which no physical manifestation would be possible. If a finite number of values is possible, and for each value, a finite number of universes based on it, then the grand total of possible universes is likewise finite, although it would be a very large number indeed. Still, the mind of God is presumed capable of imagining a finite number of worlds as if they existed and in none of which He existed or appeared to exist. Thus, acosmism honors the Principle of Sufficient Reason in a way that true physical existence cannot.

Acosmism is founded on certain premises, so it is vulnerable as a system only to the extent that any of these foundational premises are deemed untrue. As a system, it cannot be assailed solely for its conclusion. Religion discourages challenge, but systems of thought based on truth welcome it, since a disproven challenge only strengthens the original position. The bedrock premise is that answers are knowable and within the reach of human intellect. Were this not the case, every system would become mere speculation. For example, if the Universe has a particular size but the reason it is that size and not another is wholly unknowable—violating the Principle of Sufficient Reason as soon as it is invoked—then speculating what the reason might be holds little utility. For acosmism to be flatly wrong would require rethinking the very nature of true existence and abandoning any hope that existence has a purpose beyond the raw, brutal means of survival that perpetuate it.

Pantheism builds on deism by suggesting a divinity behind everything, the Universe itself being either an expression or a direct manifestation of God.[27] In a sense, pantheism equates the physical universe (or cosmos) or Nature with God but is ambiguous as to whether the identity might be individual (that is, distributed) or collective,[28] although theoretically, an overarching divinity could be achieved through the interconnectedness of the physical components that comprise the Universe. Due to the lack of anything supernatural in the pantheistic view, however, it too gives way to a form of naturalism, sometimes even mislabeled as a category of atheism.[29] With his emphasis on *natura naturata* as the modes of God's attributes and utterly dependent on God for their conception,[30] Spinoza has become among philosophers the patron saint of pantheism.[31] Nevertheless, for the pantheist, reality, even an idealistic one, is not mere appearance or the effect of a consciousness, so it remains in clear opposition to acosmism.

Combining pantheism with deism is pandeism, where a universe emerges, less as a result of creation than as God choosing to embody or become it. In one account,[32] God challenges His own omnipotence by destroying Himself in what appears as the Big Bang and hopes somehow to awaken as a consciousness in the midst of a physical universe that He, through this process, created. Some elements of pandeism are reminiscent of acosmism, such as the delusion of the phenomenal world we perceive, the role of a seemingly absent god, and the testing of omniscience as a motivating force behind the emergence, and perhaps workings, of the Universe. A clear distinction can be drawn, however, between the physical self-destruction envisioned by the pandeist and the divine mental self-reflection in acosmism—"What would it be like if I [God] did not exist?"— making it difficult to mistake the former's physicalism for the latter's genuine idealism.

Panentheism further builds on, but also veers off from, pantheism by asserting that the physical universe is what mathematically might be called a "proper" subset of God, which is to say, God is both it and more, as He transcends our world and the spatio-temporal framework within which it is believed to exist. This view serves to keep separate some otherworldly part of God, which then allows panentheists to worship Him as a supreme being, distinct from the world that He nonetheless fully embodies. In this view, God is immanently "in" rather than "equal to" Nature. Hegel saying "[w]ithout the world, God is not God"[33] is a declaration of his panentheism and an assertion of its interdependent divine-worldly relationship. If God is viewed as having both a mind and body, then for the panentheist, the physical universe is God's body.[34]

While both pandeism and panentheism avoid the cosmological impossibility of *ex nihilo* creation and thus contend as potentially viable PEQ answers, they suffer from considerable logical weaknesses that make them thoroughly inferior to acosmism. They mistake acosmism's "God ponders" for actuality; their emphasis on God having (or having had) a physical body represents their attempt to attach divinity to the science of the phenomenal world, which acosmism recognizes as a perceptual delusion, science being the consistent mechanism through which the delusion is perpetuated. They do not address, let alone solve, the problem of arbitrary extension—why is the observable universe, once a singularity at the Big Bang, the particular size it is as opposed to another size? Likewise, they fail to tackle temporal issues, such as, if God precedes in time His own creation, how could He choose to become the Universe at the particular moment He did, especially within the span of eternity?

The moralistic criticisms leveled at pantheism and panentheism, however, seem misplaced.[35] The argument, roughly, is that, because the world unavoidably contains evil, an all-good God cannot be in or equated with it. But this rationale is, in the same manner, equally applicable to nearly every other system in which God fails to swoop in like a superhero to the rescue. In deism, for example, God sets the world into motion and then watches the resulting suffering with idle indifference, while even a full-blown theism cannot reasonably explain how an omnipotent god appears powerless to prevent, or through divine planning avert, so much suffering in the world. For acosmism, God imagines a world in which He plays no role and where the suffering, no matter how illusory, is altogether real but hardly unnecessary.

Pursuing the moral thread, Canadian analytic philosopher John Leslie (1940–) promotes a system of thought he calls "axiarchism," based on platonic forms.[36] In Plato's "Cave" analogy,[37] we humans supposedly see only shadows of idealized forms whose universal reality transcends our individualized perceptions; although Plato defines "evil" as the distortion of these derivative shadows of the otherwise incorruptible forms, he recognizes existence as inherently good. Prof. Leslie contends that this goodness somehow compels a universe into existence, his critics calling this conclusion less a matter of logic and more purely "poetic fantasy."[38] Elevating "value" to become a creative force also has the effect of ensuring that a world compelled to exist in this manner would perforce conduct itself morally. The fact that the world, at least across the living realm, is full of suffering, death, and destruction may well doom axiarchism as unrealistically optimistic; in contrast, acosmism accurately predicts that a world conceived to exist on its own, apart from any regulating moral constraints, is thereby susceptible to corruption. Axiarchism, especially in its extreme metaphysical form, has not extended far beyond the ivory-towered walls of academia, where an idle discussion can be had over lunch, without a sense of irony, about the intrinsic "goodness" of the holocaust, the bubonic plague, or marauding Huns.

The system of belief that places a supernatural god in a central role is, of course, theism; when adorned with tradition, doctrine, and ritual, it becomes religion, which is more of a social structure as opposed to an intellectual one. While theism is often conceived of as a philosophy, religion instead concerns establishing some kind of relationship, often personal, between adherents and a seemingly absent deity. The Abrahamic god, through an invisible hand, is hidden in an almost cowardly way and must be pleaded with via prayer to intervene,[39] whereas acosmism's God absents Himself as the very premise of the Universe. The Lord is routinely thanked for providing food on the dinner tables of the faithful, while fully one-eighth of humanity, a fifth of them children, is starving, often to death[40]—it is not so much about recognizing that whoever may be in charge of global food distribution is doing a lousy job as it is about attributing that decidedly poor performance to a supposedly benevolent, all-powerful, divine being.[41] Similarly, that there are ever survivors of natural disasters is more the hallmark of an indifferent universe than a deity whose choices appear to us capricious or arbitrary.

Of course, theism and religion began as a way for frightened barbarians to make sense of nature and the savagery of a cruel world, which is now very nearly perfectly explained, if not quite understood, by the principles of science. The remedy for superstition is science, just as the cure for ignorance is knowledge. Theism exploits ignorance by promoting a kind of superstition and then offering its own fictitious solution, which typically involves swearing a to-the-death allegiance, routinely filling the collection plate, and condoning all manner of atrocities against enemies of the church. In contrast, for science, the only conquest is the discovery of previously unknown facts, and the only torture is of data until it surrenders some hitherto hidden truth, the only requirement being an open mind, the very thing that most threatens the control wielded by religions over the lives of their adherents.

Despite its vagueness, another contender for the least bizarre PEQ answer is a system (or systems) not yet thought of or conceived. Arguing that there may be a philosophy that will prove to be better than anything which we now know is not hard, nor can one fault someone who insists on awaiting a perfect PEQ answer. But wait for how long? Centuries? Millennia? The approach is analogous to allowing one's intellect to be frozen now and expecting it later to be thawed out when humanity finally has the long-awaited answer. One can never win a debate against a phantom, however, so, ceding to the as-yet-undiscovered perfect answer, we have little choice for now but to move on from this indeterminate alternative.

Still, we can describe the kinds of answers that are worth considering. Such answers must either be true or else, even when presumed to be false, they must possess some explanatory value that points us toward a true answer. In brief, these answers must be possible, complete, and plausible. An impossible answer is unlikely to contain much of anything instructive, and its elimination is a suitable initial threshold. An answer that is incomplete is apt to have missed the central issue and would tend more to mislead than to illuminate. A possible and complete answer that nonetheless fails to rise beyond being implausible is no better than similar answers that strain credulity. Acosmism as a philosophical system certainly has all the necessary elements to be considered both possible and complete. It is eminently possible, having been constructed from what must be true, what appears to be true, and the need to reconcile the disparity between them. In addition, it is unquestionably complete because it addresses the entirety of existence and reality. On the issue of plausibility, that imposing hill on which most PEQ answers "die" under the attentive lens of scrutiny, acosmism shows itself to be at least a bit more, if uncomfortably, probable as a working explanation than the only other known answer, the downright infeasible account of an *ex nihilo* creation of the physical universe. As one creative author observes, "Invention [...] does not consist in creating out of void, but out of chaos. [... I]t can give form to dark, shapeless substances, but cannot bring into being the substance itself."[42] Inventive thought, not physical creation, is what God has produced, and He has done so with His lonely mind, not His hands.

Acosmism is not without its critics. Their concerns center on issues like probability, falsifiability, causal simplicity, and seriousness. Because we are generally ill-equipped to evaluate speculative, metaphysical claims or hypotheses, it may not be possible fully to rebut these counterarguments, but nothing prevents us from addressing them.

In the absence of certainty, the concepts of likelihood and probability become factors shaping rational analysis. These concepts depend on conditional odds, as in the frequency with which a proposition may potentially be true given observed data or evidence; in particular, one must assess how likely corroborating data or evidence is apt to appear were the proposition true.[43] Nonetheless, such Bayesian reasoning does not constitute proof, but only relative probability.[44] Assessing the probabilities of various PEQ answers may serve as a guiding rationale but never as a substitute for proof or to steer the inquiry.

The matter of likelihood is a strong reproach against acosmism, but speaking fairly, it is similarly in opposition to every other available PEQ answer. Assuming acosmism as true, that the sole-existing omniscient Being is imagining what His absence would entail, the question then becomes: Would an apparent physical universe precisely like ours tend to arise as a result? Even if the response is "unlikely," it remains categorically no less likely than a physical universe spontaneously coming or being divinely brought into existence out of nothing for no discernible purpose. One cannot dismiss as unlikely an outcome that resulted from a causal chain of events, because each contributing event, no matter how improbable, serves as an actual but-for, if not proximate, cause of that outcome.

The philosophical problem with acosmism, however, is thornier still. Strikingly similar to religious claims that rely on faith in the authority of an unseen deity, the assertions of acosmism are not ultimately subject to verification. The apparent strength of being unassailable is actually a weakness; any hypothesis—whether concerning a physical phenomenon or a metaphysical principle—that fails to generate a testable prediction is automatically deemed "unscientific."[45] Austro-English philosopher of science Sir Karl Popper (1902–94) uses the term "falsifiable" to refer to the ability potentially, if not actually, to refute an hypothesis through testing.[46] The purpose behind falsification is to distinguish nonscience from science, although the concept of falsifiability is metaphysically a nonscientific conjecture about what constitutes a scientific claim and cannot itself be falsified.[47] There is nothing inherently wrong or less compelling about nonscientific claims, which encompass areas long understood not to be empirically testable like mathematics, metaphysics, and logic.[48] Science should not start with a conclusion, however, but must methodically deduce its interpretations from data rather than generalize overarching laws to explain them; falsification helps avoid the problem of induction and ensures science progresses by building block-by-block on facts instead of leaping to judgment based on ambiguous findings.

An unfalsifiable proposition is one whose truth-value simply cannot be determined. In a sense, it is neither true nor false, which makes it unscientific. While no accumulation of data can ever conclusively prove something to be true, a single datum or occurrence can instantly reveal it to be false. The stumbling block is learning to navigate, almost entirely by reason and intuition, in a sea of uncertainty. Perhaps falsifiability ought to be considered merely a factor, and a nondispositive one at that, in evaluating a claim. That an event occurs only rarely does not falsify the presence of causality or an hypothesized causal connection. Moreover, an association of aggregate causes can stymie the interpretation of test results. Scientific may be the best kind of knowledge in a fact-based world, but it is not necessarily the only kind. Testing is obviated if a presupposition affects testability: For example, any test presupposes that time transpires, so no test can be conceived which challenges whether time does indeed transpire.

Some will question whether metaphysics adds anything. Despite the distinction between existence (actuality) and reality (experience), these critics will see no verifiable difference between, on the one hand, a physical universe believed to have spontaneously come into existence via the negative energy of space inflating at the Big Bang, and on the other hand, an imagined universe that must be thought plausibly to have at least appeared to come into being. If the Universe is likened to a machine running in a darkened room, though, then metaphysics is akin to a light that is turned on suddenly. The machine would have continued to hum along contentedly in the dark, so the light may rightly be said to add virtually nothing to the operation of the machine. And yet, the light assists us in better understanding the machine, in this case, the Universe, and thus metaphysical observations have inherent, albeit purely explanatory, value. To those who say acosmism unnecessarily adds complexity, it is actually quite the opposite: An imagined universe would unquestionably be less, not more, complex than a physical one that would have had spontaneously to pop into existence out of either nothing or a quantum vacuum.

It may be tempting to assume outright that all unfalsifiable claims are false, because, by their not being testable, one would never come to know whether or not they were actually false. The greater danger, though, is if unfalsifiable statements are irrelevant or otherwise unusable. Thus, a nonfalsifiable statement can only be accepted on the conditions that it is both rational and useful to the understanding. Theories about cosmology (the multiverse) or quantum states (string theory) are likely out-of-reach in terms of successfully using the physical universe as a laboratory for testing, yet it would be altogether unscientific to ignore the possibility that these comprehensive and elegant solutions truly do describe the workings of the cosmos.

While metaphysical propositions are not typically capable of being tested, they surface or are called upon when science alone cannot explain an event or phenomenon, so to hold such propositions to a scientific standard like falsification is both ironic and inappropriate. Of course, they ought to clarify and must remain germane by avoiding being ridiculous or aiming for an elusive, ever-changing objective. The spontaneous emergence of a physical universe from utter nothingness is a perplexing event that seems to defy explanation. Science attempts to explain this event by denying that nothingness is even possible (i.e., that a low-energy quantum field is always present in any presumed vacuum), while acosmism explains the event by denying that it occurred at all (i.e., by insisting that the physical universe is an illusion). When it comes to explaining the event, science's denial is no more plausible than acosmism's, but the latter has the advantage by at least purporting to supply a "why" that the former likely never can. An important premise of atheism is that, to explain naturally observable phenomena, citing an invisible, intangible, or eternal entity is no better, but unnecessarily more complicated, than referencing no such being. The need for this premise evaporates under acosmism's contention that all is illusion, since denying that the phenomenon exists is even simpler than any detailed account which attempts to explain it.

Dawkins is widely known for his clear, rational, incisive analysis of religious-based beliefs. As an eminently readable science author, he characteristically possesses a unique talent for probing the truth and ferreting out the absurdities inherent in unsubstantiated or unscientific claims. His arguments are typically cogent and bitingly insightful.

One of Dawkins's lines of argument involves how improbable it is for an explanatory cause to be more complex than its simpler effect. To all appearances, he models his views on the biology of evolution, which does indeed appear to be able to account for an astonishing growth of complexity out of an original simplicity through the natural processes of hereditary selection. When Dawkins applies this line of reasoning—equating complexity with improbability, at least as a cause—to God, however, he goes a bit astray by declaring that God cannot be simple and thus is neither a sufficient explanation nor, given the circumstances, likely to exist. For example, as it relates to a designer of a universe specifically, Dawkins says, "However statistically improbable the entity you seek to explain by invoking a designer, the designer himself has got to be at least as improbable."[49] With his affinity for biology, he further states, "[A]ny God capable of intelligently designing something as complex as the DNA/protein replicating machine must have been at least as complex and organized as the machine itself."[50] One can hardly misapprehend his meaning when he asserts that "[b]y definition, explanations that build on simple premises are more plausible and more satisfying than explanations that have to postulate complex and statistically improbable beginnings [… a]nd you can't get much more complex than an Almighty God!"[51]

While it may be generally true that a cause or creator tends to be more complex than its effect or creation, this is clearly not always the case. In the area of computing and robotics, one influential founder in the field predicts that our technological innovations will outstrip us within a generation, clarifying that "[t]he singularity is that point in time when all the advances in technology, particularly in artificial intelligence (AI), will lead to machines that are smarter than human beings."[52] If we humans can eventually be viewed as simpler than our creations, then Dawkins's contention about the improbability of God based on complexity may not be entirely accurate. (Incidentally, AI also demonstrates that having a mind without a brain, or at least without a biologically based brain, is indeed possible. If electrified silicon can suddenly produce a mind, then we cannot predict where consciousness may reside. Thus, it should not surprise us that God as "that which exists" has a mind, and that, eerily, we may be the indirect product of that mind.)

Examples of relative simplicity revealing a hidden, complex interrelationship abound in the field of mathematics. A few prefatory mathematical definitions would begin with a factorial of an integer or whole number being the product of all positive integers up to the original number. The reciprocal of a number is the quotient of one and the original number. Euler's (or Napier's) number, e, is the sum to infinity of the reciprocals of all nonnegative factorials. A natural logarithm is the value to which e must be exponentiated to equal a given number. The square root of negative one is defined as the imaginary number, i. Finally, the transcendental number π is the irrational number representing the ratio of every circle's circumference to its diameter. With all these definitions in mind, a breathtakingly unexpected discovery called Euler's identity[53] is that the quotient of twice the natural logarithm of i and i itself turns out to be, magically—and perhaps, as some aesthetically minded mathematicians might allege, beautifully and elegantly—the number π. Furthermore, one-quarter of π can also be represented as the sum of an infinite series of alternating the addition and subtraction of the reciprocals of all odd integers.[54] It is remarkable that the value of π, which is the essence of every conceivable circle, can be calculated with formulae and numeric series that seemingly have nothing to do with circularity. Likewise, the computational algorithms to produce graphically the astonishingly complicated shapes of fractals and Fibonacci spirals are themselves quite simple.[55] The point is that, as with biology and other sciences, mathematics also demonstrates that complexity can quickly arise from simple beginnings.

Nevertheless, how does one measure the complexity of God's mind? Such a mind is unlike any other entity or assemblage, so we cannot apply the same standard of a large number of parts operating simultaneously in complicated relationships and/or interactions.[56] It does not consist of parts, nor does it function temporally. To attempt to adjudge its complexity with respect to material entities is therefore inappropriate. Moreover, there is also some irony in the recognition that matter can only be understood or perceived by a mind. We might encounter a machine whose unwieldy array of moving parts seem complicated to us, yet we would not necessarily regard as complex the spark of inspiration or pre-engineered insight that first motivates the inventor to visualize the innovation. The originator is God, or rather His mind.

An omniscient being might be regarded as complex, though, because its knowledge purportedly spans every atom of what has allegedly manifested into existence across the vast physical universe, yet that same omniscient being, according to acosmism, would be deemed simple were it the only entity actually to exist while all of the Universe's physical manifestations were merely imagined to exist. So, depending on how God or His mind operates, an omniscient being might prove to be quite simple and uncomplicated. Humans can neither mimic such a mind nor produce one because we are fully enmeshed in the very idea that is its product, which is to say, its conception of us does not allow us to conceive of it. If the complexities of matter and life can arise from simple beginnings, though, why not then the pure notion of them?

As Scottish empiricist David Hume (1711–76) observes:

*A mind, whose acts and sentiments and
ideas are not distinct and successive;
one, that is wholly simple, and totally
immutable; is a mind, which has no
thought, no reason, no will, no sentiment,
no love, no hatred; or in a word, is no
mind at all.*[57]

Yet, an idea may unfold, driven—not by will, reason, or emotion, but—simply by the need to know: What would it be like if the one thing that exists did not exist? It requires no extension into space, no passage of time, no human-like brain functioning, and no other thoughts than the one necessarily lacking in omniscience. One likely answer—and perhaps, *the* answer—is: a universe like ours. The irony in Hume's quote is that he fails to realize that an imagined mind is likewise hardly a mind at all; the mind that conceives it, however, along with the rest of what we call creation, certainly is.

An unfalsifiable explanation should also be comprehensive enough to fit all of the facts. The claims of acosmism might be more palatable if conceived of as an abstraction. In the same way that a Schlegel diagram projects an object into a figure at the next-lower dimension[58]—e.g., a tesseract used to convey a four-dimensional polytope as a hypercube[59]—acosmism is akin to a projection of a physical universe into a (divinely) mental space. This allows acosmism to incorporate by reference all other physical-based explanations while still denying the underlying existence of the explicated phenomena. The acosmist's view is perfectly cogent at the agreed-upon level but simply envisions it to be itself an abstraction at a different level.

Critics of metaphysics often cite Kurt Gödel's incompleteness theorem(s), in which he declares that no axiom-based "mathematical system that contains its own provability predicate can be consistent or complete."[60] He is addressing what is ultimately provable mathematically, though, not what is true philosophically. To the extent it suggests a limit on epistemology, that no "measurement from inside the observed system can be informationally complete,"[61] it concerns what is knowable rather than identifying any defect or inadequacy in what is known.

In an effort to establish a form of completeness in which nothing can exist outside temporal eternity and spatial infinity, Anglo-American philosopher W. T. Stace (1886–1967) finds acosmism hopelessly imbued with mysticism and in stark contrast with the reality of the natural world.[62] He sees all religious thought as "symbolic,"[63] clumsily referring to an ineffable god who forever remains an enigma, even to itself, and whose eternal qualities cannot be conceived, much less demonstrated to be true as literal facts.[64] According to Stace, the "infinite" in a religious sense is not measured as it might be for the numerical or spatio-temporal realms by degree or extent but rather by its steadfast resistance to being supplanted by anything else.[65] As such, it "is only by intuition that the infinite can be apprehended."[66] Nonetheless, while acosmism admittedly traffics in metaphor, that is hardly the criteria for mysticism. Envisioning the atomic orbit of an electron as a probability cloud, for example, is not by virtue of its vagueness somehow more mystical than Aristotle's four elements of nature. It is again a matter of abstraction.

The most forceful critique of acosmism might be in posing the simple question: "Are you serious?" Denying that the physical universe exists is frankly too outlandish a conclusion, even in an area admittedly plagued by considerable philosophical doubt. The denial is also seen as improbable, psychotic, self-refuting, and, worse in a sense, unnecessary. In order for acosmism to prevail, these criticisms must either be rebutted directly or shown somehow to be inapplicable.

In the acosmic state of affairs, God is both the creator of the spectacle that would be the grand illusion of a physical universe as well as its audience. Some may wonder how it is, under these circumstances, that the audience never sees the creator, while others may marvel at why the unseeing audience never comes to realize the creator is itself.[67] Even the Qur'an at 52:35 asks: "Did they come into being without any creator [o]r were they their own creators?" The key to making this consistent is by asserting, as acosmism does, that the Creator is purposely hiding from Himself; the Audience then must apprehend that It cannot exist apart from the Creator. Denying the actuality of the immanent mechanism by which the Creator deludes Himself into becoming His own Audience then no longer seems improbable.

Acosmism is emphatically not an instance of Cotard's delusion or Walking Corpse syndrome, also known as "The Delirium of Negation," in which deranged individuals suffer from an intransigent belief that they either are already dead, are immortal, or more relevantly, do not exist.[68] The fusiform gyrus and amygdala areas of the brain, which assist in the human ability, shared with other primates, to recognize faces, are thought in these cases to malfunction in their neural transmission so as to cause a disconnection; the resulting loss leads to a distortion of reality in which familiar faces, including sometimes the patient's own, fail to trigger the typical emotions, or instead elicit inappropriate responses, associated with acquaintance and recognition.[69] A similar psychological condition, Capgras delusion, also known as "impostor" syndrome, is one in which a sufferer comes to believe without foundation that an impostor or doppelganger has been surreptitiously substituted for a well-known family member or friend.[70] Likewise, someone who suffers from Fregoli syndrome irrationally asserts that a single individual is appearing in disguise as several different people[71]; this delusion has more to do with identity than facial recognition, however.

As noted, the ability to see and recognize faces has demonstrable evolutionary benefit in terms of avoiding predators and enlisting allies. The skill has also proven pernicious, however, when used to anthropomorphize natural phenomena, from the "Man in the Moon" to cultural deities themselves. But when the aptitude is compromised by brain malfunctioning, various maladies like Cotard's or Capgras delusion, Fregoli syndrome, or De Clerambault's erotomania may ensue. As psychologists maintain, in their best estimation, that the causes involved are entirely physical,[72] it becomes highly unlikely that professing acosmism is a mental disorder, as are the cited conditions.

A more apt analogy is "nihilistic" delusion, which psychologists consider the mistaken belief that everything does not exist or is unreal.[73] Any such delusion that persists despite all countervailing indications is deemed to be psychotic in nature, if not itself a form of schizophrenia.[74] Psychologists distinguish a reasonable belief, where an assertion is made amid insufficient evidence, from a delusion, where an assertion is maintained in spite of clear, convincing, and often overwhelming evidence that logically refutes it[75]; delusions are also labeled "bizarre" when doubtful, out of the ordinary, or otherwise culturally inappropriate.[76]

The hallucinations that accompany psychosis are merely mistakes of perception, while delusions are lapses in belief, which hardens enough to be resistant to challenge, regardless of how inconsistent the belief becomes in the light of evidence to the contrary.[77] Yet, the inconsistency is not only between belief and evidence but also between the specific belief and the individual's long-held, general views: An odd and suddenly adopted belief that does not fit neatly into the person's overall belief system is apt to be categorized as delusional. The preexisting belief system forms a coherent view of reality and is informed by both experience and the cultural or societal environment in which the individual lives. That is why some beliefs can be reasonable in one culture or society but, by defying expectations of credibility, nonetheless be deemed delusional in another. Abnormal brain activity can hamper how the mind interprets its experiences, although the schism between belief and reality is what truly constitutes a delusion.

By this standard, acosmism is not delusional, because its assertion that the physical universe is an illusion is not in conflict with reality: The claim is a redefinition of reality, namely, that it is the experience of something which appears to but does not actually exist. Of course, some critics will label it a self-refuting assertion[78] by mischaracterizing it, as if acosmism somehow declares reality itself to be an illusion. Such critics will emphasize that there must be an objective reality with which to contrast any purported illusion; what they are missing is the simple distinction acosmism makes between existence and reality. To the acosmist, the physical universe is all-too-real, even if, by being an idea in the mind of God, it only exists referentially.

Regardless of how we approach it, the PEQ must be deemed answerable, or else no part of the inquiry will likely be of any value to us. The major systems of thought—theism and atheism—incorporate in their beliefs or reasoning a perfunctory PEQ answer that is in line with or necessitated by their thinking, yet the PEQ is still being posed after all these centuries as if no answer, certainly not a consensus one, has been achieved or is otherwise forthcoming. Those who insist on continuing to wait for a better or compelling answer to emerge are staking not only the reputation of philosophy on a dubitable hope but their own lives, since history has shown progress on this front to be millennia in the making and beyond long successive generations of human lifetimes. Assuming the PEQ is not completely insoluble, the answer ought to be readily at hand; the failure thus far to answer it must be due then more to a lack of reason rather than to a shortage of time. The available alternatives are currently there on the table, so the task becomes simply choosing the most sensible among them. Acosmism need not be considered "sane" to qualify as a PEQ answer; it need only be a bit more convincing or plausible than every other available answer.

To say a supernatural entity conjured up the physical universe out of nothing for its own amusement is clearly irrational, as is contending that such a universe popped into existence out of nothing for no particular reason. In contrast, to envision God as existence itself, whose infinitude compels Him to imagine what it would be like if He did not exist, the seemingly godless universe being the direct result of such a thought, is consistent, explanatory, and, compared to the other hypotheses, decidedly more levelheaded as it relates to plausibility, causation, and rationale.

Ultimately, to attack acosmism successfully, one cannot simply affirm that what appears to be true (in this case, the illusion of the physical universe's existence) is true. A successful critic will have to dethrone acosmism's assertion that what must be true about existence itself quite simply is not true. Specifically, it would have to be demonstrated, as either a logical necessity or as an indisputable empirical fact, that what exists is not, nor need not be, infinite. It is by being infinite that God alone exists, that He cannot consist of parts, and that He remains unbound by any spatio-temporal framework. In characterizing an infinite "God" as "that which exists," it follows that He is alone, because anything thought to exist apart from Him would necessarily have to be within, or perhaps an expression of, Him. Since no parts can be configured to build or be subsumed under an infinite entirety, it stands to reason that something infinite could not consist of parts but rather would manifest as a single, homogeneous whole. Kant and later idealists are reasonable to insist that space and time are merely constructs of human consciousness, which the imagination uses in order to make perception sensible. At the scale of infinity—where there cannot be enough parts jammed together to make the whole infinite—there are no objects to perceive, though, thereby obviating the need for any consciousness to order its perceptions using space and time as an imaginary framework.

If "that which exists" were not infinite, acosmism would cease to add up and could not serve as an answer to any question, much less the PEQ. But were it circumscribed, what could limit existence itself? It cannot be limited by something, because that something would also have to exist and would thus be part of the existence it is limiting. Nor could it be limited by nothing, because nothingness cannot obtain or prevail and thereby cannot affect anything that does. To not be infinite, "that which exists" would thus have to be self-limiting. The basic tenet of acosmism is that the only possible limitation on existence is one that is self-imposed, and even then, only mentally, which is how God is capable of imagining what it would be like if He did not exist. Only by denying His infinitude can God conceive of a physical universe that is apart from Himself, that consists of diverse parts, and that operates within the context of a space-time continuum. In this sense, the distinction between existence and reality reasserts itself, as God is actually infinite since He cannot be limited, whereas His conception of a reality in which He does not exist is necessarily finite and is the only way through which His idea can be conceived.

Part II: Applied Acosmism

Chapter 10:

Faith

Anyone who has the power to make you believe absurdities has the power to make you commit injustices. —Voltaire[1]

Kant writes, "I have therefore found it necessary to annul [or deny] *knowledge*, in order to make room for *faith*."[2] When contrasted with knowledge, faith connotes accepting a proposition as true without knowing it to be true. To the scientist, nothing deserves to be thought of that way without the evidence proving or corroborating its truth. Einstein's adage that "[i]magination is more important than knowledge"[3] addresses their respective reach: Knowledge is a measure of what is presently understood, whereas imagination is unbounded and offers a glimpse of what has yet to be discovered. Any article of faith that involves a current understanding clearly puts itself at odds with knowledge, so what Kant means by "deny" is an acknowledgement that some truths may forever be inaccessible, and thus he is saying that, where knowledge is impossible, he relies on faith to fill in the gap.

Nonetheless, even by the Kantian standard, faith serves a very narrow purpose and remains subject to both empirical refutation and the guiding contours of reason. According to the verifiability principle of English logical positivist Sir Alfred Jules Ayer (1910–89), *aka* A. J. Ayer, the absence of any conceivable condition that would falsify an assertion, or confirm its opposite, makes it merely a pseudo-proposition, that is, nonsense.[4] Some hold a stricter view, that a proposition must be actually verified to be considered useful or meaningful.[5] Such requirements apply to not only genuine religious faith but also all metaphysical claims, which, by their very nature, transcend the empirical realm of substantiation. This is especially the case for philosophical systems like acosmism that question the existence of the celestial yardstick, namely, the physical universe itself, which logical positivists use as their proving ground.

The danger of faith generally, and of specific sweeping beliefs, is in making the individual devotee a declared enemy of the truth: A single intransigent belief can keep a believer anchored to a falsehood long after a contravening truth has come to light. A rational mind is one that strives to minimize beliefs by choosing to accept as true only what is known to be true. Beliefs can be useful placeholders which serve to round out the understanding of a structure that is only incompletely known, but beliefs should remain easy to dislodge as the information in whose stead they are embraced is finally revealed. The training wheels must come off.

Because the truth seems always eventually to surface, and because wrongs like intolerance, bigotry, and war might more easily be committed in an environment steeped in ignorance, all false beliefs need to be identified and rooted out, even if they temporarily provide the individual with some ersatz solace or comfort. While belief is accepting as true an unproven claim, skepticism is the doubting of all such claims and insisting they be subjected to scrutiny; so faith is at odds with both knowledge and skepticism. (In its extreme form, however, skepticism may question that specific knowledge or knowledge generally is even possible.)

This prompts belief holders to bolster their claims using a technique that mirrors in many ways how the scientific method approaches validation: justification. While some define knowledge as the intellectual region where belief overlaps the truth,[6] the analysis must recognize that the evidence or proof is itself the knowledge, not the original belief. Therefore, a better and more prevalently held definition of knowledge is one that incorporates some underlying reasoning, namely, justified true belief or "JTB." Again, though, one must resist equating justification with truth, as some have errantly done by suggesting the impossibility of justifying what is untrue.[7] Moreover, many false beliefs that result from prejudice, propaganda, or groupthink could be argued to have some rational basis, so justification is entirely distinct from knowledge.

Believers may justify a belief based on other knowledge they already possess (although some of that primary knowledge may have its own justification issues) or on reliable external sources (although the fact that a source can be considered "reliable" is itself also a belief), it must be rationally consistent with the broad system of beliefs to which the believers subscribe. In demanding actual evidence, a believer may stumble into a causal chain that unexpectedly stretches back in time or involves an occurrence without end, a so-called "infinite" chain.

One way of injecting a form of rationality would be to take a foundational belief axiomatically as the basis for other beliefs. In some ways, this amounts to bootstrapping, not unlike the reliance on sources or an infinite causal chain. Such bootstrapping in these various approaches creates what German critical rationalist philosopher Hans Albert (1921–) calls the "Münchhausen" trilemma[8] (named for the fictional Baron Münchhausen,[9] who, in one story, manages to extricate himself from a quagmire by pulling himself up by his own hair). The three types of approaches include: a circularity in which a conclusion, in turn, supports and is supported by, the data on which it is based; an infinite regression, where every factual demonstration evokes the need for additional fact-based explanations; and axioms, which represent debatably self-evident foundational principles.[10] In his view, none of these approaches—that is, no amount or manner of justification—is likely, or could reasonably be expected, to lead to certain knowledge.[11] At least under the auspices of the axioms of logic, uncertainty appears to be unavoidable in philosophy, not unlike in the field of physics, which embraces Heisenberg's uncertainty principle as a fundamental law governing all physical phenomena. Conceding the inevitability of uncertainty, however, does not absolve the seeker of truth from conducting investigations meticulously, being precise with measurement or language, and striving for a sense of specific, localized certainty amid an overarching, generalized ambiguity.

Focusing on the lack of a conclusion's certitude, however, ignores the connection between the methods we may use to draw that conclusion and the truth or falsity of the premises on which it is based. Could one justify a true conclusion validly based on false premises? American philosopher Edmund Gettier (1927–) says such conclusions are only accidentally true and that part of the analysis involves seeking counterexamples which may show the justification to be inapt.[12] American philosopher Robert Fogelin (1932–2016) observes that, when an information mismatch results from any justification, an invalidating "Gettierian" counterexample automatically arises.[13] In attaching a subjunctive or truth-tracking requirement, Robert Nozick insists that, to qualify as a justification, a conclusion would have to be utterly disbelieved were any of its essential premises proven false.[14]

In the spectrum of certitude,[15] a "falsehood" is a proposition no one actually believes or is ever likely to believe. A proposition that is almost certainly false but which a few happen to believe to be true despite overwhelming evidence to the contrary is what psychologists call a "delusion." A "false belief" is one that some accept as true despite strong and convincing evidence against it. Similarly, "faith" is what perhaps many or even most believe to be true but for which neither physical evidence nor logical reasons supports the contention; while it often amounts to little more than wishful thinking or a feel-good outlook, faith represents a supposed shortcut to the truth, as when a solution, condition, or arrangement is candidly revealed to an adherent rather than discovered organically as part of an active search for the truth. "Speculation" concerns what might be plausibly true, but with significant reason to doubt it; while speculation can range from unmotivated (merely a "wild" guess) to motivated (more of an educated hunch), it signals the need to wait for additional information before committing to dubious claims with little or no support. A "conjecture" is a claim that is quite plausibly true yet remains unproven; because it may be difficult to test and may never be proven, doubting such a contention under some circumstances is entirely reasonable. Similarly, an "hypothesis" is another type of unproven claim that is possibly true but that must be, and is subject to being, tested; the need to gather further evidence makes it speculative but more readily available for confirmation or rejection. As for claims believed to be true, a "theorem" is supported by strong evidence, with only a small but still nonzero likelihood of potentially being overturned or contravened; absent a seismic change in outlook, as opposed merely to further data, once established, a theory is considered proven and mostly unassailable. A "law" is not merely accepted as true but is supported by overwhelming evidence, so it has no or very little likelihood of potentially being toppled or invalidated. An accepted claim is called a "postulate" when supported by a conviction so strong that its falsity would require the redefinition of foundational concepts or at least a reexamination of underlying assumptions. An "axiom" is considered self-evidently true, although it could potentially be empirically upended under narrow circumstances. Finally, a "definition" is submitted to being automatically true by virtue of serving as a reference for other, potentially less-established concepts.

The acosmic denial that a physical universe exists at all may begin superficially as a false belief or motivated speculation, but given the additional evidence on which it is based, it becomes more of a conjecture, if not a full-blown theory. Such additional evidence includes how what appears to exist utterly fails to align with the necessary properties of existence, as well as how the required space-time framework takes on an imaginary quality once its anomalies are exposed. If viewed as self-evidently true, the denial might even serve axiomatically as the basis for an alternative worldview that reconciles the other two main worldviews of theism and atheism. This reconciliation is a fortuitous byproduct of the denial: There is no god (atheism) in any corner of the imagined realm (physical universe) of a God (theism) contemplating what it would be like if He did not exist. The conflation requires neither a reliance on the existence of an unseen world nor the detached purposelessness of a spontaneous self-creation.

It turns out that the best statistical predictor of a person's faith is simple geography, either where they were born or raised, or the ancestral homeland of their parents.[16] It cannot be a coincidence that, when people are seeking the truth, they apparently do not have to venture far from home. Due to the evolutionary benefits of survival and socialization, humans have always tended to gather in groups,[17] and part of the glue that holds such groups together consists of rule-based rituals that characterize most organized religions.[18] In addition, regional influences appear to account for the wide variety of religions and sects. To succeed, though, a religion must be promulgated through subtle persuasion and by brainwashing the society's least psychologically resistant, namely, children.[19] Some subtlety is necessary to avoid the countervailing effects of opposing points of view.[20] Geography-dependent views are not inherently false; rather, such views can only proliferate by adopting methods that suppress the truth, albeit with the noble goal of protecting the group as a whole. Moreover, because each faith claims to be the "one true" religion, nearly all of them must certainly be false, and the odds of any one of them being right come down to the randomness of terrestrial, tectonic geography.

It would be both fairer and less mentally abusive if families were not permitted to indoctrinate their offspring with any religious dogma, irrespective of its cultural relevance, until these children were sufficiently mature to be able to make their own decisions. This prohibition would not only make a child's eventual subsequent enlightenment of throwing off of the religious yoke less traumatic, but it would engender a healthier respect in each upcoming generation for the merits of science and the doctrine of thinking as true only what can be proven. Such an approach is unlikely ever to be implemented because the grip religion has on young minds supposedly promotes social cohesiveness and purports, however unverifiably, to make people more humane, with an aim somehow to accomplish these ends by breeding intolerance and stifling independent thought.

The effects of exile and colonization on the geographical spread and containment of specific religions demonstrate that doctrinal ideas can be transplanted.[21] These observations bolster the contention that religions and their strictures are absorbed organically rather than only being accepted after reasoned analysis or rational choice. Geography suspiciously remains the most accurate yet least logical determinate of religious affiliation and conviction.

Truth is neither a convention nor a tradition. It does not spread like a contagion. The geographical distribution of religion belies the way truth takes hold, as it is rooted wherever free and rational minds are open to receive it.

While currently over 4,000 unique religions are practiced world-wide,[22] about three-quarters of the population are adherents of the world's four major organized religions—Christianity (2.1 billion or 33%), Islam (1.5 billion or 21%), Hinduism (900 million or 14%), and Buddhism (376 million or 6%)—with the fifth in terms of traditional influence being Judaism (fourteen million or 0.22%).[23] The third largest affiliation by count (1.1 billion or 17%) is actually nonreligious/secular or agnostic/atheist,[24] with the remaining 865 million or 11% in mostly one of fourteen other, often ethnic or regional, religions.[25]

Even amid warring sects within a faith—e.g., Catholic versus Protestant in historical Christendom or Sunni versus Shia in Islam—there is a cohesiveness that binds its adherents to their religion in the specific rituals practiced, the traditions or directives passed down through the generations, and to the authority accorded ancient holy books and learned commentary. In terms of sacred texts, Christianity has the Holy Bible (the Old and New Testaments); Islam the Holy Qur'an (plus the Tawrat, the Zabur, and the Injil); Hinduism the Vedas, the Upanishads, and the Puranas (plus smriti literature and other hymns); non-Zen Buddhism the Tripitaka or Pali Canon (and other Sutras); and Judaism the Torah, Nevi'im, and Ketuvim (along with the Talmud).[26]

The key to understanding the power and influence of these works is acknowledging that many believe them to be infallibly inerrant. While the percentage within each faith who hold this belief is dwindling,[27] the notion that a text not only contains no errors but cannot contain any is what distinguishes revelation from mere inspiration by the divine. Divine "revelation" would consist of God deliberately divulging a hidden truth; this definition requires several contentious presumptions: that such truths lie seemingly beyond human intellect or inquiry, that an ancient text is the best way to convey these truths, that the disclosure serves some purpose (for both the conveyor and the recipient), and that a divine agency exists to counterbalance the natural arrangement in which the information is actively being withheld for some reason. In contrast, divine "inspiration" represents how a writer may be mysteriously imbued with the content of a truth or over whose writings God may hold a protective hand, whereas "illumination" refers to fully apprehending divinely revealed truths.[28]

So, if sacred texts contain truths not otherwise discoverable by humans, are those truths as vulnerable as the physical media on which they are inscribed or recorded? English comedian Ricky Gervais (1961–) and others suggest a thought experiment in which both holy books and science books are simultaneously hidden or destroyed, and then after a thousand years, one can compare which of the two might have resurfaced with essentially the same details.[29] The new science books would reemerge to establish the same laws or theories, including likely the same or similar experiments demonstrating the foundational principles on which they are based, whereas the new religious books, if any did reappear, would be substantially different, at least in the details of the allegories, poems, traditional myths or legends, and doctrinal dogma that mostly comprise them. The initial conclusion would be that scientific knowledge is genuine but that purely spiritual lore is not.

Perhaps the respective sets of knowledge with which science and religion concern themselves are not simply dissimilar in how they are obtained or tested (or corrected, as necessary, over time) but are altogether different in the type of information they represent. To say that scientific facts are discoverable—and, after privation, rediscoverable—but that religious "facts" can only be received through divine dispensation is an attempt to insulate faith from scrutiny. Moreover, to the extent that a holy book functions like a work of fiction rather than nonfiction—a forgotten imagined story would not resurface with the same details, while true-life reporting could likely be recreated—it is fair to conclude that the holy book seems more like an invention or artifact and not truly factual.

Nonetheless, recurring themes—e.g., myths and the "hero's journey"[30]—serve a psychological role in the human psyche, so those instances, such as the commandments, would almost certainly resurface, even if the related circumstances surrounding them differed. Yet, to those who view science as merely a tool that allows us to discover truths about the physical universe, as opposed to some spiritual reality, acknowledging that its claims can be consistently and unfailingly assessed without relying on the results of previous experiments would move away from the "nonfiction versus fiction" analogy and instead pit science against history. Holy books are rarely raw instruction, apart from rituals and social admonitions; they recount supposedly historical events, like the parting of the Red Sea or the virgin birth. Science insists, however, that an event which cannot be replicated in a controlled environment could never have occurred, but this maxim again claws at the difference in the kind of factual knowledge that science pursues as opposed to the (by no other means than) revealed truths of religion. Removing all corroboration for an event that did in fact occur does not make it as if the event suddenly and detachedly no longer has happened, because its effects in the cosmic chain-of-events will persist. It would be silly, then, to apply the scientific standard of reproducibility to history and thus to the circumstances in which a relationship to the divine might be forged.

Hence, the potential destruction of the history embodied in sacred texts is not what makes them false. Rather, truth, especially what passes in the holy books for ultimate truth, must lie beyond humanity's power to destroy. In the Bible, the time between when Israelite prophet Moses (1391–1271 BCE), in a fit of rage, breaks the first set of stone tablets containing the Ten Commandments, supposedly written with the finger of God, and when God later rewrites them again on new stone tablets,[31] Moses successfully destroys God's one-time, revealed truth; so, in the Bible's own view, a human did indeed have the power to demolish a truth whose only source is divine revelation, thereby undermining its own authority. No suggestion is offered that God could or ought to have prevented the initial destruction, although He is made to seem perfectly willing to reconvey the esoteric information whenever, and as many times as, necessary. Truth cannot reside exclusively in a single book that is within our power to destroy.

It would appear that the adherents' "leap of faith" is over the authorship of holy books, because once they glom onto divine revelation, they can then blindly accept any passage of scripture, no matter how outrageous or counterfactual. What remains unexplained, though, is why God would obscure a universal truth and only permit it to be approached using a method that, under other circumstances, is the most likely to lead to the wrong conclusion.

For instance, light passing through misting water droplets at certain angles produces a prism-like effect that, in combination with the light reflecting off the interior of the droplet, which is kept nearly spherical due to surface-tension forces, disperses the light in reverse order of wavelength, a display of the spectrum of colors we know as a rainbow.[32] Such rainbows would occur on the surface of any planet or moon anywhere in the Universe under these circumstances.[33] Yet, one religion claims that its deity actively participates in conjuring a rainbow every time it appears on Earth in order to signify a promise that "the waters shall never again become a flood to destroy all flesh,"[34] even suggesting that no rainbow could have occurred if "the atmosphere [were] differently constituted before the [supposed] Flood."[35] This view not only violates the rational principle that truth must be valid always and everywhere but it introduces an hypothesis for which there is no evidence[36] and for no other purpose than to bolster an already-discredited story. Such a view—that the rainbows in the sky are for us, and there were no rainbows before us—is astonishingly infantile, mirroring the preoperational stage of cognitive development in children, which is characterized by an inability to think logically while developing the use of symbols and by a kind of egocentrism that blocks the child from seeing other perspectives.[37]

Another example is the claim of some physical resemblance between a particular species of life on Earth and some eternal being[38] whose features would be either nonphysical or ones that had never evolved. The snowflake-like uniqueness of the facial appearances of the more than seven billion now-living humans[39] are already diverse enough to make the claim that we look like our Creator *prima facie* dubitable. The features of human faces might have been different—and through the course of their past and anticipated development, actually were or are expected to become substantially dissimilar—on account of fortuitous circumstances that may lead evolution in one direction or another, for instance, to introduce variability so as to make each human more identifiable in the context of social interactions.[40]

In terms of so-called revealed knowledge, the Bible and other ancient texts contain little that would astonish the Bronze Age audience for whom they were written. Imagine how credible it would have been, though, if these holy books, purporting to be the words of the Creator of the Universe, had given insights or information that went over the heads of contemporaries but spoke to later generations on topics like the configuration of the solar system (heliocentric), the medical basis for antibiotics (the distillation of penicillin), the structure of DNA (double-helix strands), the organizing principle of galaxies (supermassive black holes at their centers), or even mathematical proofs of

Goldbach's conjecture (all positive integers can be represented as the average of two prime numbers) or Fermat's "last theorem" (no integer solutions exist for like-exponentiated pairs of numbers equaling a third number with the same exponentiation where the exponent is greater than two). Those would truly have been once-hidden, revealed truths.

Do humans physically resemble God or do devout humans simply project themselves into their image of the divine? Science explains that humans look the way they do as a result of a long, evolutionary process of adaptation.[41] An eternal deity would not adapt, either as it exists outside of or is not subject to the effects of time, so the human visage hardly qualifies as a representation or mirror image. This lack of understanding epitomizes the evolution-versus-creation debate: Do humans, like all other known living organisms, adapt to their environment, or did some supernatural being fashion a designed environment in order to accommodate humans? Greek philosopher Xenophon (ca. 430–354 BCE) observes that cows and horses, if blessed with hands and the ability to sketch, would depict gods that looked like themselves.[42] The imputing of emotions to God, at least according to such a vision, also serves to demonstrate that He is no more than a human invention, in the same way human imperfections amount to proof of God's creative limitations.

An indescribably beautiful sunset occurs every day, while majestic total solar eclipses are "visible somewhere on Earth every eighteen months."[43] Those phenomena are natural processes, but given that faith requires supernatural events, why are they not as routine or as frequent as rainbows or the *aurora borealis*? Why is there not an enormous image emblazoned across the sky annually, on some especially holy day, as a reminder, or for inspiration, of the human faces of Moses, Jesus, Mohammed, Buddha, or even L. Ron Hubbard? The god of religion would appear to prefer a shell game, where faith depends on where, and importantly when, you are, since the lives of its founders are limited. In refuting that knowledge can be of different types, Galileo Galilei concludes that "the same God who has endowed us with senses, reason, and intellect [never] intended us to forgo their use and by some other means to give us knowledge which we can attain by them."[44] Truth, after all, is supposed to be valid *semper, ubique, et ab omnibus,* (Latin for "always, everywhere, and [attainable] by everyone").

Nearly every major religion has, at one time or another, practiced ritualized sacrifice[45] for the atonement of misdeeds, to curry favor for supernatural intervention, or as an act of gratitude for divine beneficence. There is no need to recount the barbarism and cruelty involved in such rituals, nor how the targeting of the weak for communal sacrifice may bolster social stratification.[46] The mentality behind unsolicited offerings of food, honey, burnt meat, or (human) blood is the furtive hope of somehow pleasing a deity without knowing its earthly proclivities.

While priests might be looked to generally for interpreting the likely desires of the mysterious gods through an awkward process of divination, the first inkling of a deity speaking directly to supplicants, although still accompanied by animal sacrifice, albeit in a more "prayerful" way, are the oracles of ancient Greece, in particular, the Pythian priestesses of the Temple of Apollo, also called the Oracle at Delphi.[47] Failure of oracular prophecy, purposefully cryptic, is solemnly accepted, either as a matter of interpretation or under the principle that the mind of the divine remains ultimately inscrutable.[48]

In the Judaic Torah, later incorporated in the Christian Old Testament and cited by the Islamic Qur'an, the priestly prophet Moses claims (Exod. 3:4) that, from within the burning bush, God spoke directly to him using the first-person pronoun "I"—here, singular, but earlier in the Bible, plural, as in the royal "we"—and engaging him in back-and-forth conversation.[49] This is very likely the first surviving written account in any mythology in human history in which God is depicted as speaking directly as Himself. One might call this an "innovation," as it eliminates the guesswork about what pleases the gods, since here, the deity conveys what is expected in terms of human behavior, both affirmatively and as prohibitions. The danger, though, lies in sanctifying such words, which become absolute and exalted to the point where they cannot be questioned. The religion's claims become truly unassailable.

Of course, making rules sacrosanct serves religion's ultimate goal of social coercion. Self-interest must be squelched, even if it results in the loss of individuality. A farmer, for example, would rather have the self-assured certainty of appeasing the gods for favorable weather than operate in a godless world where crops are at the mercy of ravenous or random misfortune; likewise for the power of prayer amidst plague-ridden communities, where the act of public entreaty by the congregation makes participants feel they can make a contribution in the face of forces they fear and do not understand.

Dutch author Mathijs Koenraadt (1980–) reckons that religion "took God away from its disciples and placed Him above them [, and t]hus, religious leaders claimed the sole right of speaking in the name of God."[50] Even in the modern era, Neale Donald Walsch is publishing books in which God is quoted *ala* Moses in transcribed conversations. Speaking as God, though, is not merely a method for seeming to don the mantle of authority; it elevates these proclamations to a level of being unassailable. Where we ought to be open to discussing contentious issues, the practice of god-speak, provided it is sufficiently believed and accepted by the plurality of a society, effectively ends all debate. It also has a tendency to run counter to natural instincts, which is why it requires the air of debate-squelching supremacy.

These instincts include ethical concerns. Does your conscience prevent you from killing your own child? You will encounter no obstacle if a god commands you to do so (Gen. 22:2–3). Apart from the moral implications of god-speak, in that one may have a hard time faulting those individuals who use the device to gain advantage over others, particularly in the past when human empathy sinks to its historical nadir, one must hold responsible those who enable the practice by adopting it as a belief system. The Bible, among other holy books, is rife with sanctioned killings and barbarities, excused almost ironically as the Word of God and readily accepted by a Bronze Age culture that predates the first inkling of individual human rights; what is appalling, instead, are the billions of supposedly enlightened people who still today embrace and exalt this catalog of cruelties.

All fear is genuine, in the sense that the emotion is lived through, however unfounded its basis may turn out to be. Causes may be disputed or perhaps altogether nonexistent, yet the one who fears will suffer all the same. The paranoid's delusions of persecution may not align with reality, but in the context of his or her world, life is unpleasantly adversarial. So, too, can it be said that faith, even if based on a falsehood, is nonetheless an authentic human experience; having convinced themselves that the religious claim is to be believed, devotees sincerely think and act as though their world operates according to the dutiful principles they embrace. Fear is a motivator and decidedly unpleasant, but fear of the unknown dissipates upon the discovery of the truth, while a false fear based on faith is far worse, inasmuch as it resists both reason and fact.

American pragmatist William James (1842–1910) declares some value to the believer in the mere act of believing, irrespective of whether sufficient evidence supports the underlying content of the belief.[51] The rationale seems to be that the claim, especially if unknowable, might possibly prove to be true and hence worth the risk of being believed. The problem, however, as with all contentions which beggar belief, is that, if we require no objective standard for truth, then truly anything is possible. Were we to use a similar pragmatic approach and abandon the "beyond a reasonable doubt" or "to a moral certainty" benchmark routinely used as a standard of proof to convict accused individuals in criminal courts every day, no defendant would ever be found guilty. Why should the criterion of truth be less burdensome for religious claims than for imprisoning those accused of a crime? James suggests there could be a truth dependency wherein a belief might be necessary in order to make a more-or-less indirect "acquaintance" with God,[52] but hardly any pragmatic reason can be offered as to why the road to truth ought to be paved with unfounded beliefs or unproven assertions. His suggestion devolves into a weak version of Pascal's wager, where the unsupported belief's benefit is the avoidance of a speculative risk of the consequences of nonbelief. Given James's background as a psychologist, it oddly ignores the mental burden of fear or guilt in the harboring of an unnecessarily false belief, while also insinuating suggestively that one specific false belief about the unknown is somehow preferable to all others.

Faith is akin to the empty-calorie snack which seems straight away to satisfy the natural hunger for knowledge that humans innately possess yet fails utterly to nourish them with genuine wisdom. Humanity must get beyond outdated, Bronze Age mysticism and rituals if we hope to be prepared to receive the truth that only scientifically enlightened discoveries about the physical universe can provide. We no longer live in the medieval Dark Ages and must strive to dispense with such notions as a god impregnating a mortal child with an incarnation of himself in order that he be offered as a blood sacrifice so as to atone for humanity's sinful imperfections with which he supposedly created them. Sacrificial redemption, no matter how magnanimous, is odious to any true morality. And those faithful to the conception of what has been called "vicarious redemption"[53]—belief in the divinity and resurrection of Jesus Christ as the only way to avoid eternal hellfire—are strangely content with it being merely a pathway to salvation rather than a final emancipation of all earthly suffering that it could have been. Faith, even in its native realm of the unknown, is a poor substitute for understanding; yet, it does not go far enough, because it superficially resolves the problems it perpetuates without readying its followers for the eventual truth.

One can endlessly debate Christianity and other redemption-based religions on their merits, but if we step back for a moment, a few aspects come into focus that render these systems highly unlikely to be true, if not outright impossible. Acosmism overcomes Descartes' declaration that he could not accept God as a deceiver, because he might have accepted the circumstance where God were only deceiving Himself: The thought of God deceiving humans or other sentient creatures is the idea he feels compelled to reject. Yet, were Christianity correct, God would have to be considered overall a deceiver, inasmuch as He made it so easy for intelligent, thoughtful, and decent human beings to renounce it or choose more appealing alternatives. By the religion's own accounting, fully 80 percent of the one-hundred billion humans who ever lived, not to mention the 60 percent of the eight billion now alive, are or will be suffering everlasting torment for falling short of its requirement blindly to believe it. That is a failure by any measure for a belief system that claims on behalf of all humanity to be the one true, redemptive religion.

As an interesting aside, for example, the serpent introduced into the Garden (Gen. 3:1) speaks directly to Eve when tempting her to disobey God; snakes at every stage of development lack a diaphragm, however, and are thus incapable of speech,[54] a fact about which Bible readers ought to feel needlessly misled. Oddly, those same readers, seeing the reference (Gen. 3:14) in which God seems to change the serpent's mode of locomotion from potentially legged to "upon thy belly shalt thou go," would correctly understand that some snakes, specifically pythons, do indeed possess a so-called dormant "Sonic hedgehog" gene, for which a biological "enhancer" generally suppresses the growth of vestigial limbs that had evolved earlier, as in lizards.[55]

English political philosopher John Gray (1948–) recasts faith as a search for meaning rather than a rationalization of the Universe's origin, history, or present state-of-affairs.[56] In Gray's view, the fact that humans uniquely have foreknowledge of their own deaths compels them to seek out ways to reconcile themselves with some form of divinity, which explains why a science built on statistics can never replace a purposeful religion that gives life its meaning.

In this way, faith becomes a means for adherents to claim a preferred version of truth without having to support the claim. Once the faithful are convinced of the divine origin and purpose of their religion, they will never be dissuaded from it merely as a result of either its unreasonableness or its consequences. Abuses in the name of religion are considered outliers and, no matter how frequent or forcefully they appear, are taken as not representative of the core beliefs of the quietly devoted. The observation by American physicist Steven Weinberg (1933–) that "for good people to do evil things, *that* takes religion"[57] is overly broad, because what truly puts the behavior of the well-intentioned at risk is when they completely mistake an evil outcome for a good one. But because religion is best at obscuring the truth by substituting the will of corrupt humans for the admonition of God, deigning even to appear to quote Him, questioning the basis for any belief is always advisable. One cannot remove religion from society, however, any more than one can convince people suddenly to stop using their opposable thumbs. Even acclaimed atheist and Anglo-American author Christopher Hitchens (1949–2011) realizes that "superstition [will forever be] part of the human condition."[58] The key is first to acknowledge the psychological need for awe and meaning and then to satisfy it with objectivity and compassion.

Only the ignorant are drawn to faith, because to the extent someone knows a fact to be true, that individual has no need for faith. The irony, however, is that those who do not know the fact in contention likewise do not require faith: What they are missing is knowledge. One assertive atheist predicts that faith "must necessarily fail in the sense that the more closely it is examined, the more its contradictions with reality are exposed."[59] The proselytizing mission of churches seems perpetually to be stoking fear, shaming doubt or skepticism, eliciting personal sacrifice for monetary gain, and offering the means for attaining an impossible end. Nevertheless, life goes on unabated. Provided the communal spirit were kept alive of wanting to help the less fortunate, it would not be at all tragic were every church permanently to close its doors, although in the absence of compulsion, whether religious or secular, it looks as though human communities do not naturally or rarely come together for even a shared purpose.[60] In the meantime, even a faith based on falsehood would nonetheless qualify as an experience and what it means to be humanly vulnerable in the face of uncertainty.

Chapter 11:

Afterlife

Life is either a daring adventure or nothing. —Helen Keller[1]

While abiogenesis is the steady process under primordial conditions by which living cells develop out of nonliving components, the configuration of these components is what actually gives rise to life.[2] Experiments confirm that the early-Earth atmosphere allows for the formation of the necessary organic compounds.[3] Moreover, NASA reports that half of the nucleobases involved in DNA and RNA structures can spontaneously appear and then fall to Earth when frozen organic compounds in space are exposed to the chemically disintegrating ultraviolet radiation of the solar wind; the reassembling fragments configure themselves in such a way as to facilitate the emergence of terrestrial life.[4]

Similarly, human life consists of useful configurations, such as the electrically connected array of brain cells from which consciousness eventually *emerges*. This concept of a phenomenon arising almost entirely out of a configuration is in sharp contrast with the view in which it develops and then imposes itself externally. An external force requires a dualistic approach and inevitably differs in kind from the system it purportedly governs. Greek physician Herophilus (325–255 BCE) notices that the pineal gland is the first gland to develop *in utero* and, by occupying the middle central location of the brain as a single organ, avoids the separation into the disparate hemispheres of most other brain functions; given its anatomy and its presence in the brains of all vertebrates as a melatonin-producing regulator of sleep patterns, and in defiance of the contemporary thinking going back to Aristotle that the heart is the seat of consciousness, Herophilus declares the pineal gland to be something of a control valve for "animal spirits" entering the brain as sensations through the nerves and for facilitating in the formation of thought.[5] Nearly two thousand years later, Descartes terms the pea-sized, pine-shaped gland the "principal seat of the soul,"[6] envisioning it as the interface between the immaterial "soul" and the physical brain. Modern neuroscience has determined that consciousness is considerably more complicated and entails the coordinated participation of neurons, synapses, and axons.[7] The concepts of "animal spirits" and a "seat of the soul" no longer serve any scientific purpose, although the precise brain processes that can or do give rise to human consciousness remain a mystery.[8]

The concept of "emergence" or an "emergent" property is based on observations where the functioning of the entirety of a composite system cannot be formally traced back to any of the individual parts that comprise it.[9] This phenomenon arises only when three conditions are met: supervenience, non-aggregation, and downward causality.[10] The supervenience criterion simply refers to the occurrence where the emergent property is observed to disappear after one or more of the component parts are removed.[11] Non-aggregation is when the whole constitutes or achieves something greater than the sum of its parts.[12] Finally, downward causality occurs when the manner in which a system acts influences either the state or behavior of its component parts.[13]

The far-from-obvious fallacy of division arises precisely because of the presence of emergent properties.[14] The following syllogism, for example, is manifestly false: This wooden table is made of atoms, and using the well-established fact that atoms individually are not visible to the naked eye, or, that is to say, they appear invisible in the absence of some aid to human vision, one concludes, therefore, that this table itself is invisible. The emergent nature of things made of atoms in our world renders the conclusion false, or at least explains how it fails to follow from its inarguably true premises. Furthermore, that the table consists almost entirely of the empty space between the molecules which comprise it, not to mention within the individual atoms themselves, belies the perception of the table as being solid; as noted, the unseen electrostatic force ensures that another object placed on the table is met with sufficient resistance that it does not "pass through" all the empty space surrounding the configuration of atoms which make up the table.

Complicated systems like swarms of bees, urban cities, and the human brain[15] all serve to demonstrate the marvel of when a totality becomes altogether and thus surprisingly distinct from its individual parts. In this sense, biologists and neuroscientists have come to regard consciousness as an emergent property of the evolved functioning of the physical brain.[16] Experiments involving fMRI imaging technology show awareness as a coordinating network in which no single, isolated area of the brain is identifiable as, or reducible to, the ultimate source.[17] Given these results, Descartes' theory that views the pineal gland as the single entry point and memory manager for the alleged "soul," and thus the center of consciousness, is unsupportable.

Of course, Descartes' dualistic view is also based on his assertion that the mind, unlike the body, cannot be divided and thus lacks extensions, or is immaterial.[18] The phrase "being of two minds" may not have had much currency in Descartes' time, and likewise, the psychology of Dissociative Identity (or Multiple Personality) disorder, but the psyche is as much prone to a kind of fracturing as any bone, particularly as a direct consequence of mental trauma.[19] Moreover, regardless of how an emergent property might manifest itself behaviorally, it could well be considered as "immaterial" insofar as its non-aggregating nature is concerned. Even Descartes admits a cohesiveness with respect to how "the mind is shown to be so closely joined to the body that it forms a single unit with it"[20]—he is unwittingly describing the emergent quality of consciousness rather than convincingly arguing that it has a separate or independent existence.

The specific atoms that comprise our bodies, including our brains, will very likely persist long after the spark of consciousness in us has been extinguished. We must recognize our experiences as merely perceptions, and the configuration or coordinated functioning of those selfsame atoms is what gives rise to our consciousness as an emergent property. Then, and only then, can we understand that nothing nonphysical of us survives our death, especially as it involves an ephemeral phenomenon like the mental discernment arising from the complicated, interconnected assemblage of our brains. Having accepted this realization, we can conclude that, apart from how any composition is imagined to occur in order to produce a synergistic whole, existence itself transcends all.

When the physical universe supposedly first appeared—an acosmist would emphasize that a universe is only imagined to have appeared—over thirteen billion years ago,[21] it might never have developed into the matter-centric Universe we observe today, with two trillion galaxies, each consisting of hundreds of billions of stars and orders of magnitude more of planets.[22] Following an initial inflationary period of space, and one second after the Big Bang, the Universe finds itself awash in the nuclear building blocks of matter, along with light and antimatter, while the passage of just three minutes introduces a process known as Big Bang nucleosynthesis, when there materializes for the first time both hydrogen, the fuel of stars, and other light elements.[23] Quite by accident, then, the presence of matter, antimatter, and light becomes the ultimate physical achievement of the burgeoning universe. Organic life, an apparent rarity in the Universe, is the highest achievement of matter. Similarly, consciousness, an emergent property of mind, is finally the unexpectedly fortuitous apex of biology. Is the merging of consciousnesses via, say, the internet, the next step?

Austrian neurologist Sigmund Freud (1856–1939), in defining the components of the human psyche as the id, the ego, and the superego, goes on to envision three distinct levels of consciousness or self-awareness: the conscious, the preconscious, and the unconscious.[24] What distinguishes these levels is the relationship of the self to its own experiences, as well as the roles of both memory (past experiences) and imagination (anticipated future experiences). Consciousness is associated with an awareness of self while a perceptual experience is occurring and with a mindfulness of existing in the present.[25] The functioning of the brain allows consciousness to emerge and then to interact with its past through its ability to memorialize the witnessed events the self has experienced or endured, in addition to being able to relive them via vivid recollection. With the mind's eye comes the uniquely human capacity for envisioning a forecasted future, including the contemplation of hypothetical events involving the self, which leads Friedrich Nietzsche (1844–1900) to call a human the "promising animal."[26] While nonhuman animals are only able to conceive of themselves ten minutes ahead in the future,[27] humans rarely live in the present moment, often spending time mentally reliving their past experiences and imagining various futures about themselves.[28]

As Freud digs deeper, he realizes that most of thought takes place in the subconscious realm.[29] The scope of the conscious mind is limited, since the majority of what we would call "cognitive" activity occurs outside the range or compass of our awareness and possibly without any deliberative effort whatsoever. The influence of the subconscious, at the preconscious and/or the unconscious level, eclipses all the exertions of consciousness in determining our behavior.[30]

The human brain is built on layers of functionality, a construction that results from an evolving development over time.[31] The oldest, or first to have developed, is the brain stem, whose function centers primarily on survival responses and autonomic processes.[32] Next, building onto the brain stem as a foundation is the limbic system, which adds the ability to store and retrieve memories, as well as to handle instincts, intuition, and emotions.[33] The latest development in the human brain is the addition of the cerebral cortex, which allows us to process language and achieve a level of consciousness or self-awareness not found elsewhere in nature.[34]

Within each layer of the brain are structures that serve specific purposes: The *thalamus* filters sensory information and relays it up to higher levels; the *cerebellum* controls voluntary movements; the *amygdala* governs emotions like aggression or fear; the *hypothalamus* links the nervous system to the endocrine system to regulate physical needs and behaviors; and the *hippocampus* helps to form long-term and spatial-oriented memories.[35] The cerebral cortex itself constitutes 80 percent of the brain's weight and is comprised of over twenty billion nerve cells with nearly 300 trillion synaptic connections and myriad billions of neuron-connecting glial cells.[36] While the cerebral cortex relies on each and every subpart of the brain in order to function, it and it alone is where actual thought takes place; more than a mere collection point for sensations, its own subcomponents—the insular cortex, the anterior cingulate cortex, and the medial prefrontal cortex—collectively serve as the true seat of consciousness, abstraction, and imagination.[37]

This sentient consciousness of ours is assuredly the result of the evolution of life on Earth[38] but is hardly necessary from a teleological standpoint. Life is teeming wherever it appears; the developmental events that lead to higher forms (i.e., conscious sentience), however, both as to when they take place or whether they even occur at all, may be either mere coincidences or else the inevitable outcome of the inexorable march of evolution.[39] Only by virtue of our ability to frame thoughts to evoke mental imagery can we conceive the possibility that the observable universe might well be an idea, but ironically, our life-preserving practices of dividing pure imagination from reality causes us to dismiss the possibility. Acosmism is exemplified in human consciousness, yet consciousness stands as the only true obstacle in accepting it. Moreover, the notion of a divine consciousness underlying reality (rather than actually pervading it, as in panpsychism) makes an individualized consciousness that we errantly claim as our own seem altogether unnecessary.

As an interesting aside, the lack of evidence that any extraterrestrial alien civilization has yet contacted us here on Earth has led Italo-American physicist Enrico Fermi (1901–54) to ask, "Where is everybody?" a query that has come to be known as the "Fermi Paradox,"[40] formulated as the Drake equation.[41] Egypto-American astronomer Yervant Terzian (1939–) and American physics and mathematics student Evan Solomonides (1966–) observe that signs of intelligent life on Earth, in the form of the broadcast of galaxy-spanning radio signals, have only been transmitted for about eighty years, beginning in 1939, whereas those signals would not be expected to reach potential extraterrestrial observers for "until at least 1,500 years."[42]

A human brain that has endured a dramatic event or has been damaged by some kind of trauma is able remarkably to alter itself structurally and/or functionally as a result, a feature known as brain "neuroplasticity."[43] The mechanism is a physical process by which such alterations, including rewiring neural connections, occur.[44] Were there some immaterial part of the brain, it would not be affected by physical events like sleep, pharmaceuticals, or concussive head trauma; a "soul," regardless of how integrally it might be conceived as interfacing with the brain, would remain untouched through the brain's physical harms and/or repairs. We can detect and observe the physical processes taking place in the brain,[45] but any effect happening to whatever immaterial part of the brain presumed by some to exist is purely speculative. The "soul" is reduced to a mere appendage, serving no purpose that is not otherwise explainable by material science.

The misconception of a "soul" appears to be based primarily on conflating it with the emergent property of consciousness. Notably, configurations of the active brain, what have been termed "mental states," ultimately produce this consciousness,[46] and they do so without requiring an interfacing supervisor, particularly one that is immaterial and undetectable. The question arises, however, whether a cloned brain would have the selfsame thoughts as the original. Or phrased more scientifically, is any given mental state sufficiently "public" as to be replicable? Imagine an experiment in the future where a human subject having a thought can have his or her mental state recorded electronically or uploaded intact into a computer or network. If the mental state were replayed or downloaded to another subject, would that someone else have precisely the same thought as the original thinker? A materialist view would likely conclude in the affirmative, with the belief that a thought is capable of being isolated context-free in this manner; the thought might be bewildering in the mind of the second subject, and his or her memories might evoke an altogether mismatched emotional response, but nonetheless, it would be, in every psychological and philosophical sense, the very same thought.

In one of Zen Buddhism's koans, the Sixth Patriarch, Hui-neng, settles an argument between two monks as to whether, when their temple flag is flapping in the wind, the flag or the wind is truly moving: Neither the flag nor the wind moves but rather it is the mind that moves.[47] This illustrates the mistaken view that consciousness must participate in an observance in order for the event to occur. Those who suggest that an observer is somehow necessary for the operation of the Universe fail to account for the period of time preceding all observers, or before life itself, although in the absence of any observer, time is not nor cannot be experienced.

In speaking of an afterlife, one must define the dividing line as to what constitutes before and after life. "Death" is the cessation or, in some instances, the absence, of life. When something that was once alive no longer is, it is regarded as dead. An area where no living thing has ever resided or no longer resides is deemed a "dead zone." Defining life may be difficult, but defining death is easy.

To quibble over this definition of death in the context of life is to take issue either with the permanence of it as an end or with it representing an end at all. Either way, such a denial amounts to an assertion that something of life remains after or survives death. Aside from discredited experiments conducted in the previous century,[48] simply no scientific evidence has come to light that any measurable part of a host persists alive or animated following its complete physical death. Exploiting what may not be known or understood about death—mysterious and macabre, yet inevitable—as some kind of evidence-free proof of a "soul" is improper gap-oriented reasoning and thus wholly unscientific.

To remain alive, humans require regular blood circulation and oxygenation, supplied naturally via a beating heart and at least one functioning lung.[49] Clinical death occurs when, in the absence of artificial support, these supplies cease, which is when the heart and lungs stop working.[50] Individual cells die or are irreparably damaged as soon as blood flow is cut off,[51] although the organ as a whole will not have irrecoverably failed until some threshold number of cells have died.[52] In contrast, biological death (or "brain death") occurs a short time later, when the organ that fails happens to be the brain itself.[53] Brain death is the irreversible loss of consciousness and where artificial life support becomes necessary to sustain cardiopulmonary functioning.[54] While consciousness can linger for a matter of seconds, perhaps up to half a minute, after clinical death, at normal body temperature, the brain is rarely able to recover beyond an additional three minutes in such a state and is considered utterly dead within ten minutes of blood ceasing to flow to it.[55]

Because cases of humans being revived following clinical death are reported routinely, albeit while the brain is still functioning to some degree, accepting such events as indirect evidence of life after death is a mistake.[56] This erroneous conclusion, however, is completely undone by the observation that, due to the irreversibility of the condition, no confirmed cases of brain recovery are known ever to have occurred following biological death.[57] After both the heartbeat and respiration/breathing finally ceases, consciousness generally persists for between two and twenty seconds,[58] yet the cells of the brain will continue to die off for considerably longer, perhaps for up to ten minutes.[59] The point at which brain death becomes irreversible, however, is not especially well-defined.[60] The patient must first be at a reasonably normal body temperature and free of drugs known to suppress brain activity. Broadly, the clinician must then determine the patient to be unresponsive to autonomic or reflexive stimuli, but in addition, the patient must be unable to breathe without the use of a ventilator (the "apnea" test) or other life-support systems.[61] In nearly all legal jurisdictions in the United States, additional, costly, and direct confirmatory testing is entirely optional and subject to the discretion of the death-certifying physician, examiner, or clinician.[62] Testing for the absence of electrical activity in the brain using an electroencephalogram (EEG) is normally not required, and in any case, may not be dispositive in establishing that the brain has truly ceased to function.[63] Transcranial Doppler ultrasound sonography (TCD) is a test that measures intracranial blood flow and pressure, which would indicate a brain's ability to sustain itself, but the test is almost exclusively used noninvasively to diagnose various medical conditions other than death.[64] When the brain via the spinal cord fails to receive the sensation that results from applying a Somatosensory-Evoked Potential (SSEP or SEP) specifically to an upper limb's median nerve, it is a very reliable and conclusive indicator of brain death, but this test is also rarely employed for death and is instead used most often in pathology to trace nerve or spinal damage.[65]

From a medical and legal standpoint, death can be complex, which makes a precise definition and determination oddly elusive, although disputes mostly center on establishing the precise moment of death as opposed to the ongoing condition of being dead. In contrast, the Bible (e.g., in James 2:26, which reads "the body without the spirit is dead"), like most other holy texts, treats the matter far more simplistically; in the religious view, death is not the annihilation of life, self, or consciousness but rather a permanent separation from the body of a "soul" or spirit. Religions are far less forthcoming on just what a "soul" or spirit is, other than describing it as incorporeal, eternal, and capable variously of unending pain and/or pleasure.

Loss of life may result from disease, senescence (age), trauma, or physical impairment. Causes of death include natural, accident or misadventure, and homicide or suicide.[66] Regardless of broad categorizations or forensics, death involves the total systemic loss of brain and sensory function. Anecdotal cases suggest consciousness and cognitive perception can be independent; people might be aware during episodes in which their senses temporarily abate, and others may perceive sensory inputs like overhearing a whispered conversation or seeing overhead objects, even while they are minimally conscious.[67]

Of course, we need eyes to see and ears to hear—patients in a near-comatose condition may acutely see or hear visual and auditory stimuli, but only if they have organs of sense intact already: Permanently blind people do not suddenly see, irrespective of their altered states of consciousness.[68] Those who envision surviving their own physical death evidently believe they will be able to see without eyeballs and to hear without ears (or an auditory system). Logistically, how would that be possible? Were it somehow possible, why would we not have evolved that form of perception to replace our eyes and ears? If those supersensible forms of perception are already in us, how does it coordinate with or override the perceptions we outwardly possess? Again, those who are ignorant of how a complex process actually works—the light-gathering, the optic nerve, the brain's internal representation of the signals—can more easily accept as possible what the informed recognize as impossible. Were there indeed an ancillary system—e.g., a "soul" capable of independently seeing, hearing, or remembering—for sight, hearing, or memory, no one would ever end up blind, deaf, or forgetful. Do those afflicted with dementia or other forms of brain damage suddenly recover all their memories when their brains completely shut down upon death? Once again, this is a topsy-turvy view: A deteriorating or damaged brain cannot logically be a launching point for the restoration of full, brain-independent memories, emotions, or knowledge.

The brain's limbic system is the center of memory storage and retrieval processes.[69] Components of the system include the following: The *hippocampus* converts short-term memories to long-term; the *amygdala* governs emotions, moods, and olfactory memories; the *cingulate gyrus* handles pain sensations and its related emotions; the *thalamus* serves as the brain's working memory; the *epithalamus* and *pineal gland* are involved in circadian and diurnal awareness; and the *hypothalamus* controls autonomic functions related to memory.[70] Furthermore, emotions are not only associated with brain activity but can be stimulated to arise spontaneously with the application of a directed electrical signal.[71]

Hence, memory is decidedly a brain function, but more than that, it is the essential key to the concept of "identity," or in this context, "self-identity."[72] Because of the way memory is processed by the brain, individual memories or types of memories are vulnerable to loss or erasure from a concussive, blunt force, as innocuous as a tap on the head.[73] Given this vulnerability, any memory is all the more unlikely to be able to survive an event as systemically catastrophic as death. No current scientific consensus is likely to be based on but scant and indirect evidence that memory in the brain can be stored at the quantum level,[74] a product of wishful thinking, but alas, no "hidden" place exists to stash the "self" in order to protect it from death, nor a mechanism for organizing any such memories, which collectively constitute what a "self" truly is.

In the case of direct past memory loss, medically termed "retrograde amnesia" (versus "anterograde amnesia," or the inability to create new memories), we retain our identity because our memory could still be intact, even when we cannot consciously access it.[75] Death, though, erases all our memories, so we cannot then retain our identity or the influences that created it. The emergence of consciousness is a transcendence, in which the whole is somehow greater than the sum of its parts. Perhaps personality—what some might call a manifestation of a "soul"—is as much an emergent property of the physical brain as the consciousness on which it is based, and this transcendent quality is what many mistakenly believe has an autonomous existence capable of surviving death.

Moreover, the continuity of the illusion of self should not be taken for an unchanging essence (or "soul"), which is simply part of how consciousness and/or personality works. One can give numerous examples of how a thing's so-called essence can be mistaken as having an independent being. Picture a bowl of fruit on a table: a common artistic still life. Now imagine, one-at-a-time, removing each individual fruit from the bowl. Envision then the bowl, and next the entire table, being carried off the scene. What, if anything, remains? Is the essence of the fruit bowl still there, or can one say that nothing of the original arrangement continues? Likewise, imagine being aboard a jet airplane that has just leveled off at cruising altitude. Can you at this point eliminate the wings or the engines? After all, the plane has achieved its ideal state or goal of traveling aloft and can shed the scaffolding that made it possible. Or visualize a train, hurtling down its track, which suddenly and catastrophically derails. A train that has jumped its tracks cannot continue to move once the infrastructure of its carriage is gone; once the foundational basis for its continuity of movement has been eliminated, the train is no longer a method of transport as originally conceived.

What these examples illustrate is that, for inanimate objects, a resultant effect cannot logically be divorced from the causes which produced it; in these circumstances, we do not propose the existence of some ephemeral essence "hanging out there" to represent the composite thing. There is no earthly reason to consider the matter any differently when the thing in question is a brain. Moreover, there must theoretically be some kind of limitation on consciousness, and mortality is the most obvious. Otherwise, an immortal consciousness might eventually become, or at least come close to being, divine. Once we accept that what some call a "soul" is both merely and miraculously the emergent property or transcendent quality of dauntingly complex neurological processes, we can come to embrace the finality and permanence of a death that temporally circumscribes the consciousness we experience in life.

The cells in our bodies either deteriorate without being replaced quickly enough or else cancerously and fatally proliferate[76]— whichever way, the death of every living organism is inevitable. The stability of cells that comprise vital organs like the brain or the heart degenerate to the point where the organs themselves cease properly to function, after which death inexorably ensues. Barring the trauma of external forces such as accident/misadventure or homicide/suicide, death is typically also considered altogether natural. That death is both inevitable and natural is not just true for living things but for the astronomical environment in which all life exists: The earth, the solar system, and the entire physical universe will all someday perish.

And yet, despite our ability to reason and prepare, most people actively fear death, a condition known clinically, particularly when characterized by irrational anxiety, as thanatophobia.[77] According to recent surveys, however, more people report fearing specifically insects, snakes, heights, open spaces, lightning or thunder, tight spaces, germs, flying, holes, or cancer than fearing death,[78] although psychologists believe the majority of people do generally, and rationally, fear their eventual demise, irrespective of their current age or religious affiliation.[79] Education appears to be one of the sole factors assuaging a fear that can, when death is imminent, become terrifying.[80]

We know that nearly all animals, including humans, possess the biological fight-or-flight survival instinct[81] for the simple reason that, were there an exception, that creature and its stoic genes would quickly disappear from the reproductive pool through natural selection. This self-preservation drive may, in fact, be our most dominant impulse, since it is a physiological reaction involving the autonomic nervous system, which operates almost entirely without our conscious participation.[82] Facing death triggers this powerful response, so understandably, we fear what intimidates us.

Phobias concern people, things, or circumstances that challenge the sufferer's "comfort zone,"[83] so, given our limited or incomplete understanding of the world, it should provoke little wonder that the all-encompassing "unknown" may be the most unsettling of phobia-inducing root causes. As far as we know, babies hardly resist being born, teenagers plunge headlong into puberty, and nearly all workers welcome taking the off-ramp into retirement; the one transition we seem universally to dread is death, the Great Unknown.

But is it death itself or the condition that leads unto death which we fear? Ancient Greek philosopher Epicurus (341–270 BCE) tries to characterize death as a static changeover by saying that "as long as we exist, death is not here[, but] when it does come, we no longer exist."[84] Holding an altogether different view, American biochemist and author Isaac Asimov (1920–92) redirects the focus by stating, "Life is pleasant. Death is peaceful. It is the transition that's troublesome."[85] In death, we permanently lose all that we have spent a lifetime acquiring in various forms, including all the knowledge we possess, every relationship we have fostered, and each material object we have come sentimentally to cherish. Fear of that overwhelming loss carries considerable weight.

That we make every effort to avoid or minimize any needless pre-death suffering, whether it be physical or emotional, is entirely prudent, but we still regard death in some sense as truly a bad thing, despite our dutiful awareness of its inevitability, as though we were witnessing the fulfillment of the terms of a contract drawn up when we were born—e.g., "you are freely given all the opportunities of life under the provision that some day, on a day not of your own choosing, you will have to surrender it." Metaphorically, we arose from dust, and to dust shall we return.[86] Other primates, elephants, and dolphins have been observed to perform funeral-like rituals over their dead, belying the myth that only humans contemplate death.[87] A respectful fear surrounding death can be considered an expression of one's love of life; confronting our mortality serves to prod us always to remember that we ought to treasure and relish life so long as we have it.

Despite whatever potential benefits may accrue from death to the individual or to society, some cope with the fear by denying its certainty. A few arrange to have themselves cryogenically frozen in the hope that, once humanity has cured all diseases, they can be thawed and revived to live forever.[88] Others blissfully latch on to the youthful myth of their own indestructibility, a fragile delusion easily shattered by the first medical emergency they encounter. The ultimate form of denial, then, is the suggestion of an afterlife, the consolation prize for a life of hardship; given that no "soul" exists independently of the brain, it amounts to little more than a booby prize.

Does the promise of—or fervent hope for—an afterlife nonetheless bring consolation to the otherwise inconsolable? Does it offer, however falsely (or negated by being under false pretenses), a feeling of comfort to those struggling to cope with life's adversities? Even assuming so, ought society to allow the gullibly vulnerable to use superstition for emotional support or reassurance, particularly during hard times for them, when they are facing death, or when they find themselves disconsolately hopeless about the future? Only a sadist could contemplate kicking the crutches or a cane out from under someone who needed these supports to assist in walking; we should consider, therefore, when religious belief serves as a crutch for some people, by what right we think entitles us to dispel whatever coping mechanism other humans have found or on which they have come emotionally to rely. Conversely, we must examine the deleterious effects that may result from failing to disabuse the millions freely running around in our midst of the dangerously false ideas to which they subscribe and on which they act as members of a civilized society.

If some individuals can only find comfort in false beliefs, we must ask whether our priority is truth or comfort. The early cave dweller can offer his shivering companion the warmth of an animal hide, or else he can redirect his efforts toward truth, leading him to discover fire, a far better, and more humane, source of life-sustaining warmth. If we are content to huddle around the comfort that a demonstrably false dogma brings, we will never strike out on our own with the adventurous human spirit that has always spelled progress for humanity. Such dogma may not only fail to encourage progress but it might squarely impede or stifle it, as when those who earnestly believe in an afterlife squander the one life they have.

This is the insidious way in which a mistaken belief in an afterlife turns our outlook topsy-turvy. The one thing we know is that we are alive on this earth for up to several decades, yet even a hundred years does not amount to a blink of an eye compared to the eternity of an afterlife that some anticipate, albeit only as pure speculation: The belief trivializes what we do know for certain (this life) by exalting or elevating what we do not or cannot know (a supposed afterlife). Any notion that distorts our level of knowledge, turning it upside down, is dangerous and serves only to discount the truth. Moreover, without a sustained belief in an afterlife, the majority of people historically might have chosen to demand better working and living conditions, so in that sense, the afflicted are hardly comforted but quite the opposite by the perpetuation of the unfairness and misery that historically has been the fate of such a large proportion of humanity.

When you see a photograph of yourself as an infant or a child at a young age, some recognition allows you to claim the picture as "you," but depending on your present age, that recognition is likely accompanied by a sense of detachment, in that you are now quite a different person. Imagine what the image of you at even a hundred years of age would evoke were you to view or recall it after a million years into your alleged afterlife, or a billion years, or a trillion. Would it not fade into oblivion? All the kingdoms of the world and their mighty empires crumble into the abyss as they stand before the timeless erosion of eternity. In the context of time without end, no finite entity or event can have any significance whatsoever; elevating what lasts forever, which can have no other effect than to belittle and utterly demean anything with limited duration. Falsely attributing infinitude to a temporally bound (i.e., mortal) being is a dangerous practice that clouds our understanding and shuffles out-of-order our epistemic priorities. Acosmism envisions only a single infinity and marshals everything else wholly within that one conception.

Many religions, and in particular the Abrahamic religions of Judaism, Christianity, and Islam, view the material earth as an area where the immortal "soul" is temporarily prepared for its eventual and everlasting afterlife in an unseen, immaterial world.[89] According to this view, our world is merely a proving ground for the "soul," whose ultimate place of residence is based on its corporeal actions, or rather the behavior of the physical body it inhabits, while on Earth.[90]

Were the world purely a laboratory to test the so-called goodness of human "souls," the observable universe would then be ridiculously oversized at a volume of 10^{31} cubic parsecs.[91] As a proving ground for just the human life forms on a small, rocky planet orbiting a mediocre star on the outer edge of a galaxy, one of two trillion such galaxies observed, would be an incalculably inefficient waste of space for this narrow purpose. Such a claim is the type made by those who either do not know or do not comprehend the unimaginable scope of the physical universe.

Even so, for what do the religious believe God would be bargaining were He trying, upon such a large physical stage as this Universe, to elicit the faith of His tiny, human creatures? It can only be, at least in part, that the truth He represents is otherwise inaccessible to human experience and reason. If the truth were manifestly visible, its acceptance would be a simple matter of observation; when any truth is forever hidden from view, faith becomes the sole route to attain it. The question then becomes: Why would God deliberately hide the truth, or if He is not actively concealing it, how can a truth we are charged to accept be beyond our natural reach?

From the religious standpoint, God bargains for us to have faith in Him, not out of a call for blind allegiance but so we will believe that, especially when the direct evidence of the circumstances appears to contradict it, He will honor the promises He has previously made to us. The problem with this outlook is it requires a god who reveals enough of his plan for us to sense his pledge toward a particular outcome without then divulging how the plan will be implemented. Moreover, such a god must be sufficiently insecure that our opinion of his promise-keeping habits actually matters to him. Faith creates an incongruity in divine motives and debases divinity in order for us to be able to relate to it. Yet, to alter our conception of God in this way so as to allow us to "relate" to Him is altogether a mistake; that diminution is the corrupting effect of every so-called faith, to which our intellect ought to remain impervious.

What the faithful always appear to ignore is the logistics involved in operating for eternity the vast machineries they call heaven and hell. These hereafter places would unavoidably require a tremendous effort to establish and maintain. Imagine devising and implementing different ways to please or torment tens of billions of "souls," constantly growing in number, forever. Despite our tendency to recognize alternately euphoria and mental anguish, our experience with sensations is entirely physical and normally constrained by duration or locale. How are incorporeal entities made to undergo any typically physical sensation, particularly in an unspecified location and in the temporal context of eternity? Perhaps the rationale is that "souls" capable of seeing without eyes can just as well experience pleasure or pain without a physical body, nervous system, or brain.

Just like the athlete's mantra, "no pain, no gain," one can say with scientific certainty, "no brain, no pain."[92] The nerve sensors that transmit pain sensations to the brain via electrical signals demonstrably cease to function at death, as does the brain itself.[93] The physical pain apparatus simply does not persist beyond our demise, so the myth of hell is purely symbolic. We can also experience other forms of pain, of course, such as the psychic anguish of regret or the pangs of remorse or the heartache of separation and loss. But the Bible depicts a physical hell as fire and brimstone, sulfur's melting point being 240 degrees Fahrenheit[94]; with the vision of bodies burning perpetually in the Lake of Fire,[95] such depictions cannot in any manner be truly real.

The concept of an afterlife, with its promise of a better life or punishment following this unjust world of ours, is as much a political invention as a religious one. The political power structures historically adopt for their own agenda the social restraints of religion.[96] When trying to convince a populace, say, how to avoid the ill effects of consuming food that is prone to spoil, rather than explaining the scientific basis for a prohibition, framing it instead as a direct edict or commandment from a god is far easier. These are the areas of life where exploiting a misinformed, god-fearing population can be at least temporarily justified. When the same religion ventures into condemning, with the same fiery invocations, innocent or innocuous behavior, then it loses its rationale as beneficently misguided; it can become a pernicious hindrance to human progress.

In the identical sense in which an admirably deft forgery loses all value upon discovery, a false or misplaced faith is ultimately worthless. Caught up in the debate over an afterlife is what genuinely constitutes death. Language can be reduced to the set of mental labels we put on the hanging folders in our own individual ontological file cabinet. To the believer, death is merely a natal-like transition from life to an afterlife, whereas in the eyes of the nonbeliever, it is the dead-stop termination of the life that has preceded it. Acknowledging the difference in these perspectives, one might view faith as a fervent hope that the apparent end is somehow not truly the end.

At the atomic level, aside from classifying the known elementary particles of physics, the Standard Model describes the three fundamental forces of the electromagnetic, weak, and strong gauge interactions.[97] Those particle physics models that theoretically consolidate these forces into a single force are called "GUTs" or grand unification theories.[98] Despite the lack to-date of any experimental confirmation, several GUTs do predict and/or require, in violation of baryon-number symmetry, that the proton, the otherwise stable subatomic building-block of all matter in the Universe, eventually decay.[99] Under these theories, the proton's expected half-life is on the order of 10^{34} years, or some ten billion, trillion, trillion years.[100] For a universe estimated to be only 13.8 billion years old so far,[101] the duration of a proton's predicted existence is an exceedingly long one. And yet, the myth of the eternal "soul" is that it will long outlive a proton; when, due to proton decay and other cosmological forces, all matter ever known or observed to exist has finally crumbled into a virtual nothingness, the "soul" of your mother's cousin's brother-in-law will supposedly still persist, either in bliss or agony, but persist it will. Once again, in the triumph of ignorance, the view of those who have not a glimmer of understanding as to how the physical universe actually works seem to prevail and will continue for the foreseeable future to represent the majority opinion of humankind.

Experiencing life is like being tortured and having nothing to confess. To die or to suffer are the sole choices, since no palliative action, thought, or belief will hasten an end to the torment. No reward is forthcoming for attending this "horror show," with its carnival-like atmosphere, apart from having, in the end, simply endured it. Fleeting moments of joy are the all-too-brief respite one has before an oppressive reality reasserts itself. Yet, all humanity strives with undistracted focus to experience precisely these types of moments.

Those who say that a "soul" is merely equivalent to a person's "essence" are trading one ambiguity for another, because every person is a far-too-complicated amalgam of genetics, experiences, routines, hopes, and beliefs to ever be predictable, let alone capable of being boiled down to a neatly understood core. Moreover, if simple essence is the key, then one may just as easily ascribe the concept of a "soul" to both nonhuman animals like insects, all the way down to bacteria and to inanimate objects, as well. Will every blade of grass in the field have an afterlife? If so, and if the world to come is populated with revivified trees and meadows supplanting all the ones that have died, of what possible use is the world in which we now live?

Moreover, in such an afterworld, be it a heaven or hell, there would be no temporal limitation. Were it possible for such a world to exist, to be assembled so-to-speak with an immunity to time, why not our world? Why could our world not be similarly constructed, thereby eschewing the need for varying levels of reality, as religions are prone to erect? It is reminiscent of the joke, "Why don't they make the whole plane out of that [indestructible] black-box stuff?"[102] Of course, a civilian aircraft constructed entirely of titanium could never fly, nor could a world of experience ever exist without the conceptual limitations of inherent finitude and the boundaries of a space-time continuum. We cannot conceive of an object without extension or a world outside of time.

If every person, much less every individual thing, is entitled to a post-death existence, it would require a "soul" to appear magically as the direct result of any number of biological processes. Do people procreating have the power to summon the creation of a "soul" whenever they choose? When a human is cloned from his or her own somatic cells, perhaps repeatedly, does each clone have its own "soul," and is it assigned automatically? Do "souls" get recycled, as is suggested by advocates of reincarnation, and if so, do they have expiration dates? Do identical twins or triplets or other single-cell siblings each have unique "souls," and if they do, are they assigned before, during, or after the splitting of the fertilized egg that produces multiple births? These questions hide no serious logic or even curiosity behind them: The point is to expose how ridiculous it is to assert, particularly without proof and for no reason, the existence of an unseen, undetectable essence somehow mysteriously attached potentially to every living thing.

Perhaps characteristic of self-awareness, the thought process is that, while we acknowledge the world existed perfectly well before we were born, we cannot quite imagine ourselves no longer existing. The salve that acosmism offers in this situation, albeit in a purely philosophical way, is to observe that, since we never truly existed, death cannot be more than an end of a delusion in which our active participation has tended to define us. What ends at death is not the idea of us but rather the imprinting of the idea on a consciousness that finally is seen to have only had an unsteady foothold in reality.

To the extent that we cannot detect a so-called "spirit world," it stands to reason that it likewise cannot affect the material world, which is subject to our instrumentation. Being neither detectable nor exerting any discernible influence ought to serve as the very definition of unreal. For religious purposes, a spirit world must exist so as to facilitate the movement of a physically undetectable "soul" and to provide a realm into which it can migrate and dwell eternally. The notion that the spirit world could influence us here on Earth, though, seems to be based on several premises, including rationalizing unexplained phenomena now understood thanks to science, imposing social control by religious leaders, and perpetuating the foundational fictions that exemplify religious dogma, such as angels, demons, and resurrection or its conquest of death.

William James, in articulating his "transmission" theory of human immortality, purports to observe that "when finally a brain stops acting altogether, or decays, that special stream of consciousness which it subserved will vanish entirely from this natural world[, … b]ut the sphere of being that supplied the consciousness would still be intact."[103] No one is apt to mistake such a pure-thought realm, however, for a true afterlife. Moreover, his theory wholly assumes a nonphysical or spirit world, for which there is no direct evidence, apart from religious claims whose motives are more focused on control than edification. Secondhand accounts, like near-death experiences, are merely indirect support of the claim and not scientifically testable. The brain is the apparent source of, not a mere portal for, consciousness; in order for it to be a portal, we would require initial proof that the unseen realm exists, as opposed to extrapolating that it exists from the equally unfounded assertion about the presence of non-brain-based memory mechanisms. Further complicating the matter is the fact that, as noted, humans possess an ability and acute propensity, driven by evolutionary influences in avoiding predators, to recognize faces almost anywhere, making inanimate objects "come alive" and understandably mistaken by the gullible and the imaginative for ghostly apparitions.

The brain as the center of consciousness is comprised of physical matter, ultimately consisting of particular molecules and atoms, yet it operates at a much higher level, as do most macroscopic systems. Those who maintain that a "soul" exists will insist that it is made of an altogether different, nonphysical substance rather than of molecules and atoms. In this manner, spiritualists presume that even the building blocks of all matter prove at long last unnecessary. Why have, in the first place, all the neurological circuitry for storing and retrieving sensory perceptions as memories if they can be imprinted on a "soul" through some indefinable and unverifiable process invented long before the physical process became known or understood? Likewise, why have evolved eyes or ears if the "soul" is equally capable of seeing or hearing (or otherwise perceiving by nonsensory means) its physical environment? (Must the "eyes" of the "soul" blink for moistening?) Spiritualists have no explanation for these manifestations; in their topsy-turvy world, they have once again made redundant what we know (physical means of perception) in order to elevate the unknown (the supposed workings of the "soul").

The logistics of an afterlife, viewed in the most favorable light that is scientifically possible, would begin with the loss of the senses of sight and hearing, the loss of consciousness, the loss of all memories, and hence, the loss of any identity that is based on memory, and finally, the loss of any corporeal connection to the material world. What remains, to the closest degree of certainty of which we are capable, would be "nothing," but for the sake of argument, let us suppose some effervescent wisp remains, not unlike the fizzy "spritz" when opening a carbonated beverage. Our wisp perceives nothing as it floats aimlessly, adrift in space, uninfluenced by the slightest breeze. More importantly, it has no thought nor self-awareness. Such an entity is not one to which any person would lay claim as representative of self or as manifesting any discernible form of existence. We resist calling it a "soul," because that word is reserved for denoting the core of essence of a sentient being, which the wisp assuredly is not. It stands defiantly against being detected by our most sensitive instruments and serves no purpose. The wisp is hardly the vision of an afterlife for which the masses of humanity yearn and have yearned, but it is all that science and reason can allow. Perhaps this realization about the post-death limits on what could remain of us is what leads some to imagine the "soul" being permanently housed in the corporeal body and thus to deny physical death altogether.

A clear instance in the Bible of a person being rapturously taken bodily to heaven is the Ascension of Christ (Luke 24:51). While the translation of the prophet Elijah up into heaven via a chariot of fire (2 Kings 2:11) might be considered another instance, some controversy surrounds the alleged timing of the event relative to his later correspondence and the contrast between the term "heaven" (meaning paradise) and "the heavens" (meaning the sky, as a channel of transportation).[104] Nevertheless, just before his Ascension, Jesus plainly states that "a spirit hath not flesh and bones, as ye see me have" (Luke 24:39), and he eats a piece of a broiled fish (Luke 24:42) to demonstrate the distinction between a physical person as opposed to a spirit. Christ's physically resurrected body is never converted into spirit form prior to his Ascension, so he is instead conveyed bodily to heaven, suggesting it to be a physical place. Why then must his faithful followers die to join him there? When Jesus tells the thieves crucified next to him that they will all be dining in heaven that first Good Friday, without citing the Sunday Resurrection or the much-later Ascension, and then "commends" his spirit (Luke 23:46), it altogether confuses the relationship among spirit, body, and death. Not even Christianity keeps the earthly and spiritual worlds entirely separate from each other, while at the same time exhorting all of humanity to hew their thoughts and behavior more toward the supposed needs of the "soul."

If all perception is ultimately an expression of God's consciousness, however, could not a "soul" be merely a manifestation of God's own awareness? The denizens of an imagined universe would not be incarnations of God, however, but rather just His avatars, in the sense of representation as opposed to corporeal materialization. Recall that time itself is embedded in the idea of the Universe, such that, it is only a fleeting idea, completed as soon as it has begun. While we and the rest of the physical universe are divine constructs, our role is strictly to epitomize the noncelestial for the benefit of God's understanding.

Some will decry any analysis skeptical of an afterlife by citing the conventional aphorism, "Absence of evidence is not evidence of absence." What this criticism ignores is that numerous scientific studies have investigated the phenomenon of death. Scientists have not stood by passively waiting for an indication of an afterlife; rather, any afterlife which might exist has withstood every effort probatively to confirm it.[105] Hawking considers "the brain as a computer which will stop working when its components fail[, so the notion that there is a] heaven or afterlife for broken down computers [...] is a fairy story for people afraid of the dark."[106]

Because we cannot be definitive about an uncertain assertion does not preclude us from declaring with assuredness what cannot in the end be the case. If someone jangles a pocketful of coins and asks you to guess how much change is in the pocket, you may be reluctant to hazard a guess; nonetheless, restrictions do govern, in that you can say with certainty that the amount in U.S. coinage cannot be less than three cents, which is the smallest number and denomination of coins capable of making the jangling sound, nor more than one-hundred dollars, which is the largest number and denomination of coins that could fit concealed in a normal-sized pocket. Similarly, even though we are constrained from saying, by virtue of it being resistant to testing, precisely what happens when a person dies, we can still deduce, based on the facts we do know, what cannot possibly ensue after death. As science demonstrates, a living brain is necessary for biological based memory, and hence, identity, yet insofar as physical death prevents the disconnected brain and all its memory from surviving, no afterlife that depends on such memory or identity is possible.

In the Bible, the disciples of Jesus hear him recite his predictions and make his personal promises concerning his own resurrection, so it is surprising that one of those disciples, Thomas, is demanding firsthand proof that his messiah had risen (John 20:27). Even more ironically, Jesus supposedly submits by offering the sought-for proof, while urging others without the opportunity for direct proof in the future simply to believe (John 20:29). This exhortation to faith, while conceding proof to one most disposed to believe, further blurs the circumstances in which it is appropriate to seek corroboration. If there were an afterlife for any of the hundred billion humans born on Earth thus far, why has not one of them, save allegedly the one asking us to believe in his resurrection, actually returned to prove it? When English politician Algernon Sidney (1623–83) declares, contrary to biblical teaching, that "God helps those who help themselves," one wonders why this same deity cannot provide the evidence precisely to those who cannot believe.

According to its common definition of continued existence after all life has ceased, an afterlife is, therefore, impossible, but as Russian playwright Anton Chekhov (1860–1904) so achingly implores:

> *"Oh, why is not man immortal?" he thought. What is the good of the brain centres and convolutions, what is the good of sight, speech, self-consciousness, genius, if it is all destined to depart into the soil, and in the end to grow cold together with the earth's crust, and then for millions of years to fly with the earth round the sun with no meaning and no object? To do that, there was no need at all to draw man with his lofty, almost godlike intellect out of non-existence, and then, as though in mockery, to turn him into clay.*[107]

The mistake in this thinking is ignoring that an individual human represents the millions of preceding generations of evolving ancestors who arose, mutated over the eons, and perished to provide the genetically encoded DNA blueprint realized in that individual. Presuming humans are not on the brink of extinction, the death of a person is not tantamount to the death of the human race. Because humans tend to live beyond the age necessary to ensure the survival of offspring, estimated at about twenty-five years,[108] no evolutionary basis has developed against life-shortening diseases that arise in the postreproductive period. There might even be instances in which a genetic disposition to an age-related affliction actually promotes health and fertility while young.[109] Basically, though, the longer you live, the more likely you will have died, and statistically, at some point, you will have. Death is a part of life, and belief in an afterlife fails utterly to recognize that undeniable fact.

One of the famous aphorisms of American writer and humorist Mark Twain (1835–1910) is: "I do not fear death. I had been dead for billions and billions of years before I was born, and had not suffered the slightest inconvenience from it."[110] This essentially restates Schopenhauer's observation that "[a]fter your death you will be what you were before your birth."[111] This is to say that, if life were truly nothing before birth, then after death, it returns to being nothing again. As Epicurus asks, "Why fear death when we can never perceive it?"[112] Potential ontological problems, referring both to a preexistence nonexistence and a prebirth nonexistence, may also be altogether different from a post-death nonexistence. Comparing the remnants of something that once lived with an inanimate thing that never did exposes a fundamental disparity, although because neither is conscious, they are effectively the same in this respect. One cannot be said to know or experience one's own nonexistence, yet to the acosmist, God's pondering it animates the phenomenal world in which we appear to live and eventually die.

Another obstacle in coming to terms with self-annihilation is that the components of life such as atoms, molecules, and energy, do themselves persist, and in light of the conservancy maxim that the matter and energy within a closed system like the physical universe are never destroyed (nor, it should be noted, created),[113] these constituent parts are, in this sense, immortal. They go on long after the life form of which they were a part has perished. What a living thing or we humans must recall, however, is that it will be strictly the organization of the component pieces that comprise us which ceases upon our death, not the components themselves. As with any entropic winding down, the result is a chaotic dispersion of organization that will never rearrange itself back into its original form[114]: the teacup shattered by gravity will not be spontaneously reassembling itself any time soon.[115]

Perhaps another way of thinking about death is that we are simply removing ourselves from the birth-to-death timeline that constitutes our lifetime. This perspective carries some logical heft, since the experience of time is subjective and represents one of the axes of the space-time framework that undergirds the illusory universe in which we appear to live. Time does not unwind, of course, as we are in the act of remembering events, although it appears to have done so when the remembered events originally occurred; God's acosmic idea similarly spans no time at all, as imagined events unfold and time seems then to transpire with regularity. In a way, death makes us timeless. All the events that occurred during our lives become, upon our death, "frozen" immortally in historic time, so in that sense, this life of ours is somehow immortal, even as it ends, and although nothing of "us" persists after death, our lifetime of experiences will seem to reverberate like an echo in the collective consciousness of God.

Chapter 12:

Free Will

It is forbidden to kill [... except] in large companies, and to the sound of trumpets.
—Voltaire[1]

Experiments repeatedly demonstrate that our unconscious impulses to act precede at least our awareness of having made a conscious decision to act, anticipatorily by perhaps as much as ten seconds.[2] The pre-awareness decision is, as noted, apparently "encoded" in the prefrontal and parietal cortices of the brain. One interpretation of these results is that our unconscious or subconscious minds actually render the decision which our conscious minds simply and involuntarily carry out, essentially leading to the conclusion that we lack free will. Even those advocating this interpretation acknowledge that the conscious mind is capable of altering or vetoing unconsciously these predecided actions,[3] so the results of the experiments may not be entirely inconsistent with freedom of choice, which remains at least a potential contributing factor in the overall decision-making process.

To suggest that our actions are either an exercise of free will or else probabilistic (at best, and at worst, random) sets up a false dichotomy, because an alternative would be a determinism based on influences that are either unseen or not understood. For some, the presence of pre-awareness impulses does not negate the existence of free will unless, however, these impulses are due to a mechanism by which the originating decisions are one-hundred percent predictable, or in the parlance of brain science, "neuro-predictable."[4] Such a level of accuracy is unlikely ever to be realized, and thus, since we will never be able to disprove that humans have free will, it would facilitate our analysis to begin by assuming that they do, indeed, have it. For a willed action to be free, however, it must either have no cause or else be contrary to all other influences; an action that follows even indirectly from an external cause or influence is fully not an exercise of free will.

At a minimum, we do seem to construct mental decision trees, if only unconsciously, which we explore only to the extent that it produces a final choice. We rarely spend precious brain time, akin to a computer's allocation of multitasked CPU time, reviewing already-pruned branches of these decision trees that we would never ultimately execute.[5] Our focus is the selection that leads to action. All thought originates in the subconscious, which cannot be directly controlled by any agency, yet we are only aware of the small percentage of thoughts, fewer than 5 percent according to cognitive neuroscientists, that actually get the attention of the conscious mind.[6] Furthermore, by studying how normal decision-making processes are compromised in accident survivors with brain injuries, scientists have been able to localize the function in the brain's frontal lobe and to map specific areas involved in reasoning and the weighing of multiple options.[7] This consistently demonstrates that something happening in the brain, and particularly in its frontal lobe, is a required precursor to post-decision actions. Perhaps free will is as much an emergent property of the brain as is consciousness or self-awareness.

Based on the estimates of neuroscientists that between 95 percent and 98 percent or more of all brain activity is completely unconscious,[8] some liken conscious thought to the tip of an iceberg, most of which lies submerged out-of-sight.[9] Although an awake brain may be conscious, other brain states decidedly are not: after death, while anesthetized, or even during nonlucid sleep, where mental images are projected to a mind unaware that it is asleep. By detecting neural activity directly, an electroencephalogram (EEG) can measure consciousness while subjects are awake, dreaming, in a dreamless sleep, or under the influence of anesthesia.[10] In particular, during sensory-driven dreams, for example, the brain is highly active without being conscious.[11] These varying brain states and levels of awareness reveal that consciousness must be entirely a brain function.

According to the "Passive Frame Theory" or PFT, consciousness is more of a mindful mediator to action than a free-will decider.[12] A clear evolutionary benefit accrues to having the unconscious mind do almost all of the work in terms of perception, memory functioning, information selection, analysis, and reasoning: The conscious mind simply "signs off" on the information presented to it and then proceeds efficiently to implement the indicated action.

When the unconscious is viewed as an information reservoir, it becomes the shared data for thoughts that are then no longer causally connected by the threads of logical reasoning and thus operates outside our conscious awareness. Moreover, because the same inputs or triggers would theoretically always yield the same cognitive result every time, there would appear in this model to be no room for free will.

At first blush, our long-term, strategic goals and/or the specific short-term tactics necessary to attain them could be thought of as having been freely chosen. The manner by which the work product of the unconscious mind is merely interpreted or indirectly acted upon, however, shows that neither goals nor tactics are the kinds of things that can be consciously or unthinkingly selected. Thus, we seem to lack genuine free will, both presently and prospectively.

Because the laws of nature are mechanically well-defined, it has become easy to think of their operation in the context of a "clockwork universe," a form of determinism mostly espoused by deists.[13] This view represents both the recognition that the Universe is comprised of material components or particles and the understanding that the behavior of these particles are governed by unvarying physical rules. Croatian mathematician and scientist Ruđer Bošković *aka* Roger Joseph Boscovich (1711–87) states the view as implying that the full knowledge of the Universe's configuration at any time would allow perfect predictability of its past and future states.[14] French mathematician and scientist Pierre-Simon de Laplace (1749–1827) builds on that view by imagining the assigning of this knowledge to an intelligence or intellect, later referred to by others as a demon, hence, the concept of "Laplace's demon."[15]

The premise for Laplace's demon seems to be based on the assertion that information in the form of matter and energy is always conserved, so that any apparent randomness which injects itself into a system is not genuine but due wholly to human ignorance or a lack of understanding. Scoto-Irish physicist Sir William Thomson, Lord Kelvin (1824–1907) would counter that, in a closed system, according to the second law of thermodynamics, however, information is indeed destroyed, as entropy in the form of disorder or heat death does irreversibly increase.[16] Nonetheless, the Universe has more recently come to be thought of as an open system, where information may actually be increasing because the rate at which its maximum possible entropy is increasing exceeds how fast actual entropy is increasing.[17]

Where the concept of Laplace's demon breaks down, though, is in the face of quantum indeterminacy and what might be called the defiance of assumed free will. These forces rob Laplace's demon of its predictive power and likely render it into the realm of the impossible. Modern physicists consider events at the quantum level to be entirely probabilistic and hence non-chaotically undetermined, largely by virtue of Heisenberg's uncertainty principle and, by extension, quantum superposition, where mutually exclusive, possible states coexist until reduced to actuality.[18] No specific information can be known or revealed, apart from observation or entanglement, which would serve to bring into sharper focus the accurate measurement of complementary properties beyond the limits that the principle has identified.[19] In addition, that more than one cause can result in identical effects presents a problem, making it impossible to "unwind" a sequence of prior causes or events from a given configuration.[20] If the information of the past is insufficient to determine even the present circumstance, then assuredly, under these constraints, the future must be completely undetermined. And as for free will, if it is assumed to exist at all, it can simply be summoned to defy any prediction: When someone claiming to have precognition predicts an occurrence that is even indirectly dependent on the actions of a free-will agent, then that agent can easily just do the opposite action so as to thwart the prediction.

Still, as noted, the many-worlds interpretation of quantum mechanics, which is akin to a never-resolved temporal superposition, negates the exercise of free will, since every possible option is realized in some world. Also, while quantum indeterminacy appears to create genuine possibilities, the results may nonetheless still be deterministic; if we can only account for six ways mathematically to make a total of seven with two dice cubes, outcomes may be predetermined even as they remain unpredictable. Quantum indeterminacy is like the radio static that disappears once the device is tuned to a specific broadcast channel: The finite number of stations amid the static represents the choices, and the continuing presence of the static does not blur the determinacy of those choices.

Those who oppose Laplace's demon contend either that, due to the limits on what an individual can know, no such creature is possible or that, for some reason, the information is ultimately unknowable which would be necessary for the creature to predict the future consistently and accurately. In other words, the obstacle is with either the ability to know or the nature of the knowledge. If an occurrence depends on a number of factors, then to the extent that these variables are hidden from view, not well understood, or too numerous to process, the event may then appear to be unpredictable. This may be especially true concerning human behavior, whose apparent unpredictability emerges out of the totality of circumstances, as though it were the product of free will.

Activity that appears unpredictable due to the complexity of its causes should not be confused with or mistaken for the uncertainty commonly associated with an entirely undetermined sequence of events. There would be a difference between an event that is predetermined but whose outcome is simply unknown, or perhaps even unknowable, and an event that is fundamentally undetermined or random. The randomness that quantum indeterminacy provides may make the future unpredictable, but it does not mean that human behavior, to the extent it is unpredictable, is an exercise of free will. While Bell's theorem seems to force us to abandon at least a localized form of determinism in favor of an objectively physical reality,[21] the notion of free will only ostensibly appears when an action is contrary to causality as opposed to being merely random.

When Hawking says "the laws of nature determine the *probabilities* of various futures and pasts rather than determining the[m] with certainty,"[22] he is suggesting what might be called a stochastic determinism. Within a range of limited probabilities lies some "wiggle room" but not the latitude of complete indeterminacy that would be essential to free choice. After all,

Heisenberg's uncertainty principle concerns only how precisely we can measure; it does not speak to the underlying laws of physics, the general predictability of events within the parameters of probability, or our ability to know or else subsequently understand either of these.

The randomness inherent in quantum indeterminacy allows the Universe in exactly the same configuration to be run multiple times theoretically without achieving the same result. This serves the acosmic purpose of simulation in which a universe is conceived while avoiding that its outcome always be immediately obvious. Even the creative process has a "sprinkling" of indeterminacy in it, exemplified by Austrian composer Wolfgang Amadeus Mozart (1756–91), who allegedly says of his musical ideas, "Whence and how they come, I know not, nor can I force them."[23] His creative method consists in immersing himself in music so as to provide his unconscious mind fertile ground for cultivating and later harvesting the seeds of his musical inspirations. Even if the quote is misattributed, the creative process of any artist seems only to gain traction when the individual, steeped in the discipline's milieu and ripened by exposure to the art's historical impact, applies himself or herself to the task with a gentle detachedness. If arguably humanity's greatest musical genius is capable of producing an arrangement of sounds that millions find emotive, expressive, and poignant, and he does so with a less than focused intent, how can anyone performing the most mundane of chores claim they act out of free will?

We act on account of our desires, but whence come these desires? Though we must own them as our own, we do not freely choose them, even as they serve utterly to define us as individuals. In a sense, we are victims, as well as observers, of our own personalities and the seemingly random ideas that, in unprovoked flashes, cross our minds. If being bereft of or actively suppressing all untoward thoughts were a requirement for virtue, no one would qualify as virtuous. Instead, decency consists of governing one's behavior in the face of such impulses and treating others with kindness and respect. To assert that we ultimately have free will, however, is to deny that we are moved at all by our emotions, which is ironic, since, were we actually devoid of such erratic feelings, we would become robotic and machine-like in our decision-making, hardly emblematic of the choice associated with free agency.

Furthermore, despite also being impossible to predict, the shaking tremors associated with Parkinson's disease or epileptic seizures can hardly be thought of as the product of free will, so randomness alone cannot be relevant as a gauge of free will. Neurologists will look in vain for a brain area or function that operates with absolute independence of the rest of the organ or its host system; there would be little evolutionary benefit for such a potentially dangerous or wayward channel of impulses to develop. Belief in free will, however, might serve a purpose by allowing the conscious mind to take credit for actions, already being freely executed by the unconscious, which it merely observes, perhaps including its own thoughts.[24]

Despite some behavior being labeled aberrant, at least in a social context, alleged free-will agents do not appear to act randomly or without reasoned motives. Even those who swear allegiance in following the commands of a leader are not mere puppets, but they instead interpose their own consciousness as an intermediary to govern their actions. Thus, the supposed cause of all our actions must originate within ourselves. If free will cannot be attributed to some externally exerted force or "will" wholly outside the neurological process, then what looks like free will is likely the result purely of personality. Scant, if any, direct evidence supports the notion that free will exists at all.

In unsuccessfully attempting to reconcile free will with determinism, compatibilists think they are free to the extent they are not being influenced by any external forces. Yet, their purportedly free decisions are based entirely on who they are, and, in turn, who they are is simply the cumulative result of all the external forces that they have so far personally encountered or to which they have been exposed, in addition to all the innate personal traits with which they have been endowed. The circumstances that bring about these encounters or exposures may seem unpredictable, so the individual's integrated personality is like a piece of driftwood being buoyed in the ocean: No one may know where it finally ends up, but each jostling influence contributes to the result.

If the simultaneity issues of special relativity guarantee that one observer's "now" event is in another observer's past, then the future must metaphysically already exist.[25] This view essentially represents the "Block Universe" model or eternalism, which envisions as equally real all events across the span of the temporal axis of the space-time continuum.[26] Eternalism is the most rigid form of determinism, in which the experience of events occurs like a computer cursor tracing a path across a monitor screen; each observer will have its own such cursor, hovering over different events and moving independently through time. Agents just play their prewritten roles. Critics of eternalism base their objections on the concept that the future is not yet here and thus cannot exist; what they gloss passed is that the "here" they reference is an entirely relative term, so in a larger, less-subjective context, events separated temporally do coexist to no lesser degree than ones separated spatially.

As noted, beyond the earth, the Universe does appear to operate like a predictable machine, in the vein of the clockwork universe espoused by the Age of Enlightenment philosophers and scientists. The planets orbit their stars with regularity, the solar systems revolve in march-like precision around their galaxies, and the galaxies majestically hoist themselves with foreseeable momentum into the void of an ever-expanding realm of space and time. When taken as a monistic whole, even the chaotic influences of quantum indeterminacy, with its cause-disrupting, entangled web of connectedness, cannot derail the predestined arrangement of these heavenly objects and their celestial movements.[27] At an extraterrestrial level, the physical universe is thus titanically unfree. Are humans, with their supposed free will and latitudes of thought, the only contrary force in all of existence, and if so, how did such a species, which constantly struggles for collective survival against the vagaries of a hostile environment, as well as its own misguided impulses, become so uniquely and remarkably free? The claim of free will has many of the same rebuttable presumptions as the assertion that the physical universe exists at all: Our choices are far more limited than they appear, and the ultimate deciding factor is driven by the necessity of our natures rather than the manifestation of an inexplicable and entirely external force of will.

Nevertheless, only through the wriggling and writhing of biological life forms can the mechanical energy of the clockwork universe be defied. The ocean-dwelling salmon, for example, swim arduously back upstream to spawn in fresh water.[28] Even the tribal social devices of human civilization that foster cooperation and altruism may run contrary to the competitive struggle for survival across the animal kingdom. And yet, in all such instances, actions proceed from nature, where the overarching goal of life is preservation of the self as an individual or the species in general. Life may resist its environment when unable to adapt, but its contrary action is hardly a true choice, given that the fight for existence and the aggregation of power are its primary, if not sole, motivations.

Regardless of whether free will is actually an illusion, as it is likely just an apparent outgrowth of the emergence of consciousness, it nonetheless might not be in the best interest of the agent entirely to abandon its belief in free will. When forced to confront the illusion, there could be a tendency toward a kind of defeatist attitude, where a fated consequence is seen inevitably to occur, despite intervening causal events.[29] In a non-fatalistic determinism, however, there remains a connection between the initial influence on an actor and the actor's eventual effect. With the actor playing a passive role, this causal correlation makes the outcome deterministic. When the cause-and-effect relationship is broken, though, the result is either the manifestation of the actor's free will or else a sort of fatalism stemming from his passivity.

To the extent that morality requires the exercise of free will, individuals must at minimum believe, even erroneously, that they are free to choose between right and wrong. Kant's duty-based morality or deontology implies that, were the world truly deterministic, it would be better ethically to believe falsely in free will, whereas were the world undetermined, it would then be worse to erroneously disbelieve in free will.[30] This resembles a Pascal's wager about morality, and the reason Kant proposes it seems to be that, despite the force of his categorical imperatives, he regards ethical principles as ultimately unknowable, in the same way his noumenal realm is unknowable to the denizens of a phenomenal world. His solution for grappling with the unknown is to minimize the regret of a mistaken belief, and thereby urges us to accept that we are free agents, irrespective of whether free will is, in fact, an illusion. Kant's reasoning falls to a similar counterargument against Pascal's wager: The supposed bargained-for benefit begs the question. Only someone who has free will can freely choose to believe in it.

If lack of free will allows us to avoid blame for our misdeeds, it likewise robs us of any credit we may take for any of our praiseworthy acts of goodness or charity. We choose neither the circumstances within which we act nor the manner in which we react to those circumstances, since, at any given moment, who we are and all the influences that determine it are collectively what brought us to, and shape how we navigate, our present situation. To a sentient being, consciousness and self-awareness might themselves be mistaken for free will. The illusion of free will is further bolstered, and we might tend to feel freer, precisely because we are able to identify more options available to us than those who grimly surrender to fate and accept the deterministic script that seems to move around all the constituent particles that make up the Universe, including us, like pieces being marshaled strategically across a chessboard.

To exert one's will means to have an aim or goal in mind. When someone plans to wield a weapon like a cudgel, that individual must, of course, first form the intent to grasp the cudgel: The will asserts itself when the arm is raised or extended, the fingers curl around the cudgel's handle, and the weapon is hoisted with the hand. What makes such a will, in the philosophical sense, free? It cannot be other than the original choice of the aim or goal that occasioned the willful action. And yet, in further regress, one might ask whether that original choice were itself freely chosen.

From the array of available choices, an agent performs a cost-benefit analysis for each one, perhaps at a subconscious level, and presuming no two are tied, the option with the greatest net benefit from the agent's perspective is ultimately selected as the basis for further thought or action. Because the analysis is subjective and not necessarily conducted with the agent's active or conscious participation, its result may not be known in advance and thus could appear as though it were unpredictable, or at least unforeseen. This indeterminacy makes it seem free, but the only actual variables in the so-called decision-making process are the agent's background, both genetic and environmental, as well as any analytical errors or improper assessments that might produce an unexpected outcome. There truly is no freedom involved, and so, as the saying goes, "No matter where you go, there you are."[31] We cannot escape the cumulative effects of our heredity and the influences to which we have been exposed over the course of a lifetime.

For English naturalist Charles Darwin (1809–82), humans lack free will because we are capable of acting without understanding our own motives.[32] From an evolutionary standpoint, the more we make decisions instinctively, particularly as it may relate to the survival instinct, the better off we will be; when we start inserting counterinstinctive judgments is precisely the moment we begin to put ourselves at risk of falling prey to a predator or of failing to secure our daily food. If we witness a bush quivering in the woods, it promotes our survival to believe it to be dangerous: An evolutionary advantage manifests in the paranoia of seeing the potential peril of free agents stalking us for their dinner at every turn, although neither prey nor predator is actually free.

Free will without a purpose—what might be called "free willy-nilly"—would be contrary to reason. In this sense, the whole concept of free will has it standing outside our biology, neurology, and evolutionary history. A choice made on a rational basis is not freely chosen, since any similarly situated, reasoning being would arrive at the same choice; when we act against the "right" choice or behave irrationally is when we exercise the greatest freedom. Is that, on the whole, how people act? People can behave erratically when they are in the grips of an emotion, which is often uncharacteristically irrational, but is the enraged or terrified individual truly free? If neither reason nor passion genuinely liberates us, the set of circumstances under which we can claim our actions to be truly free becomes difficult to identify.

Nonetheless, free will and belief in free will are two different things. The acosmist has little problem acknowledging that, even so, an illusory idea can serve some purpose in being believed or accepted as real. The illusion of free will gives way to the utility of yet believing that we and our fellow humans have free will. For the sake of personal responsibility and societal justice, we must pretend that free will exists, although ironically, the notion of, say, deterrence presumes a lack of free will because, otherwise, if free agents could defy its prohibitions by ignoring the threatened consequences, such deterrence would not work at all.[33] Recalling that our sensory perceptions are merely our own subjectively mental representations might help make more palatable the realization that our navigation through these imagined depictions is an intrinsic journey, no less an illusion, from the acosmic point of view, than is the Universe itself.

Studies tend to show that not believing in free will or believing it only weakly can lead to antisocial, unethical, and aggressive behavior.[34] As with faith in general, it will depend on society's priorities whether a false belief merits tacit support for some indirect benefit: yes, if the goal is keeping the populace docile and in conformity, but no, if truth is the ultimate aim. Some may use an inappropriate sense of fatalism as an excuse to surrender to their baser instincts or emotions. For others, suddenly aware that their conscious mind is but an agent for, rather than the originator of, their motivations, determinism evokes a feeling of connectivity to their fellow human beings, the world at large, and the history-specific times in which they live.

Some will question how any part of reality can be an illusion since, by definition, anything illusory must have a reference to the reality it is supposedly mimicking. In the acosmic realm, the whole of reality is asserted to be an illusion, but in the specific case of free will, were it an illusion, issues would remain as to how that illusion is both achieved and maintained. For a completely deterministic world, how does the notion of a free will even arise? When we as humans feel that we can exert our wills freely, how can we be consistently wrong in that belief?

While illusion may often take the form of imitation, it might more formally be defined as a condition in which something is other than as it appears. In a world where seemingly random events occur, often with devastating results and invariably beyond our control, it would not at all be surprising that we project a confidence over our at least being in charge of our own selves. But when our intentions, and even the long-term goals that are the basis of those aims, form entirely in our minds subconsciously and only then do we become aware of them, we cannot but wonder that our conscious minds constantly and mistakenly lay claim to having authored them. We look in the mirror and see ourselves; we examine our actions and recognize our agency—it is the true authorship of our intentions that we get wrong every time. The illusion is that, despite our claim of free will, our behavior follows as predictably from our personalities as the path of celestial objects do from the forces of gravitation and momentum. The personality is rendered opaque by the confusing maelstrom of the individual's conflicting emotions, thoughts, opinions, and experiences. Were we able to untangle all these influences to see clearly the direct connection each contributes collectively to our actions, we would readily abandon the pretense of volition.

For others, Gödel's incompleteness theorem precludes foreknowledge or predestination in that "there are inevitably facts about the universe that its inhabitants cannot learn by experiment or predict with a computation."[35] The observer effect in physics[36] thus becomes an epistemic boundary, since the act of knowing or predicting can profoundly affect the knower or seer. This conclusion, however, mistakes that a predetermined universe might nonetheless be unknowable or that even the outcome of a specific deterministic event could yet appear to be uncertain; the Omniscience Riddle also erects an epistemic boundary, but its border is crossed when the unattainable knowledge is acquired, to the extent it ever is, by baking the very concept of time into the structural fabric of the imagined reality. God, in the Laplacian sense of foreknowledge, is not a participant in His idea of the physical universe, by definition, and thus resides beyond its informational restrictions. He need not know in advance that a problem can be solved because even its eventual insolubility is part of the answer as to what He does not know.

Envision a psychological experiment in which a subject is presented with two distinct options from which to choose freely, say, A and B. Unbeknownst to the subject, he or she has earlier been hypnotized with two mandates: first, to cease deciding after having twice decided between A and B; and second, to forget immediately the choice after making an initial decision. If this arrangement were possible, the subject would be presented with options A and B and then charged to select one. Whatever mechanics were involved in this decision—brain activity, memories, experiences, indefinable preferences or biases—would presumably persist, at least for a time period during which the setting and conditions of the experiment are kept as unvaryingly consistent as possible. As soon as the subject effectuates the election, per the hypnosis instructions, he or she will dutifully forget having made a choice.[37] The proctor will then prod the subject to decide anew as though it were an initial pick. The subject chooses again, and, because this represents the hypnosis's termination condition, no further selection is made or repeated beyond this second choice. The results would be interpreted as a statistical analysis of how frequently the same option is selected in both choices and how likely any differences were due to free will factors. This may be the closest we can come to rerunning the decision-making process, and in the face of a high correlation between the first and second choices, we could declare, at least statistically, that so-called free will played no part in the process.

Simplistically, one might ask whether the brain controls, or even creates, the mind or rather vice versa, since were it the former, no free will would then seem possible, while were it the latter, our actions would clearly be the result of some manner of free will. The debate becomes a question of agency. The key realization is that all thought (whether concrete or abstract), all our memories, our entire sense of our own identity, and every aspect of our potentially emergent consciousness—all of these marvels of human existence—are through-and-through either brain functions or the result, however indirect, of some brain activity. Moreover, our behavior represents reactive actions, based entirely on our own personalities, which are merely an emotive outgrowth of our brain-centric minds. In a brain-imbued, materialistic world, quite simply no room remains for the antiquated notion of free will.

The anti-dualists seem to reduce human consciousness to a simple awareness of one's own body, physically interacting with one's environment.[38] To those subscribing to this view, conceptual thought is regarded as starkly a projection of language and, to a lesser extent, reason. The rationale ironically leads to a nonmaterialistic conclusion: "The human mind is structured by language[, … which] is public[, … and i]n some sense, then, the mind is itself public […i]n the sense that what we know is embodied not just in our brains [… but i]n particular, the ascription of meaning is a social process, not an individual one[, … in which s]ymbols acquire meaning insofar as they are social symbols."[39] No individual, though, can claim exclusive province over a society's collective knowledge, so the conclusion is more about the sharing of ideas than the immaterial nature of their mental source. In no ontological sense does American inventor Thomas Edison (1847–1931) spontaneously "live" whenever someone turns on a light bulb.

Perhaps the most meaningful way in which a potentially free will could be exercised is in the making of a personal choice between right and wrong. Any analysis would have to separate out the issue of actual morality, because were individuals ethically mistaken and acting on the basis of misguided beliefs, their behavior may not represent the result of fully informed decisions. Yet, a person operating under a misapprehension is hardly a free agent, and it may well turn out that doing wrong, or as religions call it, "sinning," is reducible to a fundamental misunderstanding.

Since all our thoughts, opinions, and yearnings are brain-based, we must be cognizant of the consequences when that marvelous organ malfunctions. If every instance of personally evil behavior can be traced to an apparent brain dysfunction rather than genuine malevolence, then the most fertile proving ground for free-will advocates has become compromised. These advocates must explain how a choice made under the influence of a distorted view can possibly be considered to have been selected rationally or freely.

The dilemma is a cause-or-effect problem. Evil doers necessarily lack empathy, which derails any corrective guidance that a moralistic system can provide. Inasmuch as thought precedes action, this lack of empathy, like all emotions, arises in the brain. Were the brain seen as the originating cause, the evil deeds would be its effect. Nevertheless, what if making a conscious choice to behave badly towards others is instead itself the inciting cause? Perhaps the brain chemistry associated with lack of empathy is the product of habitually choosing to disregard others' feelings and is merely a reflection, as opposed to the cause, of its choices.

Studies using functional magnetic resonance imaging (fMRI) scanners are able to monitor electrochemical activity in various areas of the brain simultaneously.[40] By showing a lack of activity in certain brain centers accompanying visual stimuli, these studies affirmatively demonstrate that emotive or non-emotive responses may not have expected cognitive precursors; for example, when a test subject is shown an image, the constellation of brain-based reactions that result will reveal whether the subject is forming a thought about the image prior to an involuntary, emotional feedback.[41] In this way, the brain's response is proven to be the ultimate source of the triggered feelings rather than the feelings being a reflection of a willed reaction.

The forces of natural selection that drive evolution among animals, including humans, tend to create a brutally competitive environment in which a cruel savagery best promotes the "survival of the fittest."[42] Thus, egocentricity characterizes the self-preservation instinct among human beings. The countervailing influences of social, wolf-pack-like cooperation and self-sacrificing altruism stand out precisely because humans are inherently selfish by nature.[43] We do not need to be taught to place our wants and desires ahead of others; quite the contrary: Selfishness is hardly an acquired attitude but is instead the natural state of individuals, who collaborate with one another only to the extent it serves their perceived long-term goals of personal sustenance and reproduction.[44] Even altruists may ultimately only be riding a "feel good" response to their own actions.

Humans seem to have no limit on their appetite for destruction, even self-destruction, if it serves their purposes. Along with our lack of concern over the threat of nuclear annihilation, we continue to degrade the habitability of the one planet in the known universe on which the human race can safely live, despite the admonitions of a consensus of climate scientists and the ready feasibility of alternative energy sources. The uninformed opinions of some are unnecessarily inviting a sixth global mass extinction of life on earth, threatening to doom the very future of humankind.[45] Only with a deeply felt compassion and abiding sense of familial connection among all of humanity can we collectively hope to stop these senseless scenarios of self-eradication.

The right *supramarginal gyrus* area of the human brain appears to provide the corrective conscience of thought that injects empathy and compassion into a person's perception of others and serves to regulate in a reformative manner our behavior toward those others.[46] Sympathy is when we feel for others based on how we recall having felt at some time about ourselves, whereas empathy is identifying with others in a way that may be entirely distinct from our own experiences.[47] When the empathic brain region fails to function properly or at all, it produces someone without the capacity for empathy who can act detachedly by treating other human beings as though they were inanimate objects. This is likely the root of all evil.[48]

Aside from brain chemistry functionality, other conditions are also known to suppress empathic response, such as hormonal imbalances, including high levels of the male hormone, testosterone, and the failure to bond with an early childhood caregiver.[49] In particular, the inverse correlation of empathy with testosterone specifically suggests that men may be naturally less empathetic, although this conclusion has yet to be borne out experimentally in any consistent way but anecdotally or according to the untested hypothesis that the hormone actively disrupts connectivity among brain regions involved in emotional sensitivity and imagery.[50] The same fMRI-scanning experiments also show subjects to be patently less empathetic in judging the misery of others when they themselves are comfortable or in situations they deem to be personally good for them.[51]

These observations confirm the direct correspondence between specific brain activities and resulting feelings of empathy, or lack thereof. Those who, due to brain malfunctioning, are incapable of having empathetic feelings toward others will act in a manner that can hardly be considered to have been chosen freely. Choosing to act evilly by mistreating others would be the most deliberate exercise of free will imaginable, so if brain chemistry wholly determines when or whether a person, lacking empathy, behaves immorally, then that individual is not free to choose.

Of particular interest are adults suffering from the identified personality disorder of psychopathy, although to speak of them as "suffering" when they do not appear to suffer at all, even as they so often consciously cause suffering in others, is ironic. Studies show that when subjects, including psychopaths, are asked to imagine themselves in pain, such thoughts trigger a heightened cognitive sense of awareness.[52] Where psychopaths are markedly different, however, is when they are shown images of others in distress or misery, and while activity in the empathy area of their brains remains ominously dark, brain scans invariably show an accompanying increase in the responsiveness of their brains' pleasure centers.[53] This explains why, in addition to feeling no empathy, psychopaths sadistically go out of their way to hurt others: They genuinely enjoy it. A consolation in these dismal discoveries is that psychopaths represent only 1 percent of the general population, but the rate is considerably higher, in some studies as high as 25 percent, among male prisoners.[54] Ruled almost entirely by their brain malfunctioning, psychopaths are incapable of freely choosing to behave in ways that betray their innate mental states, although some may learn the benefit to themselves individually of trying to conform to societal norms rather than face the potential personal ruin of giving in to their sadistic impulses.[55]

Nonetheless, even conceding that there will always be evil people in every society and that some of those individuals will attempt ambitiously to rise by seeking political power, the real evil is that these putative leaders often have many ardent followers and supporters. While these adherents may have their own agendas and obscure reasons for offering their allegiance to history's monsters, their collaboration is inexcusable unless wholly the product of a resounding ignorance. Religious beliefs can arrest the mind, mimicking a brain malfunction of reduced empathy. Zealots do not allow themselves to become radicalized, because that would suggest they do so willingly as a free choice; rather, they have come under the influence of immoral forces that aggrandize authority, despite the human suffering their single-mindedness engenders. Once an evil idea takes hold of the conscience, the believer becomes an unfeeling robot—hardly a free agent—and proceeds then to carry out the evil deeds contained in the idea and in the immediate consequences of the idea. This, too, is how evil enterprises arise: Each contributor, none of whom individually are particularly lacking in compassion, perfunctorily performs his or her job, with the result that the endeavor as a whole pursues depraved goals and ends up responsible for having committed horrible deeds, such as wartime atrocities or genocide, which could not have come to pass otherwise.[56]

Because no formula or algorithm allows us to predict with any degree of accuracy how a particular individual will behave under specific circumstances, some conclude that this unpredictability proves free agency plays a role in conscious decision-making.[57] Congenital genetic traits, a lifetime of experiences, and regimented education or training all collectively form the basis for a person's mental identity, and yet there still seems to be a missing element in accounting for individual preferences, biases, and motivations that make up a sentient being. Free-will advocates identify the missing element as volition or an animated spirit, but they are at a loss to explain the trait of contrariness, when the individual acts against the expectations of either society or the actor's own character. The missing element is instead personality, which may itself be an emergent property of consciousness and which may manifest as a hard-to-predict temperament of the psyche. Since contrariness would always be a possible product of the personality, it is no more evidence of free will than an unforeseen hiccup.

Of course, in the absence of "free will," no one can choose to try to convince others of anything, nor can anyone choose to allow himself or herself to be convinced by anyone of anything. The key is that exposure to information, as it streams sporadically and arbitrarily across the consciousness, may yet have a final, defining effect. We are not persuaded to believe by the arguer but by the argument, which could enter our sphere of awareness in bits and pieces, without any of the coherence our rational minds might demand. These exposures also become assimilated in the personality and must be included in the catalog of experiences that form the basis of behavior.

A feedback mechanism is also likely operating in which we incorporate our own emotional responses into the makeup of our personalities. A person may have a compelling reason to undertake a particular course of action, but the outcome might be unexpectedly unpleasant to the extent that feelings of guilt beset the individual; he or she will learn, not only from the experience itself but from the disconcerting response it evokes in the actor. Such an accretion of occurrences and reactions is used for informing future reasoned decision-making as opposed to the honing of a putative free will.

Free will consists of making choices, but only if the available options are substantially of our own construction. If instead the choices we habitually make are in response to circumstances we do not elect, the act of choosing is at best only partially free. Moreover, the choices seem to present themselves entirely unsolicited in our lives. Rain clouds descend, and we must "decide" whether or not to bring an umbrella with us: Regardless of our decision, we do not choose to be confronted with these particular options. We are at the mercy of the situation, or situations, in which we helplessly and unrelentingly find ourselves. Given this, our corresponding choices cannot truly be considered an exercise of the will of truly free agents.

Yet again, the mere presence of available choices does not imply that free will exists, nor does it suggest how we make our selections from among these various options. If the choices are mutually exclusive, and even if inaction were an option, we will have no choice but to choose one. Thus, the choice to choose is not free. Choosing for a reason is likewise not a free choice, since we are bound by our reasoning. If we choose for no reason, or what we think is randomly, that too is not a free choice, because it represents a surrender of having to choose; it is hardly a consolation if all that free-will advocates can salvage from this reasonless, "eeny-meeny," blindly random method of decision-making is somehow to assert that we voluntarily cede the exertion of our allegedly free will to it.

Confusing what might be called "focus" for "free will" is also an easy mistake to make. Once we decide upon a goal or course of action, we focus our efforts toward attaining it or executing the plan that will bring us closer to achieving it. The single-minded determination shown when we apply ourselves with focus does resemble a choice, but it is decidedly less than free, following the original decision on which it is based, since the focus is more akin to a robot programmed to achieve a well-defined task. So, for evidence of genuine choice or free will, we look to the action-initiating decision, what might be called the "aim." Unfortunately, that aim is purely the result of our nature, filtered through the opaque strainer of our personality: No one can know all of our thoughts, knowledge, and experiences—not even the so-called decider—or how they will coalesce and come to bear on our personal decision-making process. Unpredictability is likewise mistaken for free will, yet we must distinguish the truly unpredictable from the state of never properly being predicted; no one may know with certainty what someone will do next, however that is hardly proof that the next action is free, irrational, or capricious. Within the realms of our minds, even those afflicted with insane thoughts due to biochemical imbalances in the brain, every one of our actions is purposeful toward some end and must make relative sense to us. We control neither our aim nor our focus.

In the Bible (Gen. 2:17), God allegedly commands Adam and Eve to refrain from eating of the tree of the knowledge of good and evil, lest they die or otherwise become doomed. Later (Gen. 3:4), the talking serpent entices Eve that acquiring the knowledge of good and evil will make them "be as gods." When God discovers the supposed sin (Gen. 3:22), He declares that "man has become like one of us in knowing good and evil." This story is utterly confusing for a variety of reasons, yet it fairly epitomizes the strictly theistic view on free will.

An omniscient god would have the foreknowledge as to know already that his creatures would inevitably disobey him, so he displays a certain cruelty in placing the tree in the middle of the garden, with its fruit within easy reach. Ironically, the mere presence of the tree of the knowledge of good and evil, or else the temptation its presence represents, is what actually grants us free will, because without it, we would have lived blissfully in Eden forever. The purported disobedience is the only free act that Adam and Eve can perform in the Garden. The incongruity of the story is that, before Adam and Eve acquire the moral knowledge which the forbidden fruit would confer, God tacitly charges them with knowing that disobeying His admonition is unmistakably wrong. Furthermore, the couple's flatteringly wanting to be like God, as the talking serpent had promised, somehow constitutes an irredeemable sin. God in the Bible apparently values blind obedience over truth, which implies He truly dislikes the free will that the theists insist He has bestowed on all humans. If all the foregoing is the case, one is left to wonder why God would offer us free will only to punish us for exercising it, and also why He would set the stage so that the only way to use our free will would displease or disappoint Him.

The Universe is regulated by physical laws, although which laws we consider truly fundamental will establish whether these laws can change across space or over time or under extreme conditions. We always assume a law of physics that changes may only be a specific instance or subset of a more fundamental, unchanging law. Certain known values, such as the transcendental constant π, are necessarily invariant in every possible manifestation of reality because they are mathematically derived, whereas altering other so-called constants would create insurmountable obstacles for the development of a universe: the onset of time, the formation of stars or galaxies, and the emergence of life in a habitably conducive environment. Computer simulations over an astonishing number of variations do show that some combinations of values other than the ones governing our universe can indeed yield a life-sustaining milieu, although both the setting and the appearance of life could be difficult for us to recognize.[58]

Although governed by such inviolable physical laws, the Universe is nonetheless entirely probabilistic in nature, as demonstrated by both the theoretical or mathematical concepts and experimental outcomes of quantum mechanics. While this would appear to overturn freedom-negating determinism, the unpredictability of events actually renders uncertain the circumstances in which free will could operate, since even an intended action would only stochastically be related to, and thus unable to influence, any realized result.

Hawking uses Heisenberg's uncertainty principle to observe that "[t]here seems to be a certain level of randomness or uncertainty in nature that cannot be removed,"[59] implying that, since a given present state can never reliably be utilized to predict a future state, the Universe as a whole must be undetermined. Randomness, however, does not dispense with determinism for two reasons: (1) only the actual event is unpredictable, even though it is one of a limited number of possible outcomes, all of which were potentially known or identified in advance; and (2) any variation from a prediction can be thought of as merely a fluctuation around an average—like flipping a fair coin and expecting 50 percent odds of heads or tails, regardless of how long a streak occurs of one coin side or the other actually turning up—with the average being fully determined in the long run. An otherwise deterministic universe, with a smidgen of random fluctuations thrown in, is hardly the arena for fostering free-will agency to oppose it.

Proponents of free will often put forward scenarios to highlight the consequences of applying an actor's volition to some object,[60] but the lesson becomes completely muddled when that object is another, supposedly free agent. When one so-called free agent acts upon another, such as striking the individual or pulling the individual's hair, it utterly dilutes the claim that the first agent is somehow exercising his or her free will, when doing so fully circumscribes the second agent's supposedly independent free will. The first agent is "free" to hurt the other, but if overpowered, that other is not free to resist being hurt: Victims are not "free."[61]

When a monstrous event or natural disaster occurs, especially one that involves an horrific death toll, there is hardly ever a shortage of theists who routinely surface to declare it to be God's will.[62] Perhaps this viewpoint is cultivated out of the Old Testament's vengeful god, often depicted as smiting, drowning, or turning-to-salt a variety of innocent people or babies.[63] Frequently, God's hand is seen in the rare case of survival but generally absolved of either causing or failing to prevent the disaster in the first place. In contrast, atheists appear to view such events entirely as accidents; a series of opportunities to avert the disaster always seem expectedly to fail to materialize, so the atheist regards the matter as regrettable but inevitable.[64]

The acosmic stance considers these events deterministically, as predictable as a gathering storm, but insists on the inherent value of always having a witness to learn from the experience. An omniscient being, situated outside the temporal thread that weaves through mortal lives, ponders with complete foreknowledge all the relentless tragedies which will come to plague us; from that perspective, He cannot help but see participants as mere captives to their circumstances and to themselves. Hence, we are not free but act based on who we are and who our experiences cause us inevitably to become.

Chapter 13:

Morality

Boundless compassion for all living beings is the surest and most certain guarantee of pure moral conduct. — Arthur Schopenhauer[1]

The "Golden Rule" is the foundation of all morality. In eerily similar wording, it appears as a shimmering ideal in the laws of nearly every civilized society and is firmly embodied in the precepts of nearly every organized religion or system of morals.[2] To suggest that all evil could be completely eradicated, at least as it relates to interpersonal interactions, were the Golden Rule put fully into practice, is perhaps an overreach, but merely trying to do so would go a long way toward reducing the needless suffering that incessantly occurs at the hands of humans. Merely stating or announcing the rule, however, has never proven enough to urge people to follow it. The biblical admonitions in the New Testament, for example, though wise and well-stated, do not seem historically to have helped people, and specifically leaders, to develop their "empathy muscle" sufficiently to become moral: "[W]hatsoever ye would that men should do to you, do ye even so to them" (Matt. 7:12), "[A]s ye would that men should do to you, do ye also to them likewise" (Luke 6:31), and "[L]ove thy neighbor as thyself" (Matt. 22:39).

Also known as the Ethics of Reciprocity, the Golden Rule can be expressed either positively in its most familiar formulation, as in "Do unto others as you would have them do unto you," or negatively, as in "Do *not* do unto others as you would *not* want [to have] done unto you." Numerous variants all concisely express the same essential sentiment, but the negative form, sometimes called the "Silver Rule," ought to be considered preferable because the maxim, in calling for genuine empathy, actually represents an altruistic limitation on self-interest. When one individual begins to impose his or her will onto another, inevitably motivated by selfishness, the Golden Rule can be used to interpose itself in the spirit of cooperation by forcing the actor to think beyond his or her own interests, feelings, or desires. Any rule that incorporates a call for empathy is assuredly on a firm moral footing.

But, as worded, the Golden Rule may not be sufficient. Morality needs also to encompass higher, abstract concepts like Justice. In declaring his doctrine of Proportional Equality, for example, Aristotle observes that morality requires that each individual be treated according to his or her due.[3] Treating everyone the same may be fair, but to the extent not everyone is equally situated, to be just, such treatment must be tailored to individual circumstances. It is as though the Golden Rule were in need of an addendum, rephrased thusly: "Do unto others as you would have them do unto you *were you in their position.*" This modification does not diminish the call for empathy but merely tempers how justly it may, or perhaps must, be applied.

Another, more recent variation, dubbed the "Platinum Rule," advises: "Do unto others as they would want [to have] done to them."[4] Not addressed in this version is precisely the manner by which, despite cultural differences, one would intuit how someone wants to be treated, not to mention what one does when encountering masochists or those who ignorantly fail to understand what is in their own best interests. The negative form of this variation, what might be called the "Iridium Rule," would state: "Do *not* do unto others as they would *not* want to have done to them." Such a prohibitory version, notwithstanding its convoluted and inelegant wording, may be clearer in meaning, yet both variations suffer from being callously detached from the empathetic foundation that serves as the basis for the original Golden Rule. The reason for treating others with respect relies on the human condition being a shared experience; the Golden Rule taps into the commonality, so a variant that is indifferent to a mutual as opposed to one-sided understanding is impractical and lacks the evolutionary purpose of promoting the survival of the species.

Furthermore, dismissively interpreting the "in their position" modification against others is dangerous. Since Nazis truly, albeit ignorantly, believe the world would be better off without Jews—a morally indefensible stance—we must turn once again to empathy, or rather the lack of it, as our reliable moral guide, even, or perhaps especially, when a society wields its public power to mete out so-called "justice" to any disenfranchised minority.

As laws, customs, and social norms or mores develop, the challenging of societal standards may also have moral implications. For instance, in a culture that fosters the oppression of a group and thus establishes an expectation as to how members of that group are to be treated, the Golden Rule is especially needed to pierce through those convictions and restore empathy, even across social demarcations, as the guiding moral principle. Societal harmony may be a worthy goal, but it must never be attained at the expense of Equality and Justice.

We tend to judge an individual act or course of action by morally evaluating either the results or else the actor's motivation. Adjudicating morality focused solely on results is known as consequentialism,[5] whereas assessing intent as the primary factor is called deontology, best exemplified by Kant's "Categorical Imperative."[6] Further subdivisions, especially within consequentialism, force one perhaps also to consider the net, as opposed to the direct, effects of an act, whether the results were different from what was intended or foreseen (or even foreseeable), if there exists a law or rule to which the action must conform, or how broadly the scope of the result extends.[7]

A number of issues complicate—but thereby help better to inform or define—the consequentialist ethical system, which primarily encourages us to act so as to realize the "best" consequences; these issues include the doctrines of Negative Responsibility (DNR), Acts and Omissions (DAO), and Double Effect (DDE).[8] Under DNR, the consequentialist holds morally culpable anyone who fails—or opts not to try—to prevent an undesirable result, to the same degree as if an outcome were produced through affirmative action. In contrast, and seemingly at odds with DNR, however, is DAO, where the consequentialist regards that, under some circumstances, it may be morally worse to do an act that brings about some bad event than it would be merely to allow the event to take place by not doing anything to prevent its occurrence. DDE morally absolves the consequentialist if an otherwise ethical action has a secondary or incidentally bad (i.e., double) effect, irrespective of whether the undesired outcome were foreseeable or even foreseen as likely to occur.

The Doctrine of Double Effect (DDE) is obliquely concerned with intention, since it would label as wrong all intentional killing, while forgiving a death that results indirectly from a morally permissible act. The classic formulation of DDE is the so-called "trolley" problem, a scenario in which allowing the certain death of a pedestrian on a trolley track is deemed to be acceptable for the purpose of saving several trolley passengers from a potentially fatal crash.[9] First, the Trolley Problem is contrived. Meant to reveal the applicability of a moral system, the occurrence is simply so improbable as to be wholly irrelevant. Second, the Trolley Problem relies on a decision-maker with perfect knowledge. In actuality, we must all hazard a guess as to the potential consequences of our actions. We cannot know for certain whether the basis for our decisions will prevail: Maybe a pedestrian has time to jump aside, maybe passengers will manage to survive a sudden impact, or maybe, as in some variations, victims tied onto the tracks will wiggle out of their bonds before an unswitched, hurtling trolley runs over them. And finally, the Trolley Problem's alleged dilemma is easily solved. Both passengers and trackwalkers have each, explicitly or tacitly, assumed some level of risk in their choices that brought them into the present situation. A trespasser's expectation of safety is markedly less than that of a conductor, who owes his or her passengers a duty of action that aims to avoid crashing or causing injury. Balancing these competing expectations should not be too difficult a task.

Societies that recognize personal self-defense as a legal excuse, however, cannot acknowledge disparate motives and can only permit actions which are exclusively intended to protect someone assailed upon, even when a fatality is the foreseeable or even likely result. In contrast, the behavior of a victim-turned-aggressor can become immoral or impermissible in the eyes of the law, once a specific intent-to-kill motivation is formed independent of self-defense.

Critics of DDE declare its justification as illusory.[10] In this view, the actual effects ought to serve as a moral guide rather than inviting us to judge an actor's purported intent. The cost-benefit analysis inherent in a DDE dilemma should be weighted to achieve some proportionality, because it so often seems to be invoked as an exception to the prohibition against killing a human being.[11] An exemption must be carved out for acts of altruism and self-sacrifice, which, even when a fatal result might be both likely and intended, is always deemed morally acceptable.[12] Concerning civilian deaths, one can make a distinction—yet, is there a moral need to make it?—whether the deaths are indirect, as in the collateral damage of a war mission, usually considered regrettable but ethically tolerable, or else direct, as the targets of terrorism, universally denounced as immoral. Why would anyone, though, be they radicalized terrorists or lawfully deployed soldiers, think they have the moral right for any reason to rob noncombatants of their lives, thoughts, feelings, hopes, and experiences?

Taking the Golden Rule as a compass-like, true-north barometer of morality, there ought then to be consequences for those who violate it. A society might end up paradoxically violating it, however, in choosing to punish violators in ways that no one would want to be treated. This paradox exposes the futility or immorality of punishment *per se* and suggests that social norms may limit how a system of justice handles those who callously disrespect the rights of others.

Kicking a stone may be disruptive but hardly has moral implications; kicking a person or other sentient being is precisely when morality is invoked and when ethical questions kick in for consideration. Therefore, morality comes down to a matter of cooperation, which is why the Golden Rule is firmly its cornerstone, since it facilitates collaborative respect and fosters relationship building. Moreover, it is objective in that it operates in a way which is accessible to all who experience the vagaries of life. In addition, it is an evolved ethic, well adapted to the synergies of civilization. Finally, it reveals the corrupted egocentrism of those who fail to abide by it. For the wayward societies that tolerate enslavement or subjugation, it acts as a cleansing moral disinfectant.

This conception of the Golden Rule as an organic, objective, self-evident morality is in stark contrast to the theistic view that all moral principles are handed down from on high by the divine. In his *Euthyphro* dialogue, Plato has Socrates question whether something is moral solely because the gods say it is or whether, because this something can be considered objectively moral, the gods then feel compelled by its ethical dint to speak in support of it.[13] If authority, even a divine one, is truly the only basis for morality, then it can be arbitrary or capriciously applied, and we must guard against the possibility of being misled by a "demon" posing as a moral god. By what mechanism could every event with moral import occurring anywhere in the Universe store the power swiftly to summon a divine judge to assess it, even in altogether unforeseen circumstances? Furthermore, rigid adherence to absolutist rules and traditional textual interpretations fails at the outset to accommodate evolving circumstances, the effect of which is contra-morally to diminish feelings of sympathy and reduce any hope of a more merciful understanding; thus, inflexible fundamentalism is inherently not empathetic and prone to both injustice and misplaced zeal.

Religion's primary goal, after all, is the aggregation of power by keeping its adherents in line. It tends to achieve this goal through fear, which is how obedience oddly becomes the highest virtue, even when, as history chronicles, blind conformity in thought and deed often lead to the worst kinds of evil. While some secular autocracies also commit atrocities, there is no reason to think that a just society, harnessing an informed consensus through representative democracy rather than religious allegiance, could not resolve how to treat all its citizens equitably and in a manner that is not oppressive to either liberty or security.

In a different role, religion codifies what most individuals naturally arrive at as accepted morality, and by granting such conclusions an authoritative voice, it manages to enforce social norms in a way that has proven considerably more peaceable than through state-mandated laws. Thereby, religions exploit the tendency mistakenly to believe—a belief called the "Big Gods" concept[14]—that morality somehow requires the perpetual, ever-present watchful eye of the divine. But is not the voice of conscience less likely to be God's than simply one's own?

The "Big Gods" belief leads the faithful majority typically to mistrust nonbelievers[15] to such an extent that they often equate them with immorality or with being inherently amoral. Ethical nonbelievers, however, are genuinely moral, more so than believers, because they refuse to borrow their ethics; they have not been cajoled, violently threatened, or vainly enticed to accept someone else's morality. As one internet commenter aptly puts it: "If your religious faith is what stops you from raping and murdering, that doesn't make you a good person, that makes you a sociopath on a leash."[16]

Nevertheless, it cannot but come across as condescending to disparage religious moral systems, particularly ones to which billions of humans subscribe and thereby regard as transcendently perfect, although conversely, their "worship my god or burn forever" attitude does carry its own air of arrogance and intolerance. Yet, even these adherents claim to believe that we are all divinely granted free will so as to be able to seek and then choose the right path; by what means, then, should we find the way, if not according to the lights of our own sense of right and wrong? The Garden of Eden legend, however, suggests that the biblical god prizes blind obedience far above free will, because Adam and Eve are condemned for eating the fruit of the tree of the knowledge of good and evil, which paradoxically is the one thing that endows them with the ability to assess that their disobedient act had been wrong in the first place. We are supposedly free to choose, yet once we exercise our choice, especially if it runs contrary to our creator's arbitrary fiats, we ironically end up, as a result, losing our freedom. According to a misattributed quote, "Morality is doing right, no matter what you are told[, whereas r]eligion is doing what you are told, no matter what is right."[17] An objective morality applies to all, including and especially, to a god who is offered to the world as the most benevolent, righteous, and moral of any being conceivable.

Imagine a courtroom with a presiding judge on the raised bench, a bailiff sergeant-at-arms, two smartly dressed attorneys at their respective counsel tables, a jumpsuited criminal defendant, and a gallery of spectators. The judge is preparing to pronounce sentence on the defendant, already found guilty of murder at a lengthy and contentious trial. Just as the judge begins solemnly to issue a death sentence, a longhaired, bearded, sandal-wearing individual, completely unconnected with the foregoing proceedings, steps forward from the audience to draw the judge's attention. The individual offers to accept the forthcoming punishment in place of the convicted criminal. The judge shrugs his shoulders, orders the bailiff to take the individual into custody to await the execution order he was about to hand down, and tells the defendant that he is free to go. This imaginary scenario wholly exemplifies the Christian ethic.

To be sure, kangaroo-style courts do convene, albeit rarely, where such a scenario could conceivably play out, in third-world countries, operating more like tribal fiefdoms than the disinterested legal systems with which Western democracies are familiar. Standards of jurisprudence and due process such as the presumption of innocence, burden of proof beyond a reasonable doubt, and the attachment of legal responsibility are not universally observed, or even recognized, in every jurisdiction or society across the globe. Perhaps the defendant in the case is the son of a wealthy or politically connected person whose influence might explain the corruption exhibited by the judge in allowing an innocent individual to be punished in lieu of a guilty one. The motivations that would cause someone—in this scenario, the innocent individual stepping forward—to make a false confession or admission, or to seek punishment on someone else's behalf, have deep psychological underpinnings,[18] so the scenario, while far-fetched, is not a manifestly impossible one. Nor is it unlikely that a defendant, seeing a willing judge ready to accept someone in his place for sentencing, would turn down receiving such an offer: What remorseless crook would not shove his own mother into the furnace ahead of him if it meant he could walk out of the courtroom scot free?

Where the Christian ethic behind vicarious redemption[19] goes astray, though—notwithstanding the absurdity and moral outrageousness of an official court blithely accepting the life of an innocent individual in the stead of a known murderer—is when it declares this very judge to be, in fact, the fairest, kindest, most just, most compassionate, and most loving adjudicator ever in all the Universe. That is the contention with which no truly moral person can agree. Christians may freely say that third-party salvation is how the process is intended to work, but what they cannot proclaim is that such an arrangement is in any way moral. The premise begins with the assertion that Adam and Eve's disobedience so offends the alleged creator of the Universe that He could never stand, figuratively, to be in the same room with them: He cruelly condemns them, while engineering an eternal purgatory of torment, not only for these mortals of His own direct creation but for all their future human descendents, including babies, who are behaviorally unconnected with the event. Only a blood sacrifice, we are told, can reconcile the Creator with His creation. The demand for blood as expiation has its origins in biblical rituals, as when the Bible (Lev. 17:11) states that "it is the blood that maketh an atonement for the soul." The believer's role is to accept the offered redemption, yet inherent in that acceptance is a validation of what might be called the terms of the agreement, in which individual propitiation is achieved through the prepaid blood sacrifice of an intermediary or savior.

How supposedly does the blood sacrifice accomplish the reconciliation between Creator and sinner? How does it "heal" the rift in a way that pure forgiveness would not? Now, for the first time since the Fall of Man, God supposedly can bring Himself to be in the same room with the sinner, not because the sin has been removed, since clearly its effects persist, but because the penalty for the sin has somehow been paid, albeit indirectly by the sacrifice of the human form of the god who first creates the sinful creatures. Between what might be called divine "blood lust" and the sinner's avoidance of personal responsibility, though, is an inextricable link. Vicarious redemption is a technicality in that the sinner's willingness to avail himself of it is the very thing that ought to fail to redeem him. According to this doctrine, God rightly condemns all humans, but as a result of our killing the one allegedly perfect human among us, perhaps God Himself in the guise of His own son, suddenly with respect to those who accept the sacrifice, the condemnation is remarkably lifted, as though it had never existed. No part of this arrangement makes any moral sense, and those who claim to believe it should be afraid that the omniscient god they worship will see through the insincerity of their immoral faith.

Making original sin the basis of salvation is the classic confidence scheme in which a religion dupes you into thinking you have a disease so that it can then sell you the cure. Setting the bar at perfection renders irrefutable the declaration that "all have sinned, and come short of the glory of God" (Rom. 3:23). Yet, Jesus exhorts the crowd with "[h]e that is without sin among you, let him first cast a stone" (John 8:7), the implication being that only God can punish anyone for anything, a position reinforced when Jesus asks us as individuals to "resist not evil" (Matt. 5:38). By the time Jesus says that "no man cometh unto the Father, but by me" (John 14:6), the fix is already in, because the cure is exclusive to this particular person, to this particular religion, and to this particular moment in human history: An infinite god, eminently accessible to all rational beings in the Universe, now has a bouncer. Heaven can then be likened to a trendy nightclub, replete with a list fastened to a clipboard and a line of people queued around the corner, hoping to be admitted. What is happening out in the streets beyond the velvet ropes is of no concern to the bouncer: If your name is on the list, as the owner has decreed, you will get in, with the odd proviso that it is really a sign-up sheet open to anyone willing to check their own sense of morality at the door.

The key element of forgiveness, lest we forget, is empathy. That is why being forgiving says more about the forgiver than the transgressor: The ability to acknowledge another's state of mind, whether it involves desperation or outright callousness, is what makes forgiveness possible. Forgiveness thereby leads almost straightaway to that blessed release from the consuming fire of anger or revenge, feelings which thwart peace and harmony within, as well as among, individuals, not to mention the damaging effects on cooperation that a lack of forgiveness inevitably has on society as a whole. When we cannot forgive, we dwell in the past, as if prisoners of time, reliving those moments of anguish, preventing us from moving on or growing as human beings. Those who forgive, however, rarely condone, excuse, or forget the wrong done against them, perhaps not quite understanding the mentality, especially if rooted in psychopathy, that precipitates the pain caused by the wrongdoer; still, they recognize human imperfection and that even a remorseless individual cannot help but make mistakes, sometimes horrendous ones. Why, then, is the god of religion portrayed as so relentlessly unforgiving, at least as it concerns Adam's disobedience? Such a deity is envisioned as consigning in the billions the majority of humanity to everlasting torment, all except the chosen few who mouth, mantra-like, the incantation that the religion claims will somehow magically shield them from divine wrath.

Once again, the acosmist, skeptical of the logistics pertaining to hellfire or to any afterlife, does not directly deny out of hand the arrangement of a damning deity. Where the story ultimately breaks down, however, is in the assertion that such a god is truly all good and mercifully benevolent, exhibiting those special qualities only for those who, irrespective of bad character or misdeeds, bow their heads in obsequious surrender. A creator who is unmoved by the suffering of imperfect creatures is a mostly unforgiving god and, in that respect, is somehow less than human, being vengeful and spiteful by default. Those who subscribe to this view will find that they worship a monster who, regardless of any power it may possess, is not at the core good enough to be worth worshiping.

Discovering how, then, one can indeed be too moral to be a Christian, or any other religion that places obedience above morality, is not difficult. Apart from allegiance, such faiths have no enforceable rules because they are confident that divine absolution can be summoned, like hailing a taxicab, regardless of whom or how many one may have hurt. No transgression is too grievous as to warrant the withholding of absolute forgiveness—nothing that a deathbed conversion cannot redeem or else that a lifetime of good works will rescue from damnation—so that, if faith is all that matters, there is no point in having rules at all. Jesus implores his followers to "keep the commandments" (Matt. 19:17), meaning the Ten Commandments, but says, "I am come to set a man at variance against his father, and the daughter against her mother" (Matt. 10:34), in clear conflict with the fifth commandment (Exod. 20:12) to "[h]onor thy father and thy mother." The rules, and thus morality, no longer matter when allegiance has become the only criterion.

While moral systems may generally laud the selflessness and one-sided sacrifice of an altruistic ideal, the actual or realistic goal of morality is mutual survival through cooperation. This is most evident in a social context, where each individual's essential actions contribute to the community as a whole. Because morality is based on cooperation, moral principles are often expressed in terms that reveal their universal applicability. Morality comes down to evaluating human actions by distinguishing right from wrong; while such evaluations may be insightful after the fact, morality is most useful when it prescribes how we ought to behave. Its universality is evident in the way it is articulated, especially the Golden Rule, using, as noted, virtually the same words but always with the same meaning, across nearly all known human civilizations and cultures.

Although the process of natural selection cannot be fully equated with the concept of the "survival of the fittest," only the inheritable traits of those sufficiently fit to achieve reproductive representation in the wider gene pool will persist over time so as to serve in guiding biological evolutionary change.[20] The scientific evidence for this process is now so exceedingly well-founded as to be indisputable.[21] Nonetheless, according to a reputable poll in the United States, 70 percent of Christians reject the scientific account of human evolution due to natural processes; of those, a substantial majority deny outright that evolution transpires at all, while the remainder accept it as occurring only under divine guidance.[22] That potentially mutated genetic traits can be passed on to descendants at all—that is, the very mechanics of evolution—is what those professing a religious viewpoint typically deny, yet oddly, they continue to insist that the taint of Adam's original sin has been "inherited" by all generations, so that, until the end of time, salvation will always remain necessary.

A recurring—some might say, relentless—obstacle to communal cooperation is the specter of discrimination, in its various forms, throughout diverse or heterogeneous societies. Whether based on race, gender, age, ethnicity, affiliations, or some other, similarly irrelevant factor, the decision to treat equally situated people differently reduces the efficiency of any operation, if for no other reason than that unity fosters cohesiveness within an organization, whereas division makes the entire enterprise potentially unresponsive and difficult to manage. Of course, discrimination and prejudice are distinctly different concepts. The latter, as a form of generalized prejudgment without specific knowledge, is likely inevitable, not only because it appears to be inherent in human nature but because it is often based on some experience, albeit in an admittedly limited scope. Discrimination, on the other hand, is the real problem, because it represents a judgment rendered despite specific knowledge. As an example, consider an employer hiring for her business as between two job candidates, one of whom triggers a prejudicial reaction, either positive or negative, in the business owner. So long as the candidates are truly equal, whatever choice the business owner makes would be acceptable, even if based on a prejudgment. If the candidates are not equal, however, and if the business owner's prejudice causes her, for whatever reason, to hire the less-qualified candidate, then the decision is frankly discriminatory because it is made in spite of—that is, rationally contrary to—the relevant, available information. Victims of discrimination are harmed in many ways, including the loss of opportunities; feelings of low self-esteem, shame, guilt, fear, and stress; resentment over being stigmatized, excluded, ostracized, or made to feel less than fully human; and having to deal with deleterious health consequences, as well as the resulting lack of motivation to participate socially or develop personally through education or community service.[23] Even apart from the ill effects on individuals, both those who suffer under it and those on the other side who practice it, discrimination is detrimental to society as a whole in that it fosters bullying, fear, anger, and resentment, not to mention that it can lead to violence, mayhem, and in extreme but historically not uncommon outcomes like genocide.[24] Discrimination also fundamentally negates the Golden Rule, since people are manifestly being treated in ways no one would want to be treated;

regardless of its effects, discrimination is thus an unmitigated evil, practically so by design.

Most religions evince an inherently discriminatory attitude whenever true believers or the so-called "elect" are elevated over the baser nonbelievers and/or those unworthy of divine redemption or even the attention of the divine eye. Two passages (Matt. 3:12 and 25:32) strikingly illustrate this attitude, where, respectively, John the Baptist envisions God sifting the wheat while burning the chaff, and Jesus saying that, once enthroned, he will separate nations like "a shepherd divideth his sheep from the goats" to designate them for either preservation or destruction. While sifting of wheat is often taken as a metaphor to represent the testing of faith, the imagery makes clear that the chaff, symbolizing the unfaithful, will "burn up" in an "unquenchable fire." It evokes a process of garnering something good by disposing of the worthless. Likewise, separating sheep from goats is about exclusion: Only the worthy, God's elect, will endure. When Jesus allegedly turns water into wine at a wedding in Cana (John 2:9), he demonstrates his power to transform. Why not turn the goats into sheep? Why not refine the chaff so it becomes nourishing and edible like the wheat? In short, why not transform the wicked to become good, making them worthy, rather than disposing of them by casting them into fire? If a finely crafted work must be discarded, it impugns the crafter's skill and artisanship rather than the product: Keeping only the elect or chosen few while ultimately discarding the majority of humanity into hellfire is less of an indictment against the iniquitous than against their feckless creator. While we may want to rid ourselves of intransigents, the god of religion presumably has more power and mercy. Discrimination is fundamentally a human wrong, but it would be especially wrong at the divine level, where an omniscient deity cannot be misled by irrelevancies and an omnipotent one could flatten any disparities that undergird both unfairness and inequity.

Another area that jeopardizes survival through cooperation is personal retribution or revenge. Unlike discrimination or other forms of generalized hatred, vengeance is typically preceded by an event where the individual experiences pain at, or mistakenly perceived to be at, the hands of others.[25] Some basis in law upholds when an avenger believes he is enforcing some unwritten code of ethics; if the society consistently enforces its rules, then the individual may feel especially justified in attempting to do the same. Revenge can have many motivations, including: retaliatory, where the goal is to make the original perpetrators feel the same pain they caused the avenger; pedagogical, where the purpose of the revenge is to enlighten the original perpetrators by making them reflect on their actions and thereby teach them how they have wronged the avenger; destructive, where those who have harmed or traumatized others are themselves destroyed; and psychological, where an avenger with low self-esteem or acute egocentrism can go on a "power trip" and feel triumphant by defeating his "betters."

The Bible weighs in, from the Old Testament's "Eye for eye, tooth for tooth, hand for hand, foot for foot" (Exod. 21:24) to the New Testament's "Vengeance is mine; I will repay, saith the Lord" (Rom.12:19). The religious view is not to condemn the concept of revenge but merely to sublimate the impulse to commit it, which may have beneficial effects, but for the wrong reasons. What is missing from religion's apparent endorsement of vengeance is that, when it comes, the aggrieved person may not feel any better or have a sense of closure. The focus of the original wrongdoing is not on the victim or the wrongness of the act but on the bad actor, whose mental state or psychological inability to feel remorse might reduce an accomplished revenge to little more than a hollow victory. The initial act becomes bound up, sealed with the violence of the final act, leaving everyone worse off. The mentality of hardening one's heart, refusing to forgive, and behaving as though one is entitled to exact revenge all combine to suppress the feelings of empathy, which normally serve as guideposts for morally right action. Ironically, the compulsion for revenge often leads to the kind of conflict that is the basis for the hero's journey, on which we all tend to cheer.

Because cooperative effort at various levels is highly effective at securing resources and warding off predators, studies and psychological experiments tend to show that, in endeavoring to reap the evolutionary benefit, humans do naturally collaborate and are inclined to support one another.[26] People will contribute (or, colloquially, "pitch in") to their own families, to their tribes or other identifiable group affiliation, and to their entire communities or societies.[27] In exchange, the groups afford these individuals protection, which only serves to camouflage that humans are essentially, perhaps even innately, selfish, at least when it comes to promoting their own survival or, ultimately, the survival of their genetic blood lines. "Prisoner's dilemma" style experiments help to unmask how biologically committed we are to ourselves[28]; the survival instinct, however, is a commendable mindset, because without it, we quickly would have perished as a species. (It may be debatable whether or not the demise of humanity would have been—or still would be—a desirable outcome.) The problem is when egocentrism goes beyond mere survival and becomes destructive: Selfishness is assuredly the foundation of evil, though only when misapplied. This "sometimes yes, sometimes no" situation is a dilemma, making identifying evil and its causes surprisingly elusive.

As with most philosophical matters, the problem lies in establishing an essential definition of what is "good" and building on that so as to create a consensus. Unfortunately, even the attempt to define it logically or rationally will expose how subjective a concept it is, primarily due to the connection between "goodness" and utility. What is good must be inherently desirable or serve a purpose or accrue a benefit to someone. In the view of some religions, what constitutes good boils down simply to obedience, fealty, or surrender to authority. The vagueness of these descriptions befogs any overarching definition that might aptly encompass them.

Keying in on the concept of being desired, there might even be a disagreement on whether good, howsoever it may be defined, is better than evil, apart from how it aligns with our sense of morality. The distinction is not merely a matter of convention; it would be a mistake to assert that whatever may be better is, by definition, good. Evil is inextricably linked with suffering, so to the extent it is opposed to good, no assessment can be thought of as purely relative or contextual, although it admits of comparison when choosing the lesser of two evils in an effort to minimize suffering. The moral knot is when suffering somehow becomes the desired outcome. In the *Gorgias* dialogue, Plato has Socrates declare, "I'd rather suffer than [cause suffering]."[29] Yet, in war (as Socrates had been a soldier), inflicting the greatest casualties is often the military objective. There must be a universal principle governing what is good to which one can apply to these circumstances.

The distinction early Christians made[30] between "natural evil" and "moral evil" turns out not to be a helpful one. By the former, one understands a physical event, such as a natural disaster, which randomly or indiscriminately causes death and/or destruction, while by the latter, one means the deliberate wrongdoings of humans against other sentient beings. If there were no free will, in the Calvinistic sense, which is to say, humans act in ways that are at least theoretically predictable as a result of their nature, a complex mixture of emotions and learned behavior, then all evil deeds would be natural in the sense that they arise from a naturally occurring condition, be it the swirling wind of a tornado or the agitated mind of the sociopath. Were this the case, we would tend then to revert to a view in which we resignedly observe that we cannot experience the (subjective) beauty, say, of a rainbow without it having been preceded by the destructive capability of a rain storm, or of a sunset without it preceding the potential terrors that accompany a daily nightfall.

Isolating evil that is uniquely human thus permits religions to subject it to God's judgment. The suggestion seems to be that humans are evil by nature, from birth onward. This raises the question in the religious context whether God, seen as the Creator, could have made humans who were free of sin. The biblical view of Adam and Eve is that they were indeed sinless in the Garden of Eden until tempted to disobey, and when he in whom there "is no sin" (1 John 3:5) allows the devil in the desert to tempt him (Matt. 4:1–10), the implication is that all humans, including Jesus, are inherently corruptible, for otherwise they would not have been subjected to temptation. While the Edenites relent and the Nazarene does not, the capacity for immorality, wickedness, and depravity is firmly implanted in the human seed. Yet, if God the Creator is incapable of fashioning a creature without the seed of sin, He cannot then ethically condemn humans for the sinfulness that He cannot eliminate; conversely, if He could eliminate it, then He is as complicit in the sin as someone who hands a weapon to a known serial killer.

As a working definition, we might say that "good" is that particular state of mind which leads us to feel empathy for, and to work cooperatively with, others; this is why evil equates with a lack of empathy and why it has its basis in selfishness, which disrupts collaboration and feelings of mutual concern. Lest we think goodness is at all within the province of humankind, Jesus makes it clear that only God is genuinely good: "Why callest thou me good? None is good, save one, that is, God" (Luke 18:19). If "good" is exclusively a quality or property of the divine, then some conclude it is timeless, not to be found in the natural world, and hence, from the human perspective, utterly indefinable.[31]

Even conceding the difficulty in defining with any precision what constitutes something "good" or "goodness" itself, we might still salvage our acquaintance with it by reaffirming that its goal is the harnessing of individual self-interest to facilitate empathetic cooperation and collective harmony for the benefit of society at large. Human actions at every level may produce consequences for the actor, and the fear of such negative effects, whether in the form of the supernatural punishment envisioned by various religions or of karma as a function of the Universe in a nonreligious context, can cause actors to circumscribe their behavior or proceed to act only after cautious circumspection.[32] Fear has the power to suppress our selfishness, jostle us out of our laziness, and increase our desire for cooperation. Deep down, however, humans are innately selfish and do not help others without considerable prodding or encouragement. So, while religion exploits fear in order to manipulate its adherents into a faux-altruistic mindset, it thereby fails to make them truly moral in any real sense.

From another perspective, it may not be religion at all that unifies societies under common endeavors but rather the biology of evolution. Some scientists contend that what spurs humans into the complex interrelationships which are woven into the social fabric is the development of language.[33] In order for language to be effective as a means of communication, there must be a consensus on its vocabulary, grammatical rules, and usage. This prearranged consensus makes language the natural foundation for cooperation. Early tribes use language as a social tool to gain evolutionary advantage over less-organized rivals in the struggle for survival. The Golden Rule's intrinsic morality may thus have its basis in an evolutionary development.

Ironically, a cooperative effort could have as its aim a decidedly uncooperative effect. A torch-wielding, bloodthirsty mob ought not automatically to be deemed "moral" simply because its members are behaving cooperatively with one another. If the overall goal violates the Golden Rule's admonition to treat others with decency and respect, then the endeavor as a whole is immoral. This is where individual rights emerge as a limit on societal power; such rights serve, in essence, as a check, in order to save society from its own worst impulses. Thus, even in striving for a collective good, no society thereby becomes entitled to "roll over" individuals or trample on their rights; the social good being communally promoted must first find its representation in the goodness of the individual. Each person is nonetheless responsible for whatever part he or she contributes as a cog in the cooperative machinery. The individual, hence, is accountable in any corrupt system, but only to the extent the role is different from the one performed in a correspondingly non-corrupt system. For example, everyone pays taxes in every economy, and accordingly, doing so, even in support of a murderous government, as noted for individual contributions to depraved endeavors, would not in and of itself be participating in evil deeds; committing state-sanctioned murder or either allowing or facilitating it, however, would make the individual culpable in abetting the evil. Likewise, in a democracy, acting in antidemocratic ways amounts to evil, but only to the degree that it is underhanded by deceiving the people, using institutions against their original purpose, or sabotaging democratic processes. A further illustrative example of the moral encapsulation in the form of individual rights might be, say, capital punishment, which is typically accompanied by a popular clamor for death: Excising compassion, however, is not worthy of a beneficent society.

Another danger of society-based morality is the aggregation of power, even for a so-called noble purpose. While pursuing cooperative goals, a civilization can descend into totalitarianism, which is the second worst state of affairs, the worst being those conditions that make fascism or communism somehow appealing as a solution to social problems. Compassion has a far freer rein in a representative democracy than when the will of a single individual, no matter how magnanimous, acts as the dictator of a nation. The rudderless drive for power can provide evil with as fertile a ground as does the detached love of money. Only through the egalitarian inclusiveness of expanding the "us" to embrace the "them" can a society hope to evolve in a manner that aligns with the Golden Rule's moral precept of common purpose.

To those for whom defining "good" is too challenging, perhaps it will prove easier to define, or at least identify, "evil." Apart from the less-than-useful distinction between natural evil and moral evil, another concept can be applied to evil: the lack of justification. American philosopher William L. Rowe (1931–2015) explains the term "unjustified evil" as an evil that occurs in fact, which could have been "prevented without thereby losing some greater good or permitting some evil equally bad or worse."[34] Rowe deduces in his "evidential" argument from evil that no "omnipotent, omniscient, wholly good being" can exist, because such a being would have prevented the unjustified evil we observe actually occurring in our world.[35] The primary critique against Rowe's conclusion is in the form of a "skeptical theist" theodicy—that God works mysteriously and in ways no human could comprehend—which is a thinly veiled "god of the gaps" style argument from ignorance by denying that unjustified evil exists at all.[36]

Preventing evil is one thing, whereas doling out evil is quite another. Under the "natural evil" label, bad weather, for instance, may cause destruction and suffering but is rarely thought of as evil; though the results prove truly tragic, we tend to demand that evil be deliberate. In relation to unjustified evil, when the god of the Old Testament states an intention, later carried out, to "smite all the firstborn in the land of Egypt, both man and beast" (Exod. 12:12), it is immoral. What have innocent babies or the animals of the field done to deserve such divine wrath? Are they free agents? (Of course, the theistic notion of "free will" is a god who requires all to do as they are told or else suffer the punishment devised specifically for the disobedient: For anyone other than the god, hardly any aspect of such an arrangement could be described as "free.") While some will take umbrage at any person presuming to judge a deity as evil, it is rather those blindly ascribing monstrously evil deeds to God who are guilty of the greater offense.

Because any apparent disobedience to God—the animation of that furtive, defiant, rebellious spirit, which, at least metaphorically, represents the exercise of the free will He supposedly gave to humans—serves as the foundation of religious morality, any transgression or violation of God's purported laws is by extension a form of insubordination and, hence, a wrong. Note that the expression of God's prohibitions and laws in every religion are always indirect, written or voiced as hearsay by an intermediary, some of whom profess to speak not merely for but as God. The problem some religions have with basing their morality on the written word, however, centers around reaching the laity, given historical literacy issues and the difficulty through ministry in conveying the text in a way that is meaningful in everyday lives.

Accordingly, the concept of "sin" has been introduced as a residual, catch-all definition of wrongdoing that can function independently, albeit congruently, with holy books. The imagery used to visualize sin helps us to understand the concept concretely. White as the (unblemished) driven snow, "chaste as ice,"[37] a white cloth with a stain—all these descriptions highlight the notion of defilement, and thus, imperfection. Even those who dutifully keep the Commandments and practice all the solemn rituals are less than perfect; most adherents of a religion are not so observant, but even those who are, being imperfect, have supposedly sinned. By setting, or rather, imposing, such a default condition on humanity, a religion can wield control over everyone, not just those who disobey the rules established so far or rules not yet conceived. Furthermore, the punishment remains the same, since "the wages of sin is death" (Rom. 6:23), which suggests extermination and is oddly less cruel than the perpetual torment of hell that the Bible usually threatens to be the consequences of sin.

Sinning, according to this view, is not limited merely to action but encompasses any thought or emotion in which faith becomes less than preeminent in the mind of an individual.[38] The blanket definition is further expanded by declaring that "whatsoever is not of faith is sin" (Rom. 14:23). To the extent little or no overlap exists between faith and reason, one is left to conclude that all secular knowledge, all scientific insights, and all facts of reality must be sin. Such a pervasive outlook on humankind's flawed nature represents a departure from other biblical passages (e.g., Heb. 10:26), which would require deliberateness as a specific condition for being unworthy of salvation by stating that "if we sin wil[l]fully after ... we have received ... the truth, there remaineth no more sacrifice for sins."

The transition between defining evil as intentionally doing harm to declaring as wrong simply being imperfect must have been considered necessary, since deliberate evil might not really appear in the world. Either the good is demonstrably inferior to the bad, in which case those who aim purposively to bring about a result that others regard as evil are not truly wrong in doing so, or else those same actors made a grievous error in mistakenly choosing evil over good. They cannot then be branded as evil simply for having either made the better choice or errantly chosen the wrong one. The hereditary traits, moral environment, and other social factors that produce someone evil can no more be faulted than the root causes of, say, widespread obesity. The sadist actually jeopardizes his own survival because, in violating the Golden Rule against an individual, he erodes the functioning of a society that would otherwise protect him, all because he mistook or imagined deriving some benefit from having caused suffering in others.

In equating human imperfection with sin, however, religious advocates are invariably indicting the entirety of reality, because nothing, save God, is perfect. To look derisively down on everything is ultimately a self-defeating philosophy and one that makes true ethical judgment impossible. In contrast, acosmism celebrates imperfection as the only feasible object for divine contemplation: God, imagining what it would be like if He did not exist, inescapably conjures the idea of an imperfect, detailed, temporally bound world that deserves to be celebrated rather than condemned. Instead of the "obey or be damned" warning, the acosmic view relishes the chaos, the seeming unpredictability, and, yes, the messiness, of a less-than-divine form of reality.

The principle of sin and its connection to unavoidable imperfection also allows for no mediation, despite a number of counterexamples. For instance, lying is evil—"When a man lies, he murders some part of the world," astutely observes German theologian Paul Gerhardt (1607–76)—yet because a white lie may actually alleviate suffering, the Golden Rule would require that some balance be struck. Compulsion as against the virtue of freedom is evil, but exceptions for military or jury service are inarguably beneficial to society. Finally, there being no free will, no action whatever, much less only an evil one, could ever truly be deliberate.

Evil is not just the absence, or even opposite of, good; it requires that certain elements be present which involve a bad actor inserting himself into the causal chain that brings about an undesirable outcome. First, there must be at least one innocent victim who unwittingly steps into the path of malevolence. Second, the effect of an evil action must be one characterized by the conscious suffering, harm, loss, or nonconsensual subversion of the will of another. Third, the bad actor must insert himself into the circumstances through an affirmative act, a willful negligence, or the facilitation, support, or condoning[39] of the same. Fourth, the action must have a malevolent intent; even if a corrupted or mistaken belief is ultimately at fault, the intent to act, even when inchoate or not brought to fruition, cannot be excused or rationalized away. And finally, the bad actor must exhibit a callous indifference or remorseless lack of empathy in response to the proximate effect he produces or witnesses, whether or not it is the result he genuinely intended or wished to have occurred. When the action or its actual effect evokes an immediate and/ or sincere regret in the bad actor, however, it belies this last element. Furthermore, if, indeed, brain architecture fully explains any lack of empathy, then one ought to focus on the action rather than the actor, which is to say, since no action is freely selected, we should try to judge events rather than the actor who initiates them. Moreover, if sin is understood to be a deliberate evil that is proffered as somehow "better" than good, one can reasonably deny that it exists at all without also refuting the entire concept of evil.

Taken as a whole, these elements of evil restate more precisely the Golden Rule as a moral guide. Note how war, rarely glorified by those who directly participate in it, amounts to the worst kind of evil, as it entails an indifference to death and destruction on the grandest of scales. Every moral guide will tend to falter, though, when relied on to help choose or balance between the lesser of two evils, particularly when such a choice is unavoidable.

By definition, unfounded fear is irrational. While not necessarily contrary to fact, its connection to reality may be based on false information. Still, whether rooted in superstition or the anxiety of an unreasonable phobia, the feeling of dread underlying such a fear is all-too-real, despite the absence of any actual threat or danger. In the same way, the perceptual or mental experience of an event, especially one that engages the participant's consciousness, can be real, even when the event itself is only imagined or illusory. The apperception of the event and the emotion in the perceived that it evokes both stand, in a related way, independently of whether the event actually occurred. A distinction thus figures prominently in this context between an experienced reality and the actuality, or indeed, non-actuality, of the foundational event.

Even if all is illusion, the perceived experience of the illusion, as we have observed, is nonetheless real. Therefore, suffering is real. Thus, the Golden Rule applies morally to avoid causing suffering in others, even when the underlying mechanics itself is illusory. For example, waving a torch or brandishing a firearm near the face of another person may not represent actual endangerment, but the fear evoked in the mind of the terror-stricken victim is real and falls under the strictures of the Golden Rule. In a similar way, bending the illusion of the Universe to frighten or appear to harm a sentient being thereby produces a genuine experience of suffering that the Golden Rule admonishes us to preempt. Just because an experience is not actual in no way relieves us of accountability for the response our actions within the illusion may provoke.

One might observe that only someone with a depraved heart would willingly dream about torturing others, because strictly within the boundaries of the reverie, the suffering the dreamer conjures is real: The dreamer is more than a mere witness in that his consciousness ultimately provides the platform on which such quasi-real anguish appears to take place. In the acosmic view, God, in pondering what it would be like if He did not exist, does imagine a universe where suffering unavoidably occurs, but He is not like the torturing dreamer in two principal ways. First, what might be called the frame of mind suggests a fundamental difference. Imagining what torture might be like is not ethically equivalent to salaciously and/or deliberately fantasizing about it. Second, the dreamer is having a secondary, real-time experience of his own, perhaps even taking some sadistic enjoyment in the imagery of his visualization. Conversely, God metaphorically sits outside His imagined universe, both spatially and temporally, as those are features embedded in His own self-delusion. God does not participate, even as an active or contemporaneous witness, in the pondering that produces the Universe or in the experiences of those seemingly conscious beings who, in a contrived way, have come to occupy it.

The so-called "problem of evil" is a form of an atheological argument which juxtaposes an idealized view of divinity with the observed reality that evil has been ever-present in the world. Some philosophers use the inherent contradiction of the problem to rebut the claim that, under the circumstances, a benevolent god could even exist at all, while other, more theistic philosophers use it somewhat paradoxically to deny that what we call worldly evil may not truly be so.[40]

Whether assigned the role of creator and/or maintainer of the physical universe, a god is typically presumed to possess as qualities what is colloquially known as the "three omnis," and these would have bearing on his relationship with evil, whether occurring naturally or as a result of the conduct of potentially free agents He created. A god who is omnipotent, or all-powerful, for example, would have the ability to stop any evil or prevent it at the outset from occurring. A god who is omnibenevolent, or all-good, would want to wield his power over evil precisely in order to stop or prevent it. And a god who is omniscient, or all-knowing, would thus be aware, in great detail, and perhaps with full foreknowledge, of all the evil in the world, with no instance of it escaping the scope of his detection. The question the "problem of evil" then poses is: Why would such a god not have already stopped or prevented all the evils we observe occurring, or having historically occurred, in this world? A few philosophers think they have wrested an answer to this question by somehow explaining that all evil is an unavoidable byproduct of free will.[41] Clearly, though, if only the perpetrators of evil enjoy the latitude of action, while all of their victims remain decidedly less-than-free, then attributing evil strictly to some hypothesized autonomy is not sufficient to excuse the divine inaction that these philosophers view as somehow oddly premeditated.

The very notion of a "problem of evil" misunderstands the nature and purpose of this admittedly wicked world: According to the acosmic view, all is purely God's imagination. Thus, He wants to be unable, and conversely finds Himself unable to want, to stop any naturally occurring event, action, or deed; instead, what He really must desire is simply to see how it all works out. In wondering what it would be like if He did not exist, He considers, as a consequence, the emergence of life, the segregation of consciousness into identity, and the resulting aggressive competition for limited resources that epitomizes a finite universe. The evil we identify—what we seem to recognize in the eerie, focused, and shining glimmer of the predator's eyes—is something that is manifestly inherent in a world with few naturally occurring controls on either the selfishness or rank ambition for survival that would be exhibited by all living beings, at both the individual and collective levels. As He sits outside of His own imagination, the whole history of the Universe flashes across the lonely mind of God. It is like beholding a vast tapestry, all at once. We humans direct our attention to a small corner of the arras, where some moment of mortal agony is depicted, and we become obsessed with it; the fabric is stitched by the loom into its design, and the result and its quality are entirely independent of the weaver working the machinery. When the same entity is the designer, the weaver, the loom, the fabric, the tapestry, and the customer who ends up buying it, all rolled up into one, no discordance occurs. The "problem of evil" simply evaporates.

Adherents of religion are not made moral by its precepts or what it may call the laws of God, but likewise, secular laws do not generally have that effect, either. Among the many differences between these two systems is that, in recognizing the inherent dignity of the individual, the laws of society interpose themselves precisely where the infringement of individual rights is most likely to occur. Whereas religion invites persecution with the admonition to "not suffer a witch to live" (Exod. 22:18), a civil democracy, as in the Fifth Amendment of the U.S. Constitution, normally requires the due process of law before anyone can be deprived of life, liberty, or property. While both systems strive for conformity of behavior, only the secular system endeavors to regulate interactions among humans so as to avoid conflict.

The sentiment must have been expressed earlier by others, but a quote has been attributed in 1930 to an American cartoonist: "People are no damn[ed] good."[42] That very eloquently if bluntly characterizes the problem of evil as it relates to humans. Some may point out that this conclusion is not far from the "all have sinned" logic of religion, but the similarity ends when it comes to what to do about it. Religion demands obedience and surrender as conditions for not being punished on account of humanity's inherently selfish nature. The secular solution is quite different. It acknowledges that people would be egocentric savages were it not for the calming effect of cooperative civilization, which is why the individual must be taught, and presumably made to understand, those rules of society that foster compassion toward one's fellow humans.

Given that people are inherently bad, especially when primarily driven to act by selfishness or self-interest, morality thus consists purely of prohibitions or proscriptions on behavior that endanger self, others, or society at large. In this way, society collectively proscribes individual human behavior on behalf of, and to protect, all past or potential victims of the evil aims of those who place their own selfish interests above other humans or humanity itself.

One can imagine a setting, long before the founding of any civilization or city, when an apelike ancestor of humans, scouring a savannah or rushing through a jungle, mindlessly commits some tragic act of violence against a fellow creature of the troop or a rival group. Perhaps, using his opposable thumbs, a gift of evolution, he grabs a stone and smashes it against the skull of his adversary, killing him. Envision the rest of the troop witnessing the event, circling the scene, with the aggressor mutely holding the bloodied rock over a lifeless body. The instinct to fear, and thus despise, death is embedded in the psyche of all thinking animals. The eyes of the troop stare hauntingly at the aggressor, who quickly comes to realize he is responsible for the sense of doom that now hangs in the air over this protohuman society. He regrets what he has done, and the act represents the first step in society's censure of the type of individual behavior that threatens the group's cohesiveness and thus its ability to ensure the safety or survival of all its members.

(In analyzing the concept of "original sin," one must at the outset declare it to be a deceptively wrongheaded phrase. The way it improperly suggests that agents have total freedom of choice, that they have complete foreknowledge of the consequences of their actions, that something other than egocentrism is their primary animating motive, and that a single, historical event both defines and binds all human beings who have ever lived or ever will live, is self-contradictory. Nonetheless, one must adopt the ill-fitting phraseology, but solely in order to be able to reference it as a religious belief.)

In terms of the onset of conscience in humans, the original sin is thus one born more out of regret than defiance. The wrongness of the act is imputed retroactively, as though some divine law always existed that governs everyone's behavior and prescribes penalties for its abrogation. The creatures who populate the imagined acosmic landscape, though, must fend for themselves and learn from their mistakes so as to promote their own survival and that of their societies. In the Garden of Eden allegory, humankind is told in advance what action God has prohibited, and yet, without knowing right from wrong—the very cognizance that eating the fruit of the Tree of Knowledge of Good and Evil would, by definition, provide—Adam and Eve, in their ignorance, commit the unpardonable sin. Bear in mind that God is never depicted as actually forgiving this alleged sin, although the religion of Christianity is constructed around the notion that its effects could be, and as a result, were, in fact, expiated, albeit vicariously. The allegory does not jibe well with the likely experience of the apelike ancestor just described, being a far more probable explanation as to the origins of misconduct, social censure, and regret. Positing disobedience as humanity's first true blunder fails to inform us about the emergence of the individual's feelings of contrition and the emotional power of the ensuing guilt or shame that seem to contribute more to shaping our personalities than neglecting to observe the arbitrary demands of an unseen and ultimately pitiless deity.

The Bible, especially the New Testament, is full of wise sayings and profoundly sage advice. One cannot help but want to catalog these so that, seeing them in succession altogether, it becomes easy to see why the masses in the billions have been drawn to it and how it has affectionately endured through the centuries. If only its few nuggets of true wisdom were not attached to mountains of superstitious claptrap, it might merit its moniker of "The Good Book." We are exhorted to clothe ourselves with compassion, "kindness, humbleness of mind, meekness," and patience (Col. 3:12). Having identified that "the love of money is the root of all evil" (1 Tim. 6:10), Jesus reasons that, since "[n]o man can serve two masters[, we] cannot serve [both] God and mammon [i.e., money]" (Matt. 6:24). Earlier, Jesus insists that you "[l]ove your enemies, bless them that curse you, do good to them that hate you, and pray for them which despitefully use […] and persecute you" (Matt. 5:44), while later, "Jesus said unto him [i.e., the rich man], 'If thou wilt be perfect, go and sell that thou hast, and give to the poor[, for i]t is easier for a camel to go through the eye of a needle, than for a rich man to enter into the kingdom of God'" (Matt. 19:21–24). Jesus even says that we should "resist not evil[, …] but whosoever shall smite thee on thy right cheek, turn to him the other also" (Matt. 5:38), which is reinforced by the advice to "[s]ee that none render evil for evil unto any man; but ever follow that which is good, both among yourselves, and to all men" (1 Thess. 5:15). In declaring revenge to be unchristian, these passages offer hope that the cycle can be broken in which violence has no effect other than to beget more violence. Sadly, one all-too-rarely gets to see most of these adages actually put into practice by anyone, let alone by the mass of humanity who claim, apparently with some degree of hypocrisy, to hold fast to the tenets of a religion that otherwise promulgates such noble norms and standards.

Of course, no nation that adheres to these ideals as a basis for its foreign policy would ever survive in our dangerous world. In particular, a country that touts itself above all others as a "Christian nation" not only routinely fails to live up to these principles but seems often to go out of its way to do just the opposite: The relentless endemic racism, sexism, and xenophobia characterized in the national discourse hardly embody the compassion and tolerance for which these standards call; the economy that laudably places raw greed at its center is not one that functions in service of either the greater good or divine will; and the military of the only country to have actually used atomic weapons against civilians cannot be said to take attacks or threats of attack with the equanimity seemingly urged by the one they call their own messiah.

Nevertheless, the Bible's clear exhortation to us, "Be ye therefore perfect, even as your Father which is in heaven is perfect" (Matt. 5:48) is decidedly not a prescription for mere mortals. As already noted, people are no damned good, so any religion that rests its foundation on the perfectibility of humans instantly fails and may someday be doomed to obscurity. Churches, realizing this exhortation to be wholly impractical and wishing to stave off the despondence of flawed humans feeling unable to live up to their savior's ideal, introduce the concept of grace, whereby a spiritual power, as a divine gift of love and mercy, supposedly operates through faithful humans so they can achieve a semblance of perfection acceptable to the god who originally creates them with the unacceptable flaws in the first place. This represents yet another example of where religion "sells" you the cure for a disease you never knew you had or ever could have.

In the *Timaeus* dialogue, Plato theorizes that the sensible world in which we live is derived from an eternal, unchanging model of reason and that a demiurge, or divine artisan, corralled the initial chaos of the cosmos into an intelligent order, saying, "[T]he creator [who] made this world [...] was good, and [...thus] desired that all things should be as like himself as they could be[, ... for] God desired that all things should be good and nothing bad, so far as this was attainable."[43] Goodness, however, is not, as some Platonists assert, a "creative force,"[44] because worlds evolve out of ignorance. A newly created world can never be automatically good but is only potentially so. Misuse is not a reflection on the maker, who may lovingly craft a tool that is then abused when in the wrong hands. Untrammeled selfishness, evolution's driving force for survival, nearly guarantees such misuse of the world and its resources; in the acosmic sense, however, God could hardly have imagined it otherwise.

Kant's Categorical Imperative admonishes us to "[a]ct only according to that maxim whereby you can, at the same time, will that it should become a universal law[, and …] in such a way that you treat humanity, whether in your own person or in the person of any other, never merely as a means to an end, but always at the same time as an end."[45] This effectively creates an ever-present moral duty whose observance yields consistently admirable results, such as always telling the truth, cultivating compassion toward others, including animals, and establishing a connectedness so that individuals behave harmoniously with their environment.

In contrast to the subjectiveness of outcome-oriented utilitarianism,[46] the Categorical Imperative objectively would seek to impose an absolute duty on the individual to act as though under a universal law, or specifically, to never act in a way which, if everyone did it, would be deleterious to the community. Unfortunately, this view commits the logical fallacy of part-to-whole, as illustrated earlier with the example of a table being composed collectively of atoms, individually invisible to the naked eye, leading to the fallacious conclusion that the table must then be invisible. As a further example, while social disaster would ensue were everyone suddenly to quit their jobs all at once, surely that cannot make it wrong for some appropriately to do so at any given time. There cannot be a universal law rooted in what "everyone" does or does not do; laws are tailored to criminalize specific actions that all of society might rightly condemn.

We tend to act based on entirely who we are, not what we happen to think or even claim to know may be right. Our personalities have already absorbed the moral teachings to which we have been exposed, so relying on an innate sense of obligation as an ethical gauge is too egalitarian to be workable. A morality founded on reason over passion not only falls short of resolving the common head-versus-heart dilemma, but it dismissively fails to acknowledge this struggle or why it matters. Under Kantian morality, the failure to repay a loan, for example, would be considered wrong, not out of any feelings of empathy for the lender but rationally with the aim to preserve the financial market for borrowing. Decisions about right and wrong should be derived from reason, as Kant insists, yet in the wide expanse of human affairs, that reasoning cannot be as fully disassociated from the emotional makeup of the individual as he might hope.

Furthermore, by envisioning morality as a metaphysical principle, Kant has little choice but to portray the Categorical Imperative as an *a priori* truth. This severs moral law from empirical experience and forces his ethical judgment to focus on an actor's intent rather than on the action's outcome. That this view is a mistake is clear from the (admittedly empirical) observation that truly evil acts can be the result of something other than a wicked or corrupt intent, such as the result of neglect or ignorance.

The admonition to treat others as ends rather than means can have a positive effect by putting us in the proper mindset to do what is good or right, but it can also misdirect us improperly to reject noble deeds. What an arresting power of dissuasion the Categorical Imperative would have on, say, a murderer, who, before actually killing, urges himself to pretend that his intended victim is the last, only, or most important person on Earth. Of course, the problem in other circumstances is when, for instance, a charitable act is forsaken under the Categorical Imperative simply, and for no other reason, than that it brings joy to the giver. This is more than merely a utilitarian outlook: it may be an unnecessary loss to the community.

In transitioning between his *Critiques*, Kant makes a disingenuous and self-contradicting attempt to salvage the relationship between morality and fulfillment. The issue arises because Kant appears to have put at odds what he regards as morally well-intentioned action and what personally motivates humans to act at all. In his earlier work, Kant places the notions of God, the "soul," and immortality into the realm beyond human experience and hence unknowable to us.[47] In his later work, he seems to recognize, almost as an afterthought, that at least belief in these unknowable things becomes justifiable as necessary in order to motivate us to act morally.

Kant appears to be saying that, since one cannot disprove the existence of a punishing god or an afterlife, it would nonetheless behoove one, even errantly, to believe in them. Making faith essential for morality once again revives Pascal's wager in that both beg the question: By presuming a supposed benefit for belief, it concludes that even a misapplied belief is somehow more beneficial to the individual than intellectual honesty. When Kant contends, based on practical reason, that the highest good (or, in Latin, *summum bonum*) requires a so-called world-to-come, and thus the existence of both immortal "souls" and a god to administer them, he reveals his staid Lutheran upbringing, which he had already seemingly shelved as unknowable, according to pure reason.[48]

The Golden Rule makes all of Kant's speculations moot, however, because immediate survival will always be a stronger motivator than any other aim, such as hedonism, a vague sense of duty, or even interpersonal attachments. The instinct to live is a unifying principle in which the individual indirectly survives by not obstructing the hardy endurance of the tribe. Not even Kant can overcome this fact, as he unsuccessfully tries to bootstrap a misguided desire for immortality into a moral prerequisite.

Saying "the devil is in the details" is often an acknowledgement of the natural human tendency to look for exceptions or loopholes in any constraint placed on behavior. When the "thou shalt not kill" mandate is handed down, people scurry to declare exemptions such as "except for self-defense," or "except for the death penalty," or "except in times of war." The recognized exceptions eventually swallow the rule, as little remains of what inspired it in the first place.

Similarly, when it comes generally to ascertaining any limits that may exist on morality, a storied history unfolds of how boundaries have been drawn along the lines of gender, race, and species. On its face, slavery is patently wrong, unless, as some have said, it is a conquered people or captured enemy of war, or unless, as others have said, it is to work off financial debts, or unless, as yet other reprobates have said, it is members of an "inferior" race. Representational democracy is based on the social participation of voting by everyone, except, some miscreants have said, nonwhite citizens, or except, as others have said, women, or except, as still others have said, those without property interests in the jurisdiction. The Thirteenth Amendment ends slavery in the United States in 1865, seventy-seven years after the adopted ratification of the U.S. Constitution, while the passage of the Nineteenth Amendment in 1919 finally grants suffrage to women, nearly 131 years after adoption, although other forms of voter suppression persist.[49]

If a boundary must be drawn to circumscribe morality, where is the true ethical line? For the Golden Rule to prevail, it must have the widest berth, which suggests the line is at sentience. Using this standard highlights precisely what makes the Rule golden: empathy. A being who is sentient, as the word's Latin root (*sentient*, "feeling") suggests, is one that feels or perceives.[50] Sentience is closely associated with self-awareness or consciousness, which has essentially the same general biochemical requirements, including the presence of vertebrae and a centralized nervous system.[51] An urban definition for sentience consists of any living thing that has a face, knows its parents, or enjoys reproducing.[52] Sentience is hence a very bright line and covers virtually all species on earth with even the most limited cognitive abilities. Whether the line needs to be extended further to other living things may be debatable, but there can be no reasonable objection to setting it at sentience.

Although the Golden Rule thus applies to all sentience, it might prove helpful to rephrase it so as to make it even easier to apply. Do not do to an animal or any other sentient being what you would not do to a human infant. The Bible quite obviously gets this wrong when it implies that nonhuman animals are less than, or not as worthy of protection as, humans; the examples of cruelty, often involving needless sacrifice, are too numerous to catalog here,[53] but rereading the so-called "Good Book" with a newfound respect for sentience firmly in mind will prove just how truly immoral ritualized religions seen in this light can be. Moreover, when consciousness is viewed as a way in which the Universe transfixes its own gaze on itself, killing any sentient being becomes immoral in that it permanently shuts one (or a pair) of those eyes; an unnecessary death is truly a loss for all of us. In terms of priorities, fully 70 percent of the world's fresh surface water is used for farming, mostly for livestock and to irrigate arable feed crops.[54] If everyone adopted a vegan or plant-based diet, it would not only greatly reduce the suffering of our fellow sentient creatures at the slaughterhouse, but it would environmentally and financially benefit all members of society, especially when it comes to deforestation issues and the conservation of limited natural resources.[55]

A powerful example of a sentience-based application of the Golden Rule concerns the controversial topic of capital punishment. The death penalty typically comes into play when an offender, often a murderer, demonstrates that he or she cannot be trusted to abide by society's laws or its normative values. The natural response would be to exclude the offender altogether from society, and in fact, a number of ancient civilizations routinely utilizes the punishment of exile or banishment, but given the state of transportation and communication across the globe today, such a nation-specific, exclusionary practice is no longer feasible. Incarceration emerges as another mechanism for excluding offenders, often in the form of a lifetime prison sentence. The moral implications come into play, however, when the government ventures inside the cell in order to kill the inmate—i.e., to carry out the death penalty. In this instance, the state has gone too far, because it denies to the offender, not what it gave, which is citizenship and the right to participate in society, things it can therefore rightly revoke, but rather it denies life, which it did not grant.

What death penalty advocates must realize is that the issue is not really about the person being executed: It concerns the unfeeling, cold-hearted monsters we the public must become in order to carry out the execution. In the same way that teaching people not to kill by killing them is incongruous, the mentality it takes to shut off all empathy to execute someone is ironically the identical mentality the offender must have had when originally killing his victim(s). The Golden Rule can help to soothe our fiery passion for revenge and can serve to remind us that compassion ultimately ensures our collective survival and truly makes us better as human beings.

Chapter 14:

The Purpose of Life

Twenty years from now you will be more disappointed by the things you didn't do than by the ones you did do. So throw off the bowlines. Sail away from the safe harbor. Catch the trade winds in your sails. Explore. Dream. Discover. —Sarah Frances Brown[1]

The vast, physical universe, wrapped in an illusory spatio-temporal framework and illuminated with the fabricated light of thought, is merely an ephemeral idea in which God, as the only entity whose existence is assured, imagines what it would be like if He did not exist. Those who inhabit the idea, in the sense that they have predetermined parts to play, may well ask, "What is my purpose here?" What, indeed, is the purpose of life in a purely imagined universe?

The purpose of life is, quite simply, to live. For, in playing our assigned parts, we reify the idea and manifest its implications; in short, we vivify God's fleeting thought and, as a result, we become His idea. By living, experiencing, perceiving, feeling, and thinking—or at least, seemingly, within the context of the delusion, to do so—we flesh out the notion, not dissimilarly from actors who stage a written play: The words become more real when spoken. In this manner, we fashion a reality with our participation, even though we are but figments.

The sentiment may never find a more beautiful or concise expression as when former First Lady of the United States Eleanor Roosevelt (1884–1962) writes that "[t]he purpose of life, after all, is to live it, to taste experience to the utmost, to reach out eagerly and without fear for newer and richer experience."[2] All experiences, in the splendor of their kaleidoscopic diversity and uniqueness, collectively represent what life can be, and therefore, as they are lived, what life is. To live a life of adventure is life; to not live such a life, such as a reticent or fearful life, well, that too is life. To die in old age, or to do so courageously in youth, is all the same: It is life.

The same sentiment appears, when, in a Russian novel, a character starkly declares, "The purpose [of life] is to live."[3] In an even starker yet contrasting way, existentialists seem to take a perverse pleasure in trying to convince others that life is utterly meaningless and that any search for meaning is doomed to end in disappointing frustration.[4] While existentialism's absurdist offshoot advises us to embrace the absurdities of life,[5] acosmism allows us to do precisely that because such a knowingly deliberate resignation is a unique perspective that only a non-deity could ever possibly experience. What is more, the view that life has a purpose and it is to live actually frees the theist and the atheist alike, the former from rigid dogma and the latter from true meaninglessness. Perhaps humanity ought someday to learn just enough of life's purpose to begin treating our fellow sentient beings with respect, dignity, love, and compassion.

Religions tend to mislead adherents by suggesting that purpose is found when they follow "God's will," which would be opaquely inscrutable under the best of circumstances; from the acosmic standpoint, the notion of a divine will is nonsensical.

By substituting its history, rituals, and dogma as representative of His will, whatever that might mean, a church leads adherents astray and interferes with the lives they might have led had they not been saddled with misinformation. If individuals are brainwashed into believing whom they can love or whom they should hate, which is the kind of restrictive intolerance that a religion is apt to advocate, they may not be living life fully. So, while the purpose of life is to live, living free of negative influences may be important as well.

Happiness or contentment, as perhaps life's aim, is often proposed to be the purpose of life,[6] while helping others or living a life of sacrifice is also frequently suggested for what gives human life its true meaning. These noble aspirations might develop into useful guides for the journey, but both tend to support narrower goals than would qualify themselves alone as a true purpose. The pursuit of happiness, elusive because it seems always to retreat the more one strives to attain it, may well produce an egocentric mindset that is hardly conducive to communal interests, and, unless part of a multiplier effect, needless self-sacrifice may end up merely substituting one life for another. Seeking to leave a legacy is likewise futile, as all but a hermit will influence others in small ways and thus change the world through the inevitable connections established throughout even a short life. What resonates is an experience, granted a uniqueness by virtue of perspective, and the purpose fulfilled by having lived life.

Like other healthful and life-promoting things, however, happiness is inherently good to the extent that it proves conducive, in an assistive way, to fulfilling life's purpose; it often does so by freeing us from the negative influences that obstruct us from living life to the fullest. Furthermore, if life can be thought of as a journey, we ought then to be more focused on the "sightseeing" aspect than on the "vehicle" that happens to be transporting us, provided it is at least serviceable to our needs. Self is an illusion;

more than that, it is an illusion within an illusion. A prescription for happiness must include the observation that we should think less about ourselves than about the life experiences we are having from moment to moment. The purpose of life is indeed to live.

Terrestrial life first appears 3.5 billion years ago, well over a billion years after Earth initially formed.[7] Those first billion desolate years, without so much as a single microbe across the vast, barren desert of our rocky planet, cannot be said to have been wasted in that the specific conditions help to create the environment in which life can initially emerge and later thrive. Consciousness is rooted in a temporally based construct, founded on the inexorable biochemistry of life and the ever-advancing momentum of evolution. In an imagined universe, the virtual passage of time is less important than the coherent ordering of events; dependent prerequisites can be imputed without having had to occur in reality. The conscious mind imagines the past it requires, much as God imagines the conscious mind or the universe in which it seems to reside.

Life and consciousness are necessary to God's contemplation only to the extent to which their emergence proves to be inevitable. Experiments confirm that abiogenesis can and will occur with "an adaptive resonance" in the midst of a system with increasing entropy.[8] In fact, "atoms naturally rearrange themselves into architectures that can survive the chaos [and ...] ultimately develop the heat-exchanging characteristics of living matter."[9] The laws of thermodynamics thus seem as a matter of course to marshal inorganic atoms into processing via absorption and dissipation an external energy (and heat) source like our sun, exactly the way organic biological life forms do; the evolution of the one to the other under these conditions is thus bound to happen. It is as though God cannot imagine a world, governed by the known physical laws, which will fail to produce as a natural consequence the basis for life and eventually consciousness.

Having established that life, or at least the thought of life, cannot be said to have occurred by chance but instead appears to be the inevitable result of physical laws, it does not necessarily follow that it serves in any essential way a role in God's acosmic contemplation. Earth's "scheduled" demise several billion years hence will occur either when the Milky Way and Andromeda galaxies collide or when our sun, Sol, distends as a red giant star, expanding to the orbit of Mars and swallowing our globe in the process.[10] Yet, the earth could be destroyed at any time by some unpredictable astronomical event like a nearby supernova,[11] which supports the alternative view in which life, especially human life, is dispensable and indeed something of an accident. It may, however, be precisely that the idea of a universe being recklessly unguided which gives it its purpose, as the cycle of life and death plays out on the grandest of scales.

Depending on one's perspective, there would either be no purpose or else a heightened purpose to life if, indeed, the theists were correct in their estimate that over 80 percent of the more than one-hundred billion humans who ever lived, and two-thirds of the eight plus billion now alive, are or will be suffering everlasting torment in hell for not following a particular faith. What a waste, were this the case, just in order to reach the select few, whom their respective gods supposedly already know in advance! Profligacy is not unknown in nature, whether in the evolutionary process or the vastness of the Universe as a whole, but not when the outcome is known with such certainty.

Still, it would be an appreciably greater squandering from a teleological standpoint if the more than 10,000 generations of humans struggling to survive fail to fulfill their lives' purpose simply by not grasping quite what it might be. This is where acosmism rescues each life from the pointless oblivion of a wasted existence, because it makes altogether unnecessary the need to know life's purpose, or in the larger sense, the aim of any alleged existence, in order to fulfill it. Since God is imagining the world as existing so as to contemplate what it would be like if He did not exist, any specific manifestation of an object of thought within that idea serves a purpose. The interconnectedness of all things, the relentless march of evolution, and the clockwork coordination of chaotic events throughout the Universe all work together to render everything indispensable in the context of the larger idea. The very mental appearance of something flashing across the mind of God speaks for its essential role in His contemplation; fulfillment of the objective is thus unavoidable when the purpose of life is simply to live through and experience God's unfolding idea.

Life often appears to be intolerably cruel, but this point of view ignores that life's immediate goal, namely, survival, requires and is entirely based on the principle of endurance. We must never forget that we humans are merely organisms, clinging to a rock. The earth is regarded as habitable because it is the only planet currently known in the Universe to host life, yet, due entirely to life's adaptability, some form of life will seemingly always be present wherever it is at all possible for it to appear.[12] The triumph of life is survival through the adversity of endurance.

Urging one to live life to its fullest does not come without a few caveats, however. One must be cautious to avoid death and/or suffering, both for oneself and for others. Jumping unaided out of the window of a tall building would obviously be a vivid albeit terrifying experience, and for the unfortunate individuals who underwent such an occurrence, it must surely have provided a riveting insight into their mortality and truly clarified their non-divinity.

These types of encounters lead, however, to several problems. Once is enough; there is no particular need to repeat any devastating, fatal event. Expanding on the accomplishments and lives of others may be the only way for humanity to avoid continually making the same mistakes that bedevil humankind. Secondly, risky behavior jeopardizes the opportunity for that individual to have further experiences. A person should not be identified by a single happening but by the blossoming of many experiences, so an action that limits some or all future participation in life, including suicide, is not optimal for maximizing life-confronting or life-embracing episodes. While every potential undertaking always involves some risk, a prudent approach would be for the actor to perform some kind of cost-benefit analysis, weigh priorities, and assess a course of action against the backdrop of all future experiences that might be forgone. Third, actions should not unduly infringe on the rights of others to have their own experiences. Aside from implicating the Golden Rule, taking into consideration others' experiences when planning one's own is a sign of respect for the overall goal of the Universe: to serve as a platform on which to parade all manner of imagined characters or things and to allow for as many experiences from as many perspectives as possible.

To be sure, attempting to advocate a course of action to an agent who lacks the ability to act freely is as futile as speaking to a brick wall. If people behave in complete accordance with who they are as individuals, based on the totality of their genetic predispositions, upbringing, and experiences, then their actions are ultimately predictable, even if others are unable to recognize or process all these factors, making the behavior seem erratic or impulsive.

In the absence of free will, stating a purpose for life becomes merely a description of the "proper" mindset rather than the prescription or call to action it would represent to free agents. The saving grace is that, as noted, one need not know life's purpose in order to fulfill it. Nonetheless, exposure to the idea that the purpose of life is to live might grow to be prescriptive by embedding itself as an influence in how someone who had heard it reacts to uncommon-yet-expected events. Whether it be pursuing job or career aspirations, confronting relationship challenges, raising children, dealing with health issues, or grieving the loss of a loved one, once the shuddering acosmic awareness of their purpose dawns on us, the search for meaning becomes moot. Akin to the march of the celestial sphere across the sky due to the earth's rotation, the cycle of life serves to pave the road of humanity with individual lives, all of whom live so as to experience what existence would be like if the one thing that truly exists happened not to exist.

In this manner, all experiences are reflected in the mind of God. Since God exists atemporally, however, He neither participates in nor occasions these underlying experiences but rather He simply receives and incorporates them into His conception. What He conceives does not independently exist, so in that sense, He is alone; the reality in which we appear is thus not objective, but it is coherent, as the product of a single imagination: the lonely mind of God.

Other philosophical systems that have found a role for the mind of God seem not to build on it foundationally but instead use it to fill in a metaphysical gap. For instance, Irish empirical idealist (Bishop) George Berkeley (1685–1753), in order to guarantee that objects persist as they fall from our perception, feels that he must resort to God's omnipresent surveillance, both to fulfill the guarantee and to provide an ultimate source for our own ideas.[13] This invocation of the mind of God allows Bishop Berkeley, seemingly like an idealist, to deny the existence of mind-independent matter—*esse est percipi aut percipere*[14] (Latin for "to be is to be perceived or to perceive")—while at the same time advocating for the empirical existence of physical objects as divine-based collections of ideas. Kant's transcendental idealism purports to rescue the existence of a mind-independent world by placing it beyond human reckoning. Neither of these forms of idealism go far enough in recognizing that the lonely mind of God is all there is or need be as an explanation of the physical universe in which we find ourselves.

Conclusion

Summary

To recap the acosmist's answer to the "Primordial Existential Question," one must identify the who, how, why, and what. The "who" concerns the single, infinite, indivisible substance, which is all that exists; purely for reference purposes, the label "God" is attached. As for the "how," an important distinction must be made between the actuality of existence and the reality of experience. To reach the "why," we must solve the Omniscience Riddle: What is the one thing, by definition, you would not know if you knew everything: It is the awareness of ignorance, experiencing what it is like not to know, or divinely, what it is like not to be God. And finally, the "what," which is the illusion or delusion of the physical universe, something we all agree appears to exist; it serves as the virtual platform on which God projects the idea of a godless existence.

(1) Something exists.

As a first principle, something exists—call it "God"—which we know both *a priori* as aseity and empirically as a brute fact; Descartes' *Cogito* is misdirected, since what we know beyond all doubt is that, in doubting, a thought has occurred, not necessarily ours, and that therefore, something capable of thought, not necessarily us, exists.

(2) What exists is a single, homogenous, infinite, indivisible entity.

The second principle asserts that what exists (i.e., God) must be a single, homogenous, infinite, indivisible entity; in the thirteenth proposition of his *Ethics*, Spinoza proves this *a priori* to be the case, although some may dispute this assertion as controversial.

(3) What appears to exist is a diverse, heterogeneous, finite, and divisible world.

The third principle, which we know empirically and as a scientific fact, affirms that what appears to exist as the physical universe can be characterized as diverse, heterogeneous, finite, and divisible.

(4) Illusion (definition): something that is not as it appears.

The fourth principle is a definition that something which is not as it appears is an illusion; Kant would likely instead call this, in contrast to a noumenal actuality, a world of "phenomena," where things sensible are known to us by perception.

(5) A world that merely appears to exist must be an illusion. [from (1) through (4)]

The fifth principle is a conclusion, based on the foregoing four principles, that, therefore, what merely appears to exist must perforce be an illusion.

(6) Illusion resides in the mind.

The sixth principle declares that an illusion resides in the mind of an entity, which we know *a priori* as the self-evident "a thinker thinks," as well as empirically from our own experience with the thinking process.

(7) The illusion of the apparent world resides in the mind of God. [from (5) and (6)]

The seventh principle states as a conclusion, based on the foregoing two principles, that, therefore, the illusion of the apparent world resides in the mind of God, which is all that exists.

(8) The mind of God knows Itself. [from (6) and (7)]

(8a) God is omniscient.

The eighth principle avers, as required by the foregoing two principles, that the mind of God (a "thinker who thinks") must know Itself, since It is all that exists; to the extent that there is nothing else to know, axiomatically, God must therefore be omniscient.

(9) The Omniscience Riddle solution: The one thing an omniscient entity does not know is what it is like not to be omniscient.

The ninth principle is the Omniscience Riddle, the general solution to which professes that the one thing an omniscient entity does not know is what it is like not to be omniscient; we acknowledge this solution to be true, both analytically *a priori* by definition and empirically from the nature of knowledge.

*(10) The omniscient God does not
know what it is like not to be God.
[from (8), (8a), and (9)]*

The tenth principle is a conclusory restatement, based on the foregoing two principles, that, therefore, the omniscient God does not know what it is like not to be God.

(11) One ponders what one does not know.

The eleventh principle contends that one ponders what one does not know; this is known to be true *a priori* from the nature of thought and/or empirically as ones who are able to, and do, ponder.

*(12) God is pondering what it is like not
to be God. [from (10) and (11)]*

The twelfth principle is a conclusion, based on the foregoing two principles, that, therefore, God is pondering what it is like not to be God.

*(13) Conclusion: The apparent world is
an illusion in the lonely mind of God in
which He is pondering what it would be
like not to be God. [from (7) and (12),
where (3)'s world = (5)'s world]*

The thirteenth and final principle is the ultimate conclusion, based on the foregoing principle and the seventh principle, and by equating the third principle's apparent world or the fifth principle's illusory world with the foregoing principle's object of what God is pondering, that the apparent world is an illusion in the lonely mind of God in which He is pondering what it would be like not to be God. *QED*

In imagining what it would be like if He did not exist, God envisions a physical universe, or perhaps a finite set of possible universes, which conforms to the laws of physics that would allow it to exist. He envisions a quantum vacuum, whose fluctuations produce a singularity of matter that, through the inflation of space, suddenly manifests itself in a Big Bang. After a period of cooling, the spark of nuclear fusion begins to ignite the swirling pools of hydrogen gas, setting trillions of stars on fire. The accretions of material from mature stars are pictured caught by the gravity of another star, allowing the formation of planets into solar systems. The ice from comets may come to be trapped in a planet's gravitation, becoming oceans of water after crashing to the molten surface. Life is thought to emerge from the primordial soup, and the evolutionary process takes hold. New creatures appear amidst the struggle for survival and eventually evolve into higher forms until various species, one in particular, develop consciousness and intelligence. As entropy pervades, all activity winds down; after the heat death of the Universe, objects float silently in the darkened void so that, as the proton half-life inevitably erodes every instance of matter, the entirety of the imagined existence returns to the nothingness out of which it is conceived. Thus, God's vision maps the Universe, as though it were sketched from a template through tracing paper. The entirety of the occurrence is over as soon as it has begun, since the illusion of time is merely one of its internal features. The conception of the physical universe in this manner fulfills God's pondering and therein lies the answer to the Primordial

Existential Question: God is utterly alone, but out of His lonely mind briefly springs the visage of humanity and its civilization's ever-shifting foothold of a presence in a physical universe.

Deluding oneself into feeling better about no longer living and thus hoping that human life extends beyond its natural limits serves no legitimate purpose, nor does a logistical mechanism exist whereby it can or should be so extended. We are not immortal. There is no afterlife, because if there were, it would render the one life we know utterly meaningless. The struggle to survive in which billions perish is all the hell we need, and heaven is the contentment to which we aspire in trying to live a fulfilling life of purpose, with love, forgiveness, and compassion.

An atemporal pondering cannot produce any form of willfulness, although the belief in free will does create a mindset where a participant might feel less buoyed by the vagaries of fate. Even a preordained universe could be peppered with randomness, as is often observed at the quantum level, representing what some might consider the true tier at which reality operates. Even then, while the arbitrariness of chance may make human behavior and other events seem unpredictable, these phenomena are no more the result of "free" choice than if they were completely predestined. Free will is thus an illusion; we choose based entirely on who we are.

Morality cannot be borrowed or handed down from on high. Our need to perpetuate our species, tribes, social orders, and values compels us to behave cooperatively. Mutual survival requires empathy, so moral decisions naturally fall under the auspices of the Golden Rule.

The purpose of life, then, is to live. We may only appear to exist, but by living through our experiences, we make real the physical universe God has imagined as His own alternative. It has become incumbent on those of us, ensnared in the threads of His thought, to fulfill it by participating fully in the life we seem to have been granted. We have no choice, yet the proper mindset, whether or not we are cognizant of our purpose, will serve us in our struggle to endure.

Acosmism is not the logic of the insane; it is reasoned from incontrovertible truths and rejects the absurdities of contradiction while asserting the value of every speck that appears to have manifested in the Universe. Even if all eventually crumbles into a mirage as the pondering in the mind of God, a coherent, undeniable reality to our experiences persists. Still, as the specter of victims seem to haunt us, both throughout history and for our foreseeable future, we do evolve: The hope that empathy and compassion will someday take hold allows us to focus on nobler aspirations rather than the aggregation of wealth and power, the vengeance of hatred, or the struggle to survive. The acosmist does not contend that, because we are God's idea, somehow we are Him. We are the projection of His thought and remain confined within the bounds of our reality by the special role in which He has envisioned us to exist.

Though Earth will still be consumed by the expanding red-giant sun named Sol in some five billion years, the intervening collision between the Milky Way and Andromeda galaxies a billion years before that provides further assurance of the eventual demise of humanity, notwithstanding whether our technology might ever allow us to travel among the stars or colonize far-flung exoplanets in our own galaxy. The promethean spark of understanding granted to humans elevates us above the beasts of the field, only to help us realize that we and all terrestrial life are ultimately doomed to a fiery fate. Alas, there will be no stable place for intragalactic travelers to alit. Amidst humanity's transience, we can draw solace from life's adaptability, whose appearance in habitable spots across the Universe is rare but presumably regular and routine. Individuals know that they will expire after a lifetime, which oddly gives meaning to our temporary appearance, helping us to prioritize our experiences and the ostensible choices we believe we have. Likewise, the foreordained annihilation of humanity arrests us to fulfill our purpose: to live and to experience the unfolding of the boundless imagination of "that which exists," with the unblinking eye of God witnessing it all.

Nothing but God truly exists. In God's lonely mind, He has conjured this grand thought experiment in which we find ourselves as characters. We are not the manifestation of being but merely its effect, something of an afterthought. We are like watery ripples emanating outward when a pebble is cast into a pond; we are neither the pebble itself nor the pond. We are but the brief clap of thunder, reverberating a sound whose origin is beyond both our reach and our ken, which will, in the end, echo with a tinny ring in the empty halls of an imagined eternity.

THE END

Notes

Introduction

1. Parmenides, *Parmenides and the Way of Truth*, trans. Richard G. Geldard (Rhinebeck, New York: Monkfish Book Publishing Co., 2007), 25; *On Nature*, B 8.18–22. Or, per another translation, "how could what-is be in the future: and how could [it] come-to-be? For if [it] came-to-be, [it] is not, nor [is it] if at some time [it] is going to be." Parmenides, *Parmenides of Elea: Fragments*, trans. David Gallop (Toronto: University of Toronto Press, 1991), 67; fragment 8.19–20.

2. Lucretius, *De Rerum Natura*, trans. Rolfe Humphries with B. Feldman (Bloomington, Indiana: Indiana University Press, 1968), 35; Book 1, Line 543. See also a quote by Roman poet and satirist Aulus Persius Flaccus (34–62), "*Gigni de nihilo nihil, in nihilum nil posse reverti*" (Latin for "From nothing, nothing comes; to nothing, nothing returns"), from *The Satires*, trans. John Conington (Oxford: Clarendon Press [Oxford University Press], 1893), 66; Book 1, Satire 3, Line 83.

3. The phrase *Ex nihilo nihil fit* supposedly "derives from Parmenides," although it is called "a physical theory and hardly qualifies as a truth of logic." Kenneth Seeskin, *Maimonides on the Origin of the World* (New York: Cambridge University Press, 2006), 74. Furthermore, no specific record shows when the fragment of Parmenides's poem in Greek might have been later translated into Latin, although Lucretius similarly declares in *De Rerum Natura* that "*nullam rem e nihilo gigni divinitus umquam*" (Latin: "Nothing from nothing ever yet was born"). Lucretius (Titus Lucretius Carus), *On the Nature of Things (De Rerum Natura)*, trans. William Ellery Leonard (Mineola, New York: Dover Publications, 2004), 5; Book 1, Line 150.

4. Gottfried Leibniz, "The Principles of Nature and of Grace[, Founded in Reason]," in *Philosophical Works of Leibnitz* [sic], 2nd Edition, trans. George

Martin Duncan (New Haven, Connecticut: Tuttle, Morehouse and Taylor, 1908 [1714]), 303; original in French: *Pourquoi quelque chose plutot que rien?*

5. Implied from "For 'nothing' is simpler and easier than 'something.'" Leibniz, "The Principles of Nature and of Grace," (1714), 303; original in French: *Parce que rien n'est plus simple et facile que quelque chose.*

6. Adolf Grünbaum, "The Poverty of Theistic Cosmology," *The British Journal for the Philosophy of Science*, Volume 55, No. 4 (Oxford: Oxford University Press, December 2004), 562; doi:10.1093/bjps/55.4.561.

7. "[I]f […] Leibniz's PEQ is ill founded or demonstrably false, then PEQ is aborted as a non-starter, because in that case, it is posing an ill-conceived question." Ibid., 561.

8. *The Merriam-Webster.com Dictionary*, s.v. "acosmism (*noun*)" (Springfield, Massachusetts: Encyclopædia Britannica, Inc., ca. 3 June 2012) at **https://www. merriam-webster.com/dictionary/acosmism**, accessed November 10, 2017.

9. Baruch de Spinoza, *The Cambridge Companion to Spinoza*, ed. Don Garrett (New York: Cambridge University Press, 1996), 53.

10. Ernst Platner, *Philosophische Aphorismen nebst einigen Anleitungen zur philosophischen Geschichte*, Volume 1 (Leipzig: Schwickert, 1776), 353.

11. Solomon Maimon, *An Autobiography*, trans. J. Clark Murray (Boston: Cupples and Hurd, 1888), 114; emphasis in the original.

12. And, as Hegel declares, "Spinozism might really just as well or even better have been termed Acosmism." Georg Wilhelm Friedrich Hegel, *Lectures on the History of Philosophy: Medieval and Modern Philosophy*, Volume 3, trans. Elizabeth Sanderson Haldane (Lincoln, Nebraska: University of Nebraska Press, 1995), 281.

13. Benedict de Spinoza, *Ethics*, ed. and trans. James Gutmann (New York: Hafner Press, 1949 [1677]), 117; Part 2 (of the Nature and Origin of the Mind): Proposition XLV.

14. Ibid., 63; Part 1 (of God): Corollary to Proposition XXV.

15. J. Allanson Picton, *Pantheism: Its Story and Significance* (Chicago: Archibald Constable and Co., Ltd., 1905), Foreword.

16. Paul Deussen, *Sixty Upanishads of the Veda*, Volume 2, trans. V. M. Bedekar and Gajanan Balkrishna Palsule (Delhi: Motilal Banarsidass Publishers, 1997), 618 [stanza 19].

17. Rachel Elior, *The Paradoxical Ascent to God: The Kabbalistic Theosophy of Habad Hasidism*, trans. Jeffrey M. Green (Albany, New York: SUNY Press,

1993), 56; Part 2 (The Doctrine of Divinity, The Mystical Theology), emphasis in the original.

18. Thomas Valone, *Practical Conversion of Zero-Point Energy: Feasibility Study of the Extraction of Zero-Point Energy from the Quantum Vacuum for the Performance of Useful Work* (Beltsville, Maryland: Integrity Research Institute, 2005), 10.

Chapter 1: Something Exists aka "Aseity," or The Axiom of Existence

1. Lucius Annaeus Seneca, *Delphi Complete Works of Seneca the Younger*, Illustrated (Hastings, England: Delphi Classics [Delphi Publishing], 2014), ii.

2. "Kant was slender and short, scarcely five feet tall, a man of eccentrically regular habits, of whom it is said that his neighbors could set their clocks by the moment he emerged for his daily afternoon walk." Walt Truett Anderson, *The Next Enlightenment: Integrating East and West in a New Vision of Human Evolution* (New York: St. Martin's Press, 2003), 30. "[B]arely five feet tall, Kant subjected himself to a strict regime of regular exercise, mainly walks." Carl Sagan and Ann Druya, *Comet* (New York: Ballantine Books [Random House], 1985), 83.

3. In declaring that "without reason, [we] would have no coherent use of the understanding," Kant means the understanding we possess of what can be experienced is governed by reason. Immanuel Kant, *Critique of Pure Reason*, trans. Werner S. Pluhar (Indianapolis, Indiana: Hackett Publishing, 1966 [1781/1787]), 624; A651/B679.

4. Jason S. Baehr, "A Priori and A Posteriori," *IEP.utm.edu*, Internet Encyclopedia of Philosophy (Martin, Tennessee: University of Tennessee, ca. 9 March 2010) at **https://www.iep.utm.edu/apriori/**, accessed September 3, 2019.

5. Ibid. Also, "such cognition is possible *a priori* and precedes all experience." Immanuel Kant, *Prolegomena to Any Future Metaphysics: That Will Be Able to Come Forward as Science*, ed. and trans. Gary Hatfield (Cambridge: Cambridge University Press, 2004 [1783]), 48.

6. Peter Markie, "Rationalism vs. Empiricism," *The Stanford Encyclopedia of Philosophy*, Fall 2017 Edition, ed. Edward N. Zalta (Palo Alto, California: Metaphysics Research Lab, Stanford University, 2017) at **https://plato. stanford.edu/archives/fall2017/entries/rationalism-empiricism/**, accessed September 3, 2019.

7. Ibid.

8. John R. Searle, *Speech Acts: An Essay in the Philosophy of Language* (New York: Cambridge University Press, 1969), 77.

9. Aloysius Martinich and Avrum Stroll, *Much Ado about Nonexistence: Fiction and Reference*, of *G - Reference, Information and Interdisciplinary Subjects Series* (Lanham, Maryland: Rowman and Littlefield, 2007), 18.

10. Immanuel Kant, *Critique of Pure Reason*, (abridged), trans. Werner S. Pluhar (Indianapolis, Indiana: Hackett Publishing Company, 1999 [1781/1787]), 200; A599/B627, emphasis in the original.

11. Ayn Rand, *Atlas Shrugged* (New York: Signet [Penguin], 2005), 1201.

12. Among many examples: "[A] meaningless tautology—'Existence exists,'" William F. O'Neill, *With Charity Toward None: An Analysis of Ayn Rand's Philosophy* (New York: Philosophical Library, 2015), 224. Cf. "[I]n the tautology that existence exists[, t]here is no possibility of getting anything more out of it." Paul Carus, "Mysticism and Immortality," *The Open Court*, Volume 28, No. 692 (Chicago: Open Court Publishing, January 1914), 361.

13. René Descartes, *Discours de la Méthode* (Paris: Tandou et Cie., 1863 [1637]), 46.

14. René Descartes, *Meditations on First Philosophy: With Selections from the Objections and Replies*, ed. and trans. John Cottingham (Cambridge: Cambridge University Press, 2013 [1641]), 136 and 176.

15. René Descartes, *Meditations on First Philosophy*, trans. Donald A. Cress (Indianapolis, Indiana: Hackett Publishing, 1993 [1641]), 10.

16. Ibid., 72.

17. Term coined by David Premack and Guy Woodruff, "Does the Chimpanzee Have a Theory of Mind?" in *Behavioral and Brain Sciences*, Volume 1, No. 4 (Cambridge: Cambridge University Press, December 1978), 515–26; doi:10.1017/S0140525X00076512.

18. Heinz Wimmer and Josef Perner, "Beliefs about Beliefs: Representation and Constraining Function of Wrong Beliefs in Young Children's Understanding of Deception," *Cognition*, Volume 13, No. 1 (Amsterdam: Elsevier, January 1983), 103–28; doi:10.1016/0010-0277(83)90004-5. Cf. Carl Zimmer, "How the Mind Reads Other Minds," *Science*, Volume 300, No. 5622 (Washington, D.C.: American Association for the Advancement of Science, 16 May 2003), 1079–80; doi:10.1126/science.300.5622.1079. Another observation relates to how it "is impossible to be a good teacher, for example, until you can separate what you know and understand from what other people know and

understand." Art Markman, "When Children Learn About Other's Minds, They Learn to Lie," *PsychologyToday.com*, ed. Kaja Perina (New York: Sussex Publishers, 1 December 2015) at **https://www.psychologytoday.com/us/blog/ulterior-motives/201512/when-children-learn-about-others-minds-they-learn-lie**, accessed October 31, 2019.

19. Thomas Colligan, "Did the Stoics Really Say That?" on *ModernStoicism.com*, ed. Gregory Sadler (Exeter, England: Modern Stoicism UK #10950027, 18 August 2018) at **https://modernstoicism.com/did-the-stoics-really-say-that-by-thomas-colligan/**, accessed September 4, 2019.

20. John Stuart Mill, *An Examination of Sir William Hamilton's Philosophy* (London: Longman, Green, Longman, Roberts and Green, 1865), 208.

21. "[O]ur thinking presupposes our existence." David Weissman, *Intuition and Ideality* (Albany, New York: State University of New York Press, 1987), 265. And, "the moment I say to you, 'I don't exist,' [I prove] that I do exist[, meaning that] god could never speak an untruth, especially against himself[, so… b]eing able to say 'God does not exist' proves that god does not exist." Karry Lynn Dayton, *Saint Horz, The Stone Saint: The New Addition* (Morrisville, North Carolina: Lulu.com, 2009–16), 299–300.

Chapter 2: The Necessary Properties of What Exists

1. Herman Melville, "Hawthorne and his Mosses," *Piazza Tales and Other Prose Pieces, 1839–1860*, ed. Harrison Hayford, et al. (Evanston, Illinois: Northwestern University Press / The Newberry Library of Chicago, 1987 [1980]), 247.

2. "[T]here can be no fact[,] real or existing, no statement true, unless there be a sufficient reason, why it should be so and not otherwise." Gottfried Wilhelm Freiherr von Leibniz, *The Monadology and Other Philosophical Writings*, trans. Robert Latta (Oxford: Clarendon Press, 1898), 235; section 32 [from the French, *La Monadologie* (1714)]. Compare to Leibniz's earlier formulation of the "principle […] of the *determinate reason*: [N]othing ever comes to pass without there being a cause or at least a reason determining it." Gottfried Wilhelm Leibniz, *Theodicy: Essays on the Goodness of God, the Freedom of Man and the Origin of Evil*, ed. Austin M. Farrer, trans. E. M. Huggard (New York: Cosimo, 2010), 147; section 44 [from the French, *Essais de Théodicée sur la bonté de Dieu, la liberté de l'homme et l'origine du mal* (1710)].

3. The PSR's contentious history following Leibniz's formulaton include: Hume's taking issue with causation generally, Wolff's attempt to derive the PSR from the Aristotelian LNC, Euler's complaint that the PSR is often arbitrary

in its application, Kant's identifying the PSR as an essential part of what makes experience (objectively and relationally) possible, and Schopenhauer's connecting his four variants of the PSR on the same philosophical grounds. See Yitzhak Y. Melamed and Martin Lin, "Principle of Sufficient Reason," *The Stanford Encyclopedia of Philosophy*, Spring 2017 Edition, ed. Edward N. Zalta (Palo Alto, California: Metaphysics Research Lab, Stanford University, 2017) at **https://plato.stanford.edu/archives/spr2017/entries/sufficient-reason/**, accessed November 21, 2017.

4. The PSR "*implies that nothing can exist unless it can be potentially understood by a sentient being*[, … and t]his principle is psychological, not metaphysical, since it expresses our hubris and fear of death." Benjamin Cain, "Why Is There Something Rather Than Nothing?" on *RantsWithinTheUndeadGod. blogspot.com* (Mountain View, California [Canada]: Google [weblog], 22 January 2017) at **http://rantswithintheundeadgod.blogspot.com/2017/01/ why-something-rather-than-nothing.html**, accessed October 6, 2017; emphasis in the original.

5. "If the only information available from quantum mechanics concerns the probabilities of certain outcomes, then causality and determinism are abandoned[; … Furthermore, q]uantum mechanics established the final failure of causality[, with t]he uncertainty principle [having] sounded the death knell for causality, [just as] Heisenberg believed." Jim Baggott, *The Quantum Story: A History in 40 Moments* (New York: Oxford University Press, 2011), 75, 93–94. And "[there is a] lack of local causality associated with quantum entanglement." Gregg Jaeger, *Entanglement, Information, and the Interpretation of Quantum Mechanics* (Berlin: Springer-Verlag [Springer Science+Business Media], 2009), 47.

6. "[I]t must (if finite) be limited by another substance of the same nature, which also must necessarily exist[, …] which is absurd [and] exists therefore as infinite substance." Benedict de Spinoza, *Ethics*, ed. and trans. James Gutmann (New York: Hafner Press, 1949 [1677]), 44; Part 1 (of God): Proposition VIII.

7. "[If, through division, the parts do] not retain the nature of substance absolutely infinite[…], then […] substance absolutely infinite can cease to be, which [… is…] absurd." Ibid., 51; Part 1 (of God): Proposition XIII.

8. Aristotle, *The Physics, or Physical Auscultation*, trans. Thomas Taylor (London: Robert Wilks, 1806), 390–92; Book 6, 239b14–16.

9. "[T]he set of positive rational numbers is countably infinite." John F. Lucas, *Introduction to Abstract Mathematics* (New York: Ardsley House Publishers [Rowman and Littlefield], 1985), 121.

10. "[E]very infinite set can be placed in a one-to-one correspondence with some proper subset of itself." Ibid. An infinite set starts with innumerable proper subsets, at least one of which would be expected, according to this definition, to correspond directly with the original set's membership.

11. One ought rather to deny that any infinite whole exists than to consider whether any such infinite whole could consist of parts, themselves either infinite or finite. As Euclid observes, "The whole is greater than the part." Euclid, *(The Thirteen Books of Euclid's) Elements*, Volume 1, trans. Sir Thomas Little Heath (Cambridge: Cambridge University Press, 1908), 232; from Book 1, Common Notion 5, where Euclid admittedly states this observation as an unproven mereological axiom.

12. Aristotle, *The Metaphysics*, trans. John H. McMahon (Mineola, New York: Courier Corporation [Dover Publications], 2013), 84; Book 4, Chapter 6 (1011b).

13. Ravi Zacharias, *Can Man Live Without God* (Nashville, Tennessee: Thomas Nelson, 2004), 130.

14. "McTaggart believed that the most extreme kind of monism, namely the doctrine that there is exactly one thing, is incoherent[, f]or if there were exactly one thing, it could have no attributes or features, and hence, on McTaggart's view, would really be nothing." Kris McDaniel, "John M. E. McTaggart," *The Stanford Encyclopedia of Philosophy*, Winter 2016 Edition, ed. Edward N. Zalta (Palo Alto, California: Metaphysics Research Lab, Stanford University, 2016) at **https://plato.stanford.edu/archives/win2016/entries/mctaggart/**, accessed September 12, 2017; citing John McTaggart Ellis McTaggart, *Philosophical Studies*, ed. Stanley Victor Keeling (Freeport, New York: Books for Libraries Press, 1966), 61.

15. The "god of the gaps" concept is used variously either as a theological argument, where the existence of a supernatural being is offered in response to science's explanatory shortcomings, or as a response to theological arguments in the form of an argument-from-ignorance fallacy, in which a temporary lack of knowledge invites speculation about supernatural explanations. As the-then Bishop of Birmingham innovatively states, "They have made him God of the gaps in human knowledge." Ernest W. Barnes, *Scientific Theory and Religion: The World Described by Science and its Spiritual Interpretation* (Cambridge: Cambridge University Press, 1933), 409.

16. Calvin Helin, *Dances with Spirits: Ancient Wisdom for a Modern World* (New York: Open Road Media, 2014), 117. Also, Rosenberg acknowledges that "[s]cientism is my label for [...] accepting science's description of the nature of reality." Alex Rosenberg, "The Disenchanted Naturalist's Guide to Reality,"

NationalHumanitiesCenter.org (Research Triangle, North Carolina: National Humanities Center, November 2009) at **https://nationalhumanitiescenter. org/on-the-human/2009/11/the-disenchanted-naturalists-guide-to-reality/,** accessed September 4, 2019.

17. Based on a survey of the brushstroke techniques used in prehistoric art, humans have been 93% right-handed for between 5,000 and 10,000 years. Clare Porac and Stanley Coren, "Fifty Centuries of Right-Handedness: the Historical Record," *Science,* Volume 198, No. 4317 (Washington, D.C.: American Association for the Advancement of Science, 11 Nov 1977), 631–32; doi:10.1126/science.335510.

18. Brian Greene, *The Fabric of the Cosmos: Space, Time, and the Texture of Reality* (New York: Vintage Books [Random House], 2004), 302. Cf. NASA's 2010 Wilkinson Microwave Anisotropy Probe results data, *NASA.gov* (Greenbelt, Maryland: NASA's Goddard Space Flight Center, 13 May 2008) at **https://map.gsfc.nasa.gov/universe/WMAP_Universe.pdf,** accessed October 6, 2017, which confirms these figures.

19. "About 80% of the mass of the present Universe is made up of the unknown (dark matter)." Masahiro Ibe, et al., "Baryon-Dark Matter Coincidence in Mirrored Unification," *Physical Review D,* Volume 100, No. 7 (College Park, Maryland: American Physical Society, October 2019); doi:10.1103/ PhysRevD.100.075022. Also, "[t]he SN Ia observations have shown that about 70% of the present energy of the Universe consists of dark energy." Luca Amendola and Shinji Tsujikawa, *Dark Energy: Theory and Observations* (Cambridge: Cambridge University Press, 2010), 1. Cf. The Dark Energy survey (or DES) at the **https://www.darkenergysurvey.org/the-des-project/overview/** webpage, journaling a multinational, collaborative project funded in part by the U.S. Department of Energy and the U.S. National Science Foundation.

20. "The sun's surface is blisteringly hot at 10,340 degrees Fahrenheit— but its atmosphere is another 300 times hotter[, … which] has led to an enduring mystery for those who study the sun: What heats the atmosphere to such extreme temperatures?" on *NASA.gov* (Washington, D.C.: National Aeronautics and Space Administration, 30 April 2015) at **https://www.nasa. gov/feature/goddard/sounding-rockets/strong-evidence-for-coronal- heating-theory-presented-at-2015-tess-meeting,** accessed October 6, 2017.

21. "I shall use the phrase 'time's arrow' to express this one-way property of time which has no analogue in space." Sir Arthur Eddington, *The Nature of the Physical World: The Gifford Lectures (1927)* (Cambridge: Cambridge University Press, 1928), 69. Cf. Stephen Hawking, *A Brief History of Time* (New York: Bantam Books, 1988), 147–58.

22. Sean Carroll, *The Big Picture: On the Origins of Life, Meaning, and the Universe Itself* (New York: Dutton [Penguin Random House], 2016), 58–59.

23. Joseph Silk, *The Big Bang* (New York: W. H. Freeman [Henry Holt] and Company, 2001 [1980]), 134–37. A recent restatement of the observation is recounted in "The Matter-Antimatter Asymmetry Problem," *CERN* (Geneva, Switzerland: The European Organization for Nuclear Research, ca. 7 November 2018) at **https://home.cern/science/physics/matter-antimatter-asymmetry-problem**, accessed March 21, 2019.

24. Guy Kahane, "Our Cosmic Insignificance," *Nous*, Volume 48, No. 4 (Detroit, Michigan: Wiley-Blackwell, 2014), 745–72; doi:10.1111/nous.12030. See also, *The Origin and Evolution of the Universe*, ed. Ben Zuckerman and Matthew Arnold Malkan (Sudbury, Massachusetts: Jones and Bartlett Publishers, 1996), 8–9.

25. "[I]n an effort to measure how much the universal expansion has slowed over the last few billion years[, …] observations indicate that the universal expansion is speeding up, or accelerating!" on *NASA.gov* (Greenbelt, Maryland: NASA's Goddard Space Flight Center, 10 March 2008) at **https://map.gsfc.nasa.gov/universe/uni_accel.html**, accessed November 19, 2019.

26. Neil deGrasse Tyson, Michael Strauss, and J. Richard Gott, *Welcome to the Universe: The Problem Book* (Princeton, New Jersey: Princeton University Press, 2017), 198.

27. Herbert Spencer, *First Principles* (New York: D. Appleton and Company, 1896 [1864]), 48.

28. "A cornerstone of the scientific method is that the results from good science must be reproducible." James M. Hyman, "Future Directions in Large Scale Scientific Computing," *Large Scale Scientific Computation*, ed. Seymour V. Parter (Orlanda, Florida: Academic Press [Harcourt Brace Jovanovich], 1984), 78. "[T]he scientific method [… involves the requirement that e]xperimental results must be *reproducible* by others." Martin Silberberg, *Chemistry: The Molecular Nature of Matter and Change With Advanced Topics* (New York: McGraw-Hill Education, 2016 [2012], 12; emphasis in the original. Yet, in a survey of scientists, "less than 31% think that failure to reproduce published results means that the result is probably wrong, and most say that they still trust the published literature." Monya Baker, "1,500 Scientists Lift the Lid on Reproducibility," *Nature*, Volume 533, No. 7604 (London: Nature Research [Springer Nature], 25 May 2016), 452–54; doi:10.1038/533452a. And "[d]ata from many fields suggests reproducibility is lower than is desirable." Marcus R. Munafò, et al., "A Manifesto for Reproducible Science," *Nature Human Behaviour*,

Volume 1, Article 21 (Berlin: Springer Nature, January 2017); doi:10.1038/ s41562-016-0021.

29. Darren Hewer, "Five Things Science Can't Explain," *TheLife.com* (Langley City, British Columbia, Canada: Power to Change Ministries, 24 March 2011) at **https://thelife.com/five-things-science-cant-explain**, accessed October 6, 2017.

30. Clifford J. Stevens, "Science or Nonsense," *Amazon.com* (Seattle, Washington: Amazon, 19 May 2012) at **https://amzn.to/3y32uE0**, accessed August 4, 2019; review of Victor J. Stenger, *Has Science Found God? The Latest Results in the Search for Purpose in the Universe* (Amherst, New York: Prometheus Books, 2003).

31. Stevens, "Science or Nonsense;" emphasis in the original.

32. "[O]ur rational cognition applies only to appearances, and leaves the thing in itself uncognized by us[; … hence,] the unconditioned is […] to be met with in them (only) insofar as was are not acquainted with them, viz., insofar as they are things in themselves." Immanuel Kant, *Critique of Pure Reason*, trans. Werner S. Pluhar (Indianapolis, Indiana: Hackett Publishing, 1966 [1787]), 24; Bxx, Preface (Second Edition).

33. "The possibility of a thing, however, can never be proved merely from the fact that a concept of this thing is not contradictory, but can be proved only by supporting the concept through an intuition [or sensation] corresponding to it." Ibid., 317–18; A253/B308.

34. "Since we are speaking here only of the cognitive powers and so of ideas (not of the feeling of pleasure and displeasure), *sensation* will mean only sense representations (empirical intuitions), as distinguished both from concepts (thoughts) and from pure intuitions (ideas of space and time)." Immanuel Kant, *Anthropology from a Pragmatic Point of View*, trans. Mary J. Gregor (The Hague, Netherlands: Martinus Nijhoff, 1974 [1798]), 24; 143, footnote, emphasis in the original. "Because imagination, which submits a matter to understanding so as to provide content for its concepts (so that we have knowledge), seems, by virtue of the analogy between its (invented) intuitions and real perceptions, to give our concepts reality." Ibid., 46; Section 28, 169.

35. "Kant argued that absolute space is 'not some adumbration or schema of the object, but only a certain law implanted in the mind by which it coordinates for itself the sensa that arise from the presence of the object.'" Paul Guyer, "[Editor's] Introduction: The Starry Heavens and the Moral Law," for *The Cambridge Companion to Kant* (New York: Cambridge University Press, 1992), 10; citing Section 4, 2:393 of "On the Form and Principles of the Sensible and Intelligible World," *Inaugural Dissertation* (1770). "Kant's transcendental idealism holds that space and time are not

mind-independent features of reality, but structural features of experience specific to human cognition; they are the 'forms of intuition,' or the forms of human perception[, … and t]he fact that our experience has structural features that are due to our cognitive faculties introduces a distinction between objects as they appear to us ('appearances' or 'phenomena') and objects as they are in themselves, considered apart from the conditions under which they appear ('things-in-themselves' or 'noumena')." Andrews Reath, "Introduction" for Immanuel Kant's *Critique of Practical Reason*, ed. and trans. Mary Gregor (Cambridge: Cambridge University Press, 1997 [1788]), xi.

36. "[A]nalytic judgments are those in which the predicate's connection with the subject is thought by (thinking) identity, whereas those judgments in which this connection is thought without (thinking) identity are to be called synthetic." Kant, *Critique of Pure Reason*, 51; A7/B11.

37. "Motion of an *object* in space does not belong in a pure science, and consequently not in geometry[, …f]or the fact that something is movable cannot be cognized a priori, but can be cognized only through experience." Kant, *Critique of Pure Reason*, 193; B155, emphasis in the original. That the categories are not illusory is evident by contrasting them with transcendental ideas: "[W]hereas the categories lead to truth, i.e., to the agreement of our concepts with the object, the transcendental ideas bring about a mere illusion—although an irresistible one." Ibid., 617; A643/B671.

38. "I am conscious of my own existence as determined in time[, … which] presupposes something *permanent* in the perception[, … made] possible only through a *thing* outside me and not through a mere *presentation* of a thing outside me[; … h]ence determination of my existence in time is possible only through the existence of actual things that I perceive outside me." Ibid., 290; B276, emphasis in the original.

39. "Kant's […] transcendental idealism minimally rejects supposed truths about things in themselves from pure reason alone." Graham Bird, *The Revolutionary Kant: A Commentary on the Critique of Pure Reason* (Peru, Illinois: Open Court Publishing [Carus Publishing], 2006), 186. "[N]oumena […] is a conception of objects considered by pure reason alone, which […] results from our having 'abstracted from all conditions of (sensory) intuition under which alone objects can be given' (A499–500/B528–9)." James O'Shea, *Kant's Critique of Pure Reason: An Introduction and Interpretation* (Chesham, England: Acumen Publishers, 2012), 69. "Thoughts without content are empty; intuitions without concepts are blind." Kant, *Critique of Pure Reason*, 107; A52/B76. Although, "properties belonging to things in themselves [… cannot] ever be given to us through the senses." Ibid., 90; A53/B36.

40. "[L]earning is nothing but imitation." Immanuel Kant, *Critique of Judgment*, trans. Werner S. Pluhar (Indianapolis, Indiana: Hackett Publishing, 1987 [1790]), 176; Section 47. Despite our ability to cognize something "independently of experience, yet we do not cognize it independently of all reference to the form of experience as such, and to the synthetic unity in which alone objects can be cognized empirically[; … with regard to such knowledge, we] can acquire it only a posteriori, as concepts given by experience itself[, …] and hence their possibility must either be cognized a posteriori and empirically, or it cannot be cognized at all." Kant, *Critique of Pure Reason*, 285. Specifically as to the future of humanity, "we cannot infer a priori from what we have seen of its natural predispositions[, … but] can infer it only from experience and history." Kant, *Anthropology*, 189; paragraph 329.

41. "Only those forms of propositions which have genuine counterparts in the empirical world are to be admitted in the logical schematicism of admissible (i.e., significant) concepts." Julius Rudolph Weinberg, *An Examination of Logical Positivism* (London: Kegan Paul, Trench, Trübner, and Co., Ltd., 1936), 34.

42. "[A] developed use of the concept of space in geometry must itself require appeal to a priori concepts as well as a priori intuition[; … in particular, the Transcendental] Aesthetic outlines a precondition in sense experience, a sensory manifold[, …] and proves the a priori character of its central intuitions." Bird, *Revolutionary Kant*, 186. "[O]n Phenomena and Noumena, Kant contended that the idea of an appearance implies that it is the appearance of some reality[; … in] his Transcendental Aesthetic, he declared: Sensibility deals with the *mode* in which things-in-themselves appear [… and] 'that something which is not in itself appearance must correspond to it.'" Gary Dorrien, *Kantian Reason and Hegelian Spirit: The Idealistic Logic of Modern Theology* (Chichester, England: John Wiley and Sons, 2012), 45; emphasis in the original. "[S]pace and time […] are merely phenomenal, […] being 'forms of intuition' rather than features of things in themselves." James Van Cleve, *Problems from Kant* (New York: Oxford University Press, 1999), 135. Nonetheless, "Kant's distinction between phenomena and things in themselves is very far from being a phenomenalistic distinction between mental representations and things independent of the mind." Rae Langton, *Kantian Humility: Our Ignorance of Things in Themselves* (Oxford: Clarendon Press [Oxford University Press], 1998), 20. And merely by "formulating the notion of an appearance[,] Kant believes we do in fact form an idea or a thought of the thing in itself." J. V. Buroker, *Space and Incongruence: The Origin of Kant's Idealism* (Dordrecht, Netherlands: D. Reidel Publishing [Kluwer Group / Springer Science+Business Media], 1981), 109. "For otherwise an absurd proposition would follow, viz., that there is appearance without anything that appears." Kant, *Critique of Pure Reason*, 28; Bxxvii.

43. Kant presents ordinally four of what he calls a "Conflict of Transcendental Ideas" in a chapter entitled "The Antinomy of Pure Reason," each in the form of thesis and antithesis, both sides of which Kant offers proof and disproof: "[t]he world has a beginning in time" (an ambiguity relating to an act of creation), "[e]very composite substance in the world consists of simple parts" (an ambiguity relating to composition), "[t]he causality according to the laws of nature is not the only causality from which the appearances of the world can thus one and all be derived [, … but] it is necessary to assume also a causality through freedom" (an ambiguity relating to causation), and "[t]here belongs to the world something that, either as its part or as its cause, is absolutely necessary being" (an ambiguity relating to contingency). Kant, *Critique of Pure Reason*, 458, 464, 473, and 479.

44. "[T]he entire universe was squashed into a single point with zero size, like a sphere of radius zero[, at] the time we call the big bang[, which itself] was the beginning of time." Stephen Hawking and Leonard Mlodinow, *A Briefer History of Time* (New York: Bantam Books, 2005), 68–69.

45. "All cognition of things merely from pure understanding or pure reason is nothing but sheer illusion, and only in experience is there truth." Immanuel Kant, *Prolegomena to Any Future Metaphysics*, trans. Paul Carus, rev. James W. Ellington (Indianapolis, Indiana: Hackett Publishing, 1977 [1783]), 107; original translation's page number 375.

46. "Thinking constitutes one part of experience[, … and if we] omit everything empirical, then pure intuition remains, i.e., space and time remain." Immanuel Kant, "Metaphysik Mrongovius: Ontology," *Lectures on Metaphysics*, ed. and trans. Karl Ameriks and Steve Naragon (New York: Cambridge University Press, 1997), 154; *gesammelte Schriften* (Academy edition [1782–83]), Volume 28, 801. "Space is a necessary a priori presentation that underlies all intuitions[; … in particular, w]e can never have a presentation of there being no space, even though we are quite able to think of there being no objects encountered in it." Kant, *Critique of Pure Reason*, 78; A24/B39. "Time is a necessary presentation that underlies all intuitions [… and] is given a priori[; …] time itself […] cannot be annulled." Ibid., 86; A31/B46. "[W]e dispute that time has any claim to absolute reality." Ibid., 89; A53/B36. "For time and space, taken together, are pure forms of all sensible intuition, and thereby make synthetic propositions possible a priori[, … or, in other words,] make synthetic a priori propositions possible." Ibid., 92; A39/B56, with reference to B19 footnote 234.

47. "There is no possible intuition which we can have apart from space and time[, … allowing us to hold] their *empirical reality*, but assert their

transcendental ideality[, … and to declare] that they are nothing, if we omit the conditions of experience, and regard them as belonging to things in themselves[; … w]e also deny their *absolute reality*, which can never be revealed to us, and which is in some senses absurd." Immanuel Kant, *The Kritik of the Pure Reason Explained and Defended*, ed. and trans. John P. Mahaffy and John H. Bernard (London: Macmillan, 1889), 55; emphasis in the original. As is the case for time, likewise "space is *real* (i.e., objectively valid) in regard to everything that we can encounter externally as object, but [...] space is *ideal* in regard to things when reason considers them in themselves, i.e., without taking into account the character of our sensibility." Kant, *Critique of Pure Reason*, 82; A28/B44, emphasis in the original.

48. Donald K. McKim, *The Westminster Dictionary of Theological Terms* (Louisville, Kentucky: Westminster John Knox Press, 2014), 132; the "God, aseity of" entry. See also, Mortimer J. Adler, *How to Think About God* (New York: Simon and Schuster, 2008 [1980]), 114. Additional online resources include **https://www.merriam-webster.com/dictionary/aseity, https://www. yourdictionary.com/aseity**, and **https://plato.stanford.edu/entries/divine-simplicity/**, all accessed November 19, 2019.

49. "God [...] just exists in and of Himself, independent of everything else." William Lane Craig, *God Over All: Divine Aseity and the Challenge of Platonism* (Oxford: Oxford University Press, 2016), 10.

50. A definition of aseity that "avoids any circular reasoning" involves identifying it as a divine property rather than saying God has or possesses it. Yann Schmitt, "The Deadlock of Absolute Divine Simplicity," *International Journal for Philosophy of Religion*, Volume 74, No. 1 (The Hague, Netherlands: Springer Netherlands, August 2013), 117–30; doi:10.1007/s11153-012-9336-7. Cf. Paul Tillich, *Systematic Theology* (Chicago: Chicago University Press, 1951), 252 et seq.

51. William F. Vallicella, "Divine Simplicity," *The Stanford Encyclopedia of Philosophy*, Spring 2019, ed. Edward N. Zalta (Palo Alto, California: Metaphysics Research Lab, Stanford University, 2019) at **https://plato. stanford.edu/archives/spr2019/entries/divine-simplicity/**, accessed June 26, 2019.

52. Alvin Plantinga, *Does God Have a Nature?* (Milwaukee, Wisconsin: Marquette University Press, 1980); generally.

53. George Harold Medley III, "History, Cosmos and Field Theory: A Critically Constructive Re-examination of Wolfhart Pannenberg's Theology of History with a View to the Question of Divine Sovereignty and Human Freedom," PhD diss. (London: King's College, January 2018), 249 at **https://kclpure.kcl.**

ac.uk/portal/files/95763694/2018_Medley_Lii_George_0933266_ethesis. pdf, accessed November 21, 2019.

54. "[B]esides God no substance can be nor can be conceived." Spinoza, *Ethics*, 51; Part 1 (of God): Proposition XIV. "[T]he intellect of God [is] the cause of things, both of their essence and of their existence." Ibid., 58.

55. Nicholas Rescher, *Nature and Understanding: The Metaphysics and Method of Science* (New York: Clarendon Press [Oxford University Press], 2000), 174–79.

56. Reasoning that something exists based on the assertion that something must exist sounds like circular logic, and one could characterize the use of that potential circularity to justify the wholesale abandonment of the PEQ as a form of philosophical pessimism; those philosophers "think the question stumps us by imposing an impossible explanatory demand, namely, *Deduce the existence of something without using any existential premises.*" Roy Sorensen, "Nothingness," *The Stanford Encyclopedia of Philosophy*, Spring 2020, ed. Edward N. Zalta (Palo Alto, California: Metaphysics Research Lab, Stanford University, 2020) at **https://plato.stanford.edu/archives/spr2020/entries/ nothingness/**, accessed August 28, 2017. The cited quotation might have originally appeared as: "[T]he question is still unanswerable, as it imposes an impossible explanatory demand; it asks one to deduce the existence of something without using any existential premises." Thomson von Stein, "What Man Knew, or Thought He Knew," (Chronological Outline of a History of Knowledge and Beliefs, with Key Events, Rev. 6–11: 2010), 121, at **http://history-of-knowledge.com/yahoo_site_admin/assets/docs/1-23- 11chron.161205822.pdf**, accessed August 28, 2017.

57. The Thomist view considers "*Deus sit ipsum esse subsistens*" (Latin for "God, [W]ho is subsistent existence itself"). (Saint) Thomas Aquinas, *Summa Theologiae*, Volume 2, Existence and Nature of God: 1a. 2–11, ed. Timothy McDermott (Cambridge: Cambridge University Press, 2006 [1485]), 52–53. In contrast, McTaggart eschews this view, saying, "[T]he quality of being [...] is simple and undefinable." John McTaggart Ellis McTaggart, *The Nature of Existence*, Volume 2, ed. C. D. Broad (Cambridge: Cambridge University Press, 1988 [1900]), 76. Spinoza originally declares that "God is a substance[, ...] from whose definition existence itself follows." Spinoza, *Ethics*, 44; Part 1 (of God): Proposition XIX (proof). Even the Bible envisions the divine as the basis for existence, "[f]or in [God] we live, and move, and have our being" (Acts 17:28). (Note: Unless otherwise indicated, all Bible references are to the King James Version.) An entirely different position detaches God from any association with existence, as in, "God is blasphemed if [H]is existence is discussed because [H]e is beyond existence." Paul Tillich, *Writings in the Philosophy of Religion (Religionsphilosophische Schriften)*, ed. John Clayton (Berlin: Walter de Gruyter and Co., 1987), 393.

58. *The Hymns of the Rigveda*, Volume 2, trans. Ralph Thomas Hotchkin Griffith (Benares, India: E. J. Lazarus and Co., 1897), 575; (Mandala) Book 10, Hymn CXXIX: Creation. For a composite-translated version of the hymn, see Keerthi Kumar Patangay, *Creation of Universe God or Big Bang* (Chennai, India: Notion Press, 2017), 128–29.

Chapter 3: Reality Consists of Multiple Things that Appear to Exist

1. Isaac Asimov, "My Turn: A Cult of Ignorance," *Newsweek* (Washington, D.C.: The Washington Post, 21 January 1980), 19.

2. Sir Fred Hoyle, "A New Model for the Expanding Universe," *Monthly Notices of the Royal Astronomical Society*, Volume 108, No. 5 (Oxford: Oxford University Press, October 1948), 372–82; doi: 0.1093/mnras/108.5.372.

3. Ibid. See also, Hermann Bondi and Thomas Gold, "The Steady State Theory of the Expanding Universe," *Monthly Notices of the Royal Astronomical Society*, Volume 108, No. 3 (June 1948), 252–70; doi:10.1093/mnras/108.3.252.

4. "Earlier theories … were based on the hypothesis that all the matter in the universe was created in one big bang at a particular time in the remote past." Sir Fred Hoyle, *The Listener*, Volume 41 (London: BBC, 7 Apr 1949), 567–68; transcript of radio talk on the BBC Third Programme (28 Mar 1949 at 6:30 P.M.).

5. "[D]etection of the primordial B-modes of the CMB (cosmic microwave background) polarization by NASA's BICEP2 telescope at the South Pole provides […] direct support for the cosmic inflation theory of how the Universe came into being." Jose W. F. Valle and Jorge C. Romao, *Neutrinos in High Energy and Astroparticle Physics* (Weinheim, Germany: Wiley-VCH Verlag, 2015), 307. See also "Figure 17.1" for the Big Bang timeline; Ibid., 308. "The very existence of the cosmic microwave background led to the widespread acceptance of big bang cosmology[; … one rationale is that] excess noise in their radio antenna turned out to be the crucial piece of evidence that destroyed the Steady State Theory and led to the primacy of the Hot Big Bang Theory which remains the central paradigm to this day." Andrew R. Liddle, "Fingerprinting the Universe-Future Cosmic Microwave Background Experiments," *Contemporary Physics*, Volume 39, No. 2 (London: Taylor and Francis, April 1998), 95–105; doi:10.1080/001075198182053. "[T]he cosmic microwave background is polarized[, … and though w]e do not yet know what this matter consists of, but the 'best bet' is exotic particles left over from

the big bang." Jay M. Pasachoff and Alex Filippenko, *The Cosmos: Astronomy in the New Millennium*, 4th Edition (New York: Cambridge University Press, 2001), 516. "WMAP's [or Wilkinson Microwave Anisotropy Probe's] precision strongly confirms the standard inflationary big bang scenario." Karl F. Kuhn and Theo Koupelis, *In Quest of the Universe* (Sudbury, Massachusetts: Jones and Bartlett Learning, 2004), 611–12.

6. "[O]f series which are infinite[, …] all the parts down to that now present are alike intermediates; so that if there is no first there is no cause at all." Aristotle, *The Works of Aristotle*, Volume 8: Metaphysica, ed. and trans. John Alexander Smith and W. D. Ross (Oxford: Clarendon Press, 1908), 994; Book 2, Chapter 2, Lines 17–19. Based on Aristotle, the Thomist view states that "an infinite series is infinite precisely insofar as it has no primary cause." *Revisiting Aquinas' Proofs for the Existence of God*, ed. Robert Arp (Leiden, Netherlands: Brill Rodopi [Koninklijke Brill], 2016), 80. Even centuries later, an American philosopher declares, "[In] the absurdity of an infinite series of causative acts[, …] we are driven to the conclusion, that there is no cause whatever." Henry Philip Tappan, *A Treatise on the Will* (Glasgow: Lang, Adamson, and Co., 1857), 94. In the same era, another states succinctly, "[A]s an eternal series has no beginning, it can have no cause." *The Popular Educator*, Volume 6 (London: John Cassell, 1855), 605.

7. Bertrand Russell and Fr. Frederick C. Copleston, "Debate: The Existence of God," BBC radio Third Programme (originally aired January 28, 1948); transcript available, as of October 18, 2019, on *BiblicalCatholic.com* (St Petersburg, Florida: Phil Vaz dba Vaz Software, ca. 31 December 2014) at **http://www.biblicalcatholic.com/apologetics/p20.htm** and reprinted in *Bertrand Russell on God and Religion*, ed. Al Seckel (Amherst, New York: Prometheus Books, 1986), 131 et seq.

8. "[T]here is no possibility of a creator, because there is no time for a creator to have existed in." Stephen Hawking, *Brief Answers to the Big Questions* (New York: Bantam Books, 2018), 38.

9. "[E]very radiation mode has an irreducible ground state energy, consistent with quantum fluctuations in the electric and magnetic fields, and representing as such the vacuum expectation value of the radiation Hamiltonian when no observable light is present." David L. Andrews, *Photonics*, Volume 1: Fundamentals of Photonics and Physics (Hoboken, New Jersey: John Wiley and Sons, 2015), 13. Furthermore, "massive bosons [...] are given mass by interacting with a *Higgs field*[, … directly] proportional to the value of the Higgs field in a vacuum[, making it] therefore necessary that the Higgs field [have] a value different from zero in the vacuum (the *vacuum expectation value* must be non-zero)." Øyvind Grøn, *Lecture Notes on the General Theory*

of Relativity: From Newton's Attractive Gravity to the Repulsive Gravity of Vacuum Energy (New York: Springer Science+Business Media, 2010), 233; emphasis in the original.

10. Albert Einstein, "Ist die Trägheit eines Körpers von seinem Energieinhalt abhängig?" in *Annalen der Physik*, Volume 323, No. 13 (September 1905), 639–41; doi:10.1002/andp.19053231314; English title: "Does the Inertia of a Body Depend upon Its Energy Content?" in *The Annals of Physics*.

11. Ilya Prigogine with Isabelle Stengers, *The End of Certainty* (New York: The Free Press [Simon and Schuster], 1996), 179. The concept is further explained by Pasachoff and Filippenko, *The Cosmos*, 532. The term "ultimate free lunch" was coined to describe a net-zero total energy cosmology by Alan Guth, *The Inflationary Universe* (New York: Basic Books, 1998), 15.

12. Alexander Vilenkin, "Creation of Universes from Nothing," *Physics Letters B*, Volume 117, Nos. 1–2 (Singapore: World Scientific Publishing, 4 November 1982), 25–28; doi:10.1016/0370-2693(82)90866-8.

13. "Vilenkin has suggested that [… o]ur universe may have quantum-tunneled from 'nothing' [which itself] turns out to be a sort of spacetime foam." Nick Bostrom, "A Review of Anthropic Reasoning," *Anthropic-Principle.com* (London and New York: Routledge [Nick Bostrom], 29 September 1998) at **http://anthropic-principle.com/preprints/alit/review.doc**, accessed August 30, 2017.

14. A. F. J. Levi, *Applied Quantum Mechanics* (New York: Cambridge University Press, 2006), 145–49.

15. "Quantum tunneling is common in the tiny world of the atom but is highly improbable in our human world." Alan Lightman, "What Came before the Big Bang?" in *Harper's Magazine* (New York: Harper's Magazine Foundation [John R. MacArthur], December 2012) at **https://harpers.org/archive/2016/01/what-came-before-the-big-bang/3/**, accessed November 26, 2019. It also appears as a reprint in *The Best American Essays 2017*, ed. Leslie Jamison (and Robert Atwan) (Boston: Houghton Mifflin Harcourt, 2017), 72–81. A potential counterexample but still on the tiniest of scales can be found in experimental results. Youngwook Park, et al., "The Frequency-Domain Infrared Spectrum of Ammonia Encodes Changes in Molecular Dynamics Caused by a DC Electric Field," *Proceedings of the National Academy of Sciences*, Volume 116, No. 47 (Washington, D.C.: the United States National Academy of Sciences, 5 November 2019), 23444–47; doi:10.1073/pnas.1914432116.

16. "Experiments in nuclear physics use large accelerators that collide particles at nearly the speed of light, producing short-lived forms of matter." *Energy.gov*

(Washington, D.C.: U.S. Department of Energy, ca. 19 May 2019) at **https:// www.energy.gov/science/np/nuclear-physics**, accessed November 30, 2019.

17. "The processes described here do not represent the creation of matter out of nothing, but the conversion of pre-existing energy into material form." Paul Davies, *God and the New Physics* (New York: Simon and Schuster, 1983), 31. Furthermore, "after the initial creation of the universe itself, no matter has ever been created out of absolutely nothing[, while n]o empirical evidence at all supports the theory of continuous creation *ex nihilo.*" Rem B. Edwards, *What Caused the Big Bang?* (Amsterdam: Rodopi, 2001), 63.

18. "Today, conservation of energy is one of the most firmly established principles of physics, and no violation of it has ever been observed." Sadri Hassani, *From Atoms to Galaxies: A Conceptual Physics Approach to Scientific Awareness* (Boca Raton, Florida: CRC Press [Taylor and Francis], 2010), 267.

19. "[N]o mental phenomenon can have the property of provoking another mental phenomenon by an act of true causality" Alfred Binet, *The Mind and the Brain* (London: Kegan Paul, Trench, Trübner and Co., Ltd., 1907), 218.

20. Immanuel Kant, "A New Elucidation of the First Principles of Metaphysical Cognition," [Lat. *Principiorum primorum cognitionis metaphysicae nova dilucidatio*] in *Theoretical Philosophy, 1755–1770*, trans. and ed. David Wolford (New York: Cambridge University Press, 1992 [1755]), 14; 1:394.

21. G. W. F. Hegel, *Science of Logic* (London: Routledge, 1969), 831. Moreover, Hegel merely cites rather than adopts, as Fichte does, Kant's antinomy structure. Georg Wilhelm Friedrich Hegel, *Lectures on the History of Philosophy*, Volume 3, trans. Elizabeth Sanderson Haldane and Frances H. Simson (London: Kegan Paul, Trench, Trübner, and Co., Ltd., 1896), 449.

22. Werner Heisenberg, "Über den anschaulichen Inhalt der quantentheoretischen Kinematik und Mechanik," *Zeitschrift für Physik*, Volume 43, Nos. 3–4 (1927), 172 et seq.; doi:10.1007/BF01397280; English title: "About the Descriptive Content of Quantum Theoretical Kinematics and Mechanics" in *Journal for Physics*.

23. "[T]he quantum vacuum energy density is the fundamental, ultimate physical reality characterizing the [entirety of] gravitational space." Davide Fiscaletti and Amrit Sorli, "Space-Time Curvature of General Relativity and Energy Density of a Three-Dimensional Quantum Vacuum," *Annales Universitatis Mariae Curie-Sklodowska, Sectio AAA-Physica*, Volume 69, No. 1 (Warsaw: Walter de Gruyter and Co., 2014), 56; doi:10.1515/ physica-2015-0004. "[A]n accelerating universe['s …] kinematics are consistent with a constant vacuum energy density that permeates the universe." W. Michael Wood-Vasey, "The Future of Supernova Cosmology,"

Dark Energy: Observational and Theoretical Approaches, ed. P. Ruiz-Lapuente (Cambridge: Cambridge University Press, 2010), 202.

24. Quantum Field Theory would "predict a vacuum energy density that is some 122 orders of magnitude larger than what is observed[, ... referred to] as the 'vacuum catastrophe.'" Tristan Hübsch, *Advanced Concepts in Particle and Field Theory* (Cambridge: Cambridge University Press, 2015), 266. And to "calculate the energy density of the vacuum [...] involves summing the quantum mechanical zero-point energies of all the fields[, ... yielding] an answer about 120 orders of magnitude higher than the upper limits [...] set by cosmological observation[... and] the worst theoretical prediction in the history of physics!" M. P. Hobson, G. P. Efstafthiou, and A. N. Lasenby, *General Relativity: An Introduction for Physicists* (Cambridge: Cambridge University Press, 2006), 187.

25. "The energy stored in the false vacuum [or the curvature of empty space] became larger and larger as the universe inflated, and was then released when the phase transition took place at the end of the inflationary period[, ... while a]t the same time, however, the energy stored in the cosmic gravitational field—the field by which everything in the universe is attracting everything else—became more and more negative[, ... with the result that t]he total energy of the system was conserved, remaining constant at a value at or near zero." See "Inflationary Universe," *Encyclopedia of Cosmology: Historical, Philosophical, and Scientific Foundations of Modern Cosmology*, ed. Norriss S. Hetherington (New York: Garland Publishing, 1993), 316. "[Any] definition of energy [...] would have to include the energy stored in the gravitational field, which in general relativity means the curvature of space-time." Jon Butterworth, *Smashing Physics* (London: Headline Publishing, 2014), 119–120; reissued as *Most Wanted Particle: The Inside Story of the Hunt for the Higgs, the Heart of the Future of Physics* (New York: The Experiment, 2015). "[O]ur best data prefers a spatially flat universe, and we can expect inflation theory to adapt to these findings[; ... indeed,] now most inflation models result in a flat universe." Joseph Silk, *Horizons of Cosmology: Exploring Worlds Seen and Unseen* (West Consohocken, Pennsylvania: Templeton Press, 2011), 39.

26. "Zero-point energy is the *ground-state mechanical energy* associated with oscillations retained in a matter [...] at zero K at which all thermal motions of the particles of the matter cease [...] in the lowest de Broglie energy state." J. X. Zheng-Johansson and P.-I. Johansson, *Unification of Classical, Quantum, and Relativistic Mechanics and of the Four Forces* (New York: Nova Science Publishers, 2006), 38; emphasis in the original. "Quantum Fluctuations and Zero Point Energy [... is] referred to as the vacuum state, [... or] the state of lowest energy [... that] corresponds to the state for which all the

occupation numbers are zero[, ... but a]lthough no excitations are present, the total energy does not vanish [... and] is a divergent quantity (equal to infinity)." Vlatko Vedral, *Modern Foundations of Quantum Optics* (London: Imperial College Press, 2005), 140. "[A] zero-point energy of the vacuum, [t]hat it is not empty but teeming with virtual particles[, ...] has given rise to [the idea] that Heisenberg's uncertainty principle requires that the vacuum have zero point energy, so that its energy is not zero but finite or perhaps infinitely large." R. Mirman, *Quantum Mechanics, Quantum Field Theory* (Huntington, New York: Nova Science Publishers, 2001), 256–57. Cf. R. B. Dingle, "LI. The Zero-Point Energy of a System of Particles," *The London, Edinburgh, and Dublin Philosophical Magazine and Journal of Science*, Volume 40, No. 304 (London: Taylor and Francis, 15 March 1949), 573–78; doi:10.1080/14786444908521743.

27. "[R]eflecting the unified wave–corpuscle viewpoint at objects of nature[, ... e]ach kind of elementary particle is correlated with the corresponding wave field[, ... whose quantization] means to set up a correspondence between field and discrete energy quanta (we call them 'quanta of the given field')." O. M. Boyarkin, *Advanced Particle Physics: Particles, Fields, and Quantum Electrodynamics*, Volume 1 (Boca Raton, Florida: CRC Press [Taylor and Francis], 2011), 4. "All particles, including elementary particles, are divided into fermions and bosons[, ... where t]he particles of the elementary matter fields are fermions and the interaction carriers of the gauge force fields are bosons." Gordon McCabe, *The Structure and Interpretation of the Standard Model* (Amsterdam: Elsevier, 2007), 6. "Matter fields correspond to particles which at the given level of resolution are assumed to be without structure[, ... such as] fermions (i.e., the leptons and quarks)[, ... representing] vector bundles on Minkowski space-time[, ... wherein then] the matter field is a section of the direct sum of all these vector bundles." Yuri I. Manin, *Gauge Field Theory and Complex Geometry* (Berlin / Heidelberg, Germany: Springer-Verlag, 1988 [1984]), 3. "The wavicles of the electromagnetic and asthenonic fields are photons and asthenons; the wavicles of the [...] electronic field are electrons and positrons[, ... and these] descriptions based on quantum fields make sense of the otherwise mysterious wave–particle dualism of physical quanta." Ugo Amaldi, *Particle Accelerators: From Big Bang Physics to Hadron Therapy* (Cham, Switzerland: Springer International Publishing [Springer Science+Business Media], 2014), 134.

28. Based on "the mean density of ordinary matter in the Universe[, ...] if we 'spread' the matter uniformly in space, one cubic meter would contain only one hydrogen atom." Igor D. Novikov, *Black Holes and the Universe*, trans. Vitaly Kisin (Cambridge: Cambridge University Press, 1990), 131–32. Another reputable, yet even sparser, estimate invites us to "imagine that all matter

would have been scattered evenly through space, making the universe a[n] homogeneous cloud of gas, with an average density of about one hydrogen atom every ten cubic meters." (Nobel laureate) George Smoot and Keay Davidson, *Wrinkles in Time: Witness to the Birth of the Universe* (New York: Harper Collins, 2007 [1993]), 9. According to yet another estimate, however, the Universe's average "density corresponds to about five hydrogen atoms every cubic meter." Neil deGrasse Tyson, Michael Strauss, and J. Richard Gott, *Welcome to the Universe: The Problem Book* (Princeton, New Jersey: Princeton University Press, 2017), 198.

29. As for the "atomic nucleus[, …i]ts diameter is about one hundred-thousandth (10^5) the diameter of the whole atom, so it takes up only one thousand-trillionth (10^{15}) of the atom's volume" Jack Challoner, *The Atom: The Building Block of Everything* (London: Ivy Press, 2018), 38.

30. "The apparent solidity and stability of matter is proof of the existence of other forces, […] such as the magnetic and electrostatic forces." Vincent Icke, *The Force of Symmetry* (Cambridge: Cambridge University Press, 1995), 5. Also, "solidity is […] largely an illusion[, since] like every other form of material substance, it is composed primarily of 'empty space.' The only thing that in reality prevents us from falling through this substrate is the electrostatic repulsion between the particles in our bodies and those in the ground itself." *Conceptual and Contextual Perspectives on the Modern Law of Treaties*, ed. Michael J. Bowman and Dino Kritsiotis (Cambridge: Cambridge University Press, 2018), 1042, citing the quote that "[s]olidity arises when we try to push the cloud of electrons whizzing around the nucleus through the cloud of a neighboring atom." Brian Cox and Jeff Forshaw, *Why Does E=mc2?: (And Why Should We Care?)* (Boston: Da Capo Press [Perseus Books Group], 2009), 107.

31. "The Planck scale corresponds to […] a size of 10^{-35} meters, and a time of 10^{-43} seconds." Dennis D. McCarthy and P. Kenneth Seidelmann, *Time: From Earth Rotation to Atomic Physics* (Cambridge: Cambridge University Press, 2018 [2009]), 126. Furthermore, "these values, [on the order of] 10^{-35} meters for the Planck length and […] 10^{-43} seconds for the Planck interval, are absurdly small quantities." Thomas Grissom, *The Physicist's World: The Story of Motion and the Limits to Knowledge* (Baltimore, Maryland: Johns Hopkins University Press, 2011), 250.

32. "[N]o measurement can be made of distances smaller than the Planck length[, as it] would require the use of probes with a wave length smaller than the Planck length[, which] would result in a total energy exceeding the Planck energy, inside a volume smaller than the Planck volume[, …] all conditions for the occurrence of gravitational collapse[:] A black hole will form[, …] bigger than the Planck length." Gerard 't Hooft, "The Giant Leap

to the Planck Length," *Perspectives on High Energy Physics and Cosmology—Proceedings of the Conference*, ed. Antonio Gonzalez-Arroyo and Cayetano Lopez (Singapore: World Scientific Publishing, 1993), 7. Stated flatly, "[t]here is no distance smaller than the Planck length, no time shorter than the Planck time." Jim Baggott, *The Quantum Story: A History in 40 Moments* (New York: Oxford University Press, 2011), 365. Furthermore, "fluctuations of spacetime curvature make the concept of length meaningless on scales smaller than the Planck [...] length, 10^{-33} centimeters[, ...] so also the curvature fluctuations should make the concept of time meaningless on scales smaller than 10^{-43} second[s]." Kip S. Thorne, *Black Holes and Time Warps: Einstein's Outrageous Legacy* (New York: W. W. Norton and Company, 1994), 518. And to the extent "space is quantised at the level of the Planck length, that is to say that it is not possible to measure a distance less than it[, so t]he very idea of a distance smaller than the Planck length is, in fact, meaningless." Rhodri Evans, *The Cosmic Microwave Background: How It Changed Our Understanding of the Universe* (Cham, Switzerland: Springer International Publishing [Springer Science+Business Media], 2015), 196.

33. "The brain gives a precise representation of what the mind is experiencing[, whereas] Spirituality deals with your state of awareness[, ... and a] message from the liver is just as valid as information sent by the brain, and just as intelligent." Deepak Chopra, *Spiritual Solutions: Answers to Life's Greatest Challenges* (New York: Harmony Books [Random House], 2012), 9–10 and 37.

Chapter 4: The Nature of Illusion or Delusion

1. Wisdom has many parents; the quote is variously attributed to Woody Allen, Franz Kafka, Stephen Hawking, Robert Beauvais, Charles-Maurice de Talleyrand, and many others.

2. "A foolish consistency is the hobgoblin of little minds, adored by little statesmen and philosophers and divines." Ralph Waldo Emerson, "Self-Reliance," *Self-Reliance and Other Essays*, ed. Stanley Applebaum (Mineola, New York: Courier Corporation [Dover Publications], 2012 [1841–44]), 24.

3. "[T]he Upanishads teach that this universe is not the *atman*, the proper 'self' of things, but a mere *maya*, a deception, an illusion, and that the empirical knowledge of it yields no *vidya*, no true knowledge." Paul Deussen, *The Philosophy of the Upanishads* (Edinburgh: T. and T. Clark, 1906), 227; emphasis in the original. "[T]he followers of his [i.e., Kant's] theory were at last forced to fall back [...] on the mere phrase Maya, 'illusion', which turns the supreme lord into a conjurer." Arthur Berriedale Keith, *The Religion and Philosophy of the Veda and Upanishads*, Volume 2, ed. Charles Rockwell Lanman (Cambridge,

Massachusetts: Harvard University Press, 1925), 594. "[T]he upanishads or vedanta […] by and large promoted theism, more pointedly monotheism[, … as] the concept of a single God was the central message of the upanishads[, … though a]ll phenomena animate and inanimate is maya (illusion) which conceals the supreme spirit." S. N. Sadasivan, *A Social History of India* (New Delhi, India: APH Publishing, 2000), 202.

4. "'Illusion' is a misleading rendering of the word '*Maya*' by those who did not know sufficiently Sanskrit or English[; … m]*aya* is not 'illusion' but power." Sir John George Woodroffe and Swami Pratyagatmananda Saraswati, *The World as Power: Power as Matter* (Madras [Chennai], India: Ganesh and Company, 1923), x.

5. "[T]he Indian term for 'illusion,' *maya*—from the verbal root *ma*, 'to measure, to measure out, to form, to create, construct, exhibit or display'— refers to both the power that creates an illusion and the false display itself." Joseph Campbell, *The Mythic Image* (Princeton, New Jersey: Princeton University Press, 1974), 52. Also, the "Sanskrit word *maya* means 'that which is measured (from the root *ma*, 'to measure,' 'to give form,' 'to limit')." Astrid Fitzgerald, *Being Consciousness Bliss: A Seeker's Guide* (Great Barrington, Massachusetts: Lindisfarne Books, 2001), 54. "*Maya* comes from the Sanskrit root *ma*, meaning 'to measure,' 'mete out' or 'mark off' [… and] is the illusion inherent in the world, by which we constantly seek to limit the limitless." *The Uddhava Gita: The Final Teaching of Krishna*, trans. Swami Ambikananda Saraswati (Berkeley, California: Seastone [Ulysses Press], 2002 [2000]), 52.

6. "[T]he essence, or true Self, or Atman, of each of us is ultimately identical with the one Reality, Brahman, the nature of which is eternal, unimpeded […] consciousness." *Philosophy of Religion: Indian Philosophy*, ed. Roy W. Perrett (New York: Routledge, 2001), 77. Bringing it all together, "[o]ur true Self (Atman) is […] the higher consciousness which transcends ego [and thus] is connected to all created consciousness." Richard L. Corliss, *Making Sense of Religion: A Study of World Religions and Theology* (Eugene, Oregon: Wipf and Stock Publishers, 2014), 165.

7. Arthur Schopenhauer, *Parerga and Paralipomena: Short Philosophical Essays*, Volume 1, trans. and ed. E. F. J. Payne (Oxford: Clarendon Press, 2000), 12.

8. Arthur Schopenhauer, *The World as Will and Representation*, Volume 1, trans. E. F. J. Payne (New York: Dover Publications, 2012 [1958; 1966]), 3.

9. Ibid., Volume 3, 395.

10. "[T]he thing-in-itself, the will-to-live, exists whole and undivided in every being." Schopenhauer, *Parerga and Paralipomena*, Volume 2, 221.

11. "[T]he manifestation of the will [is] the thing in itself[, which] allow[s] an idea of things and of the world to precede their actual existence[; ...] desire [...] is clearly an affection of the will [...] which, if it take outward effect, exhibits itself as an act of will proper." Schopenhauer, *World as Will/ Idea*, Volume 2, 180 and 412.

12. Spencer, *First Principles*, 48.

13. Ibid., 145; Part 2, Chapter 2, Section 43.

14. Frederic B. Fitch, "A Logical Analysis of Some Value Concepts," *Journal of Symbolic Logic*, Volume 28, No. 2 (Storrs, Connecticut: Association for Symbolic Logic,June 1963), 135–42; doi:10.2307/2271594.

15. "[T]he scientific method is the basis of science [... and is] braced by immutable pillars, such as by knowability and objectivity." Sophie C. Lewis, *A Changing Climate for Science* (Cham, Switzerland: Palgrave Macmillan [Springer Nature], 2017), 4.

16. "[A]ssume a principle of quantization of information: An elementary system is the manifestation of one bit of information." Johannes Kofler and Anton Zeilinger, "Quantum Information and Randomness," *European Review*, Volume 18, No. 4 (Cambridge: Cambridge University Press, 2010), 474; doi:10.1017/S1062798710000268. The point is originally made in an earlier article. Anton Zeilinger, "A Foundational Principle for Quantum Mechanics," *Foundations of Physics*, Volume 29, No. 4 (New York: Springer Science+Business Media, April 1999), 631–43; doi:10.1023/A:101882041.

17. "A qubit is the smallest unit of information in a quantum computer." Shabnam Siddiqui, *Quantum Mechanics: A Simplified Approach* (Boca Raton, Florida: CRC Press [Taylor and Francis], 2019), 212.

18. "[A] particle can exhibit wave properties, [... and according to] the famous probabilistic interpretation of the wave function[, one can envision a particle] 'probability cloud' [...] for an electron." Moses Fayngold and Vadim Fayngold, *Quantum Mechanics and Quantum Information: A Guide through the Quantum World (Physics Textbook)* (Weinheim, Germany: Wiley-VCH, 2013), 396. Furthermore, given "the probabilistic nature of quantum mechanics[, ... t]he electron is not a particle but a fuzzy probability cloud described by Schrödinger's wave." Valerie Calderbank, *Cruising the Cosmos* (East Haney, UK: Calderbank Books, 2018), 117.

19. Werner Heisenberg, "The Representation of Nature in Contemporary Physics," *Daedalus*, Volume 87, No. 3 (Cambridge, Massachusetts: MIT Press [American Academy of Arts and Sciences], 1958), 99–100.

20. Heisenberg, "The Representation of Nature," 100.

21. "[T]he [conscious] proposition *I think* precedes the experience that is to determine the object of perception through the category in regard to time." Immanuel Kant, *Critique of Pure Reason*, trans. Werner S. Pluhar (Indianapolis, Indiana: Hackett Publishing, 1966 [1787]), 435; B423, emphasis in the original. "[E]ven *unity of synthesis* of the manifold outside or within us, and hence also a *combination* to which everything that is to be presented determinately in space or time must conform, is already given a priori as condition of the synthesis of all *apprehension*[, ...] conforming to the categories but applied to our *sensible intuition*, of the manifold of a given *intuition as such* in an original consciousness." Ibid., 198; B161, emphasis in the original.

22. "[A]ll things which exist [...] can never cease to be, unless God [H]imself, by refusing [H]is concurrence to them, reduce them to nothing." René Descartes, *The Meditations, and Selections from the Principles of Philosophy*, trans. John Veitch (Edinburgh: Sutherland and Knox, 1853 [1641]), 13; Meditation 2: Of the Nature of the Human Mind.

23. "You can't get to a time before the Big Bang because there was no time before the Big Bang." Stephen Hawking, *Brief Answers to the Big Questions* (New York: Bantam Books, 2018), 37.

24. "[T]he five senses—visual/sight, tactile/touch, auditory/hearing, gustatory/taste, olfactory/smell." *Handbook of Remotivation Therapy*, ed. Jean A. Dyer and Michael L. Stotts (Philadelphia, Pennsylvania: Haworth Press, 2005), 130. See also the online article "Sight, Sound, Smell, Taste, and Touch: How the Human Body Receives Sensory Information," *VisibleBody.com* (Newton, Massachusetts: Argosy Publishing/Visible Body, ca. 27 March 2018) at **https://www.visiblebody.com/learn/nervous/five-senses**, accessed December 12, 2019.

25. John M. Henshaw, *A Tour of the Senses: How Your Brain Interprets the World* (Baltimore, Maryland: Johns Hopkins University Press, 2012), 10.

26. Claudia Krebs, Joanne Weinberg, and Elizabeth Akesson, *(Lippincott's Illustrated Review of) Neuroscience* (Hong Kong: Lippincott Williams and Wilkins, 2012), 303.

27. "Located on the dorsal surface of the superior temporal gyrus, the primary auditory cortex shows tonotopic organization for the processing of sound [... and] equilibrium." William W. Orrison, *Atlas of Brain Function* (New York: Thieme Medical Publishers, 2008), 5; the "Auditory cortex" entry in Glossary of Structures and Definitions. "[T]he control of equilibrium [... and] conscious awareness of vestibular sensation [... along an] ascending auditory pathway [... is] situated on the dorsal surface of the superior temporal gyrus."

Alan R. Crossman and David Neary, *Neuroanatomy: An Illustrated Colour Text* (London: Churchill Livingston [Elsevier], 2002 [1995]), 112.

28. "Olfactory receptor cells [...] help to differentiate among odors [... via] the olfactory complex of the brain[, while s]ensory adaptation is the ability to ignore unimportant [or enhance relevant] stimuli." Jahangir Moini, *Anatomy and Physiology for Health Professionals* (Burlington, Massachusetts: Jones and Bartlett Learning [Ascend Learning], 2016), 317. For more on "precise discrimination of olfactory signals from the environment," see "Cortical Feedback Decorrelates Olfactory Bulb Output in Awake Mice," *Neuron* (Cambridge, Massachusetts: U.S. Cell Press [Elsevier], 17 June 2015), Volume 86, No. 6, 1461–77; doi:10.1016/j.neuron.2015.05.023.

29. Edith Applegate, *The Anatomy and Physiology Learning System* (St. Louis, Missouri: Saunders [Elsevier], 2011 [1995]), 203–4. Cf. Sharon Rady Rolfes, Kathryn Pinna, and Ellie Whitney, *Understanding Normal and Clinical Nutrition* (Belmont, California: Wadsworth [CENGAGE Learning], 2012 [2009]), 388; *Health and Safety Aspects of Food Processing Technologies*, ed. Abdul Malik, Zerrin Erginkaya, and Hüseyin Erten (Cham, Switzerland: Springer Nature, 2019), 40. Peter Macinnis, *Poisons: From Hemlock to Botox to the Killer Bean of Calabar* (New York:Arcade Publishing, 2004–5), 88; Danielle Renee Reed and Antti Knaapila, "Genetics of Taste and Smell: Poisons and Pleasures," *Progress in Molecular Biology and Translational Science*, Volume 94 (San Diego, California: Elsevier Academic Press, 2010), 213–40, doi:10.1016/B978-0-12-375003-7.00008-X; and Paul Robert, *The End of Food* (New York: Houghton Mifflin, 2008), 84.

30. "Transcranial magnetic stimulation of the posterior parietal cortex [...] demonstrates a direct role of the parietal lobe in modulating tactile perception." T. Ro, et al., "Visual Enhancing of Tactile Perception in The Posterior Parietal Cortex," *Journal of Cognitive Neuroscience*, Volume 16, No. 1 (Cambridge, Massachusetts: MIT Press, January/February 2004), 24–30; doi:10.1162/0898929042322755520.

31. In speaking of the "broad spectrum of functional localizations in [...] the brain" related to perception, "[i]nteroception works along with proprioception and exteroception to provide [inputs to] the brain." Giovanni Berlucchi and Salvatore M. Aglioti, "The Body in the Brain Revisited," *Experimental Brain Research*, Volume 200, No. 25 (New York: Springer Science+Business Media, 19 August 2009); doi:10.1007/s00221-009-1970-7. Cf. Erik Ceunen, Johan W. S. Vlaeyen, and Ilse Van Diest, "On the Origin of Interoception," *Frontiers in Psychology*, Volume 7, No. 743 (Lausanne, Switzerland: Frontiers Media, 23 May 2016); doi:10.3389/fpsyg.2016.00743.

32. "[T]he first production of a living organism [... might have taken place] in some warm little pond." Charles Darwin, "Letter to Joseph Hooker," as a

footnote in *The Life and Letters of Charles Darwin*, Volume 2, ed. Sir Francis Darwin (New York: D. Appleton and Company, 1887 [1 February 1871]), 202–3. Ironically, this concept evolved into that of a primordial soup, first delineated in a not widely published, 1924 Soviet book and independently in a brief 1929 English journal article. A. I. Oparin, *The Origin of Life*, trans. Sergius Morgulis (New York: The Macmillan Company, 1938), being a revision of that initial 1924 work later translated in 1967 by Ann Synge; and J. B. S. Haldane, "The Origin of Life," *The Rationalist Annual*, Volume 148 (London: Watts and Company, 1929), 3–10.

33. Emily Monosson, *Evolution in a Toxic World: How Life Responds to Chemical Threats* (Washington, D.C.: Island Press [Center for Resource Economics], 2012). Cf. John Raven and Keith Skene, "Chemistry of the Early Oceans: The Environment of Early Life," *Evolution on Planet Earth: Impact of the Physical Environment*, ed. Lynn Rothschild and Adrian Lister (Academic Press [Elsevier], London and San Diego, California, 2003), 55–64; and Robert J. P. Williams, "The Natural Selection of the Chemical Elements," *Cellular and Molecular Life Sciences* Volume 53, No. 10 (Basel, Switzerland: Springer Science+Business Media, October 1997), 816–29, doi:10.1007/s000180050102.

34. Rodolfo R. Llinas, "Chapter 5: Lessons from the Evolution of the Eye," *i of the Vortex: From Neurons to Self* (Cambridge, Massachusetts: MIT Press, 2001), 93–109. Conservatively, "it would take [no more than] 364,000 generations for a [cupped] fish eye to evolve," from which a vertebrate, lens-based pinhole eye could later emerge. Dan-Eric Nilsson and Susanne Pelger, "A Pessimistic Estimate of the Time Required for an Eye to Evolve," *Proceedings of the Royal Society of London B*, Volume 256, No. 1345 (London: The Royal Society, 22 April 1994), 53–58; doi:10.1098/rspb.1994.0048.

35. "Vision is the primary sensory modality in primates such as ourselves[, … as] reflected in the complexity of the visual system and the extent of the cerebral cortex used for the analysis of visual information." Martin J. Tovée, *An Introduction to the Visual System* (Cambridge: Cambridge University Press, 1996), 59. Cf. Thomas Politzer, O.D. and former president of the Neuro-Optometric Rehabilitation Association, "Vision Is Our Dominant Sense," *BrainLine.org* (Washington, D.C.: WETA, 6 November 2008) at **https://www.brainline.org/article/vision-our-dominant-sense**, accessed January 10, 2020.

36. "Sound vibrations [out of the air] bend the cilia, which causes the [ear's] membrane potential to change—thus transducing sound into a neural signal[—so that w]hen a particular portion of the basilar membrane bulges upward, the cilia on hair cells attached to that particular area are stimulated, and ultimately, sound of a particular pitch is perceived." Kevin T. Patton and

Gary A. Thibodeau, *Anatomy and Physiology* (St. Louis, Missouri: Elsevier, 2016 [1987]), 539.

37. For a general discussion of how sight and sound as survival mechanisms factor into the evolution of mammals specifically, see Doris M. Kermack and Kenneth A. Kermack, "Chapter 6: The Evolution of Mammalian Sight and Hearing," *The Evolution of Mammalian Characters* (Sydney, Australia: Croom Helm, 1984), 89–99.

38. Our senses are truly limited (e.g., humans hear only sounds between 12 Hz and 28 kHz), and while that fact alone does not necessarily make our perceptions inherently unreliable, optical illusions and mistaken naked-eye observations support the fallibility of the senses and how the brain, honed for survival by evolution, fills in the gaps to avoid potential threats. An example of a disturbing optical phenomenon is the famous Adelson Checker-Shadow illusion on *IllusionsIndex.org* (Glasgow, Scotland: University of Glasgow's Centre for the Study of Perceptual Experience, ca. 1 November 2017) at **https://www.illusionsindex.org/ir/checkershadow**, accessed January 11, 2020. Also, mistaken observations might include how the earth appears motionless as the sun moves across the sky. Or, consider how the brain ignores sensory input for the sake of processing more information than it can handle—refer to Arien Mack and Irvin Rock, *Inattentional Blindness* (Cambridge, Massachusetts: MIT Press, 1998); and note how the brain's "amygdala receives input directly from the senses, so its responses are designed to be fast, not accurate" from Sandra Aamodt and Sam Wang, *Welcome to Your Brain: Why You Lose Your Car Keys but Never Forget How to Drive and Other Puzzles of Everyday Life* (New York: Bloomsbury Publishing, 2008), 2. The mere fact that our perceptions are subjective further renders them unreliable until they are or can be objectively corroborated.

39. J. Kevin O'Regan and Alva Noë, "A Sensorimotor Account of Vision and Visual Consciousness," *Behavioral and Brain Sciences*, Volume 24, No. 5 (Cambridge: Cambridge University Press, October 2001), 939–73; doi:10.1017/S0140525X01000115. Cf. in the same issue, Paul Bach-y-Rita and Steven J. Hasse, "The Role of the Brain in Perception," *Behavioral and Brain Sciences*, Volume 24, No. 5 (Cambridge: Cambridge University Press, October 2001): 975 et seq.; doi:10.1017/S0140525X01240114.

40. "The retina contains two types of light receptors[:] the rods and the cones [that] contain pigments which are broken up when light falls upon them [... and which] send impulses [... through] the axons of the ganglion cells [... from] the eyeball via the optic nerve and go to the brain." D. F. Horrobin, *Essential Physiology* (Lancaster, England: MTP Press, 1973), 42. Once "the light [...] reach[es] the retina, it [...] activate[s] the rods and cones of the

retina, which will send a nerve signal via the optic nerve to the occipital lobe of the brain." Steven Bassett, *CliffsStudySolver: Anatomy and Physiology* (Hoboken, New Jersey: Wiley Publishing, 2005), 198.

41. "[C]ones […] require about 1000 times more light than rods[, … which] are very sensitive to changes in light intensity caused, for example, by something moving; this ability is potentially vital because that 'something' could be an enemy or predator[; moreover, s]ensory information from rods and cones passes to the brain via the optic nerve." Michael Kent, *Advanced Biology* (Kuala Lumpur, Malaysia: Oxford University Press, 2000), 204.

42. "Light rays strike the retina, forming an image that is upside down; the sensitive nerves of the retina send this inverted impulse to the brain through the optic nerve[, so t]he brain 'sees' the inverted image as right side up." Edward P. Ortleb and Richard Cadice, *The Human Body* (Dayton, Ohio: Milliken Publishing, 1986), iv. A fascinating example of the human brain's neuroplasticity with regard to the eye's inverted imagery is an experiment involving a pair of reversing eyeglasses; after four days of continuously wearing the eyeglasses, the brain's interpretation of the inverted vision adapts, and remarkably, from then on, the imagery flips right-side up. George M. Stratton, "Some Preliminary Experiments on Vision without Inversion of the Retinal Image," *Psychological Review*, Volume 3, No. 6 (Washington, D.C.: American Psychological Association, 1896), 611–17; doi:10.1037/h0072918.

43. Gavin Buckingham and Melvyn Goodale, "When the Predictive Brain Gets It Really Wrong," *Behavioral and Brain Sciences*, Volume 36, No. 3 (New York: Cambridge University Press, May 2013), 28–29; doi:10.1017/S0140525X12002233.

44. Jan Dirk Blom, *A Dictionary of Hallucinations* (New York: Springer Science+Business Media, 2010), 32. See also, William Pryse-Phillips, *Companion to Clinical Neurology* (New York: Oxford University Press, 2009), 62.

45. Space and time collectively "concerns only the pure form of intuition and hence includes no sensation whatever (nothing empirical); and all kinds and determinations of space [and time] are capable of being presented a priori[, … and through them] alone is it possible for things to be external objects for us." Kant, *Critique of Pure Reason*, 83; A29. Despite this indication, it is controversial to interpret that Kant regarded space and time as "mere constructs" because, as noted, he acknowledges their "empirical reality," while also choosing to "assert their transcendental ideality" in his philosophy; the interpretation is bolstered by his denial of "their absolute reality."

46. "[T]he spacetime-interval […] is a combination of distances in space and in time [that] measures the spacetime distance between events [a]nd

is invariant." Bernard Schutz, *Gravity from the Ground Up: An Introductory Guide to Gravity and General Relativity* (Cambridge: Cambridge University Press, 2003), 217. Moreover, "time cannot be separated from space." Edwin F. Taylor and John Archibald Wheeler, *Spacetime Physics* (New York: W. H. Freeman and Company, 1992), 7.

47. "[It] is now, all together, one [and] continuous [...n]or is it divisible." Parmenides, *Parmenides of Elea: Fragments*, trans. David Gallop (Toronto: University of Toronto Press, 1991), 67–68; *On Nature*, fragments 8.5–6 and 8.22.

48. "Eternalists accept what is known as the B-theory of time[, which] is the view that the world is a static block of events ordered by the earlier than, later than, and simultaneous with, relations." *A Companion to the Philosophy of Time*, ed. Heather Dyke and Adrian Bardon (Chichester, England: John Wiley and Sons, 2013), 347.

49. Julian Barbour, *The End of Time: The Next Revolution in Physics* (New York: Oxford University Press, 2001), 18–19, 141.

50. René Descartes, *Principles of Philosophy*, Part 2, Article XVIII, trans. John Veitch (New York: Start Publishing, LLC [Simon and Schuster], 2012 [1644]), 53.

51. The "little argument, advanced by Melissus, [... observes that saying] 'There is vacuum in this flask' [... actually] means the same as 'There is nothing in this flask.'" C. J. F. Williams, "The Ontological Disproof of the Vacuum," *Philosophy*, Volume 59, No. 229 (Cambridge: Cambridge University Press [Royal Institute of Philosophy], July 1984), 382–84; doi:10.1017/ S0031819100069977, citing fragment 7.7: "Nor is there any void, for void is nothing, and nothing cannot be" from W. K. C. Guthrie, *A History of Greek Philosophy*, Volume 2 (Cambridge: Cambridge University Press, 1965), 104. "Since a vacuum was considered to be absolutely empty, the innocent observation that 'there is a vacuum in this flask' was seen as a contradiction, since, as Melissus said, 'A void is nothing, and nothing cannot be,' so how could there be something that doesn't exist in the flask?" Ronald Green, *Nothing Matters* (Alresford, England: Iff Books [John Hunt Publishing], 2011), 220. "Melissus is right[: ...] The vacuum in my flask is not a part of my flask any more than the water in a bucket is a part of the bucket." Jonathan Barnes, *The Presocratic Philosophers* (London and New York: Routledge [Taylor and Francis], 1982 [1979]), 172.

52. One must interpret the concession by not taking his words literally, that he cannot have meant an impossible result, as in: "Melissus [in fragment B7.7] rejects [the concept of the void], then points out that without void, motion is not possible." *The Oxford Handbook of Presocratic Philosophy*, ed. Patricia

Curd and Daniel W. Graham (New York: Oxford University Press, 2008), 343. Other interpretations focus on an anti-materialist stance, as in: "The only way to explain movement, Melissus is saying [in fragment F6], is to assume the existence of void and matter to move into the void; but in fact there is no such thing as void, nor as movement, and so we have no need to think of what-is as corporeal." *The First Philosophers: The Presocratics and Sophists*, ed. and trans. Robin Waterfield (New York: Oxford University Press, 2000), 83. The literal words are there, however, in the following fragments. B7.7: "Nor does it [i.e., what-is] move, for it does not have anywhere to withdraw to [... such as] the void[, b]ut since there is no void, it does not have any place to withdraw to." *The Oxford Handbook of Presocratic Philosophy*, 343. "[T]here exists no empty space in which [an infinite being] can move, since such a space, if it existed, would be an existing nothing." Friedrich Ueberweg, *History of Philosophy*, Volume 1: History of the Ancient and Mediaeval Philosophy, ed. Henry B. Smith and Philip Schaff (London: Hodder and Stoughton, 1872), 59–60.

53. "[T]here are 10^{79} protons and as many electrons in the universe." Arthur Eddington, *New Pathways in Science: Messenger Lectures (1934)* (Cambridge: Cambridge University Press, 1935), 221. And also "10^{80} is roughly found for the total number of nucleons in the Universe [...] by multiplying the estimated mass density of the Universe by the cube of Hubble's length and then divid[ing] by the proton's mass." Marcelo Samuel Berman, *Introduction to General Relativistic and Scalar-Tensor Cosmologies* (Hauppauge, New York: Nova Science Publishers, 2007), 123.

54. Adam G. Riess, et al., "A 2.4% Determination of the Local Value of the Hubble Constant," *The Astrophysical Journal*, Volume 826, No. 1 (Philadelphia, Pennsylvania: IOP Publishing [Institute of Physics], 10 June 2016), 56; doi:10.3847/0004-637X/826/1/56. Some studies contradict that the expansion is accelerating. See Jeppe T. Nielsen, Alberto Guffanti, and Subir Sarkar, "Marginal Evidence for Cosmic Acceleration from Type Ia Supernovae," *Scientific Reports*, Volume 6 (London: Springer Nature, 21 October 2016); Article 35596, doi:10.1038/srep35596.

55. "[I]magine that your entire worldline from birth to death was contained in the absolute elsewhere." Pieter Thyssen, "Conventionality and Reality," *Foundations of Physics*, Volume 49, No. 12 (Cham, Switzerland: Springer Nature, December 2019), 1336–54; doi:10.1007/s10701-019-00294-8; citing an objection to eternalism by Steven F. Savitt, "There's No Time Like the Present (in Minkowski Spacetime)," *Philosophy of Science*, Volume 67, No. 3 (Chicago: The University of Chicago Press, September 2000), S563–74; doi:10.1086/392846.

56. "[T]he differential geometry of an arbitrary world line in flat Minkowski spacetime is given by a covariant set of Serret-Frenet equations, which are differential equations (in proper time) of a set of four covariant unit vectors which form an orthonormal set at any point along the curve." M. A. Trump and W. C. Schieve, *Classical Relativistic Many-Body Dynamics* (Dordrecht, Netherlands: Springer Science+Business Media, 1999), 325.

57. Internet comment by Xaqron (**https://philosophy.stackexchange.com/users/3191/xaqron**), *Stack Overflow* (New York: Stack Exchange, 19 February 2013) at **https://philosophy.stackexchange.com/questions/6096/what-was-the-impact-of-the-discovery-of-non-euclidean-geometry-on-kantian-though**, accessed October 6, 2017. Also, the "precession [is ...] something like 4 seconds of arc per century in the case of the earth" from Richard Feynman, *Feynman Lectures On Gravitation*, ed. Brian Hatfield (Boca Raton, Florida: CRC Press [Taylor and Francis], 2018 [Pasadena, California: California Institute of Technology, 1995]), 73.

58. "[T]ime is unreal." John McTaggart Ellis McTaggart, *The Nature of Existence*, Volume 2, ed. C. D. Broad (Cambridge: Cambridge University Press, 1988), 9.

59. John Earman, "Tracking Down Gauge: An Ode to the Constrained Hamiltonian Formalism," in *Symmetries in Physics: Philosophical Reflections*, ed. Katherine Brading and Elena Castellani (Cambridge: Cambridge University Press, 2003), 152. Cited by Michael Silberstein, W. M. Stuckey, and Timothy McDevitt, *Beyond the Dynamical Universe: Unifying Block Universe Physics and Time as Experienced* (New York: Oxford University Press, 2018), 58.

60. "The notion of a [temporal] 'velocity' of one hour per hour, for example, is troubling." *The Oxford Handbook of Philosophy of Time*, ed. Craig Callender (Oxford: Oxford University Press, 2011), 72. For a contrary view, see Tim Maudlin, "Remarks on the Passing of Time," *Proceedings of the Aristotelian Society*, New Series, Volume 102 (London: Oxford University Press, 2002), 259–274.

61. Barbour, *End of Time*, 4.

62. Ibid., 313.

63. "[M]olecules themselves are not hot entities, but their movement generates heat[, ... as t]he temperature of a gas [or any substance in another state of matter] is reduced to the average kinetic energy of its molecules." Richard H. Jones, *Reductionism: Analysis and the Fullness of Reality* (Cranbury, New Jersey: Associated University Presses, 2000), 13.

64. "[E]lectrons cannot emit or absorb electromagnetic radiation in arbitrary amounts[, … which] would force the electron to move to an orbit that [is not allowed … or to] cross the space between the orbits [that are permitted; … instead, t]hey simply appear or disappear within the allowed states[:] a phenomenon referred to as a quantum leap or quantum jump[, … and thus, s]ince the orbits are discrete and quantized, so are their energies." Tatjana Jevremovic, *Nuclear Principles in Engineering* (New York: Springer Science+Business Media, 2005), 27.

65. "[A]n electron jumps to a higher orbit when it absorbs a photon, and falls back to a lower orbit when it emits a photon[: …] The event is called a *quantum leap* or *quantum jump*[; … however,] instead of thinking of electrons as microscopic planets circling the nucleus, we now see them as probability waves sloshing around the orbits like water in some kind of doughnut-shaped tidal pool, governed by SCHRÖDINGER'S EQUATION." James Trefil, *The Nature of Science: An A-Z Guide to the Laws and Principles Governing Our Universe* (Boston: Houghton Mifflin Harcourt, 2003), 51; emphasis in the original. When the "probability function [of the electron, or rather, …] its mathematical representation[, …] has undergone [some kind of] discontinuous change[, …] we speak of a 'quantum jump.'" Karoly Simonyi, *A Cultural History of Physics*, trans. David Kramer (Boca Raton, Florida: CRC Press [Taylor and Francis], 2012), 469.

66. "The height of a wave function at some point, so says quantum theory, determines how often one would take this place as the actual position of the particle[, … or i]n mathematical terms, this distribution is a probability[, …] deriving from the individual results for all points in space the shape of the wave function." Martin Bojowald, *Once Before Time: A Whole Story of the Universe* (New York: Alfred A. Knopf [Random House], 2010), 48; originally published, in German, as *Zurück vor den Urknall: Die ganze Geschichte des Universums* (Frankfurt, Germany: S. Fischer Verlag GmbH, 2009).

67. "Wormholes […] are also allowed by the equations of general relativity which give a description of them as theoretical entities[, …b]ut, unlike black holes, wormholes remain theoretical curiosities." Jim Al-Khalili, *Black Holes, Wormholes and Time Machines* (New York: Taylor and Francis, 1999), 196. Furthermore, "[w]ormholes have been introduced in physics by Wheeler[, … and each] consists of a throat (corridor) connecting two holes in asymptotically flat space[, … where] the throat of the wormhole pinches off so quickly that it cannot be traversed even by light." I. D. Novikov, "Physics in the Presence of a Time Machine," *2001: A Relativistic Spacetime Odyssey*, ed. Ignazio Ciufolini, Daniele Dominici, and Luca Lusanna (Singapore: World Scientific Publishing, 2003), 89.

68. "Solid particles [like electrons or photons] have a wave nature[, …] but do not actually exist as real entities in real places until they are observed, and they aren't observed until they hit the […] detection." Robert Lanza, *Beyond Biocentrism: Rethinking Time, Space, Consciousness, and the Illusion of Death* (Dallas, Texas: Ben-Bella Books, 2016), 49.

69. Conversely, since no iteratively generated subset of an infinite set can ever be finite, it stands to reason that no inverse function can transform a finite set into an infinite one, which is borne out by noting that the "fundamental observation of Dedekind is that when you say that S is an infinite set you are implying the existence of a reflection […] of S which maps it on a proper subset S'[, … which] by the same reflection, S' is mapped onto S", and S" onto S‴, and so on[, … wherein all] are infinite." Arie Hinkis, *Proofs of the Cantor-Bernstein Theorem* (Basel, Switzerland: Birkhäuser [Springer Basel], 2013), 91.

70. "[E]ach universe [in the multiverse] may [… be] governed by different laws (and with different physical constants) from other members of the ensemble." Martin J. Rees, "Life in Our Universe and Others: A Cosmological Perspective," *Many Worlds: The New Universe, Extraterrestrial Life, and the Theological Implications*, ed. Steven J. Dick (Philadelphia, Pennsylvania: Templeton Foundation Press, 2000), 76.

71. "If the universe has no edge, then it cannot have a center." Michael A. Seeds and Dana E. Backman, *Horizons: Exploring the Universe* (Belmont, California [Boston]: Brooks/Cole [CENGAGE Learning], 2008), 297. The implication that a no-edge universe must therefore be infinite ignores at least two countervailing facts. As it relates to refuting the so-called "Stoic cosmos" model—the idea of unoccupied space residing outside any potential edge of a matter-filled universe—because such a universe would collapse into a gravity well appears not to take account of dark-matter and dark-energy forces propelling the Universe's accelerating expansion. Furthermore, with a truly unbounded "spherical geometry[, however, …] the Universe is finite— and at the same time, it has no edge." George Greenstein, *Understanding the Universe: An Inquiry Approach to Astronomy and the Nature of Scientific Research*, (Cambridge: Cambridge University Press, 2013), 542.

72. "Dark matter is [solely] detectable by its gravitational influence, but appears neither to emit nor absorb light nor any other form of electromagnetic radiation [… and while s]ome of the dark matter may be dense, non-luminous, baryonic matter, […] much of the dark matter is non-baryonic." See "The Milky Way - Our Galaxy," *An Introduction to Galaxies and Cosmology*, ed. Mark H. Jones and Robert J. Lambourne (Cambridge: Cambridge University Press, 2004), 10. "[T]he dark matter hypothesis: [… T]he matter content of the Universe is dominated by an unseen, non-luminous substance that interacts

with ordinary matter, protons, neutrons and electrons, primarily through the force of gravity." Robert H. Sanders, *The Dark Matter Problem: A Historical Perspective* (New York: Cambridge University Press, 2010), 1. "[D]ark matter candidates are hypothetical particles that move slowly, such as WIMPs (weakly interacting massive particles) that hardly interact with normal matter except through their gravitational attraction." Bradley W. Carroll and Dale A. Ostlie, *An Introduction to Modern Astrophysics* (Cambridge: Cambridge University Press, 2017), 1233. Dark matter does not "appear to interact with regular matter[, … nor does it] appear to interact with other dark matter either[; … moreover,] dark matter seems to interact through only one of [the four fundamental focres]: gravity[, … meaning] possible candidates include neutrinos, axions, the gravatino, MACHOs, and WIMPs." Kristi Lew, *Dark Matter Explained* (New York: Enslow Publishing, 2019), 45.

73. "[A]ll laws of physics break down or become totally inapplicable either at the initial singularity or at Planck Time[, … and, as John Wheeler puts it, 'w]ith the collapse of space and time the framework falls down for everything one ever called a law of physics.'" Rem B. Edwards, *What Caused the Big Bang?* (Amsterdam: Rodopi, 2001), 4. "The laws of physics are useless to say what would emerge from the singularity[, … because a]t that singularity all our laws of physics break down[, … and the fact that a]ny sort of universe could come out of a singularity [… means t]here would be no way to predict that it would be a universe like ours[; … furthermore,] in imaginary time there would be no singularity at the origin of the universe where the laws of physics as we know them would break down." Kitty Ferguson, *Stephen Hawking: An Unfettered Mind* (New York: Palgrave Macmillan [St. Martin's Press], 2012), 64, 103, and 155. Viewed another way, "a singularity [… is] a region of infinite density and space-time curvature where the laws of physics break down." Jim Baggott, *The Quantum Story: A History in 40 Moments* (New York: Oxford University Press, 2011), 373.

74. "Right after the Big Bang, the expansion rate [… of inflation] is almost infinite, so galaxies were flying apart at that time faster than the speed of light." Q. Ho-Kim, N. Kumar, and C. S. Lam, *Invitation to Contemporary Physics* (Singapore: World Scientific Publishing, 2004), 401. "Within 10^{-30} second, the universe enlarged by a factor of at least 10^{25} in every direction[, … and i]t expanded at an accelerated rate, pulling regions of space apart faster than the speed of light." Paul J. Steinhardt, "The Inflation Debate: Is the Theory at the Heart of Modern Cosmology Deeply Flawed?" in *Scientific American*, Volume 304, No. 4 (New York: Nature Research [Springer Nature], April 2011), 39. "In the standard big bang theory, however, the universe evolves so quickly that it is impossible for the uniformity [of temperature] to be created by any physical process […] but is instead a direct consequence of

the principle that no information can propagate faster than the speed of light." Alan H. Guth, "The Big Bang and Cosmic Inflation," *The Oskar Klein Memorial Lectures*, Volume 2, ed. Gösta Ekspong (Singapore: World Scientific Publishing, 1994), 42. One essentially untestable hypothesis that sidesteps violating the limit involves VSL, or the "variable speed of light" over time, allowing inflation to occur with a different lightspeed limit than permitted under the current one. John W. Moffat, "Superluminary Universe: a Possible Solution to the Initial Value Problem in Cosmology," *International Journal of Modern Physics D*, Volume 2, No. 3 (Singapore: World Scientific, 1993), 351–65, doi:10.1142/S0218271893000246; and John W. Moffat, "Quantum Gravity, the Origin of Time and Time's Arrow," *Foundations of Physics*, Volume 23, No. 3 (New York: Springer, March 1993), 411–37; doi:10.1007/BF01883721. A less-controversial explanation posits that "inflation can be thought of as the mechanism that 'launched' the big bang[, … yet i]n the inflationary universe, space itself expands faster than the speed of light[, … and] Einstein's theory of relativity permits space to expand faster than the speed of light; it only restricts the transmission of information *through* space to a speed no greater than that of light[, … and importantly,] the expansion of space does not allow particles to pass each other [at all, at any speed]." Jay M. Pasachoff and Alex Filippenko, *The Cosmos: Astronomy in the New Millennium* (New York: Cambridge University Press, 2001), 528.

75. "[T]he big bang happened everywhere [… and] was not a bomb going off at a particular spot that we can identify as the center of the explosion[; …] in the balloon analogy, there is no special place on the surface of the balloon that is the center of the expansion." Charles H. Lineweaver and Tamara M. Davis, "Misconceptions about the Big Bang," *Scientific American*, Volume 292, No. 3 (New York: Nature Research [Springer Nature], March 2005), 37; doi:10.1038/scientificamerican0305-36. Cf. Alan Guth and Paul Steinhardt, "The Inflationary Universe (1997)," *The New Physics*, ed. by Paul Davies (Cambridge: Cambridge University Press, 1989), 34–60.

76. "Dark energy is distinguished from ordinary matter species such as baryons and radiation, in the sense that it has a negative pressure[, … and t]his negative pressure leads to the accelerated expansion of the Universe by counteracting the gravitational force." Luca Amendola and Shinji Tsujikawa, *Dark Energy: Theory and Observations* (Cambridge: Cambridge University Press, 2010), 1. "Positive dark energy will lead to *exponential* expansion; the Universe will expand forever with (almost) constant acceleration[, … meaning that] the nature of dark energy [represents] the precise reason for the accelerated expansion of the Universe at present)." Dmitry S. Gorbunov and Valery A. Rubako, *Introduction to the Theory of the Early Universe: Hot Big Bang Theory* (Singapore: World Scientific Publishing, 2011), 19; emphasis in the original.

"A key element of the New Standard Cosmology is dark energy, the causative agent for accelerated expansion[; … accordingly, d]ark energy is my term for the causative agent of the current epoch of accelerated expansion." Michael S. Turner, "Dark Energy and the New Cosmology," *arXiv preprint* (Ithaca, New York: Cornell University, 7 August 2001), 1 and 3; retrieved April 15, 2020 from the arXiv database at **https://arxiv.org/abs/astro-ph/0108103**.

77. "[A] contracting universe which bounces due to quantum cosmological effects […] can produce an almost scale invariant spectrum of perturbations [… if] produced during an almost matter dominated era in the contraction phase[, … which] is achieved using Bohmian solutions of the canonical Wheeler-DeWitt equation." Patrick Peter, Emanuel J. C. Pinho, and Nelson Pinto-Neto, "Noninflationary Model with Scale Invariant Cosmological Perturbations," *Physical Review D*, Volume 75, No. 2 (College Park, Maryland: American Physical Society, January 2007); doi:10.1103/PhysRevD.75.023516. In a decidedly less scientific analysis, another theorist reasons that "at some time in the past, all galaxies were at the same place[, …] not only moving directly away from each other, but they also had sideway velocities[; … t]hus, in reality they need never have been exactly in the same place, only very close together[, so p]erhaps then the current expanding universe resulted not from a 'big bang singularity' but from our earlier 'contracting phase' as the universe had collapsed." Narendra D. Sharma, "The Theory of Evolution of the Universe and Cosmic Consciousness: Scientific and Spiritual Viewpoints," *Journal of Consciousness Exploration and Research*, Volume 9, No. 6 (Stony Brook, New York: QuantumDream, June 2018), 552.

78. Theorists supporting the discredited Steady State model "imply that the arrow of time would reverse at the moment the universe hit its maximum size," but the existence of dark matter and the non-isotropic (non-homogenous) nature of gravitational collapse make such a reversal unlikely. Sean Carroll, *From Eternity to Here* (London: Oneworld Publications, 2010), 245. The Weyl tensor (called WEYL) of a sphere's tidal distortion leads to the Weyl curvature hypothesis, which identifies a lack of symmetry as the reason a Big Crunch singularity's high entropy would not mirror the low entropy of the Big Bang, meaning the entropy-following, thermodynamic Arrow of Time would not reverse its direction. (Nobel laureate) Roger Penrose, *The Emperor's New Mind: Concerning Computers, Minds, and the Laws of Physics* (Oxford: Oxford University Press, 1989), 439.

79. "The second law [of thermodynamics] requires that the entropy of the entire system must increase, but it allows for a local entropy decrease as long as the [overall] entropy of the universe increases." Tom Fenchel, *The Origin*

and Early Evolution of Life (New York: Oxford University Press, 2002), 32. "Life and evolution do not violate the second law of thermodynamics; we know of nothing in nature that violates this absolute law[, ... and thus, t]he entire fabric of life on Earth necessitates an intricate balance of *organization* involving a highly ordered, low entropy state [...] and dynamic interconnected structures[, ...] which do not violate the thermodynamic laws as applied to the *whole* system." Wassim M. Haddad, *A Dynamical Systems Theory of Thermodynamics* (Princeton, New Jersey: Princeton University Press, 2019), 644; emphasis in the original. "[A] gradient can lead to the organization of form[, ... but we do not] violate the second law of thermodynamics because the form helps dissipate a larger kind of order: the energy differential." Raymond L. Neubauer, *Evolution and the Emergent Self: The Rise of Complexity and Behavioral Versatility in Nature* (New York: Columbia University Press, 2012), 183. "[R]eplace the ordinary second law of thermodynamics by the generalized second law (GSL): The total generalized entropy of the universe never decreases with time[; ... then,] the local entropy density of matter is bounded in a suitable manner by the energy density of matter." Robert M. Wald, "The Thermodynamics of Black Holes," *Living Reviews in Relativity*, Volume 4, No. 1 (Potsdam, Germany: Albert-Einstein-Institut, July 2001), 6.

80. "Because of the symmetry of the Einstein equations, a time-reverse black hole—not very appropriately called a *white hole*[...—]would be excluded by the Weyl tensor hypothesis[, ...] emerging from a past horizon[, ... and thus] inconsistent with an arrow of time that is valid everywhere." H. Dieter Zeh, *The Physical Basis of The Direction of Time* (Berlin / Heidelberg, Germany: Springer-Verlag [Springer Science+Business Media], 2007), 142. "A white hole is the time reverse of a black hole[, ... and j]ust as nothing can escape from a black hole horizon without going faster than light, nothing can *enter* a white hole horizon without going faster than light[; ...] Einstein's field equation is time reversal invariant, so it admits while hole solutions[, ... while a] black hole that forms from collapse is of course not time reversal invariant, but the time reverse of this spacetime is also a solution to Einstein's equation." Ted Jacobson, "Black Holes and Hawking Radiation in Spacetime and Its Analogues," *Analogue Gravity Phenomenology: Analogue Spacetimes and Horizons, from Theory to Experiment*, ed. Daniele Faccio, et al. (Cham, Switzerland: Springer International Publishing [Springer Science+Business Media], 2013), 26; emphasis in the original. "Einstein's General Theory of Relativity describes the curvature of space-time in the vicinity of a black hole[, ... predicting] that if you fell toward a black hole your time slows down and[, ... a]s you near the edge of the black hole, the 'event horizon,' your time almost stops." Neil deGrasse Tyson, *Merlin's Tour of the Universe* (New York: Main Street Books [Bantam Doubleday Dell Publishing], 2011), 234.

Chapter 5: The Discrepancy between What Must Be True and What Appears to Be True

1. Sylvia Plath, *The Unabridged Journals of Sylvia Plath: 1950–1962*, ed. Karen V. Kukil (New York: Anchor Books [Random House], 2000 [1955–56]), 199.

2. "The Eagle Nebula is much larger than the star cluster [inside it], with a diameter of about 70 light years [or about 412 trillion miles]." Martin Rees, *Universe: The Definitive Visual Guide* (London: Dorling Kindersley Ltd., 2012 [2005]), 244. Imagery is part of NASA's catalog (Washington, D.C.: National Aeronautics and Space Administration, 21 October 2017) at **https://www. nasa.gov/feature/goddard/2017/messier-16-the-eagle-nebula**, in addition to the original press release with photographs, *Hubblesite.org* (Baltimore, Maryland: Space Telescope Science Institute [STScI], 2 November 1995) at **https://hubblesite.org/contents/news-releases/1995/news-1995-44.html**, both accessed December 16, 2019.

3. "[A] misleading image presented as a visual stimulus[,] something that deceives or misleads intellectually[, or] perception of something objectively existing in such a way as to cause misinterpretation of its actual nature." *The Merriam-Webster.com Dictionary*, s.v. "illusion (*noun*)" (Springfield, Massachusetts: Encyclopædia Britannica, Inc., ca. 26 November 2005) at **https://www.merriam-webster.com/dictionary/illusion**, accessed November 10, 2017. Moreover, "it is fairly common for people to misperceive or misinterpret the world around them[, … as in an optical illusion, which is an] example of how direct sensory experience can deceive us." Frederick J Gravetter and Lori-Ann B. Forzano, *Research Methods for the Behavioral Sciences* (Boston: Cengage Learning, 2018 [2016]), 8. And "change of the sort believed in by most people may well be an illusion[; … indeed, a] divine mind could contemplate an entire life, and its thoughts about the life could be the only reality which the life possessed, while that mind was itself eternally unchanging." John Leslie, *Infinite Minds: A Philosophical Cosmology* (Oxford: Clarendon Press [Oxford University Press], 2001), 111.

4. "An illusion is a false mental impression derived through the senses[, … although] the false perception can soon be corrected by an appeal to the senses, or to the judgment[; … i]f, however, it is persistently believed to have a positive existence, and this belief is not removed either by reflection, or by a reference to the other senses, then the illusion becomes a delusion, or a misleading of the mind." John J. Reese, *Text-book of Medical Jurisprudence and Toxicology* (Philadelphia, Pennsylvania: P. Blakiston's Son and Co., 1894), 550–51. One "may have an illusion or hallucination, and yet be able to correct it, but it becomes a delusion when [one's] reason and judgment accept it as

real." See "Insane Impulse," *The Medical News*, Volume 41 (Philadelphia, Pennsylvania: Henry C. Lea's Son and Co., 18 November 1882), 575.

5. *The Udana, or The Solemn Utterances of the Buddha*, trans. Major General D[awsonne] M[elanchthon] Strong (London: Luzac, 1902), 94–96; Udana 6.4.

6. John Godfrey Saxe, *The Poems of John Godfrey Saxe: Complete in One Volume* (Boston: Ticknor and Fields, 1868), 260.

7. William Lane Craig and Quentin Smith, "Debate: Does God Exist?" (Cambridge, Massachusetts: Harvard University [Harvard Science Center], April 2003) at **https://www.reasonablefaith.org/media/debates/does-god-exist-the-craig-smith-debate-2003/**, accessed August 28, 2017.

8. The concept of a perpetually oscillating universe emerges primarily in the context of being scientifically insupportable. Moisey A. Markov, "Problems of a Perpetually Oscillating Universe," *Annals of Physics*, Volume 155, No. 2 (San Diego, California: Academic Press [Elsevier Science], July 1984), 333–57; doi:10.1016/0003-4916(84)90004-6. An initial analysis—in a preprint of M. A. Markov, "Is [a] Perpetually Oscillating Friedman Universe Possible that Passes through the Region Near the Classical Singularity in a State of Metastable de Sitter Universe?" in *Institute for Nuclear Research* (Moscow: Academy of Sciences of the USSR, 1981)—identifies the main issue of entropy increase, which an earlier examination had raised by Richard C. Tolman, *Relativity, Thermodynamics and Cosmology* (Oxford: Clarendon Press [Oxford University Press], 1934). Both analyses are cited in a chapter by M. A. Markov, "Some Remarks on the Problem of the Very Early Universe," *The Very Early Universe: Proceedings of the Nuffield Workshop, Cambridge, 21 June to 9 July 1982*, ed. G. W. Gibbons, S. W. Hawking, and S. T. C. Siklos (Cambridge: Cambridge University Press, 1983), 370.

9. "If you try to invent a cosmology in which you straightforwardly replace the singular Big Bang by a smooth Big Bounce continuation into a previous spacetime, you have one of two [nonsensical] choices: either the entropy continues to decrease as we travel backwards in time through the Bang, or it changes direction and begins to increase." Sean Carroll, "Against Bounces," *PreposterousUniverse.com* (Pasadena, California: Sean Carroll, 2 July 2007) at **https://www.preposterousuniverse.com/blog/2007/07/02/against-bounces/**, accessed January 24, 2020. Others have invoked "phantom dark energy" in connection with "Come Back Empty (CBE)" contraction as a way to overcome the "Tolman Entropy Conundrum (TEC)." Paul H. Frampton, "Bang or Bounce," *arXiv preprint* (Ithaca, New York: Cornell University, 26 November 2014); retrieved January 24, 2020 from the arXiv database at **https://arxiv.org/abs/1411.7887**.

10. Paul J. Steinhardt and Neil Turok, *Endless Universe: Beyond the Big Bang* (New York: Doubleday [Random House], 2007), 149. For further mathematical treatment in five dimensions, see the Cyclic Ekpyrotic Universe model. Gianluca Calcagni, *Classical and Quantum Cosmology* (Cham, Switzerland: Springer International Publishing [Springer Science+Business Media], 2017), 776–83; Section 13.7.7.

11. "Cosmologists Neil Turok and Paul Steinhardt put forward a model of a five-dimensional spacetime in which the four special dimensions are bounded by two three-dimensional walls, that is to say, by two 3-branes." David A. J. Seargent, *Weird Universe: Exploring the Most Bizarre Ideas in Cosmology* (Cham, Switzerland: Springer International Publishing [Springer Science+Business Media], 2014), 208; citing Neil Turok and Paul J. Steinhardt, "Beyond Inflation: A Cyclic Universe Scenario," *Physica Scripta*, Volume 2005, No. T117 (Philadelphia, Pennsylvania: IOP Publishing [Institute of Physics for the Royal Swedish Academy of Sciences], January 2005), 76; doi:10.1238/Physica.Topical.117a00076. Extrapolating to higher dimensions, "spacetime is approximately a narrow five dimensional layer bounded by four-dimensional walls[, … indirectly] a consequence of the preservation half of the spacetime supersymmetry." Michael Duff, "A Layman's Guide to M-Theory," *Mathematical Sciences After The Year 2000*, ed. Khalil Bitar, Ali Chamseddine, and Wafic Sabra (Singapore: World Scientific Publishing, 2000), 32.

12. "[B]rane collision events define an infinite number of flat spacelike surfaces[, … where, a]s in inflation, a horizon is present, preventing an observer from seeing the entire universe[; …] the system would be restored to thermal equilibrium and would no longer possess an arrow of time[, … contravening the] standard wisdom that a high energy inflationary phase is the *only* way to solve the conundra of the hot big bang." Neil Turok and Paul J. Steinhardt, "Beyond Inflation: A Cyclical Universe Scenario," *String Theory and Cosmology*, Proceedings of the Nobel Symposium 127, ed. U. Danielsson, A. Goobar, and B. Nilsson (Stockholm and Singapore: Physica Scripta and World Scientific Publishing, 2005), 84; emphasis in the original. And "even if the inflation ends, in this case the D-branes do not disappear, and they remain almost parallel to each other[; … moreover,] because of this thermal energy, D-branes and anti-D-branes should have pair-created one after another[, … and thus,] the big bang is a pair-annihilation with a collision of higher-dimensional D-branes." Koji Hashimoto, *D-Brane: Superstrings and New Perspective of Our World* (Berlin / Heidelberg, Germany: Springer-Verlag [Springer Science+Business Media], 2012), 119. "A cosmological scenario in which the hot big bang universe is produced by the collision of a brane in the bulk space with a bounding orbifold plane, beginning from an otherwise

cold, vacuous, static universe[, …] as with inflation there are […] thermal excitations of the light degrees of freedom, and the hot big bang phase begins[; … h]ence, the brane collision is not only responsible for initiating the expansion of the universe, but also for spontaneously breaking symmetries and for producing all of the quarks and leptons." Justin Khoury, et al., "Ekpyrotic Universe: Colliding Branes and the Origin of the Hot Big Bang," *Physical Review D*, Volume 64, No. 12 (College Park, Maryland: American Physical Society, 15 December 2001); doi:10.1103/PhysRevD.64.123522. "[P]article production at the collision of two domain walls in 5-dimensional Minkowski spacetime […] may provide the reheating mechanism of an ekpyrotic (or cyclic) brane universe, in which two BPS branes collide and evolve into a hot big bang universe." Yu-ichi Takamizu and Kei-ichi Maeda, "Collision of Domain Walls and Reheating of the Brane Universe," *Physical Review D*, Volume 70, No. 12 (College Park, Maryland: American Physical Society, 15 December 2004); doi:10.1103/PhysRevD.70.123514.

13. The incompatibility between ekpyrotic (or Big Splat) cosmologies and the confirmed discovery of gravitational waves is revealed when those promoting a new non-inflationary cosmological theory must admit that "[r]elic gravitational waves will […] be therefore strongly suppressed on large scales[, … just as in or] very close to ekpyrotic/cyclic models[, … which likewise result in a situation where] no detection is possible in the foreseeable future." Paolo Creminelli and Leonardo Senatore, "A Smooth Bouncing Cosmology with Scale Invariant Spectrum," *Journal of Cosmology and Astroparticle Physics*, Volume 2007, No. 11 (London: Institute of Physics Publishing, November 2007), 10.6; doi:10.1088/1475-7516/2007/11/010. Even more pointedly, "[i]f primordial gravitational waves are observed, certain bouncing cosmologies, such as the cyclic scenario, are in trouble." Diana Battefeld and Patrick Peter, "A Critical Review of Classical Bouncing Cosmologies," *Physics Reports*, Volume 571 (Amsterdam: North-Holland Publishing, April 2015), 1–66; doi:10.1016/j.physrep.2014.12.004. Cf. Ian Harry, et al., "Searching for Gravitational Waves from Compact Binaries with Precessing Spins," *Physical Review D*, Volume 94, No. 2 (College Park, Maryland: American Physical Society, 2016); doi:10.1103/PhysRevD.94.024012.

14. "[T]o detect something as ethereal as ripples in spacetime [… requires the] Laser Interferometer Gravitational-Wave Observatory [… or LIGO, which uses interference rather than direct detection,] like detecting the water wave generated by a passing speedboat a thousand miles away." A. Zee, *On Gravity* (Princeton, New Jersey: Princeton University Press, 2018), 66. Cf. Govert Schilling, *Ripples in Spacetime: Einstein, Gravitational Waves, and the Future of Astronomy* (Cambridge, Massachusetts: Belknap Press [Harvard University Press], 2017); and W. Wayt Gibbs, "Ripples in Spacetime," *Scientific*

American, Volume 286, No. 4 (New York: Nature Research [Springer Nature], April 2002), 62–71, doi:10.1038/scientificamerican0402-62.

15. "Aristarchus of Samos brought out a [no longer extant] book[, hypothesizing] that the fixed stars and the sun remain unmoved [… while] the earth revolves around the sun." Archimedes, "The Sand Reckoner," *The Works of Archimedes*, ed. Sir Thomas Little Heath (Cambridge: Cambridge University Press, 1897), 221–22.

16. "[T]he heliocentric hypothesis of Aristarchus was too revolutionary for the early Greeks[, … given that no less an authority than] ARISTOTLE personally championed the then widely accepted geocentric model." Joseph A. Angelo Jr., *Encyclopedia of Space and Astronomy* (New York: Facts On File [Infobase Publishing], 2006), 153, capitalization in the original; entry entitled "Copernicus, Nicholas (Nicolaus)" about how he "first became fascinated with the little-known hypothesis of Aristarchus of Samoa that the Earth revolved around the Sun" in lectures at the University of Bologna.

17. "In 1616, [more than seventy years after Copernicus's death,] the Inquisition ruled Copernicus's opinion erroneous and formally heretical, and the Congregation of the Index placed Copernicus's *De revolutionibus* on the list of books banned by the church." James E. McClellan III and Harold Dorn, *Science and Technology in World History: An Introduction* (Baltimore, Maryland: Johns Hopkins University Press, 2015), 249.

18. "[T]he sun and all its smaller companions are known as the solar system[, which] orbits the center of the Milky Way galaxy, completing one revolution about every 225 million years." *New Views of the Solar System* (Chicago: Encyclopaedia Britannica, Inc., 2013), 1

Chapter 6: Bridging Existence and Reality, or The World as an Idea in the Mind of God

1. H. L. Mencken, *Prejudices: Third Series* (New York: Alfred A. Knopf, 1922), 93.

2. "[As for] the wondrous symmetry and simplicities of Nature[, …i]ronically, it is the departure from those simplicities that makes life possible[, … and i]t is upon the flaws of Nature, not the laws of Nature, that the possibility of our existence hinges." John D. Barrow, *The Artful Universe* (New York: Oxford University Press, 1995), 37.

3. Nick Bostrom, "Are You Living in a Computer Simulation?" in *Philosophical Quarterly*, Volume 53, No. 211 (2003), 243–55.

4. The probabilistic representation of the wave function is outlined in Erwin Schrödinger, "An Undulatory Theory of the Mechanics of Atoms and Molecules," *Physical Review*, Volume 28, No. 6 (New York: American Physical Society, December 1926), 1049–70; doi: 0.1103/PhysRev.28.1049. Predating possible modern rapid-entanglement explanations, the notion of an observer effect, or collapsing wave functions into the deterministic certainty of particles, is illustrated in a later article (in German): Erwin Schrödinger, "Die gegenwärtige Situation in der Quantenmechanik," *Naturwissenschaften*, Volume 23, No. 48 (November 29, 1935), 807–12, doi:10.1007/BF01491891; English title: "The Current Situation in Quantum Mechanics" in *Natural Sciences*.

5. Erwin Schrödinger, *My View of the World*, trans. Cecily Hastings (New York: Cambridge University Press, 1964), Chapter 5. Cf. Erwin Schrödinger, "The Oneness of Mind," *Quantum Questions: Mystical Writings of the World's Great Physicists*, ed. Ken Wilber (Boston: Shambhala Publications, 2001), 87.

6. Emerging Technology from the arXiv, "A Quantum Experiment Suggests There's No Such Thing As Objective Reality," *TechnologyReview.com* (Cambridge, Massachusetts: Massachusetts Institute of Technology's [MIT] Technology Review, 12 March 2019) at **https://www.technologyreview.com/s/613092/a-quantum-experiment-suggests-theres-no-such-thing-as-objective-reality/**, accessed March 14, 2019; referencing Nobel Prize–winning physicist Eugene Wigner's 1961 thought experiment about "how the strange nature of the universe allows two observers [...] to experience different realities."

7. Thomas Young, "The Bakerian Lecture: On the Theory of Light and Colours," *Philosophical Transactions of the Royal Society of London*, Volume 92 (London: The Royal Society, 1802 [read: November 12, 1801]), 12–48. Cf. Thomas Young, "The Bakerian Lecture: Experiments and Calculations Relative to Physical Optics," *Philosophical Transactions of the Royal Society of London*, Volume 94 (London: The Royal Society, December 31, 1804); doi: 0.1098/rstl.1804.0001.

8. "The 'particles' of light are called *quanta of light* or *photons*, the co-existence of waves and particles [is called] wave–particle duality[, ... and t]he ejection of electrons from a metal surface by light is called the photoelectric effect[, ... which later] Einstein interpreted [... as the] discrete quanta of light (photons)." Walter Greiner, *Quantum Mechanics: An Introduction* (Berlin / Heidelberg, Germany: Springer-Verlag, 1989), 1–2; emphasis in the original.

9. Both photons and electrons "behave somewhat like waves, and somewhat like particles[, so i]n order to save ourselves from inventing new words like 'wavicles,' we have chosen to call these objects 'particles' [in some instances, or 'waves' in other instances,]" as they both variously exhibit the qualities

of each designation. Richard P. Feynman, *QED: The Strange Theory of Light and Matter* (Princeton, New Jersey: Princeton University Press, 1985), 85.

10. "[T]he hypothesis that the interaction between mind and matter causes the collapse of the wave function [… cannot be experimentally disproven and may indeed be] unfalsifiable." J. Acacio de Barros and Gary Oas, "Can We Falsify the Consciousness-causes-collapse Hypothesis in Quantum Mechanics?" in *Foundations of Physics*, Volume 47, No. 10 (New York: Springer Science+Business Media, October 2017), 1294–1308; doi:10.1007/s10701-017-0110-7. For a further description of "the deep relationship between the complementarity principle and the superposition principle," see Jian-Shun Tang, at al. "Realization of Quantum Wheeler's Delayed-Choice Experiment," *Nature Photonics*, Volume 6, No. 9 (London: Nature Publishing Group, September 2012), 600; doi:10.1038/nphoton.2012.179. Others see no paradox to resolve. Johannes Fankhauser, "Taming the Delayed Choice Quantum Eraser," *Quanta*, Volume 8, No. 1 (New York: Simons Foundation, 2019), 44–56; doi:10.12743/quanta.v8i1.88.

11. "Quantum woo is the justification of irrational beliefs by an obfuscatory reference to quantum physics," as defined on *RationalWiki.org* (Albuquerque, New Mexico: RationalWiki Foundation, ca. 6 May 2010) at **https://rationalwiki.org/wiki/Quantum_woo**, accessed December 17, 2019.

12. Einstein wrote in German, "spukhafte Fernwirkung," later translated into English as "spooky actions at a distance," about quantum entanglement. Albert Einstein, "Letter to Max Born," in *The Born-Einstein Letters: Correspondence between Albert Einstein and Max and Hedwig Born from 1916 to 1955*, trans. Irene Born (London: Macmillan Press Ltd, 1971 [3 March 1947]), 158.

13. Since its introduction, "Bell's inequalities which showed that quantum theory could not be explained by any local hidden variables theory [… has come under attack, and in t]he intervening years have also seen experimental verification of the violation of Bell's inequalities[, whose] conclusion cannot be that the equations are deficient, but that quantum theory is either inexplicable or requires a non local unifying theory." Mark J. Hadley, "Time Machines and Quantum Theory," *Proceedings of the Eleventh Marcel Grossmann Meeting on General Relativity*, Part A, ed. Kleinert Hagen and Robert T Jantzen (Singapore: World Scientific Publishing, 2008), 778.

14. Paul Davies, *The Goldilocks Enigma: Why Is the Universe Just Right for Life?* (New York: Houghton Mifflin, 2008), 250–51.

15. "[T]he universe has organized its own self-awareness." Paul Davies, *The Cosmic Blueprint: New Discoveries in Nature's Ability to Order the Universe* (Philadelphia: Templeton Foundation Press, 2004), 203.

16. "Earth is the only planet that is known to have hosted life." Shuhai Xiao and James D. Schiffbauer, "Microfossil Phosphatization and its Astrobiological Implications," *From Fossils to Astrobiology: Records of Life on Earth and the Search for Extraterrestrial Biosignatures*, ed. Joseph Seckbach and Maud Walsh (Cham, Switzerland: Springer International Publishing [Springer Science+Business Media], 2008), 91. "At the moment, life on Earth is the only known life in the universe[, ... but t]o declare that Earth must be the only planet with life in the universe would be inexcusably bigheaded of us." Neil deGrasse Tyson, *Death by Black Hole: And Other Cosmic Quandaries* (New York: W. W. Norton and Company, 2007), 229. "[I]f one includes all planets around all stars, including free-floating planets, then the total number [of such exoplanets] could be in the trillions." Michael Inglis, *Astrophysics Is Easy!* (Springer International Publishing [Cham, Switzerland: Springer Science+Business Media], 2015 [2007]), 226; doi:10.1007/978-3-319-11644-0_13. "[R]ecent powerful telescopes [... are set] along with the Search for Extraterrestrial Intelligence (SETI) to search among the trillions of exoplanets." Richard H. Schlagel, *Three Scientific Revolutions: How They Transformed Our Conceptions of Reality* (Amherst, New York: Humanity Books [Prometheus Books], 2015), 14.

17. Sir James Hopwood Jeans, *The Mysterious Universe* (Cambridge: Cambridge University Press, 1930), 137.

18. Robert Nozick, *Philosophical Explanations* (Cambridge, Massachusetts: Harvard University Press, 1981), 116.

19. Barrow himself labels his observation "Barrow's Uncertainty Principle." John D. Barrow, *100 Essential Things You Didn't Know You Didn't Know: Math Explains Your World* (New York: W. W. Norton and Company, 2008), 71.

20. Sir Arthur Conan Doyle, *The Sign of the Four* (New York: Quality Paperback Book Club, 1993 [1890]), 42; emphasis in the original.

21. "In the case of asexual reproduction, i.e., cloning, the only variation in genetic material between a single parent and the progeny will be the result of relatively infrequently occurring mutations; otherwise, all individuals in an entire lineage, over many generations, would be genetically identical." James F. Harris, *The Ascent of Man: A Philosophy of Human Nature* (New Brunswick, New Jersey: Transaction Publishers, 2011), 76. More pointedly, "[p]arthenogenesis [i.e., cloning] is simply not an option available to mammals[, because] although it is possible to activate a mammalian egg (including a human egg) in the complete absence of spermatozoon, such that it undergoes the early processes of development and may even implant in the uterus, these parthenogenetic conceptuses always fail and die eventually." Martin H. Johnson, *Essential Reproduction* (Detroit, Michigan: Wiley-Blackwell, 2013), 4.

22. Cloning an opposite-gender version is possible "only for a female version of the male, not the other way around[, … since i]f you were to create [the] male version of a particular female individual, you would need to obtain a Y chromosome and its associated DNA, which is missing from the original woman's genome[, … but] by replacing an X with a Y chromosome, you may express phenotypes from the remaining maternal X chromosome that were previously overridden or influenced by the paternal X." Internet comment by Stephen Hou (**https://www.quora.com/profile/Stephen-Hou**), *Quora. com* (Mountain View, California: Quora Inc., 13 February 2014) at **https:// www.quora.com/Genetic-Engineering-Is-it-possible-to-clone-an-opposite- gender-version-of-yourself**, accessed December 31, 2019; answering "Is it possible to clone an opposite-gender version of yourself?" and upvoted by Matt Russell, Ph.D. in Biochemistry, Cellular and Molecular Biology from the University of Tennessee. For an analysis of the genetic issues involved in the rare but naturally occurring XX-male or de la Chapelle syndrome, see T. Wang, et al., "46, XX Male Sex Reversal Syndrome: A Case Report and Review of the Genetic Basis," *Andrologia*, Volume 41, No. 1 (Hoboken, New Jersey: Wiley-Blackwell, February 2009): 59–62; doi:10.1111/j.1439-0272.2008.00889.x.

23. Albert Einstein, *The Einstein Reader* (New York: Citadel Press Books [Kensington Publishing Corp.], 2006), 54.

24. "*[P]luralitas non est ponenda sine necessitate*" (Latin for "plurality should not be posited without necessity"). William of Ockham, *Philosophical Writings: A Selection*, trans. Philotheus Boehner (Indianapolis, Indiana: Hackett Publishing, 1990), 97.

25. "There are actually four primary facets or *canons* (i.e., rules or principles that guide a field of study) that define the scientific method[: …] empricism [or observation], determinism [as to causation], parsimony [in the form of Occam's Razor], and testability [or falsifiability]." Dawn M. McBride, *The Process of Research in Psychology* (Los Angeles [Thousand Oaks, California]: SAGE Publications, 2010), 6; emphasis in the original. Cf. Nancy Levit, "Listening to Tribal Legends: An Essay on Law and the Scientific Method," *Fordham Law Review*, Volume 58, No. 3 (1989), 263–307.

26. "Especially in the EEA [or environment of evolutionary adaptedness] imagine the consequences of failing to see an oncoming predator versus seeing a predator that really is not there[, … where a]lthough the latter behavior might be deemed foolish or wasteful, the consequences of the former predisposition could be deadly[; …] the tendency of modern humans to see patterns that are not real […] is called *apophenia*[, … a] subcategory of [which] is *pareidolia*[, … or] the tendency for humans to perceive a face or pattern where one does not exist[, … although e]volutionarily, it would

be critically important to recognize faces (and other objects, both animate and inanimate)." Frederick L. Coolidge, *Evolutionary Neuropsychology* (New York: Oxford University Press, 2020), 217.

27. "[H]aving the wrong opinions first set forth, it might be proved that the disciples had received the truth." (Saint) Thomas Aquinas, *Catena Aurea*, Volume 1, Part 2: St. Matthew (Oxford: John Henry Parker, 1841 [ca. 1262–67]), 581.

28. "[L]awyers and judges can point to many instances where circumstantial evidence has proven to be more reliable than testimonial evidence." John M. Scheb II, *Criminal Law and Procedure* (Belmont, California: Wadsworth [CENGAGE Learning], 2013), 620. Direct evidence proves a fact, whereas indirect evidence, by requiring that a logical inference be drawn, only tends to support rather than prove a fact, although circumstantially, it may become impossible to deny the supported fact. Moreover, in term of trial tactics, "a robust strategy, which is in line with the accepted principles of evidence synthesis, would be to combine all relevant and appropriate information, whether direct or indirect." Jason Madan, et al., "Consistency between Direct and Indirect Trial Evidence: Is Direct Evidence Always More Reliable?" in *Value in Health*, Volume 14, No. 6 (Lawrenceville, New Jersey: International Society for Pharmacoeconomics and Outcomes Research [Elsevier], September–October 2011), 953–60; doi:10.1016/j.jval.2011.05.042. See also a study tending to show sometimes how "the availability of more evidence for a conclusion provides a reason [counterintuitively] to believe in its falsity." Ofer Malcai and Ram Rivlin, "Reasonable Self-Doubt," *Criminal Law and Philosophy* (The Hague/Kluwer: Springer Netherlands, 14 February 2020); doi:10.1007/s11572-020-09528-7. In any event, "the single most important factor leading to wrongful conviction in the United States [...] is eyewitness misidentification." C. Ronald Huff, *Convicted but Innocent: Wrongful Conviction and Public Policy* (Los Angeles [Thousand Oaks, California]: SAGE Publications, 1996), 66.

29. Jeffrey Goldstein, "Emergence as a Construct: History and issues," *Emergence: Complexity and Organization*, Volume 1, No. 1 (Marblehead, Massachusetts: Institute for the Study of Coherence and Emergence, 1999), 49–72. Cf. Benyamin Lichtenstein, *Generative Emergence: A New Discipline of Organizational, Entrepreneurial, and Social Innovation* (New York: Oxford University Press, 2014); see especially Chapter 4, pp. 107–30.

30. Among many such declarations stands Schelling's analysis of Descartes, namely, that "the most perfect being can only exist necessarily." F. W. J. von Schelling, *On the History of Modern Philosophy*, trans. Andrew Bowie (Cambridge: Cambridge University Press, 1994), 50.

31. "To be a good person, one must suffer—suffering is necessary to make a person virtuous." Alan Page Fiske and Tage Shakti Rai, *Virtuous Violence* (Cambridge: Cambridge University Press, 2015), 12. "Gregory reflects on Job's virtuous suffering by explaining that 'strength is never shown except in adversity and therefore patience immediately leads to strength.'" Susan E. Schreiner, *Where Shall Wisdom be Found?: Calvin's Exegesis of Job from Medieval and Modern Perspectives* (Chicago: University of Chicago Press, 1994), 35. "A [...] troublesome biblical theme is the ideal of virtuous suffering[, ...] upheld as a praiseworthy disposition." Nancy Eiesland, "Encountering the Disabled God," *Publications of the Modern Language Association*, Volume 120, No. 2 (New York: Modern Language Association, March 2005), 585. "Because God suffers man must suffer." Ludwig Feuerbach, *The Essence of Christianity*, trans. Marian Evans (London: Trübner and Co., 1881), 292; appendix Section 7. Yet "[t]o be perfect is to be unchanging and self-sufficient[, ... making it] therefore impossible for such a perfect being to be affected or changed by anything outside itself[: ...] Whoever is capable of love is also capable of suffering, because he is open to the suffering that love brings." Jürgen Moltmann, "The Suffering of God," *Theology: The Basic Readings*, ed. Alister E. McGrath (London: Blackwell Publishing, 2008), 35. Solely through imperfection can one suffer, for "[f]rom the Gospel record we see that this Logos [or the Word in the Beginning] is not an absolutely perfect being, but is capable of suffering." *Encyclopædia of Religion and Ethics*, Volume A-Art, ed. James Hastings, et al. (New York: Charles Scribner's Sons, 1908), 777; the "Arianism" entry beginning on page 775. "Since [H]e[, namely, God,] is a perfect being, [...] to ascribe to [H]im grief or suffering is to impugn [H]is perfection[, ... for if God] is capable of sorrow[, ... then H]e is capable of suffering." Washington Gladden, *Where Does the Sky Begin?* (Boston and New York: Houghton, Mifflin and Company, 1904), 157. Hence, if being capable of suffering is necessary to being virtuous, and no perfect being such as God can or does suffer, the surprising yet inescapable conclusion is that God cannot then be virtuous.

32. "[T]here was a time, called the big bang, when the universe was infinitesimally small and infinitely dense." Stephen Hawking, *A Brief History of Time* (New York: Bantam Books, 1998), 9. "Time itself began at the moment of the Big Bang." Peter Shaver, *Cosmic Heritage: Evolution from the Big Bang to Conscious Life* (Berlin / Heidelberg, Germany: Springer-Verlag [Springer Science+Business Media], 2011), 55. "[T]he spontaneous creation of our universe [...] is an absolute accident that just popped into being out of pure nothingness devoid of all causal conditions whatsoever." Rem B. Edwards, *What Caused the Big Bang?* (Amsterdam: Rodopi, 2001), 172.

33. David Kyle Johnson, "Why 62 Percent of Philosophers Are Atheists Part III: 'Did God Fine Tune the Universe?' A reply to Alvin Plantinga," *PsychologyToday.com* (New York: Sussex Publishers, 14 February 2014) at **https://www.psychologytoday.com/us/blog/logical-take/201402/why-62-percent-philosophers-are-atheists-part-iii**, accessed September 10, 2019.

34. "Complex systems are usually defined as an integrated set of interconnected components." Guy André Boy, *Orchestrating Human-Centered Design* (London: Springer-Verlag [Springer Science+Business Media], 2013), 89. Specifically, "a complex system consists of two or more interconnected components and these components react together and[, because] it is very complicated to separate them[, ...] the system's behaviour is impossible to deduce from the behaviour of its individual components." Eva Volná, et al., "Methodology for System Adaptation Based on Characteristic Patterns," *Robotic Systems: Applications, Control and Programming*, ed. Ashish Dutta (Rijeka, Croatia: InTechOpen, 2012), 612. "[B]y a complex system [is] mean[t] one made up of a large number of parts that interact in a nonsimple way." Herbert A. Simon, "The Architecture of Complexity," *Proceedings of the American Philosophical Society*, Volume 106, No. 6 (Philadelphia, Pennsylvania: American Philosophical Society, 12 December 1962), 468. Furthermore, "the complex organization [or system] is a set of interdependent parts which together make up a whole because each contributes something and receives something, which in turn is interdependent with some larger environment." James D. Thompson, *Organizations in Action: Social Science Bases of Administrative Theory* (New York: McGraw-Hill, 1967), 6.

Chapter 7: What is the "Idea" in the Mind of God?

1. Edgar Allan Poe, "A Dream within a Dream," *The Works of the Late Edgar Allan Poe*, Volume 2 (New York: Redfield, 1857), 40.

2. "Einstein penned the letter on January 3 1954 to the philosopher Eric Gutkind who had sent him a copy of his book *Choose Life: The Biblical Call to Revolt.*" James Randerson, "Childish Superstition: Einstein's Letter Makes View of Religion Relatively Clear," *TheGuardian.com* (London: Guardian Media Group [Scott Trust Limited], 13 May 2008) at **https://www.theguardian.com/science/2008/may/13/peopleinscience.religion**, accessed September 10, 2019.

3. Benedict de Spinoza, *Ethics*, ed. and trans. James Gutmann (New York: Hafner Press, 1949 [1677]), 188; Part 4 (of Human Bondage): Preface.

4. "Thought thinks the absolute existence; such existence is to it absolute thought." Georg Wilhelm Friedrich Hegel, *Lectures on the History of*

Philosophy, Volume 3, trans. Elizabeth Sanderson Haldane and Frances H. Simson (London: Kegan Paul, Trench, Trübner, and Co., Ltd., 1896), 419.

5. Internet comment by jk54321 (**https://www.reddit.com/user/jk54321**), *Reddit.com* (San Francisco: Advance Publications, 27 October 2015) at **https://www.reddit.com/r/DebateReligion/comments/3qcllg/theists_so_how_does_your_god_think_without_a_brain/**, accessed October 2, 2019.

6. "Literal modes of thought and literal language are simply not adequate for characterizing God[, Who] can be understood only through metaphorical thought and communicated through metaphorical language[, as He] after all, is ineffable—beyond human comprehension." George Lakoff, *Moral Politics: How Liberals and Conservatives Think* (Chicago: University of Chicago Press, 2016 [1996]), 245. Furthermore, "any human conceptual system is mostly metaphorical in nature, [meaning] there is no fully objective, unconditional or absolute truth." George Lakoff and Mark Johnson, *Metaphors We Live By* (Chicago: University of Chicago Press, 1980), 185.

7. Ludwig Wittgenstein, *Tractatus Logico-Philosophicus*, trans. C. K. Ogden (New York: Harcourt, Brace, and Company, 1922), 149; proposition 5.6.

8. The balloon analogy first appears in a post-interview cartoon sketch by Dutch cosmologist Willem de Sitter (1872–1934), showing him blowing up a galaxy-festooned balloon in *Algemeen Handelsblad*, Volume 103, No. 33543 (Amsterdam: 9 July 1930). P. J. E. (Phillip James Edwin) Peebles, *Principles of Physical Cosmology* (Princeton, New Jersey: Princeton University Press, 1993), 81. Prof. Greene also cites this source and remarks that the balloon analogy is "superbly useful [… and one] that physicists often invoke." Brian Greene, *The Fabric of the Cosmos: Space, Time, and the Texture of Reality* (New York: Alfred A. Knopf [Random House], 2004), 231 and 515–16.

9. "The oracle at Delos declared [Socrates] the wisest of mortals[, and he accepts it as true b]ecause other people in general believe that they know something[, whereas Socrates is] sensible, however, [to] acknowledge, that all [his] knowledge amount[s] to this—that [he] know[s] nothing." Plato, *Phaedon: or The Death of Socrates*, trans. Moses Mendelssohn (London: J. Cooper, 1789), xvii–xviii. Or, "Socrates said that it was his *awareness of ignorance*, his own and others', that made him the wisest person in ancient Greece." Alan R. Drengson, "The Virtue of Socratic Ignorance," *American Philosophical Quarterly*, Volume 18, No. 3 (Champaign, Illinois: University of Illinois Press, July 1981), 237; emphasis added.

10. "[The] neutron star[:] the densest object known in the universe." *Energy and Movement* (Chicago: Encyclopaedia Britannica, Inc., 2013), 41. Also, a "neutron star[, …] matter's last line of defense against gravity[, …] is the

densest known form of matter in the universe." Charles Liu, *The Handy Astronomy Answer Book* (Canton, Michigan: Visible Ink Press, 2014), 113.

11. "[A] neutron star is ten trillion times denser than water[, meaning a] single teaspoon of neutron star material would weigh about five billion tons!" Liu, *Handy Astronomy Answer Book*, 113.

12. Clive Staples Lewis, *The Joyful Christian* (New York: Macmillan, 1977), 36–37.

13. Heraclitus (of Ephesus), *The Fragments of the Work of Heraclitus of Ephesus on Nature; Translated from the Greek Text of Bywater, with an Introduction Historical and Critical*, trans. George Thomas White Patrick (Baltimore, Maryland: N. Murray, 1889 [ca. 500 BCE]), 94; fragment 41.

Chapter 8: The Purpose of the Universe, or the Acosmist's Answer to the Primordial Existential Question

1. Milan Kundera, *The Unbearable Lightness of Being*, trans. Michael Henry Heim (New York: Harper and Row, 1984), 139; Part 4, Section 6.

2. "In the Big Bang singularity, space and time do not exist, so causality cannot be operative [… and thus] the Big Bang was an uncaused event[, …] which was the beginning of time itself." Peter R. Bahn and Steven H. Pravdo, "The Big Bang at Time Zero," *From Fossils to Astrobiology: Records of Life on Earth and the Search for Extraterrestrial Biosignatures*, ed. Joseph Seckbach and Maud Walsh (Cham, Switzerland: Springer International Publishing [Springer Science+Business Media], 2008), 445.

3. "This might suggest that the so-called imaginary time is really the real time, and that what we call real time is just a figment of our imaginations[, … s]o what we call imaginary time is really more basic, and what we call real is just an idea we invent to help us describe what we think the universe is like." Stephen Hawking, *A Brief History of Time* (New York: Bantam Books, 1988), 139.

4. "[T]he universe could continue through the singularity to another expansion period, although the classical concept of time would break down so that one could not say that the expansion happened after the contraction[; … i]f this were the case, one would have solved the problem of the initial boundary conditions of the Universe: the boundary conditions are that it has no boundary." J. B. Hartle and S. W. Hawking, "Wave Function of the Universe," *Physical Review D*, Volume 28, No. 12 (New York: American Physical Society, 15 December 1983), 2974–75; doi:10.1103/

PhysRevD.28.2960. Carried to its logical conclusion, "[t]he suggestion by Hawking and Hartle […] that the universe could have existed before the big bang indefinitely in imaginary time implies that the universe did not exist physically[, … inasmuch as] imaginary time is not a physically measurable quantity." Mohammed Basil Altaie, "Creation and the Personal Creator in Islamic Kalam and Modern Cosmology," *Humanity, the World and God: Studies in Science and Theology*, Volume 11 (Lund, Sweden: Lund University's European Society for the Study of Science and Theology, 2008), 160. However, "the Big Bang is not an event at all [… because a]n event takes place within a space-time context[, … while] the Big Bang has no space-time context; there is neither time prior to the Big Bang nor a space in which the Big Bang occurs[, … and h]ence, the Big Bang cannot be considered as a physical event occurring at a moment of time[; a]s Hawking notes, the finite universe has no space-time boundaries and hence lacks singularity and a beginning[, … meaning that t]ime might be multi-dimensional or imaginary, in which case one asymptotically approaches a beginning singularity but never reaches it[, … a]nd without a beginning the universe requires no cause[, … so, t]he best one can say is that the universe is finite with respect to the past, not that it was an event with a beginning." Bruce Reichenbach, "Cosmological Argument", *The Stanford Encyclopedia of Philosophy*, Fall 2019 Edition, ed. Edward N. Zalta, (Palo Alto, California: Metaphysics Research Lab, Stanford University, 2019) at **https://plato.stanford.edu/ archives/fall2019/entries/cosmological-argument/**, accessed April 20, 2020.

5. Some conclude, though, that "the various 'no-boundary' attempts to interpret the transition from imaginary to real time in a logically consistent and physically significant way all fail [… and are thus] incoherent." Robert J. Deltete and Reed A. Guy, "Emerging from Imaginary Time," *Synthese*, Volume 108, No. 2 (Dordrecht, Netherlands: Kluwer Academic Publishers, August 1996), 185.

6. "The Kaluza-Klein idea of extra spacetime dimensions continues to pervade current attempts to unify the fundamental forces." M. J. Duff, "Kaluza-Klein Theory in Perspective," *The Oskar Klein Centenary: Proceedings of the Symposium*, ed. Ulf Lindström (Singapore: World Scientific, 1995), 22; at the Oskar Klein Centenary Nobel Symposium held in Stockholm, Sweden, 19–21 September 1994. "[E]xtra dimensions are needed to make the [grand-unification] theory both mathematically consistent and capable of describing [the forces involved]." Eric Adelberger, Blayne Heckel and C. D. Hoyle, "Testing the Gravitational Inverse-Square Law," *Physics World*, Volume 18, No. 4 (London: Institute of Physics Publishing, April 2005), 41.

7. "This is the Hartle-Hawking suggestion that the initial state of the Universe could be a region where time did not exist: instead of three spatial dimensions and one time dimension, there were four spatial dimensions." George F. R. Ellis, "Modern Cosmology and the Limits of Science," *Transactions of the Royal Society of South Africa*, Volume 50, No. 1 (Cape Town, South Africa: Royal Society of South Africa [Taylor and Francis], 1995), 43855; doi:10.1080/00359199509520326. Such an analysis is a realization that beginnings and causations disappear when the temporal dimension itself is removed; it is likely based on Hawking's observation that "[w]hen we combine quantum mechanics with general relativity, there seems to be a new possibility that did not arise before: that space and time together might form a finite, four-dimensional space without singularities or boundaries, like the surface of the earth but with more dimensions." Hawking, *Brief History of Time*, 189–90.

8. "*[T]ime itself began with the big bang*[, ... meaning] there was no time (or place) before the big bang for a causative agency to exist." Paul Davies, *The Goldilocks Enigma: Why Is the Universe Just Right for Life?* (New York: Houghton Mifflin, 2008), 69; emphasis in the original.

9. Blaise Pascal, *Pensées*, [Dover Thrift Editions] (Mineola, New York: Courier Dover Publications, 2018 [1670]), 72; #242.

10. (documentary film), "Expelled: No Intelligence Allowed," *IMDb.com* (Seattle, Washington: Amazon [Internet Movie Database], 18 April 2008) at **https://www.imdb.com/title/tt1091617/characters/nm1468026**, accessed July 3, 2019; dialogue available at the URL.

11. *Bertrand Russell on God and Religion*, [Great Books in Philosophy], ed. Al Seckel (Amherst, New York: Prometheus Books, 1986), 11 [Preface]; quoting "The Talk of the Town," in *The New Yorker* (New York: Condé Nast Publications, 21 February 1970), 29 at **http://archives.newyorker.com/?i=1970-02-21#folio=029**.

12. "Sensory input may be routed both to the cortex for analysis and directly to the amygdala for a more instant emotional reaction[; ... r]esearch on neurological processes shows how we can experience emotion before cognition[, ... where] some of emotion's neural pathways [... create a mental wormhole, ... and this] shortcut, bypassing the cortex, enables our greased-lightning emotional response before our intellect intervenes." David G. Myers, *Exploring Psychology* (New York: Worth Publishers [Macmillan Learning], 2004), 382. And "[w]hen one is in an elevated mood state, that emotional feeling is a shortcut to memory, making it easier to both encode and retrieve it later when in that same mood state." Chris Lierman, "Experiential EQ and the Power of Experience: Human Need, Emotion and its Effect on Brand Memory," *Journal of Brand Strategy*, Volume 8, No. 3 (London: Henry Stewart Publications, Winter 2019-20), 229–40.

13. Neale Donald Walsch, *Conversations with God: An Uncommon Dialogue,* Complete (New York: G. P. Putnam's Sons [Penguin], 2005), 28, 63, and 497.

14. Ibid., 426.

15. The quote appears to be a misattributed amalgam of "God is revealed just as excellently in the effects of nature as in the sacred sayings of Scripture." Galileo Galilei, "Letter to the Grand Duchess Christina" (1615), *Selected Writings,* trans. William R. Shea and Mark Davie (Oxford: Oxford University Press, 2012), 67; and the quote of the following endnote.

16. Ibid., "The Assayer" (1623), 115.

17. Quoting Paul Dirac's widow, "My husband wasn't an atheist[; …] once, he said, 'If there is a God, he's a great mathematician.'" Denis Brian, "Chapter 3: Paul Dirac," in *The Voice of Genius: Conversations with Nobel Scientists and Other Luminaries* (Cambridge, Massachusetts: Perseus Publishing, 1995), 69.

18. Hugh Everett III, "'Relative State' Formulation of Quantum Mechanics," *Reviews of Modern Physics,* Volume 29, No. 3 (New York: American Physical Society [American Institute of Physics], July - September 1957), 454–62; doi:10.1103/RevModPhys.29.454 and reprinted in *Many-Worlds Interpretation of Quantum Mechanics,* ed. Bryce Seligman DeWitt and Neill Graham (Princeton, New Jersey: Princeton University Press, 1973), 141–50. "In the cosmological multiverse, the other universes are simply far away; in [Everett's Many Worlds Interpretation of] quantum mechanics, they're right here, but in different possibility spaces (i.e. different parts of Hilbert space)." Sean Carroll, "Are Many Worlds and the Multiverse the Same Idea?" on *PreposterousUniverse.com* (Pasadena, California: Sean Carroll, 26 May 2011) at **http://www.preposterousuniverse.com/blog/2011/05/26/ are-many-worlds-and-the-multiverse-the-same-idea/**, accessed April 22, 2020; reprinted in *Discover Magazine* (Waukesha, Wisconsin: Kalmbach Publishing, 26 May 2011).

19. "There is no such thing as two individuals indiscernible from each other." Gottfired Wilhelm Leibniz, *Philosophical Papers and Letters: A Selection,* Volume 2, trans. Leroy E. Loemker (Dordrecht, Netherlands: Kluwer Academic Publishers, 1989), 687; Part 4, Leibniz's Fourth Letter, Section 4.

20. The Fermi-LAT (Large-Area Telescope) Collaboration (Marco Ajello, et al.), "A Gamma-Ray Determination of the Universe's Star Formation History," *Science,* Volume 362, No. 6418 (Washington, D.C.: American Association for the Advancement of Science, 30 Nov 2018), 1031–34; doi:10.1126/science.aat8123.

21. "[T]he night in which, as we say, all cows are black." G. W. F. Hegel, "Preface: On Scientific Knowledge," *The Phenomenology of Mind,* trans. Sir

James Black Baillie (Mineola, New York: Dover Publications, 2003 [1910]), 9. The 1549 adage, "when all candles be out, all cats be grey," had been artfully translated as "at night all cows are black," so the sayings have been taken as equivalent and sometimes transposed. *A Dictionary of Proverbs*, ed. Jennifer Speake (Oxford: Oxford University Press, 2008), 122.

22. Peter van Inwagen, *Ontology, Identity, and Modality: Essays in Metaphysics*, ed. Ernest Sosa (New York: Cambridge University Press, 2001), 67–70. See also, Peter van Inwagen and E. J. Lowe, "Why is There Anything At All?" in *Proceedings of the Aristotelian Society*, Supplementary Volumes, Volume 70 (1996).

23. Ludwig Wittgenstein, *Tractatus Logico-Philosophicus*, trans. C. K. Ogden (New York: Harcourt, Brace, and Company, 1922), 79; proposition 4.122.

24. A false belief is a mistake, whether it is affirmative or negative. So, "materialism is rendered inevitable by disbelief in a personal God and a future life." G. M. Trevelyan, "Should Agnostics be Miserable?" in *Hibbert Journal: A Quarterly of Religion*, Volume 12, ed. L. P. Jacks (London: Williams and Norgate, 1905), 672. By way of contrast, "[t]o the Pantheist God is everything, and besides him there is nothing[; and whereas] Atheism says there is no God, Pantheism says all is God[, and while] Materialism says there is no spirit, Pantheism says all is spirit." William Tucker, "Theories of Skepticism— Pantheism," (Article 26), *The Universalist Quarterly and General Review*, Volume 19, ed. Thomas B. Thayer (Boston: Universalist Publishing House, October 1882), 427–28. As an illustration, in Ancient Greece, the concept of fated tragedy figures prominently in establishing "the human–divine relationship[, … although its effect […] portrays a godless world." Richard Rader, "The Fate of Humanism in Greek Tragedy," *Philosophy and Literature*, Volume 33, Number 2 (Baltimore, Maryland: Johns Hopkins University Press, October 2009), 442–54; doi:10.1353/phl.0.0063.

25. Michael Brannigan, "There Is No Spoon: A Buddhist Mirror," (Chapter 9), *The Matrix and Philosophy: Welcome to the Desert of the Real*, Volume 3: Popular Culture and Philosophy, ed. William Irwin (Chicago: Open Court Publishing, 2002).

26. Quote cited on *IMDB.com* (Seattle, Washington: Amazon [Internet Movie Database], 31 March 1999) at **https://www.imdb.com/title/tt0133093/ quotes/**, accessed June 20, 2019. See also commentary by David J. Chalmers, "The Matrix as Metaphysics," *Cons.net* (New York: David Chalmers [New York University's Department of Philosophy], ca. 15 March 2003) at **http:// consc.net/papers/matrix.html**, also accessed June 20, 2019, although the conclusion seems to ignore the possibility of a virtual spoon.

27. "[T]he unconditioned necessity in a being's existence absolutely cannot be comprehended by us; hence subjectively it rightly resists every speculative proof of a necessary supreme being, but resists wrongly the possibility of such an original being in itself[; …] if one presupposes that the world of sense is given in itself in its totality, then it is false to say that this world must either be infinite as regards space or be finite and bounded, because both alternatives are false." Immanuel Kant, *Critique of Pure Reason*, trans. Werner S. Pluhar (Indianapolis, Indiana: Hackett Publishing, 1966 [1781/1787]), 725; ca. A794/ B822. "According to Kant's *Critique of Pure Reason*, God is as hidden and unknowable as the [… thing-in-itself] because he is not an object of possible experience[; … t]he limits of reason itself have actually made it impossible for him to reveal himself and to manifest himself in the world of experience." Jürgen Moltmann, *The Spirit of Life: A Universal Affirmation*, trans. Margaret Kohl (Minneapolis, Minnesota: Fortress Press [1517 Media], 2001 [1992]), 31.

28. "[A]n unprovable rule or first principle accepted as true because it is self-evident or particularly useful." *The Merriam-Webster.com Dictionary*, s.v. "axiom (*noun*)" (Springfield, Massachusetts: Encyclopædia Britannica, Inc., ca. 3 May 2006) at **https://www.merriam-webster.com/dictionary/axiom**, accessed February 5, 2020. Gödel speaks of hypotheses being "consistent with the other axioms of set theory if these axioms are [themselves] consistent." Kurt Gödel, *The Consistency of the Axiom of Choice and of the Generalized Continuum-Hypothesis with the Axioms of Set Theory* (Princeton, New Jersey: Princeton University Press, 1940). Historically, "it was not enough that an axiom set should be internally consistent: it was generally assumed that they should be true in the sense of a correct representation of reality." *The Oxford Handbook of the History of Mathematics*, ed. Eleanor Robson and Jacqueline Stedall (New York: Oxford University Press, 2009), 13.

29. "Objectivism holds that existence exists." *Objectively Speaking: Ayn Rand Interviewed*, ed. Marlene Podritske and Peter Schwartz (Lanham, Maryland: Lexington Books [Rowman and Littlefield], 2009), 15; quoted from Columbia University's WKCR radio series "Ayn Rand on Campus" (1962–66).

30. "[T]hat something exists is simply a brute fact for which we have no explanation, causal or otherwise." Richard H. Jones, *Mystery 101: An Introduction to the Big Questions and the Limits of Human Knowledge* (Albany, New York: State University of New York Press, 2018), 56–57. Or phrased differently, "the universe just exists; its existence is a brute fact." Reichenbach, "Cosmological Argument."

31. "Intelligence (and the related notions like 'thinking' and 'cognition') is a complicated phenomena mainly observed only in the human brain at the current time[, so] the very idea of '*artificial* intelligence' assumes that the same

phenomena can be reproduced in something that is different from the human brain[, which is a]n attempt to 'get a mind without a brain', i.e., to describe mind in a medium-independent way, [and] is what makes AI important and attractive." Pei Wang, *Rigid Flexibility: The Logic of Intelligence* (Dordrecht, Netherlands: Springer, 2006), 12; emphasis in the original.

32. There exists a "consciousness which is tied to the perceptual awareness of phenomena." Paul J. Thibault, *Brain, Mind and the Signifying Body: An Ecosocial Semiotic Theory* (London: Continuum, 2004), 300. See also the development and use in consciousness studies of the Perceptual Awareness Scale (PAS). Thomas Zoëga Ramsøy and Morten Overgaard, "Introspection and Subliminal Perception," *Phenomenology and the Cognitive Sciences*, Volume 3, No. 1 (Cham, Switzerland: Springer Nature, March 2004), 1–23; doi:10.1023/B:PHEN.0000041900.30172.e8.

33. "According to Critical Realism, in veridical perception the subject's conscious experience is an inner state that is distinct from the perceived object." Paul Coates, *The Metaphysics of Perception: Wilfrid Sellars, Perceptual Consciousness and Critical Realism* (London and New York: Routledge [Taylor and Francis], 2007), 52. From a contrasting view, "[t]he Buddhist idealist recognizes the distinction of subject and object only within consciousness[, … not] any permanent self apart from the ever-changing stream of consciousness." Jadunath Sinha, *Indian Psychology Perception* (London: Kegan Paul, Trench, Trübner and Co., Ltd., 1934), 222.

34. "[Charles] Hartshorne and Paul Tillich described God as 'not less than conscious' or superconscious." David H. Nikkel, *Radical Embodiment* (Eugene, Oregon: Pickwick Publications [Wipf and Stock Publishers], 2010), 135. "[O]nly [a] superconscious God would be God in any degree of reality." Alexander Campbell Fraser, *Philosophy of Theism* (Edinburgh and London: William Blackwood and Sons, 1899), 159. "[I]f God is to be conceived as superpersonal, superconscious—as God above God, as Tillich says—then those who do so should tell us what 'super' is supposed to add to our wisdom." Peter A. Bertocci, "A Rationale for a Cosmoteleological Argument for God," *The Journal of Religion*, Volume 56, No. 4 (Chicago: The University of Chicago Press, October 1976), 332. On the spectrum of awareness, there are "unselfconscious puppets [...] at one extreme of the continuum, the superconscious god is at the other." Christopher Roland Trogan, "Rilke's Fourth Duino Elegy as Philo-Poetic Dialectic," *Interdisciplinary Literary Studies*, Volume 16, No. 2 (University Park, Pennsylvania: Pennsylvania State University Press, 2014), 265–81; doi:10.5325/intelitestud.16.2.0265.

35. "Collectively, neurons exhibit intelligence in roughly the same way that bees exhibit a 'hive mind' [... as] the interaction of billions of neurons and

trillions of synapses gives rise to consciousness and cognition." Warren W. Tryon, *Cognitive Neuroscience and Psychotherapy: Network Principles for a Unified Theory* (San Diego, California: Academic Press [Elsevier], 2014), 99. "[I]n a hive insects seem to lose [… their] individuality and become subsumed into the group in a way that goes far beyond co-operation[, …] as though the hive itself becomes conscious—a consciousness, perhaps that 'emerges' from the interaction of its parts[, …] much as neuronal activity in a human brain." Rita Carter, *Exploring Consciousness* (Berkeley, California: University of California Press, 2002), 296.

36. "[A]ll possibilities are realized [and thus, a]ll possible worlds obtain." Robert Nozick, *Philosophical Explanations* (Cambridge, Massachusetts: Harvard University Press, 1981), 127–33.

37. Internet post in the affirmative by Scott Owen (**http://www.ScottOwen. org/**) on *Debate.org* (Swansea, Illinois: Juggle, LLC, ca. 6 April 2015) at **https:// web.archive.org/web/20180917125402/http://www.debate.org/opinions/ is-the-universe-the-mind-of-god**, accessed June 17, 2022.

38. "Appearances, insofar as they are thought as objects according to the unity of the categories are called phenomena[, … b]ut if I assume things are objects merely of the understanding and that, as such, nonetheless be given to an intuition—even if not to sensible intuition[…]—then such things would be called noumena." Kant, *Critique of Pure Reason*, 312; A249. "[W]e would, after all, have taken a step beyond the world of sense [or phenomena]; we would have entered the realm of noumena." Ibid., 427. As one translator aptly puts it, Kant invokes "the notion of noumena lying beyond the boundary of possible knowledge, thinkable but unknowable." Gary Hatfield, et al., "Translator's Introduction" for *Theoretical Philosophy after 1781*, ed. Henry Allison and Peter Heath (Cambridge: Cambridge University Press, 2002), 37.

39. "Quantum discreteness must come into play even in the structure of time and space[; … i]f the amount of information during inflation is small enough, it […] will show signs of quantum discreteness[, … allowing us to] think of spacetime itself as an active quantum object." Craig J. Hogan, "Observing the Beginning of Time: New Maps of the Cosmic Background Radiation May Display Evidence of the Quantum Origin of Space and Time," *American Scientist*, Volume 90, No. 5 (Research Triangle Park, North Carolina: Sigma Xi [The Scientific Research Honor Society], September–October 2002), 425–26; doi:10.1511/2002.5.420. Nonetheless, based on data collected over a year by the Fermilab Holometer in a particular configuration, an "irreducible space-time noise arising from a putative fundamental Nyquist frequency[, … which normally] grows via diffraction over macroscopic distances[, …] is thus excluded with [high] statistical significance, [even when the expectation

has been] reduced by the 10% calibration uncertainty." Aaron S. Chou, et al., "First Measurements of High Frequency Cross-Spectra from a Pair of Large Michelson Interferometers," *Physical Review Letters*, Volume 117, No. 11 (College Park, Maryland: American Physical Society, 9 September 2016), 111102; doi:10.1103/PhysRevLett.117.111102.

Chapter 9: Critiques of Acosmism

1. George Orwell (Eric Arthur Blair), *Orwell on Truth* (London: Harvill Secker [Penguin Random House], 2017 [1940s]).

2. René Descartes, *The Meditations, and Selections from the Principles of Philosophy*, trans. John Veitch (Edinburgh: Sutherland and Knox, 1853 [1641]), 38; Meditation 3: Of God, that He Exists.

3. Ibid., 46–51.

4. René Descartes, *The Method, Meditations, and selections from the Principles*, trans. John Veitch (Edinburgh: William Blackwood and Sons, 1880 [1637–41]), 205; Part 1: Of the Principles of Human Knowledge (XXVII).

5. Perhaps because the subject of children's independent or natural attitudes toward cultural-specific concepts is a sensitive one, little experimental evidence on record confirms (or refutes) that their minds are a "blank slate" when it comes to spirituality generally; even Piaget's work on child development depicts children grappling to understand the concept of God abstractly so as to be more amenable to religious indoctrination. The support for the conclusion is thus anecdotal and often expressed in the form of opinion, as follows. "All children are born Atheists; they have no idea of God." Paul Henri Thiry, Baron d'Holbach (as, perhaps inadvertently, Jean Meslier), *Le Bon Sens* (English title: *Good Sense*), an abridgement of *Système de la Nature* (Amsterdam: 1772), 36; paragraph 30. "Nobody is born with the idea[s ... of religious particulars, familiarity with which] has to be learned—though such learning might have interesting and non-intuitive properties that distinguish it from other types of social information gathering." Paul Bloom, "Religious Belief as an Evolutionary Accident," *The Believing Primate: Scientific, Philosophical, and Theological Reflections on the Origin of Religion*, ed. Jeffrey Schloss and Michael J. Murray (New York: Oxford University Press, 2009), 120. "We are not born with a specific belief in God, or for that matter, any religious belief[, ... but i]nstead we learn to believe or disbelieve in God." Andrew Newberg and Mark Robert Waldman, *Born to Believe: God, Science, and the Origin of Ordinary and Extraordinary Beliefs* (New York: Free Press [Simon and Schuster], 2006), xviii. "[A]ll humans are born atheists." Phil Zuckerman, "Are Humans Naturally Religious?" in *Homo Religiosus?:*

Exploring the Roots of Religion and Religious Freedom in Human Experience, ed. Timothy Samuel Shah and Jack Friedman (Cambridge: Cambridge University Press, 2018), 55; quoting David Eller, *Natural Atheism* (Parsippany, New York: American Atheist Press, 2004). "All babies are born atheists [… and] would remain atheists for all or most of their lives except for the immediate teachings and constant brainwashing of their parents and others who bombard them weekly with the idea that the fairy tales and fiction of the Bible are true." C. Boyd Pfeiffer, *A Cure for Christianity* (New York: Algora Publishing, 2015), 52. "We are all born atheists[, … which] is not an opinion: it is a fact." Tommy Rodriguez, *Diaries of Dissension: A Case Against the Irrational and Absurd* (Bloomington, Illinois: iUniverse, 2012), 1. "Children born into religious homes are exposed to religious acculturation along with language, social expectations and all the other things that children learn from the family and their society[; … however, the i]ntelligent and inquisitive children find that religion is not good at providing intelligent and reasonable answers to their questions." Internet comment by Barry Hampe (**https://www.quora.com/profile/Barry-Hampe**), *Quora.com* (Mountain View, California: Quora Inc., 23 May 2018) at **https:// www.quora.com/What-makes-some-babies-convert-thoughtlessly-to-atheism-and-others-to-remain-Christian-for-their-entire-life**, accessed March 25, 2020. But others, based on so-called "empirical evidence," doubt that "the default assumption about human nature is that we are born atheists who come to subscribe to a specific faith through socialisation into a religious culture[; … instead, they believe that h]uman beings appear to be born with an inbuilt spiritual awareness that in normal circumstances expresses itself via the religious culture in which we are nurtured [… and that] spiritual awareness is a human universal, part of our biological make up that has evolved through the process of natural selection because it has survival value." David Hay, *Why Spirituality is Difficult for Westeners* (Exeter, England: Imprint Academic, 2017), 9.

6. "[C]hildren show remarkable natural affinities for thinking about and believing in gods[, … causing them to] naturally develop minds that encourage them to embrace belief in the god or gods of their culture[; … they] may practically be *born believers*." Justin L. Barrett, *Born Believers: The Science of Children's Religious Belief* (New York: The Free Press [Simon and Schuster], 2012), 3; emphasis in the original. "God was largely conceived as ignorant 'man in the sky' by younger and increasingly as 'supernatural agent in the sky' by older children." Florian Kiessling and Josef Perner, "God-Mother-Baby: What Children Think They Know," *Child Development*, Volume 85, No. 4 (Malden, Massachusetts: Wiley-Blackwell [the Society for Research in Child Development], July/August 2014), 1601–16; doi:10.1111/cdev.12210. "[Pre-school] children (ages 3 to 7) [...] distinguished God [...] as having greater perceptual access than humans[, a result which serves to] offer further

support for the theory that in developing a concept of God, even young children differentiate God from humans." Rebekah A. Richert and Justin L. Barrett, "Do You See What I Young Children's Assumptions About God's Perceptual Abilities," *The International Journal for the Psychology of Religion*, Volume 15, No. 4 (Hillsdale, New Jersey: Lawrence Erlbaum Associates, 2005), 283–95; doi:10.1207/s15327582ijpr1504_2. And "[c]hildren who used God as an explanation for the events showed higher levels of belief in the factuality of those events." Victoria Cox Vaden and Jacqueline D. Woolley, "Does God Make it Real? Children's Belief in Religious Stories from the Judeo-Christian Tradition," *Child Development*, Volume 82, No. 4 (Malden, Massachusetts: Wiley-Blackwell [the Society for Research in Child Development], July 2011); doi: 10.1111/j.1467-8624.2011.01589.x.

7. That a lack of "emotional expression is found in the documents on religion presented by the public school children" suggests they accept it as realistic, for "as soon as religious reality is replaced by metaphysical imagination[, … such characters] no longer appear as figures of fairy tales or in a mystic composition such as is stimulated by the language of religion." Ernest Harms, "The Development of Religious Experience in Children," *American Journal of Sociology*, Volume 50, No. 2 (Chicago: The University of Chicago Press, September 1944), 112–22. "Fairy tales, folktales, myths, and religious stories share common elements that make them memorable: events or entities that do not behave as we expect[; …i]n fact, it may be argued that fairy tales, folktales, and myths are themselves religious stories, containing information about the transcendent and the mysterious." Kevin J. Eames, *Cognitive Psychology of Religion* (Long Grove, Illinois: Waveland Press, 2016), 63. "[C]ultural figures such as the Tooth Fairy and Santa Claus do seem to have an impact on children's factuality judgments." Huseyin Kotaman and Ali Kemal Tekin, "The Impact of Religion on the Development of Young Children's Factuality Judgments." *North American Journal of Psychology*, Volume 17, No. 3 (Winter Garden, Florida: North American Journal of Psychology, December 2015), 525. "[C]hildren's endorsement of God's existence seems unproblematic to them[, … especially when] God ought to belong to the world of fairy tales." Paul L. Harris, "Fairy Tales, History, and Religion," *The Oxford Handbook of the Development of Imagination*, ed. Marjorie Taylor (New York: Oxford University Press, 2013), 38.

8. Heisenberg recollects Dirac's quote at the Fifth Solvay International Conference, held in Brussels, Belgium in October 1927. Werner Heisenberg, *Physics and Beyond: Encounters and Conversations* (New York: Harper and Row, 1971), 85.

9. Peter Van Inwagen, *Metaphysics* (Boulder, Colorado: Westview Press [Perseus Books Group], 2009), 336–38.

10. Characterizing the solipsistic view, Russell observes that "we can never *prove* the existence of things other than ourselves and our experiences[, so n]o logical absurdity results from the hypothesis that the world consists of myself and my thoughts and feelings and sensations, and that everything else is mere fancy." Bertrand Russell, *The Problems of Philosophy* (London: Williams and Norgate, 1912), 34; emphasis in the original. Moreover, the "solipsist regards only himself—that is, his thoughts and perceptions—as real; the outside world and other people 'disappear' as independently real and meaningful entities." Allard den Dulk, *Existentialist Engagement in Wallace, Eggers and Foer* (London: Bloomsbury Academic, 2015), 58. The stronger form of solipsism substitutes "exists" for "real" in these contexts. Historically, the "'methodic doubt' [… of] René Descartes created the backdrop against which solipsism subsequently developed," although he likely means it as an epistemological challenge to help us hone our grasp of what we claim to know rather than a genuine skepticism of the objective reality with which he and his fellow rationalist are so enamored. Stephen P. Thornton, "Solipsism and the Problem of Other Minds," *IEP.utm.edu* (Martin, Tennessee: University of Tennessee's Internet Encyclopedia of Philosophy, ca. 2 March 2010) at **https://www.iep.utm.edu/solipsis/**, accessed February 8, 2020.

11. "We can, it seems, have direct knowledge only of ourselves[; accordingly, i]n philosophy, this argument is aptly termed solipsism (from the Latin *solus*, alone, and *ipse*, self)." Terrence W. Deacon, *The Symbolic Species: The Co-evolution of Language and the Brain* (New York: W. W. Norton and Company, 1997), 424.

12. For a survey of historical refutations of solipsism, see Eric Schwitzgebel and Alan T. Moore, "Experimental Evidence for the Existence of an External World," *Journal of the American Philosophical Association*, Volume 1, No. 3 (New York: Cambridge University Press, Fall 2015), 564–82; doi:10.1017/apa.2014.27. Furthermore, according to Russell, "although this [solipsism] is not logically impossible, there is no reason whatsoever to suppose that it is true." Russell, *Problems of Philosophy*, 35.

13. "The children […] all really imagine that the doll's perspective is the same as their own, [… and] make every perspective a facsimile of [their] own momentary viewpoint." Jean Piaget and Bärbel Inhelder, *Child's Conception of Space*, trans. F. J. Langdon and J. L. Lunzer (London and New York: Routledge [Taylor and Francis], 1956 [1948]), 220. And "[y]oung children are also more egocentric—that is, they are more centered on their own perspective than are older children." Ross D. Parke, Glenn I. Roisman, and Amanda J. Rose, *Social Development* (Hoboken, New Jersey: John Wiley and Sons, 2019 [2011]), 26.

14. "[M]ost Americans actually do not perceive religion and science as being inherently in conflict[, … but] those most likely to a hold a conflict view are the religiously unaffiliated[, …] almost all of [… whom] say they side with science." Elaine Howard Ecklund and Christopher P. Scheitle, *Religion Vs. Science: What Religious People Really Think* (New York: Oxford University Press, 2018), 16. In various specific scientific or philosophical fields, "most psychologists and neuroscientists are materialists." Paul Thagard, *The Brain and the Meaning of Life* (Princeton, New Jersey: Princeton University Press, 2010), 42. And "[m]ost current commentators [on the mind–body distinction] are materialists." George Mandler, "Consciousness and Mind as Philosophical Problems and Psychological Issues: Yes, Virginia, There Is a Brain: The Mind–body Distinction," *Perception and Cognition at Century's End: History, Philosophy, Theory*, ed. Julian Hochberg (London: Academic Press [Harcourt Brace], 1998), 62. Some contend, though, that "in fact[,] most philosophers are dualists." David Bourget and David J. Chalmers, "What Do Philosophers Believe?" in *Philosophical Studies: An International Journal for Philosophy in the Analytic Tradition*, Volume 170, No. 3 (Dordrecht, Netherlands: Springer Science+Business Media, September 2014), 466; doi:10.1007/s11098-013-0259-7.

15. "As late as the 1990s nearly 40 percent of American scientists continued to believe in a personal God[; … s]cience may have become godless, but the masses—and many scientists—privately cling tenaciously to the supernatural." Ronald L. Numbers, *Science and Christianity in Pulpit and Pew* (New York: Oxford University Press, 2007), 58. "The majority of physicians believe in God (65.2%), and 51.2% reported themselves as religious, 24.8% spiritual, 12.4% agnostic, and 11.6% atheist." Kristin A. Robinson, et al., "Religious and Spiritual Beliefs of Physicians," *Journal of Religion and Health*, Volume 56, No. 1 (New York: Springer Nature [Academy of Religion and Mental Health], February 2017), 205–25; doi:10.1007/s10943-016-0233-8. See also *The Faith of Scientists: In Their Own Words*, ed. Nancy K. Frankenberry (Princeton, New Jersey: Princeton University Press, 2008) and Gregory W. Graffin and William B. Provine, "Evolution, Religion and Free Will: The Most Eminent Evolutionary Scientists Have Surprising Views on How Religion Relates to Evolution," *American Scientist*, Volume 95, No. 4 (Research Triangle Park, North Carolina: Sigma Xi [The Scientific Research Research Society], July–August 2007), 294ff.

16. To "prove their claim by scientific method […] means publicity exhibited, as a physical fact[, … a viewpoint that can only] drive straight into materialism, the doctrine that all verified truth is of physical events and properties alone." Wilmon H. Sheldon, "Critique of Naturalism," *The Journal of Philosophy*, Volume 42, No. 10 (New York: The Journal of Philosophy, Inc. [Columbia University], 10 May 1945), 253–70; doi:10.2307/2019588.

17. "[I]t would make no sense to create a model that encompasses time before the big bang, because what existed then would have no observable consequences for the present, and so we might as well stick with the idea that the big bang was the creation of the world." Stephen Hawking and Leonard Mlodinow, *The Grand Design* (New York: Bantam Books, 2010), 51. "[B]lack holes cannot just appear out of nothing[, b]ut a whole universe can[, … and b]ecause there is a law like gravity, the universe can and will create itself from nothing." Ibid., 180. Although others declare that "the universe cannot be its own cause of existence, as Hawking claims." Arthur Gibson, *God and the Universe* (New York: Routledge, 2000), 195. Yet, "to affirm a self-created universe, one must reject the law of non-contradiction[, … because f]or something to create itself, or to be its own effect as well as its own cause, it would have to exist before it existed." R. C. Sproul, *Defending Your Faith: An Introduction to Apologetics* (Wheaton, Illinois: Crossway [Good News Publishers], 2003), 110. It has long been accepted that "a thing cannot be its own cause." (Saint) Thomas Aquinas, *Summa Theologica*, Volume 1 (New York: Cosimo, 2007 reprint of 1911 [1485]), 107; The Will of God (God and the Divine Attributes): Part 1, Q. 19, Article 5. And, specifically, that "matter cannot be its own cause." *The Bhagavad-Gita*, trans. J. Cockburn Thomson (Hertford, England: Stephen Austin, 1855 [ca. 200]), lxxviii; preface. Logically, "[a]n effect cannot be its own cause[, … so, t]he universe, therefore, could not be its cause." Leander S. Keyser, *A System of Natural Theism* (Burlington, Iowa: The German Literary Board, 1917), 55.

18. "[U]ntil very recently, almost all modern materialists had assumed that matter is unoriginated and everlasting, [… but with a consensus around Big Bang cosmology, s]cience, however, now seems to have laid to rest the idea of an eternally existing universe." John F. Haugh, *Science and Religion* (Mahwah, New Jersey: Paulist Press, 1995), 101.

19. The PEQ "is unanswerable by science […] because the question, as it stands, is ill-posed[; … once reformulated,] it has an answer that naturalism can in principle provide." Stephen Maitzen, "Stop Asking Why There's Anything," *Erkenntnis*, Volume 77, No. 1 (Dordrecht, Netherlands: Springer Nature, July 2012), 51–63; doi:10.1007/s10670-011-9312-0. But see John Danaher, "Maitzen on Why Is There Anything?" on *Philosophical Disquisitions weblog* (Mountain View, California: Google, 26 June 2012) at **http://philosophicaldisquisitions.blogspot.com/2012/06/maitzen-on-why-is-there-anything.html**, accessed August 29, 2017; and Peter Lupu, "The Modified Leibniz Question: The Debate So Far," *Maverick Philosopher weblog* (Bill Vallicella, 17 June 2012) at **http://maverickphilosopher.typepad.com/maverick_philosopher/2012/06/**

the-modified-leibniz-question-the-debate-so-far.html, also accessed August 29, 2017.

20. David Wiggins, *Identity and Spatio-Temporal Continuity* (Oxford: Blackwell, 1967), 33.

21. Stephen Maitzen, "Questioning the Question," *The Puzzle of Existence: Why Is There Something Rather Than Nothing?* ed. Tyron Goldschmidt (New York: Routledge, 2013), 252–71.

22. "We have no evidence of any minds except human minds[, … and m]aking up an idea of an 'infinite mind' does not make such a thing a reality." Internet comment (third comment) by J. Blilie, *Amazon.com* (Seattle, Washington: Amazon, 2011) at **https://amzn.to/3uakMSj**, accessed September 12, 2017; reviewing Victor J. Stenger, *The New Atheism* (Amherst, New York: Prometheus Books, 2009).

23. "Since we only know appearances, anything outside of time is for Kant 'metaphysical,' and we can have no knowledge of it[, … which] rules out supernatural, and so atemporal, causes such as the will of God, laws of nature, the transcendental structure of the human mind, and even logical forms[; … i]ndeed, there is on this basis no such thing as a cause which begins a series of events but does not itself have a specific place within that series." John McCumber, *On Philosophy: Notes from a Crisis* (Palo Alto, California: Stanford University Press, 2013), 76; citing B50–51 of the *Critique of Pure Reason*. "[T]he understanding is itself the source of the laws of nature, and hence the source of nature's formal unity[; … thus,] all empirical laws are only particular determinations of the pure laws of understanding." Immanuel Kant, *Critique of Pure Reason*, trans. Werner S. Pluhar (Indianapolis, Indiana: Hackett Publishing, 1966 [1781]), 173; A128. "[I]f everything occurs according to mere laws of nature, then there is always only a subsidiary but never a first beginning, and hence there then is on the side of causes originating from one another no completeness of the series at all." Ibid., 474; A446/B474. "[T]he proof [of the physicoteleological or 'argument from design'] could not establish (the existence of) a creator of the world, to whose idea everything is subjected; but it could establish at best (the existence of) an architect of the world, who would always be greatly limited by the suitability of [the material on which he works]." Ibid., 606; A627/B655. The same passage rendered by a different translator reads: "All that the argument from design can possibly prove is an *architect* of the world, who is very much limited by the adaptability of the material in which he works: it cannot prove a *creator* of the world, to whose

idea everything is subject." Immanuel Kant, *The Philosophy of Kant: As Contained in Extracts from His Own Writings*, trans. John Watson (New York: Macmillan and Co., 1888 [1781]), 220; A627/B655, emphasis in the original.

24. "[D]eism is a subset of [...] naturalism[, ...b]ut the drift from theism to deism was certainly accelerated by the rise of naturalism." D. A. Carson, *The Gagging of God* (Grand Rapids, Michigan: Zondervan [HarperCollins], 2009), 61. "In deism, the world is ordered by its divine creator, but this tends to be limited to a general pattern that provides the setting for the exercise of creaturely freedom[, ... while a] divine imprint is believed to be evident in the order of nature." David Fergusson, *Creation* (Grand Rapids, Michigan: William B. Eerdmans Publishing, 2014), 63. "Deism is the view that there is a God, but [H]e remains 'at a distance' and doesn't intervene at all in the natural workings of the universe[, ... and thus,] there are no supernatural events such as miracles or divine revelation." James N. Anderson, *What's Your Worldview?* (Wheaton, Illinois: Crossway [Good News Publishers], 2014), 61–62; Worldview: Deism. As one self-published author succinctly expresses it, "[d]eism is the doctrine or view of God which asserts that the universe is like unto a clock, made then wound up by the Creator, subsequently left to run by means of laws He's established for its orderly operation[, ... while] God Himself remains distant, ineffable, aloof—utterly transcendent and unknowable except by inference through our discovery of said laws." James Barlow, *God and Eternity* (Indianapolis, Indiana: Dog Ear Publishing, 2009), 1.

25. "Deism [...] refers to what can be called natural religion or the acceptance of a certain body of religious knowledge acquired solely by reason as opposed to knowledge gained either through revelation or the teaching of a church." *Evangelical Dictionary of Theology*, ed. Walter A. Elwell (Grand Rapids, Michigan: Baker Academic [Baker Book House], 2001 [1984]), 329; Deism entry. "Deism is knowledge of God based on the application of our reason [... and] is therefore a natural religion and is not a 'revealed' religion." See "Welcome to Deism!" on *Deism.com* (Clearwater, Florida: World Union of Deists, 9 May 2008) at **https://www.deism.com/post/the-true-and-false-definitions-of-deism**, accessed March 2, 2020.

26. Multiverses can even be assigned levels based on distance, observability, spatial parallelism, and physical laws; Everett's Many Worlds Interpretation, for example, inevitably results if "the wavefunction never collapses." Max Tegmark, *Our Mathematical Universe: My Quest for the Ultimate Nature of Reality* (New York: Vintage Books [Random House], 2014), 139 and 179. See also Alex Vilenkin, *Many Worlds in One: The Search for Other Universes* (New York: Hill and Wang [Farrar, Straus and Giroux], 2006); Brian Greene,

The Hidden Reality: Parallel Universes and the Deep Laws of the Cosmos (New York: Vintage Books [Random House], 2011); and Tom Siegfried, *The Number of the Heavens: A History of the Multiverse and the Quest to Understand the Cosmos* (Cambridge, Massachusetts: Harvard University Press, 2019).

27. "Pantheism, therefore, merges everything into God[, … so that t]he universe is the existence-form of God; that is, the universe is [H]is existence[, … and] He is only the substance of which the universe and all that it contains are the ever[-]changing manifestation." Charles Hodge, *Systematic Theology*, Volume 1, ed. Anthony Uyl (Woodstock, Ontario, Canada: Devoted Publishing, 2016 [Grand Rapids, Michigan: William B. Eerdmans Publishing, 1940 from Princeton, New Jersey: Charles Scribner and Co., 1871]), 145.

28. One "version of pantheism holds that there are many distinct things in our universe, but all of them collectively make up the being of God[, …] according to which God exists in [H]is totality nowhere[… and by which e]ach individual has its own place as part of the whole of God." John S. Feinberg, *No One Like Him: The Doctrine of God* (Wheaton, Illinois: Crossway [Good News Publishers], 2001), 52; citing Colin Gunton, "Transcendence, Metaphor, and the Knowability of God," *The Journal of Theological Studies*, Volume 31, No. 2 (Oxford: Oxford University Press, October 1980), 501–16, and Douglas Hedley, "Pantheism, Trinitarian Theism and the Idea of Unity: Reflections on the Christian Concept of God," *Religious Studies*, Volume 32, No. 1 (Cambridge: Cambridge University Press, March 1996), 61–77; doi:10.1017/S0034412500024070.

29. The "denial of direct supernaturalism is […] seen in pantheism[, … although admittedly, o]ver against such forms of naturalism, an idealistic pantheism might be called supernaturalistic in asserting a reality other than physical nature." Caspar Wistar Hodge Jr., "The Finality of the Christian Religion," *Biblical and Theological Studies* (New York: Charles Scribner's Sons, 1912), 456. "While later thinkers beginning with Herder distinguish atheism from pantheism, for Jacobi and Mendelssohn Spinoza's pantheism is synonymous with atheism." Michah Gottlieb, *Faith and Freedom: Moses Mendelssohn's Theological-Political Thought* (Oxford: Oxford University Press, 2011), 67. "Pantheism is sexed-up atheism." Richard Dawkins, *The God Delusion* (London: Bantam Press, 2006), 40. Cf. "Pantheism as 'Sexed-up Atheism,'" *Pantheism.net* (Colorado: World Pantheist Movement, 19 September 2016) at **https://www.pantheism.net/atheism/**, accessed March 3, 2020.

30. "[B]y *nautra naturata* we are to understand that which is in itself and conceived through itself." Benedict de Spinoza, *Ethics*, ed. and trans. James Gutmann (New York: Hafner Press, 1949 [1677]), 65; Part 1 (of God): note to Proposition XXIX.

31. "[T]he patron Saint of unbelievers […ю is the pantheist] Spinoza." *The Athenaeum: Journal of Literature, Science, the Fine Arts, Music, and the Drama*, No. 2921 (London: John C. Francis, 20 October 1883), 492–93; review of *Spinoza Essays*. "To some, Spinoza was espousing straightforward pantheism, equating God with the whole of reality." Demian Wheeler, "Deus Sive Natura: Pantheism as a Variety of Religious Naturalism," *The Routledge Handbook of Religious Naturalism*, ed. Donald A. Crosby and Jerome A. Stone (London and New York: Routledge, 2018), 107. Some relegate Spinoza's status below others, as when a graphic "novel opens with what many consider to be the 'patron saint' of pantheism, Giordano Bruno, being burned at the stake for heretical views." Charles Beebe, "New Graphic Novel Details the Dawn of Modern Western Philosophy," *Pantheism.com* (Los Angeles [Venice, California]: The Paradise Project, 12 May 2017) at **https://pantheism.com/new-graphic-philosophy-novel/**, accessed March 3, 2020, reviewing Steven Nadler, *Heretics!: The Wondrous (and Dangerous) Beginnings of Modern Philosophy* (Princeton, New Jersey: Princeton University Press, 2017), 8; graphic depicting Giordano Bruno being burned at the stake by the Roman Inquisition in 1600. "The most famous pantheist of the age was Spinoza." David Byrne, "Anne Conway, Early Quaker Thought, and the New Science," *Quaker History*, Volume 96, No. 1 (Haverford, Pennsylvania: the Friends Historical Association, Spring 2007), 28; doi:10.1353/qkh.2007.0011. "PANTHEISM: […] Spinoza (q.v.), was perhaps the most famous pantheist philosopher." Irina Pollard, "UNESCO/IUBS/ EUBIOS Bioethics Dictionary," *Bioscience-Bioethics.org* (Sydney, Australia: Macquarie University, 10 August 2006) at **http://www.bioscience-bioethics. org/p.htm**, also accessed March 3, 2020.

32. Scott Adams, *God's Debris: A Thought Experiment* (Kansas City, Missouri: Andrews McMeel Publishing, 2001).

33. Georg Wilhelm Friedrich Hegel, *Lectures on the Philosophy of Religion: Together with a Work on the Proofs of the Existence of God*, Volume 1, trans. Ebenezer Brown Speirs and J. Burdon Sanderson (London: Kegan Paul, Trench, Trübner, and Co., Ltd., 1895 [1821–31]), 200.

34. "[T]he panentheist holds that the world of material reality is only a part of God[, … Who] is not wholly identical with the universe but rather includes the universe as a portion of its constitution[, … so that the] universe is something like God's body." John Marmysz, *The Path of Philosophy* (Boston: Wadsworth [CENGAGE Learning], 2012), 260. Or explicitly, "the material universe is God's Body; [H]e is in everything but greater than everything (panentheism)." Alan W. Gomes, *Truth and Error* (Grand Rapids, Michigan: Zondervan [HarperCollins], 1998), 53. And "imagining the world as God's body […] necessarily entails a form of panentheism." Adam Pryor, *The*

God Who Lives (Eugene, Oregon: Pickwick Publications [Wipf and Stock Publishers], 2014), 153.

35. Pantheism or, and by extension, "panentheism rejects [...] the assumption that God is a being than can freely choose to eliminate evil [... since] all possible worlds [... are] identical with God [... and] are ontologically on a par." Yujin Nagasawa, "Modal Panentheism," *Alternative Concepts of God*, ed. Andrei A. Buckareff and Yujin Nagasawa (Oxford: Oxford University Press, 2016), 100. "Pantheism [...] offers its own formulation(s) of a 'problem of evil[', ... while] the very idea of evil may be [...] essentially a metaphysical rather than a moral concept." Michael Levine, "Pantheism," *A Companion to Philosophy of Religion*, ed. Charles Taliaferro, Paul Draper, and Philip L. Quinn, (Oxford: Blackwell Publishing, 2010 [1997]), 341.

36. John Leslie, "The Theory That the World Exists Because It Should," *American Philosophical Quarterly*, Volume 7, No. 4 (Champaign, Illinois: University of Illinois Press, October 1970), 286–98.

37. Plato, *The Republic*, ed. Andrea Tschemplik [original trans. John Llewelyn Davies and David James Vaughan] (Lanham, Maryland: Rowman and Littlefield, 2005 [376 BCE]), 250–53; 514a-517a.

38. "Goodness is a strong enough force to pull the universe into existence[, ... and] Leslie understands that this explanation of existence is a poetic fantasy rather than a logical argument." Freeman Dyson (1923–2020), "What Can You Really Know?" in *New York Review of Books* (New York: Penguin Random House, 8 November 2012), 18–20 at **https://www.nybooks.com/articles/2012/11/08/what-can-you-really-know/**, accessed October 15, 2019; review of Jim Holt, *Why Does the World Exist?: An Existential Detective Story* (New York: W. W. Norton and Company, 2012).

39. "[T]he weakness of our evidence for God is not a sign that God is hidden; it is a revelation that God does not exist." J. L. Schellenberg, *Divine Hiddenness and Human Reason* (Ithaca, New York: Cornell University Press, 1993), 1. "God is ensconced in mystery, hidden in the depths[, ... and p]rayer is pleading with God to come out of the depths[, ... as in a biblical passage (Ps. 130), which begins with] 'Out of the depths have I [cried unto] Thee, O Lord." Abraham Joshua Heschel, "On Prayer," *The Jewish Philosophy Reader*, ed. Daniel H. Frank, Oliver Leaman, and Charles H. Manekin (London and New York: Routledge [Taylor and Francis], 2000), 589; from Abraham Joshua Heschel, "On Prayer," *Conservative Judaism*, Volume 25, No. 1 (New York: Rabbinical Assembly of America [and the Jewish Theological Seminary of America], Fall 1970), 2. Also, Jesus at Gethsemane, confronting the prospect of his atoning sacrifice to appease God, "fell on his face, and prayed, saying, 'O my Father, if it be possible, let this cup pass from me'" (Matt. 26:39).

40. "The number of undernourished people in the world has been on the rise since 2014, reaching an estimated 821 million in 2017." See "Figure 1" in The Food and Agriculture Organization, *The State of Food Security and Nutrition in the World* (Rome: the United Nations, 2018), 3. "Nearly 151 million children under five—or over 22 percent [of the undernourished]—are affected by [hunger-driven] stunting in 2017." Ibid., xii. This means roughly one-fifth of the hungry are children and that one in every fourteen children worldwide experience chronic hunger. Note that the undernourished category is easier to count; there may be many, many more who go to bed hungry (estimated at one billion). The percentage of humans going hungry (11%) is the same as the proportion who are racially white. "Global hunger continues to rise, new UN report says." *WHO.int* (Geneva, Switzerland: World Health Organization, 11 September 2018) at **https://www.who.int/news-room/detail/11-09-2018-global-hunger-continues-to-rise---new-un-report-says**, accessed December 16, 2018. "About 19 percent of the world population was undernourished in 1990[, but t]hat number had dropped to 11 percent by 2014." Rick Noack, "For Decades Global Hunger Was on the Decline. Now It's Getting Worse Again—and Climate Change Is to Blame," *The Washington Post* (Washington, D.C.: Nash Holdings, 11 September 2018) at **https://www.washingtonpost.com/world/2018/09/11/decades-global-hunger-was-decline-now-its-getting-worse-again-climate-change-is-blame/**, accessed December 16, 2018. "Undernutrition in childhood is estimated to cause 3.1 million [under age 5] child deaths annually." Kelsey D. Jones, et al., "Childhood Malnutrition: Toward an Understanding of Infections Inflammation and Antimicrobials," *Food and Nutrition Bulletin*, Volume 35, No. 2, Supplement 1 (Tokyo: the United Nations University's World Hunger Programme, June 2014), S64–70; doi:10.1177/15648265140352S110. Overall, over nine million people die of starvation annually. John Holmes, "Losing 25,000 to Hunger Every Day," *United Nations Chronicle*, Volume 45, No. 3 (New York: the United Nations Department of Public Information, December 2009), 14–20; doi:10.18356/4db709e5-en.

41. "[A]groecology delivers advantages that are complementary to better known conventional approaches." Olivier, Baron De Schutter, *Report Submitted by the Special Rapporteur on the Right to Food*, General Assembly's Sixteenth session, Agenda item 3 (Geneva, Switzerland: the United Nations, 17 December 2010). Thus, world hunger is a problem that theoretically has been solved, in that we are able to grow enough to feed everyone; it's the distribution system that is broken, a condition that grace-sayers somehow errantly attribute to God. Furthermore "[h]unger is caused by poverty and inequality, not scarcity[; … f]or the past two decades, the rate of global food production has increased faster than the rate of global population growth[,

… meaning t]he world already produces more than 1½ times enough food to feed everyone on the planet[, … which is] enough to feed 10 billion people, the population peak we expect by 2050." Eric Holt-Gimenez, "We Already Grow Enough Food for 10 Billion People—and Still Can't End Hunger," *The Huffington Post* (New York: AOL [Verizon Media], 2 May 2012) at **https:// www.huffpost.com/entry/world-hunger_b_1463429**, accessed April 2, 2020.

42. Mary Wollstonecraft Shelley, *Frankenstein, or, The Modern Prometheus* (Boston: Sever, Francis, and Co., 1869), 10; Preface.

43. "[C]onditional odds [...] should equal the prior odds adjusted by the likelihood." Kevin B. Korb, Nicholas Geard, and Alan Dorin, "A Bayesian Approach to the Validation of Agent-Based Models," *Ontology, Epistemology, and Teleology for Modeling and Simulation*, ed. Andreas Tolk (Berlin: Springer-Verlag [Springer Science+Business Media], 2013), 258; doi:10.1007/978-3-642-31140-6_14.

44. Bayesian reasoning "does not take the task of scientific methodology to be that of establishing the truth of scientific hypotheses, but to be that of confirming or disconfirming them to degrees that reflect the overall effect of the available evidence." Richard C. Jeffrey, "Probability and Falsification: Critique of the Popper Program," *Synthese*, Volume 30, Nos. 1–2 ["Methodologies: Bayesian and Popperian"] (Dordrecht, Netherlands: Kluwer Academic Publishers, February/March 1975), 102. And so, "with an infinity of possible results, probability 0 does not always mean impossible, and probability 1 not certainty." Jan von Plato, *Creating Modern Probability* (New York: Cambridge University Press, 1994), 7. Moreover, "probabilities of hypotheses are calculable by the doctrine of 'inverse probability' (Bayes's theorem) [… as] subjective probabilities." Deborah G. Mayo, *Error and the Growth of Experimental Knowledge* (Chicago: University of Chicago Press, 1996), 77. Specifically, recall that "[p]roof 'beyond a reasonable doubt' is not proof to absolute certainty." Charles Weiss, "Expressing Scientific Uncertainty," *Law, Probability and Risk*, Volume 2, No. 1 (Oxford: Oxford University Press, March 2003), 31; doi:10.1093/lpr/2.1.25.

45. That an hypothesis is untestable does not necessarily make it untrue, only unscientific. Indeed, "[i]t is the ability of an explanation to generate new predictions, which then serve as a check on the explanation, that improves the accuracy of our scientific explanations." Heather E. Douglas, "Reintroducing Prediction to Explanation," *Philosophy of Science*, Volume 76, No. 4 (Chicago: The University of Chicago Press, October 2009), 454–55; doi:10.1086/648111. For example, "[s]olipsism is unscientific precisely because no possible evidence could stand in contradiction to its predictions." Douglas Theobald, "29+ Evidences for Macroevolution: The

Scientific Case for Common Descent," Version 2.89, Usenet newsgroup *TalkOrigins.org* (Houston, Texas: The TalkOrigins Foundation, 4 June 2003 [Version 2.7]) at **http://www.talkorigins.org/faqs/comdesc/**, accessed February 19, 2020. Nonetheless, some scientists like Sean Carroll, in declaring that "[s]cience is not merely armchair theorizing," advocate abandoning falsifiability in favor of a kind of explanatory empiricism. Sean Carroll, "Falsifiability," in answer to the annual question, "What Scientific Idea Is Ready for Retirement?" by *Edge.org*, ed. John Brockman (Seattle, Washington: Edge Foundation, 2014) at **http://edge.org/response-detail/25322**, accessed February 19, 2020.

46. "In so far as a scientific statement speaks about reality, it must be falsifiable: and in so far as it is not falsifiable, it does not speak about reality." Sir Karl Raimund Popper, *The Logic of Scientific Discovery* (London: Hutchison and Co., 1959), 314.

47. This is not necessarily, however, a fatal flaw. As some have observed, "[f]alsificationism is not itself falsifiable[, ... but] because it is a philosophical or logical theory of the scientific method and not itself a scientific theory, [such an] objection, although often made, misses its target." James Ladyman, *Understanding Philosophy of Science* (London and New York: Routledge [Taylor and Francis], 2002), 85.

48. Popper speaks of falsifiability "as a criterion of demarcation between empirical science on the one hand and pure mathematics, logic, metaphysics, and pseudo-science on the other." Sir Karl Raimund Popper, *Realism and the Aim of Science*, ed. W. W. Bartley III (London: Hutchinson, 1983), 175.

49. Dawkins, *God Delusion*, 138.

50. Richard Dawkins, *The Blind Watchmaker: Why the Evidence of Evolution Reveals a Universe Without Design* (New York: W. W. Norton and Company, 1996), 141.

51. Richard Dawkins, "The Improbability of God," *RichardDawkins.net* (Washington, D.C.: Richard Dawkins Foundation for Reason and Science, 17 June 2014) at **https://www.richarddawkins.net/2014/06/the-improbability-of-god/**, accessed July 1, 2019.

52. Christianna Reedy, "Kurzweil Claims That the Singularity Will Happen by 2045," *Futurism.com* (New York: Futurism, 5 October 2017) at **https://futurism.com/kurzweil-claims-that-the-singularity-will-happen-by-2045**, accessed July 3, 2019; quoting Ray Kurzweil.

53. "The World's Most Beautiful Equation[, ... according to multiple polls taken of scientists and mathematicians over two decades, is] Euler's Identity." John

M. Henshaw, *An Equation for Every Occasion: Fifty-Two Formulas and Why They Matter* (Baltimore, Maryland: Johns Hopkins University Press, 2014), 58.

54. Gottfried Wilhelm Leibniz, "De vera proportione circuli ad quadratum circumscriptum in numeris rationalibus expressa," *Acta Eruditorum, février* (1682), 41–46—English title: "On the True Proportion of the Circle to the Circumscribed Square, Expressed in Rational Numbers" in *Acts of the Erudite, February*—as cited by Amrik Nimbran and Paul Levrie, "[100.29] Some Odd Series for [pi]," *The Mathematical Gazette*, Volume 100, No. 549 (Cambridge: Cambridge University Press, 2016), 496–500; doi:10.1017/mag.2016.116. In a similarly eerie linking of the geometry of pi with the convergence of the sum of an infinite series, one-sixth of the square of pi can be expressed as the sum of the reciprocals of the squares of all positive integers. Leonhard Euler, "De summis serierum reciprocarum," *Commentarii*, Volume 7, No. 41 (St. Petersburg: Academiae Scientiarum Imperialis Petropolitanae [The St. Petersburg Academy], 1740), 123–134; English title: "On the Sums of the Series of Reciprocals" in *Commentaries*.

55. Through the "use of relatively simple algorithms[, one can] generate complex fractals that reproduce patterns that we see in nature." Lewis M. Branscomb, *Confessions of a Technophile* (Woodbury, New York: American Institute of Physics, 1995), 57. For an example of a fractal-generating algorithm, see the programs of Austrian software developer Zimmermann Stephan, "The Beauty of Fractals - A Simple Fractal Rendering Program Done in C#," *CodeProject.com* (Toronto, Ontario, Canada: Code Project, 27 July 2009) at **https://www.codeproject.com/Articles/38514/The-beauty-of-fractals-A-simple-fractal-rendering**, accessed January 22, 2020.

56. It is unlike a human brain that "[i]nsofar as the Mindscape [of the totality of all thought] is God's mind, […] one of the objects in the Mindscape should be the Mindscape itself[, … where] any such object [… is] something that one can perceive through one's consciousness." Rudy Rucker, *Infinity and the Mind* (Princeton, New Jersey: Princeton University Press, 2019), 45. And "[i]f God does not have a brain, then there is no physical mechanism to determine which things he knows[, … so that, u]nlike us, God knows things directly, rather than by the mediation of a perceptual apparatus[; …] if an omniscient being knew things by representation, then he would need an exact identical copy of the entire Universe in his brain." Aron Wall, "Fundamental Reality VII: Does God Need a Brain?" on *Undivided Looking weblog* (Cambridge: Aron Wall, 28 December 2014) at **http://www.wall.org/~aron/blog/fundamental-reality-vii-does-god-need-a-brain/**, accessed March 7, 2020.

57. David Hume, *Dialogues concerning Natural Religion* (London: William Blackwood and Sons, 1907 [1779]), 63.

58. Günter M. Ziegler, *Lectures on Polytopes* (New York: Springer-Verlag [Springer Science+Business Media], 2012), 134.

59. G. M. Acklom, "Some Fourth-Dimension Curiosities," *The Fourth Dimension Simply Explained: A Collection of Essays Selected from Those Submitted in the Scientific American's Prize Competition*, ed. Henry Parker Manning (New York: Munn and Company, 1910), 135.

60. Kurt Gödel, *On Formally Undecidable Propositions of Principia Mathematica and Related Systems*, trans. B. Meltzer (New York: Dover Publications, 2012 [1931]). The quote is a version of Gödel's incompleteness theorem as expressed in an internet comment by zentiger (**https://zentiger. livejournal.com/**), *LiveJournal.com* (Moscow: SUP Media, 5 May 2007) at **https://philosophy.livejournal.com/1667929.html**, accessed July 21, 2017.

61. Thomas Breuer, "The Impossibility of Accurate State Self-Measurements," *Philosophy of Science*, Volume 62, No. 2 (Chicago: The University of Chicago Press, 1995), 214; doi:10.1086/289852.

62. W. T. Stace, *Mysticism and Philosophy* (New York: Macmillan, 1960), 237–38.

63. "[A]ll religious thought and speech are through and through symbolic[, … and] all religious language is symbolic." Walter T. Stace, *Time and Eternity: An Essay in the Philosophy of Religion* (Princeton, New Jersey: Princeton University Press, 1952), vi and 62.

64. "[None of the] names of natural nonreligious qualities of natural objects […] is literally applicable to God." Stace, *Mysticism and Philosophy*, 293.

65. "The religious infinite, or in other words the infinity of God, means *that than which there is no other*." Stace, *Time and Eternity*, 47; emphasis in the original.

66. Ibid., 46–47.

67. "[W]hen God plays hide and pretends that [H]e is you and I, [H]e does it so well that it takes [H]im a long time to remember where and how [H]e hid himself[, b]ut that's the whole fun of it—just what [H]e wanted to do[:] He doesn't want to find [H]imself too quickly, for that would spoil the game[, … which] is why it is so difficult for you and me to find out that we are God in disguise, pretending not to be [H]imself." Alan Watts, *The Book: On the Taboo against Knowing Who You Are* (New York: Colllier Books [Pantheon Books/Random House], 1966), 12. Admittedly, Watts's interpretation of Zen Buddhism has a decidedly acosmic bent, with God playing hide-and-seek with Himself, but the distinction is apparent as it concerns God's motivation: Watts suggests that God is merely playing an amusing "game" within the confines of a temporal world, while Acosmism asserts that the imagined world

is itself a direct, epistemological consequence of God's atemporal awareness of His own ignorance.

68. John Pearn and Christopher Gardner-Thorpe, "Jules Cotard," (1840–89): His Life and the Unique Syndrome which Bears His Name, *Neurology*, Volume 58, No. 9 (Hagerstown, Maryland: Lippincott Williams and Wilkins, 14 May 2002), 1400–3; doi:10.1212/wnl.58.9.1400. "The Cotard delusion is often referred to as the belief that one is dead or does not exist [… and] is the only self-certifiable delusion[, …] insofar as to declare I am dead or do not exist is self-evidently a contradiction." Garry Young, *Philosophical Psychopathology: Philosophy without Thought Experiments* (London: Palgrave Macmillan, 2013), 150–60. Cf. Andrew W. Young, Kate M. Leafhead, and T. Krystyna Szulecka, "The Capgras and Cotard Delusions," *Psychopathology*, Volume 27, No. 3–5 (Basel, Switzerland: S. Karger AG, 1994): 226–31, doi:10.1159/000284874; and Nancy Butcher, *The Strange Case of the Walking Corpse* (New York: Avery [Penguin], 2004), 98 et seq.

69. "[T]he amygdala and fusiform gyrus [… are] brain areas that participate in face processing and social cognition." David J. Grelotti, et al., "fMRI Activation of the Fusiform Gyrus and Amygdala to Cartoon Characters but Not to Faces in a Boy with Autism," *Neuropsychologia*, Volume 43, No. 3 (Oxford: Pergamon Press, 2005), 373–85; doi:10.1016/j. neuropsychologia.2004.06.015. "[D]ysfunction in the amygdala leads to emotional processing problems, and the dysfunction in the fusiform gyrus leads to a kind of prosopagnosia, or face blindness." Matthew Rouse, *Neuroanatomy for Speech-Language Pathology and Audiology* (Burlington, Massachusetts: Jones and Bartlett Learning, 2020), 330. "[A brain] region, located primarily in the right lateral fusiform gyrus, is activated specifically by faces." Gregory McCarthy, et al., "Face-Specific Processing in the Human Fusiform Gyrus," *Journal of Cognitive Neuroscience*, Volume 9, No. 5 (Cambridge, Massachusetts: Cognitive Neuroscience Institute [MIT Press], Fall 1997), 605–10; doi:10.1162/jocn.1997.9.5.605. Cf. Nouchine Hadjikhani and Beatrice De Gelder, "Neural Basis of Prosopagnosia: An fMRI Study," *Human Brain Mapping*, Volume 16, No. 3 (New York: Wiley-Liss [John Wiley and Sons], July 2002), 176–82; doi:10.1002/hbm.10043. "The visual memory ability to remember and recognize faces may be unique to people and perhaps other primates as well[, … since p]rimates are animals with visual abilities well suited to living in social groups." Robert Ornstein and Richard F. Thompson, *The Amazing Brain* (Boston: Houghton Mifflin, 1984), 141.

70. Michael H. Connors, Robyn Langdon, and Max Coltheart, "Misidentification Delusions," *Troublesome Disguises: Managing Challenging Disorders in Psychiatry* (Chichester, England: John Wiley and Sons, 2015

[1997]), 169–85. "*Delusional misidentification* [...] is a catch-all phrase for Capgras syndrome, Fregoli delusion, and other misidentification syndromes." Barry Wright, Subodh Dave, and Nisha Dogra, *100 Cases in Psychiatry* (Boca Raton, Florida: CRC Press [Taylor and Francis], 2017), 200; definitional emphasis in the original.

71. "[A] rare form of delusional misidentification, the Frégoli syndrome, is [... a] delusional misidentification [that] has been reported in affective, neurological, and toxic-metabolic disorders[, ... indicating] a diagnosis of paranoia (delusional disorder) secondary to predominantly right hemisphere pathology." Karel W. de Pauw, T. Krystyna Szulecka, and Tracy Poltock, "Frégoli Syndrome after Cerebral Infarction," *Journal of Nervous and Mental Disease*, Volume 175, No. 7 (Baltimore, Maryland: Williams and Wilkins, July 1987), 433–38; doi:10.1097/00005053-198707000-00008. See the chart from Cornelius Katona, Claudia Cooper, and Mary Robertson, *Psychiatry at a Glance* (Oxford: Wiley-Blackwell, 2012 [1995]), 38. Cf. Sally Wright, et al., "Frégoli Delusion and Erotomania," *Journal of Neurology, Neurosurgery, and Psychiatry*, Volume 56, No. 3 (London: BMJ Publishing [British Medical Association], March 1993), 322–23; doi:10.1136/jnnp.56.3.322-a.

72. The following citations refer to studies in which various delusional misidentification syndromes arise as a result of brain injury or trauma. Daryl Fujii and Iqbal Ahmed, "Characteristics of Psychotic Disorder Due to Traumatic Brain Injury: an Analysis of Case Studies in the Literature," *The Journal of Neuropsychiatry and Clinical Neurosciences*, Volume 14, No. 2 (Washington, D.C.: American Psychiatric Press, Spring 2002), 130–40; doi:10.1176/jnp.14.2.130. Todd E. Feinberg, et al., "Multiple Fregoli Delusions after Traumatic Brain Injury," *Cortex*, Volume 35, No. 3 (London: Elsevier, June 1999), 373–87; doi:10.1016/s0010-9452(08)70806-2. Miles E. Drake Jr., "Cotard's Syndrome and Temporal Lobe Epilepsy," *Psychiatric Journal of the University of Ottawa: Revue de Psychiatrie de L'universite D'ottawa*, Volume 13, No. 1 (Ottawa, Canada: University of Ottawa's Psychiatry Department's Journal Management Committee, March 1988), 36. Andrew W. Young, Kate M. Leafhead, and T. Krystyna Szulecka, "Cotard Delusion after Brain Injury," *Psychological Medicine*, Volume 22, No. 3 (Cambridge: Cambridge University Press, August 1992), 799–804; doi:10.1017/S003329170003823X. David Bienenfeld and Thomas Brott, "Capgras' Syndrome Following Minor Head Trauma," *The Journal of Clinical Psychiatry*, Volume 50, No. 2 (Memphis, Tennessee: Physicians Postgraduate Press, February 1989), 68–69. Martin A. Hayman and Richard Abrams, "Capgras' Syndrome and Cerebral Dysfunction," *The British Journal of Psychiatry*, Volume 130, No. 1 (London: Headley Brothers [Cambridge University Press], January 1977), 68–71. Margaret O'Connor, et al., "A Neuropsychological Analysis of

Capgras Syndrome," *Cognitive and Behavioral Neurology*, Volume 9, No. 4 (Philadelphia, Pennsylvania: Lippincott-Raven Publishers, October 1996), 265–71. Michael J. Weston and Francis Antony Whitlock, "The Capgras Syndrome Following Head Injury," *The British Journal of Psychiatry*, Volume 119, No. 548 (London: Headley Brothers [Cambridge University Press], July 1971), 25–31; doi:10.1192/bjp.119.548.25.

73. "[N]ihilistic delusion[:] A delusion that nothing exists, or that a significant aspect of the self (such as one's brain or the outside world) does not exist." Andrew M. Colman, *Oxford Dictionary of Psychology* (Oxford: Oxford University Press, 2015 [2001]), 507. Also, "NIHILISTIC DELUSION[:] Considered an existential delusion that raises the question Do we exist or not? In this delusion the answer is a resounding 'not.'" Henry Kellerman, *Dictionary of Psychopathology* (New York: Columbia University Press, 2009), 159; definitional capitalization in the original. And earlier medical texts cite "a nihilistic delusion that nothing longer exists, that everything has been destroyed." Richard (von) Krafft-Ebing, *Textbook of Insanity: Based on Clinical Observations for Practitioners and Students of Medicine*, trans. Charles Gilbert Chaddock (Philadelphia, Pennsylvania: F. A. Davis Co., 1905), 311.

74. "Cotard syndrome is a rare condition characterized by nihilistic delusions concerning body or life[, ... which appeared in] a case of Cotard syndrome without depressive symptoms in the context of known paranoid schizophrenia." Pedro Morgado, Ricardo Ribeiro, and João J. Cerqueira, "Cotard Syndrome without Depressive Symptoms in a Schizophrenic Patient," *Case Reports in Psychiatry*, Volume 2015, Article 643191 (New York: Hindawi Publishing, 25 May 2015); doi:10.1155/2015/643191. In other cases, the "experience of losing the self can become manifest in an extreme and sometimes bizarre way in the course of psychotic depression, particularly as nihilistic delusion." *Neuropsychodynamic Psychiatry*, ed. Heinz Boeker, Peter Hartwich, and Georg Northoff (Cham, Switzerland: Springer International Publishing [Springer Nature], 2018), 233.

75. "*Delusions* are fixed beliefs that are not amenable to change in light of conflicting evidence." *Diagnostic and Statistical Manual of Mental Disorders (DSM-5)* (Washington D.C.: American Psychiatric Association, 2013), 87; emphasis in the original. An earlier definition characterizes delusion as a "false personal belief based on incorrect inference about external reality and firmly sustained in spite of what almost everyone else believes and in spite of what constitutes incontrovertible and obvious proof or evidence to the contrary." Brendan A. Maher, "Delusions: Contemporary Etiological Hypotheses," *Psychiatric Annals*, Volume 22, No. 5 (Thorofare, New Jersey: Slack, 1 May 1992), 260–68; doi:10.3928/0048-5713-19920501-11.

76. "Delusions are deemed bizarre if they are clearly implausible and not understandable to same-culture peers and do not derive from ordinary life experiences." *Diagnostic and Statistical Manual*, 87. These include "[p]ersistent delusions of other kinds that are culturally inappropriate and completely impossible." *Neurobiology of Mental Illness*, ed. Dennis S. Charney, et al. (Oxford: Oxford University Press, 2013), 227; citing *International Statistical Classification of Diseases and Related Health Problems (ICD-10)*, Schizophrenia #G1d (Geneva, Switzerland: World Health Organization, 2004).

77. "A *functional hallucination* is a true hallucination originating in a perception, but independent of perception itself[, … whereas] *[i]llusions* are misinterpretations of perceived objects [… and] are found in many psychotic disorders." *The Assessment of Psychosis*, ed. Flavie Waters and Massoud Stephane (London and New York: Routledge [Taylor and Francis], 2015), 66; emphases in the original. But "[t]o say simply that a delusion is a mistaken idea […] gives only a superficial and incorrect answer." Karl Jaspers, *Gesammelte Schriften zur Psychopathologie* (Berlin / Heidelberg, Germany: Springer-Verlag, 1963), 93; English title: *Collected Writings on Psychopathology*.

78. "[T]he truth or falsity of a non-tautologous proposition [is] determined by experience[, … and if] *some* knowledge is acquired by experience[, … then perhaps] *all* knowledge is so acquired." A. Cornelius Benjamin, "Is Empiricism Self-Refuting?" in *The Journal of Philosophy*, Volume 38, No. 21, ed. The Columbia University Philosophy Department (New York: The Journal of Philosophy, Inc. [Columbia University], 9 October 1941), 571; doi:10.2307/2018321, emphases in the original. The view that "'existence is an illusion, and reality isn't real' […] is self-refuting[, in that i]t leads to solipsism, the idea that only oneself exists." David F. Coppedge, "Does the Mind Create Reality or Discover It?" on *Creation-Evolution Headlines at CrEv.info*, ed. David F. Coppedge (California: Master Plan Association, 21 July 2013) at **https://crev.info/2013/07/does-the-mind-create-reality-or-discovery-it/**, accessed February, 20, 2020. "Acosmism, then, would seem to be self-refuting." Kristor Lawson, "A Prayer for Lawrence Auster", *The Orthosphere*, ed. Richard Cocks (San Francisco, California: Automattic, Inc., 6 January 2013) at **https://orthosphere.wordpress.com/2013/01/06/a-prayer-for-lawrence-auster/**, also accessed February, 20, 2020.

Chapter 10: Faith

1. Translation of the original French, "qui est en droit de vous rendre absurde est en droit de vous rendre injuste," often obliquely paraphrased as "those who can make you believe absurdities can make you commit atrocities." Voltaire

(François-Marie Arouet), *Oeuvres Completes de Voltaire*, Volume 8 (Paris: F. Didot freres, 1875), 691; from *Questions sur les Miracles* (1765).

2. Immanuel Kant, *Critique of Pure Reason*, trans. Werner S. Pluhar (Indianapolis, Indiana: Hackett Publishing Company, 1966 [1787]), 31; Bxxx, Preface, emphasis in the original.

3. Albert Einstein, *Einstein on Cosmic Religion and Other Opinions and Aphorisms* (Mineola, New York: Dover Publications [Covici-Friede], 2009 [1931]), 97.

4. Alfred Jules Ayer, *Language, Truth and Logic* (New York: Dover Publications, 2012 [1936]), 36.

5. The pragmatic outlook of William James has been said to involve a "requirement that a true proposition be actually verified." Richard M. Gale, *The Divided Self of William James* (New York: Cambridge University Press, 1999), 130. "[B]efore a proposition is actually verified it is only possibly true[; furthermore t]he requirement that a true proposition be actually verified amounts to equating truth with knowledge." Richard M. Gale, *The Philosophy of William James* (New York: Cambridge University Press, 2005), 34 and 107.

6. [W]e cannot distinguish knowledge from (mere) belief by the fact that knowledge entails truth[, nor can we] say that knowledge is merely true belief[, … which] could be true by accident. William P. Alston, *A Realist Conception of Truth* (Ithaca, New York: Cornell University Press, 1996), 248. Specifically, "[t]here needs to be something that connects your belief to the truth, some way in which belief is sensitive to the truth, and doesn't just stumble over it by accident." Steven D. Hales, *This Is Philosophy* (Chichester, England: Wiley-Blackwell [John Wiley and Sons], 2013), 245. "In order for a belief to count as knowledge, a person needs to have a good *reason* for a true belief[, … so] knowledge is true, *justified* belief." Jason Lisle, *The Ultimate Proof of Creation* (Green Forest, Arizona: Master Books [New Leaf Publishing], 2009), 41; emphasis in the original. See the "Figure 1" Venn diagram illustration and its description about the relationship between belief, truth, and knowledge in Kevin S. Krahenbuhl, *The Decay of Truth in Education* (Newcastle upon Tyne, England: Cambridge Scholars Publishing, 2018), 3.

7. "[J]ustification of basic or nonbasic beliefs will never yield a justified false belief[, … thereby serving to] ensure that no justification essentially depends on error or is defeated by it." Keith Lehrer, *Theory of Knowledge* (London: Routledge, 1990), 44. Cf. Peter Unger, *Ignorance: A Case for Scepticism* (Oxford: Oxford University Press, 1975). "One way to avoid the Gettier Problem is to simply deny that it is possible to have justified

false beliefs." Kevin McCain, *The Nature of Scientific Knowledge* (Cham, Switzerland: Springer International [Springer Nature], 2016), 122. Furthermore, "[m]isleading testimony can justify untrue epistemic beliefs in the presence of conflicting epistemic facts that are not apparent." Richard Feldman and Earl Conee, "Between Belief and Disbelief," *Believing in Accordance with the Evidence: New Essays on Evidentialism*, ed. Kevin McCain (Cham, Switzerland: Springer International [Springer Nature], 2018), 89. But from an altogether different perspective, "[one can] establish a connection between justification and truth without making it impossible to have a justified false belief [… by turning our] focus on the processes that produce belief." Richard Fumerton, *Metaepistemology and Skepticism* (Lanham, Maryland: Rowman and Littlefield, 1995), 97. In a specific case, "you can have a justified false belief, since this is crucial to the Gettier cases[, … like when a] stopped clock just happens to be 'telling' the right time." Duncan Pritchard, *What is this Thing Called Knowledge?* (London: Routledge [Taylor and Francis], 2006), 27. Moreover, "one can insist that justification for false beliefs is impossible[, … and such a] view amounts to a form of infallibilism[, … which, from the perspective of this author,] is not an accurate descriptive account." Alex Broadbent, *Philosophy for Graduate Students: Metaphysics and Epistemology* (London and New York: Routledge [Taylor and Francis], 2016), 127.

8. Hans Albert, *Treatise on Critical Reason*, trans. Mary Varney Rorty (Princeton, New Jersey: Princeton University Press, 1985 [1968]), 18.

9. "The right emblem for *causa sui* is Baron Münchhausen, sinking on horseback into the water, clinging by the legs to his horse and pulling both himself and the animal out by his own pigtail, with the motto underneath: *Causa sui*." Arthur Schopenhauer, *On the Four-Fold Root of the Principle of Sufficient and On the Will in Nature: Two Essays by Arthur Schopenhauer* (London: George Bell and Sons, 1891), 17.

10. Albert, *Treatise on Critical Reason*, 18.

11. Certainty appears only to be possible through a "justification by *recourse to dogma*." Ibid., 18–20; emphasis in the original.

12. Edmund L. Gettier, "Is Justified True Belief Knowledge?" in *Analysis*, Volume 23, No. 6 (June 1963), 121–23; doi: 0.1093/analys/23.6.121.

13. Robert J. Fogelin, *Pyrrhonian Reflections on Knowledge and Justification* (Oxford: Oxford University Press, 1994), 22–23.

14. Robert Nozick, *Philosophical Explanations* (Cambridge, Massachusetts: Harvard University Press, 1981), 176 and 234.

15. Internet comment by Nat (**https://english.stackexchange.com/ users/225288/nat**), *Stack Overflow* (New York: Stack Exchange, 13 April 2017) at **https://english.stackexchange.com/a/384358**, accessed February 22, 2020.

16. Refer to the "Prevailing Belief" map on *CloudFront.net* (Seattle, Washington: Amazon, ca. 12 March 2019) at **http://d3tt741pwxqwm0.cloudfront.net/ WGBH/sj14/sj14-int-religmap/index.html**, accessed March 5, 2019.

17. "[G]roups give a survival edge to their members[, … and since] humanity's ancestors lived in an environment that favored those who lived in groups, […] over time those who affiliated would gradually outnumber those who were self-reliant loners." Donelson R. Forsyth, *Group Dynamics* (Belmont, California: Thomson Wadsworth [Thomson Learning], 2006), 75. "It is the crowd[, …] the vast human herd, that exerts a baneful attraction on those outside it." William McDougall, *An Introduction to Social Psychology* (Boston: John W. Luce and Co., 1909), 296.

18. "[H]umans before agriculture [… were ones whose] lives depend on killing prey, and on not being killed by predators[, …s]o rituals connected with hunting and avoiding predators are prominent[, … and because h]uman death is a major concern, […] they mark it with rituals." John Morreall and Tamara Sonn, *The Religion Toolkit: A Complete Guide to Religious Studies* (Chichester, England: Wiley-Blackwell [John Wiley and Sons], 2012), 115. Moreover, "rituals have usually left behind cultic paraphernalia that can be unearthed and analyzed[, … and as] religion is a mechanism for the coordination and control of groups of peoples[, … a] community that practises religion is more efficient over time and survives better than a community without it." Yosef Garfinkel, "Dancing with Masks in the Proto-historic Near East," *Ritual, Play and Belief, in Evolution and Early Human Societies*, ed. Colin Renfrew, Iain Morley, and Michael Boyd (Cambridge: Cambridge University Press, 2017), 144. And "group rituals would have enhanced survival through physical and emotional healing, enforcement of group norms, and resource management." Hervey C. Peoples, et al., "Hunter-Gatherers and the Origins of Religion," *Human Nature*, Volume 27 (New York: Springer Nature, 6 May 2016), 261–82; doi:10.1007/s12110-016-9260-0.

19. "[T]he best time to indoctrinate people is early in life […] because skepticism has yet to develop[; … i]f religions had factual evidence or a basis in truth, it would not be necessary to brainwash children [… by t]elling children that Jesus loves them[, which] is exactly what they wish to hear at a young age." Lawrence Allen, *Future Cost of Today's Religion* (Lincoln, Nebraska: iUniverse, 2006), 35. And "religions survive mainly because they brainwash the young." A. C. Grayling, *Against All Gods* (London: Oberon Books [Bloomsbury], 2007).

20. Even in the face of resistance, "religion is an instrument of social control that works in a subtle way through internalized value- and belief-systems." Christian P. Scherrer, *Structural Prevention of Ethnic Violence* (New York: Palgrave Macmillan, 2002), 234.

21. "[A]doption of […] dietary laws helped the church spread[, … especially through those] dispersed from their homeland by colonization and the slave trade." *National Geographic Concise History of World Religions*, ed. Tim Cooke (Washington, D.C.: National Geographic Society [Book Division], 2011), 303. As an example, "the spread of Christianity […] illustrates the connections between religion, trade, and imperial politics." Richard Bulliet, et al., *The Earth and Its Peoples* (Boston: Wadsworth [CENGAGE Learning], 2011 [2005]), 225.

22. The world has "over 4,200 religions[, … or more accurately, data collected contain] 43,940 adherent records [representing] 4,351 groups." *Adherents.com* (Dallas, Texas: Preston Hunter, ca. 22 April 1999) at the now-defunct **https://www.adherents.com/**, accessed February 24, 2020. A more exhausting analysis, however, reveals "the world's 12,600 ethnic peoples and their 10,000 distinct religions." Todd M. Johnson and David B. Barrett, "Quantifying Alternate Futures of Religion and Religions," *Futures*, Volume 36, No. 9, ed. Ted Fuller (London: Elsevier, November 2004), 953; doi:10.1016/j.futures.2004.02.009. Citations are to a scholarly work, published every nineteen years, which covers "at least 10,000 distinct religions, 12,600 peoples, 13,500 languages, 7,000 cities, and 3,030 major civil divisions in 238 countries." *World Christian Encyclopedia: A Comparative Survey of Churches and Religions in The Modern World*, Volume 3, ed. David B. Barrett, George T. Kurian, and Todd M. Johnson (Oxford: Oxford University Press, 2001).

23. "Major Religions of the World Ranked by Number of Adherents," *Adherents.com* (Dallas, Texas: Preston Hunter, ca. 4 March 2000) at the now-defunct **https://www.adherents.com/Religions_By_Adherents.html**, accessed February 24, 2020.

24. Ibid. at the now-defunct **https://www.adherents.com/Religions_ By_Adherents.html#Nonreligious**, accessed February 24, 2020. Cf. Pew Research Center, "The Global Religious Landscape: A Report on the Size and Distribution of the World's Major Religious Groups as of 2010," under "Forum on Religion and Public Life" (Washington, D.C.: The Pew Charitable Trusts, December 2012) at **https://www.pewforum. org/2012/12/18/global-religious-landscape-exec/**, also accessed February 24, 2020.

25. Op cit. "Major Religions … Ranked," *Adherents.com*.

26. See "Appendix 1: Table of Religions," showing the primary "Holy books" for each religion. Roger Whiting, *Religions for Today* (Cheltenham, England: Stanley Thornes Publishers, 1983), 251. See also Sue Penney, *Christianity* (Oxford: Heinemann Educational Publishers [Harcourt Education], 1999), 22. "[T]he Bible as contained in the Tawrat, Zabur and Injil is spiritually subsumed within the essence of the Qur'an." Stephen N. Lambden, "Islam," *The Blackwell Companion to the Bible and Culture*, ed. John F. A. Sawyer (Oxford: Blackwell Publishing, 2006), 141. "[P]rophets were given books of divine revelation[: …] Moses, who was given the Tawrat (Torah), David, who was given the Zabur (Psalms), Jesus, who was given the Injil (Gospel), and Muhammad, who was given the Qur'an." Dean Halverson, *The Compact Guide To World Religions* (Bloomington, Minnesota: Bethany House Publishers, 1996), 106. Cf. Paul Gwynne, *World Religions in Practice* (Hoboken, New Jersey: John Wiley and Sons, 2018), 65; Michael McDowell and Nathan Robert Brown, *World Religions At Your Fingertips* (New York: Alpha Books [Penguin], 2009), 171, 208, and 19; and Sue Penney, *Judaism* (Oxford: Heinemann Educational Publishers [Harcourt Education], 1995 [1987]), 12.

27. "[Just] 24% believe [that the] Bible is [the] literal word of God, the lowest in Gallup's 40-year trend." Lydia Saad, "Record Few Americans Believe Bible Is Literal Word of God," *Gallup's annual Values and Beliefs poll* (Washington, D.C.: The Gallup Organization, conducted May 3–7, 2017) at **https://news. gallup.com/poll/210704/record-few-americans-believe-bible-literal- word-god.aspx**, accessed April 3, 2020. Cf. trends in Pew Research Center, "Religious Landscape Study: Interpreting Scripture" (Washington, D.C.: The Pew Charitable Trusts, 2014) at **https://www.pewforum.org/religious- landscape-study/interpreting-scripture/#religious-tradition**, also accessed April 2, 2020.

28. "Revelation means, 'God disclosing to humanity truths they would not otherwise know'[, … while d]ivine inspiration means that God preserved the writers from recording error[; … in contrast,] what we call illumination [refers to] the ability to understand the truths that God has already revealed." Don Stewart, "Is There a Difference between Revelation and Divine Inspiration?" on *Blue Letter Bible* (Lake Forest, California: Sowing Circle, ca. 25 November 2011) at **https://www.blueletterbible.org/faq/don_stewart/ don_stewart_800.cfm**, accessed October 26, 2018; later revised at **https:// www.blueletterbible.org/Comm/stewart_don/faq/bible-authoritative-word/ question9-revelation-and-divine-inspiration.cfm**. Surprisingly, some assert that what constitutes divine inspiration has definable standards, as when "the Quran and the book of Mormon claim to be inspired by God[, … yet] we have good reasons to believe otherwise." Jason Lisle, "The Bible vs. other Holy Books," *BiblicalScienceInstitute.com* (Colorado Springs, Colorado: Biblical

Science Institute, 21 September 2018) at **https://biblicalscienceinstitute. com/apologetics/the-bible-vs-other-holy-books/**, also accessed October 26, 2018. Cf. William Evans, *The Great Doctrines of the Bible* (Chicago: The Bible Institute Colportage Association, 1912), 194–210; and Augustus Hopkins Strong, *Systematic Theology* (New York: A. C. Armstrong and Son, 1889), 95.

29. Making the point that scientific information is discoverable, while religious information is not, Gervais speculates that "[i]f you took every holy book, every holy book there's ever been, every religious book, every bit of spirituality, and hid them or destroyed them[,] then you took every science book and destroyed that, in a thousand years' time, those science books would be back exactly the same, because the tests would always turn out the same[, … yet] those religious books would either never exist or they'd be totally different, because there's no test." Hemant Mehta, "Ricky Gervais: If Holy Books and Science Books Disappeared, Only One Would Return with the Same Info," *Patheos.com* (Virginia Beach, Virginia: BeliefNet [BN Media Associates], 9 February 2017) at **http://friendlyatheist.patheos. com/2017/02/09/ricky-gervais-if-holy-books-science-books-disappeared- only-one-would-return-with-the-same-info/**, accessed October 19, 2018; referencing interviews with Sean Evans by First We Feast, "Ricky Gervais Pits His Mild British Palate Against Spicy Wings," *YouTube* video, 22:09 (New Haven, Connecticut: Yale University Press, 9 February 2017) at **https:// www.youtube.com/watch?v=3qrNRzkwlbU**; and with Stephen Colbert by Hemant Mehta, "Ricky Gervais to Stephen Colbert: 'You Don't Believe in 2,999 Gods. I Don't Believe in Just 1 More'" (Virginia Beach, Virginia: BeliefNet [BN Media Associates], 2 February 2017) at **https://friendlyatheist.patheos. com/2017/02/02/ricky-gervais-to-stephen-colbert-you-dont-believe-in- 2999-gods-i-dont-believe-in-just-1-more/**. From another perspective, others counter that the destruction of the proof of an event doesn't alter the fact that the event occurred, especially as long as the ongoing effect of the event lives on; science may thus be merely a tool we use to discover truth about the present world. Danielle Camorlinga, "Science vs. History: The Great Gervais Book Burning," *YouthApologeticsNetwork.com* (La Mirada, California: Youth Apologetics Network, 3 February 2017) at **http://www. youthapologeticsnetwork.com/2017/02/science-vs-history-great-gervais- book-burning/**, also accessed October 19, 2018.

30. Joseph Campbell, *The Hero with a Thousand Faces* (New York: Pantheon Books [Random House], 1949).

31. "And the tables were the work of God, and the writing was the writing of God, graven upon the tables" (Exod. 32:16); "[when] he saw the calf, and the dancing[, …] Moses' anger waxed hot, and he cast the tables out

of his hands, and brake them beneath the mount" (Exod. 32:19); "[a]nd the Lord said unto Moses, [...] 'I will write upon these [newly prepared] tables the words that were in the first tables, which thou brakest'" (Exod. 34:1). In another characterization, "Moses raises the Ten Commandments, inscribed by the finger of God[, ... and, w]hether Moses intended it or not, shattering the tablets graphically symbolized what the people had done[, ... in that] the Hebrews probably broke the first and most important of the Ten Commandments." Stephen M. Miller, *Incredible Mysteries of the Bible: A Visual Exploration* (Grand Rapids, Michigan: Zondervan [HarperCollins], 2008), 26.

32. "A rainbow is a multicolored arc made by light striking water droplets[, ... as when] sunlight strikes raindrops in front of a viewer at a precise angle (42 degrees)[, ... but actually] is an optical illusion—it does not actually exist in a specific spot in the sky[; ... t]he sun or other source of light is usually behind the person seeing the rainbow[s, ... which] are the result of the refraction and reflection of light" that is seen above the horizon. "Rainbow," *National Geographic* (Washington, D.C.: National Geographic Society, 31 May 2016) at **http://www.nationalgeographic.org/encyclopedia/rainbow/**, accessed November 1, 2018. Due to surface tension, two-millimeter drops form which are spherical, while the sun must be behind the water at or above forty-two degrees on the horizon; "refraction of sunlight in falling water droplets plus reflection of the light from the back of the droplet" causes the light to focus at the points of both the entrance of the droplet and in its post-reflection. Federica Volpi, "On the Physics of Rainbow," *Interdisciplinary Encyclopedia of Religion and Science*, ed. Advanced School for Interdisciplinary Research (Rome, Italy: Pontifical University of the Holy Cross, 18 August 2015) at **http://inters.org/physics-of-rainbow**, also accessed November 1, 2018. For a sophisticated mathematical treatment, see John A. Adam, "The Mathematical Physics of Rainbows and Glories," *Physics Reports*, Volume 356, Nos. 4–5 (Amsterdam: North-Holland Publishing, January 2002), 229–365; doi:10.1016/S0370-1573(01)00076-X.

33. "[The] Venus Express [spacecraft], which has been orbiting Earth's sister planet since 2006, observed [rainbow-like] glories in April and July 2011[, ...] the first sighting of a full extraterrestrial glory[; ...] for conditions in the Venusian clouds, which [are] made of sulphuric acid and completely enveloping the planet, [...] that a glory can form at all suggests that the cloud droplets are spherical in shape and uniform in size[, ... roughly] 2.4 micrometres in diameter." George Musser, "Why the 'Venus Rainbow' is Actually a Glory," *Nature News* (London: Nature Research [Springer Nature], 14 March 2014) at **https://www.nature.com/articles/nature.2014.14869**, accessed November 1, 2018; doi:10.1038/nature.2014.14869. Still, "[t]he ingredients required to make a rainbow are sunlight and raindrops[, ... but

c]urrently, there is no other planet known to have liquid water on its surface or in sufficient quantities in the atmosphere to make rain." Alastair Gunn, "Are There Rainbows on Other Planets?" in *BBC Science Focus Magazine* (London: Immediate Media Company [BBC Studios], 21 April 2020) at **https://www.sciencefocus.com/space/are-there-rainbows-on-other-planets/**, accessed April 24, 2020. With respect to exoplanets, "liquid water clouds covering as little as 10–20% of the planetary surface, with more than half of these covered by ice clouds, still create a polarized rainbow feature in the planetary signal[, … while] calculations of flux and polarization signals of an exoplanet with a realistic Earth-like cloud coverage, show a strong polarized rainbow feature." Theodora Karalidi, Daphne M. Stam, and Joachim W. Hovenier, "Looking for the Rainbow on Exoplanets Covered by Liquid and Icy Water Clouds," *Astronomy and Astrophysics*, Volume 548 (Berlin: European Southern Observatory [Springer-Verlag], December 2012), A90; doi:10.1051/0004-6361/201220245. See also Joe Rao, "Rainbows: How They Form and How to See Them," *LiveScience.com* (New York: TechMedia Network [Purch Group], 15 March 2011) at **https://www.livescience.com/30235-rainbows-formation-explainer.html**, also accessed November 1, 2018.

34. God is said to have declared, "I do set My [rain]bow in the cloud, and it shall be for a token of a covenant between Me and the earth[, … that] the waters shall no more become a flood to destroy all flesh[, … and thus,] the bow shall be in the cloud; and I will look upon it, that I may remember the everlasting covenant" (Gen. 9:13–16). "So the next time you see a rainbow, remember that God judges sin[, … which He did] with a global flood at the time of Noah[, … b]ut He is merciful, and He made a covenant of grace with Noah and the animals that He would never again judge with a worldwide Flood." Ken Ham, "Taking Back the Rainbow," *Answers in Genesis* (Hebron, Kentucky: Answers in Genesis, Inc., 27 March 2007) at **https://answersingenesis.org/the-flood/taking-back-the-rainbow/**, accessed November 1, 2018.

35. "[Entry for] Rainbow: Caused by the reflection and refraction of the rays of the sun shining on falling rain[, … which] existed indeed before [but that some argue did not because] the atmosphere was differently constituted before the Flood." Matthew George Easton, *Illustrated Bible Dictionary, and Treasury of Biblical History, Biography, Geography, Doctrine, and Literature* (New York: T. Nelson and Sons, 1894), 572; citing Franz Delitzsch, *A New Commentary on Genesis*, Volume 1, trans. Sophia Taylor (Edinburgh: T. and T. Clark, 1888), 288–89.

36. Some acknowledge that "the rainbow must have existed prior to the flood," but its designation as "a symbol or sacramental sign" first occurred at

the event occasioning the divine covenant (or promise) that it would never happen again. John Cumming, *Is Christianity from God? A Manual of Christian Evidence* (London: Arthur Hall and Co., 1847), 202. Cf. Jason Kruger, "Proof That Religion Is a Man-Made Device and Why It Is Outdated," *MyNews24* (Cape Town, South Africa: Naspers, 17 October 2014) at **https://www.news24. com/News24/MyNews24/Proof-that-religion-is-a-man-made-device-and-why-it-is-outdated-this-article-mainlyuses-Christiani-20141017**, accessed October 19, 2018; and Laurence A. Turner, "The Rainbow as the Sign of the Covenant in Genesis IX 11–13," *Vetus Testamentum*, Volume 43, No. Fasc. 1 (Leiden, Netherlands: Brill Publishers, January 1993), 119–24. Others have noted that the scripture's use of "[t]he term 'My rainbow' implies that it had existed earlier." Michael Hattin, "The Rainbow," *etzion.org.il* (Alon Shvut, Israel [Jerusalem]: Yeshiva Publications, April 2016) at **https://www. etzion.org.il/en/rainbow-0**, accessed October 19, 2018. Meanwhile, still others advance the so-called "Canopy Theory," which posits—without citing any supporting evidence—that the pre-Flood earth was hydrated with a rainless mist and that an atmospheric layer of water was released to initiate the worldwide flooding. Danny R. Faulkner, *The Expanse of Heaven: Where Creation and Astronomy Intersect* (Green Forest, Arizona: Master Books [New Leaf Publishing], 2017), 98–100.

37. Jean Piaget, *The Construction of Reality in the Child* (London: Routledge and Kegan Paul, 1954).

38. The various (Old Testament, and specifically, Genesis) biblical passages supporting the contention include: "And God said, 'Let us make man in Our image, after Our likeness.'" (Gen. 1:26); "So God created man in His *Own* image, in the image of God created He him; male and female created He them." (Gen. 1:27), emphasis in the original; "God created man, in the likeness of God made He him." (Gen. 5:1); and "in the image of God made He man." (Gen. 9:6). Usually taken as the "royal 'we,'" some interpret the reference differently by observing that "[t]he term 'let us' prevents the image being referred directly to God alone[, ... and perhaps] refers there to the angels." Gerhard von Rad, *Old Testament Theology*, Volume 1: The Theology of Israel's Historical Traditions, trans. D. M. G. Stalker (San Francisco, California: Oliver and Boyd [HarperCollins], 1962), 145. Others reinterpret the meaning by rationalizing that, although "humans are made in the image and likeness of God[, ... i]t is widely accepted that the image is not primarily a physical one[; ... r]ather it is often suggested that humans reflect God in their capacity for rational thought, in their ability to communicate or even as moral agents, able to freely choose their actions and to anticipate the moral consequences of them." See "The Doctrine of Humanity," *Christian Doctrine*, ed. Lindsey Hall, Murray Rae, and Steve Holmes (London: SCM Press [Student Christian Movement], 2010), 280.

39. "The uniqueness of each human face, with the possible exception of monozygotic twins, allows for identification [… for purposes of] facial recognition." Karen Gripp and Luis Fernando Escobar, "Facial Bones," *Human Malformations and Related Anomalies*, ed. Roger E. Stevenson and Judith G. Hall (Oxford: Oxford University Press, 2006), 267.

40. "[W]ith deeper implications in human interaction and, more important, in social functioning[, …t]he human facial form results from the interaction between the skeletal and soft tissue elements[, … which, based on t]he skeletal framework provides the structural support of the face and is largely responsible for size, shape, and proportions of each facial structure." Ibid.

41. John Gurche, *Shaping Humanity: How Science, Art, and Imagination Help Us Understand Our Origins* (New Haven, Connecticut: Yale University Press, 2013). See also this same "paleoartist's" accompanying video: John Gurche, "Shaping Humanity: How Science, Art, and Imagination Help Us Understand Our Origins," *YouTube* video, 2:40 (New Haven, Connecticut: Yale University Press, 18 October 2013) at **https://www.youtube.com/ watch?v=ru8ifph_q9o**, accessed April 24, 2020. Additionally, "[a]lthough humans seem to vary a great deal in physical appearance, we are actually a genetically homogeneous species." Lynn B. Jorde, Michael Bamshad, and Alan R. Rogers "Using Mitochondrial and Nuclear DNA Markers to Reconstruct Human Evolution," *Bioessays*, Volume 20, No. 2 (Cambridge: ICSU Press [Cambridge University Press], February 1998), 126–36; doi:10.1002/ (SICI)1521-1878(199802)20:2%3C126::AID-BIES5%3E3.0.CO%3B2-R.

42. "But if cattle and horses or lions had hands, or were able to draw with their hands and do the works that men can do, horses would draw the forms of the gods like horses, cattle like cattle, and they would make their bodies such as they each had themselves." G. S. Kirk, J. E. Raven, and M. Schofield, *The Presocratic Philosophers: A Critical History with a Selection of Texts* (New York: Cambridge University Press, 1983), 175; fragment B 15; KRS 169.

43. Ian Morison, *Introduction to Astronomy and Cosmology* (Chichester, England: John Wiley and Sons, 2008), 67.

44. "I do not consider it necessary to believe that the same God who has endowed us with senses, and with the power of reasoning and intellect, should have chosen to set aside and to convey to us by some other means those facts which we are capable of finding out by exercising these faculties." Galileo Galilei, "Letter to the Grand Duchess Christina," *Selected Writings*, trans. William R. Shea and Mark Davie (Oxford: Oxford University Press, 2012 [1615]), 68.

45. "[T]o religious societies the sacrifice seems like the conclusion of the mimetic crisis enacted by the ritual[, ... where often,] everyone assembled is required to participate [... or] in the name of everyone involved[, ... and t]he community affirms its unity in the sacrifice[, ... which] is simply another act of violence." René Girard with Jean-Michel Oughourlian and Guy Lefort, *Things Hidden Since the Foundation of the World* (London: Athlone Press [University of London], 1987), 24. "Religion [...] regulates and even authenticates violence in the form of ritualized sacrifice." Mark Juergensmeyer and Margo Kitts, *Princeton Readings in Religion and Violence* (Princeton, New Jersey: Princeton University Press, 2011), 96. "Ritualized sacrifice is thus institutionalized in human cultures, alongside myths that justify it." Scott Cowdell, et al., *Violence, Desire, and the Sacred*, Volume 2: René Girard and Sacrifice in Life, Love, and Literature (New York: Bloomsbury Academic [Bloomsbury Publishing], 2014), xviii. "All religions consider sacrifice, more or less transformed, as pre-eminently the means of realizing the union of man with the divinity." Albert Réville, *Prolegomena of the History of Religions*, trans. A. S. Squire (London: Williams and Northgate, 1884), 128. "Sacrifice constitutes an essential part of every religion in the world." John Bate, *A Cyclopædia of Illustrations of Moral and Religious Truths* (London: H. J. Tresidder, 1865), 714. On the other hand, "sacrifice is not a central component to all religions[; ...] Buddhism, for example, does not have sacrifice as one of its tenets[, ... while] Girard's theory explains *subconscious* human desire and the actions that these thoughts produce." Heather Selma Gregg, *The Path to Salvation: Religious Violence from the Crusades to Jihad* (Lincoln, Nebraska: Potomac Books [University of Nebraska Press], 2014), 24; emphasis in the original. Although, one "theory contends that channeling violence onto a victim—be it in the form of ritualized sacrifice or spontaneous scapegoating—does not 'work' any more after it has been unmasked." Nikolaus Wandinger, "Religion and Violence," *Journal of Religion and Violence*, Volume 1, No. 2 (Charlottesville, Virginia: Philosophy Documentation Center, 2013), 127–46. And lest we think the barbarism of animal sacrifice in the name of religion is a thing of the past, a modern-day example is the Gadhimai festival in Nepal: "In 2009, during a particularly brutal festival, up to 500,000 animals were slaughtered[, ... while f]ive years later, the number was reduced to 30,000[; ...] on [...] this year's heaviest day for sacrifices, about 3,500 buffalo were killed[, ... although t]hose numbers will increase when the rest of the sacrificed animals are counted." Bhadra Sharma, "Nepal's Animal-Sacrifice Festival Slays On[, ...] But Activists Are Having an Effect," *New York Times* (New York: The New York Times Company, 6 December 2019) at **https://www.nytimes.com/2019/12/06/world/asia/nepal-animal-sacrifice-gadhimai.html**, accessed April 25, 2020. "Chandan Dev Chaudhary, a Hindu priest, said he was pleased with the [2009] festival's high turnout and insisted tradition

had to be kept[, … adding,] 'The goddess needs blood.'" Olivia Lang, "Hindu Sacrifice of 250,000 Animals Begins," *TheGuardian.com* (London: Guardian Media Group [Scott Trust Limited], 24 November 2009) at **https://www. theguardian.com/world/2009/nov/24/hindu-sacrifice-gadhimai-festival-nepal**, accessed April 20, 2019.

46. "Through the collective expression of ritualized sacrifice, violence is removed from the group and directed against a safe 'victim,' [… revealing that s]ome form of ritual expression of aggression is part of every religion." Charles Selengut, *Sacred Fury: Understanding Religious Violence* (Lanham, Maryland: Rowman and Littlefield, 2017), 43. "One such cultural institution is religion, which shelters the expression of cathartic violence in the guise of ritualized sacrifice[, … and t]hrough religion, Girard claims, the death of a sacrificial victim becomes a saving death." Mark Juergensmeyer, *God at War: A Meditation on Religion and Warfare* (New York: Oxford University Press, 2020), 90.

47. "Apollo speaks to us through the Pythia[, or the priestess of Temple of Apollo]." Shaul Tor, "Heraclitus on Apollo's Signs and His Own: Contemplating Oracles and Philosophical Inquiry," *Theologies of Ancient Greek Religion*, ed. Esther Eidinow, Julia Kindt, and Robin Osborne (Cambridge: Cambridge University Press, 2016), 94. "At Delphi, for example, Apollo sent oracles delivered in garbled speech by the Pythia[, … or the priestess of Temple of Apollo, whose] words, in turn, were 'translated.'" Jennifer Eyl, *Signs, Wonders, and Gifts* (New York: Oxford University Press, 2019), 52. "Zeus gehören die bedeutendsten Zeichenorakel, Apollon die Spruchorakel, der Wille des Zeus wird aus Zeichen und Erscheinungen erkannt, Apollon spricht durch den Mund des von ihm erfüllten Propheten" (German for "Zeus owns the most important oracles of signs, Apollo the oracles of speech; the will of Zeus is recognized from signs and phenomena, while Apollo speaks through the mouth of the prophet whom he has chosen"). Paul Stengel, *Die Griechischen Kultusaltertümer* (Munich: C. H. Beck'sche Verlagsbuchhandlung [Oskar Beck], 1920), 68; English title: *The Greek Cultural Antiquities*. "[A]s a sign that it is no human wisdom and art which reveals the divine will, Apollo speaks through the mouth of feeble girls and women." Ernst Curtius, *The History of Greece*, Volume 2, trans. Adolphus William Ward (New York: Charles Scribner and Company, 1871), 14.

48. "[M]isinterpretation is key to oracular failure[; … such heroes are those whose] stories are consistently over-confident[, … and by mistakenly] assuming the oracle's language to be straightforward, they never acknowledge differences between mortal and divine knowledge and perceptions of time and causality." Lisa Raphals, *Divination and Prediction in Early China and Ancient*

Greece (Cambridge: Cambridge University Press, 2013), 285. "Divinity, it seems, communicates readily with humanity, through dreams and omens, through the utterances of oracles, [… a]nd yet the messages of divinity are imagined as being systematically ambiguous, inscrutable, opaque: they require the interpretive resources of those specially endowed to understand and transmit them, and more significantly they are systematically misunderstood by those to whom they are addressed." John Gould, *Myth, Ritual, Memory, and Exchange* (Oxford: Oxford University Press, 2001), 224.

49. Muslims have even named these conversations between Moses and God (Allah) the Munajat Musa or Masa'il Musa, as in The Qur'an verses Q. 4:164 which claims "God [Allah] spoke to Moses directly" (Arabic: "wa kallama Allahu Musa takliman") and Q. 19:52 which voices the action of God (Allah) in "We brought him near to converse" (Arabic: "wa qarrabnahu najiyyan"). Other instances in the Bible where God speaks directly to humans include to Adam and Eve (Gen. 2:16–17); to their son, Cain (Gen. 4:6); to Noah (Gen. 6:12–13); to the prophet Samuel (1 Sam. 3:10); to David (1 Sam. 23:2); and as a voice to Saul or the later Apostle Paul (Acts 9:3–4).

50. Mathijs Koenraadt, *Ignorant God: Thoughts about Time and Eternity* (Amsterdam: Morningtime, 2017), 74.

51. William James, "The Will to Believe," *The New World*, Volume 5 (Boston and New York: Houghton, Mifflin and Company, 1896), 327–47.

52. Ibid., 345.

53. The phrase 'vicarious redemption' appears to have been first mentioned prior to the U.S. Civil War. James Martineau, *Studies of Christianity*, ed. William R. Alger (Boston: American Unitarian Association, 1858), 83. The concept is further explored in a scathing analysis by a late Anglo-American author. Christopher Hitchens, *God Is Not Great: How Religion Poisons Everything* (New York: Twelve [Hachette Warner], 2007), 209.

54. "Like all reptiles, snakes lack a diaphragm[, … using] the muscles in the body wall to do the same job, which is to push air in and out[, and a]lthough snakes have larynxes, and some species even possess vocal chords, the only sound regularly made by snakes is the hiss and, in rattlesnakes, the rattle[, … regardless that] myth supplies snakes with powers that natural snakes do not possess." Diane Morgan, *Snakes in Myth, Magic, and History: The Story of a Human Obsession* (Westport, Connecticut: Praeger Publishers [Greenwood Publishing], 2008), 55. And "to be able to speak[, … s]ound is generated when air moves from diaphragm[, which snakes lack,] to lungs through the throat and causes the vocal cords to vibrate." Mikail Widagda, Tri Arief Sardjono, and Ronny Mardiyanto, "Design of Intonation Control on Electrolarynx Using

Electromyograph (EMG)," in *International Seminar on Intelligent Technology and Its Applications (ISITIA)* (Bali, Indonesia: Institute of Electrical and Electronics Engineers [IEEE], 30–31 August 2018), 443–47; doi:10.1109/ISITIA.2018.8711156.

55. Evgeny Z. Kvon, et al., "Progressive Loss of Function in a Limb Enhancer during Snake Evolution," *Cell*, Volume 167, No. 3 (Amsterdam: Elsevier, 20 October 2016), 633–42; doi:10.1016/j.cell.2016.09.028.

56. John Gray, *The Silence of Animals: On Progress and Other Modern Myths* (London: Allen Lane [Penguin UK], 2013), 48–49. Cf. John Gray, *Heresies: Against Progress and Other Illusions* (London: Granta Books, 2004), 44; and John Gray, *The Immortalization Commission: Science and the Strange Quest to Cheat Death* (Toronto: Doubleday Canada [Random House of Canada], 2011), 119.

57. Steven Weinberg, debate during an address at the Conference on Cosmic Design, American Association for the Advancement of Science, Washington, D.C. (April 1999) and restated in "A Designer Universe?" on *PhysLink.com* (Long Beach, California: Anton Skoruca, ca. 23 November 2001) at **http://www.physlink.com/Education/essay_weinberg.cfm**, as quoted by Carey Goldberg, "Crossing Flaming Swords Over God and Physics," *New York Times* (New York: The New York Times Company, 20 April 1999) at **https://www.nytimes.com/1999/04/20/science/crossing-flaming-swords-over-god-and-physics.html**, accessed August 5, 2019; emphasis added for context.

58. "[S]uperstition [… as an] irrationality [is an] inevitable part[] of the human condition." Christopher Hitchens, *Letters to a Young Contrarian* (New York: Basic Books, 2001), 27. Also, "The cause of my life has been that of combating superstition." Christopher Hitchens, *Hitch-22: A Memoir* (Toronto: Signal [McClelland and Stewart], 2010), xiii (Preface). Another, possibly misattributed version of this quote by Christopher Hitchens is: "The cause of my life has been to oppose superstition[; …i]t's a battle you can't hope to win—it's a battle that's going to go on forever[,… as i]t's part of the human condition." David Graham, *The Wit and Wisdom of Christopher Hitchens: Thoughts of an Outspoken Atheist* (UK: Ben Berger, 2014).

59. Rick Wingrove, "The Assertive Atheist: FaithCraft," *FlameWarrior.com* (Reston, Virginia: Beltway Atheists, Inc., ca. 12 December 2002) at **https://www.flamewarrior.com/faith.htm**, accessed June 22, 2019.

60. "[Y]ou can't just meet for the sake of community itself[; y]ou need a very powerful motivating element to keep people coming, something that attendees have in common." Faith Hill, "They Tried to Start a Church Without God [and f]or a While, It Worked," *TheAtlantic.com* (Washington, D.C.: Emerson Collective, 21 July 2019).

Chapter 11: Afterlife

1. Helen Keller, *Let Us Have Faith* (New York: Doubleday, 1940), 50–51.

2. The latent configuration of nonliving components in RNA (ribonucleic acid) molecular strands would later allow DNA (deoxyribonucleic acid) to copy and hold genetic information; in such an "RNA world, the structure that would be replicated [...] would convert to functional molecules, the ribozymes[, ... while a] remnant of this process may be the structure of transfer RNA." Walter Gilbert, "Origin of Life: The RNA World," *Nature*, Volume 319, No. 6055 (London: Nature Research [Springer Nature], 20 February 1986), 618; doi:10.1038/319618a0. "[T]here is compelling evidence for such an 'RNA world', notably in the structure of the ribosome as a likely molecular fossil from that time [... and its] functional potential [...] with respect to self-replication, catalysis and assembly into simple protocellular entities." Falk Wachowius, James Attwater, and Philipp Holliger, "Nucleic Acids: Function and Potential for Abiogenesis," *Quarterly Reviews of Biophysics*, Volume 50 (London: Cambridge University Press, 9 March 2017); doi:10.1017/S0033583517000038. And "because a lot can happen in 3.5 billion years[, ...] abiogenesis (life from not life) [...] is still the leading theory of how biology got started on Earth." Bill Nye, *Undeniable: Evolution and the Science of Creation*, ed. Corey S. Powell (New York: St. Martin's Press [Macmillan], 2014), 286.

3. Stanley L. Miller, "A Production of Amino Acids Under Possible Primitive Earth Conditions," *Science*, Volume 117, No. 3046 (Washington, D.C.: American Association for the Advancement of Science, 15 May 1953), 528–29; doi:10.1126/science.117.3046.528. See also Stanley L. Miller and Harold C. Urey, "Organic Compound Synthesis on the Primitive Earth," *Science*, Volume 130, No. 3370 (Washington, D.C.: American Association for the Advancement of Science, 31 July 1959), 245–51; doi:10.1126/science.130.3370.245. Characterizing the experimental conditions as "requiring the presence of liquid water, a supply of prebiotic organic compounds, and a source of energy[, ... m]any of the protein-building amino acids have been synthesized abiotically in laboratory experiments of the early Earth's atmosphere from simple precursors." E. Pierazzo and C. F. Chyba, "Impact Delivery of Prebiotic Organic Matter to Planetary Surfaces," *Comets and the Origin and Evolution of Life*, ed. Paul J. Thomas, et al. (Amsterdam: Springer-Verlag [Springer Science+Business Media], 2006), 138. And "slow hydrogen escape and volcanic outgassing could have maintained a hydrogen mixing ratio of more than 30%[, ... leading to a situation in which t]he organic soup in the oceans and ponds on early Earth would have been a more favorable place for the origin of life." Feng Tian, et al., "A Hydrogen-rich Early Earth Atmosphere," *Science*, Volume 308, No.

5724 (Washington, D.C.: American Association for the Advancement of Science, 13 May 2005), 1014–17; doi:10.1126/science.1106983.

4. Christopher K. Materese, Michel Nuevo, and Scott A. Sandford, "The Formation of Nucleobases from the Ultraviolet Photo-Irradiation of Purine in Simple Astrophysical Ice Analogs," *Astrobiology*, Volume 17, No. 8 (Larchmont, New York: Mary Ann Liebert, August 2016), 761 et seq.; doi:10.1089/ast.2016.1613.

5. "[T]he human pineal gland was discovered by Herophilus[, … who observed that] the melatonin-generating system may be established *in utero* prior to the development of the necessary anatomic pathways." Stephanie S. Erlich and Michael L. J. Apuzzo, "The Pineal Gland: Anatomy Physiology and Clinical Significance," *Journal of Neurosurgery*, Volume 63, No. 3 (Park Ridge, Illinois [Rolling Meadows, Illinois]: American Association of Neurological Surgeons, September 1985), 321–41; doi:10.3171/jns.1985.63.3.0321. Moreover, the "cerebral hemispheres [as s]ectional anatomy originated […] probably with Herophilus of Alexandria[,] who paid particular attention to the ventricles [… and] noticed that the ventricles are filled with fluid (i.e., liquor) which he considered the origin of the 'animal spirits' or 'soul' that flows through the nerves and moves the muscles." Marco Catani and Michel Thiebaut de Schotten, *Atlas of Human Brain Connections* (New York: Oxford University Press, 2012), 26. See also Du-Xian Tan, et al., "Pineal Calcification, Melatonin Production, Aging, Associated Health Consequences and Rejuvenation of the Pineal Gland," *Molecules*, Volume 23, No. 2 (Basel, Switzerland: Molecular Diversity Preservation International, January 2018), 301; doi:10.3390/molecules23020301. Specifically, "Herophilus proposed the idea that the pineal gland was a valve, similar to a sphincter, that regulates the flow of vital spirits from medial ventricles to the back." Daniel Pedro Cardinali, *Ma Vie en Noir: Fifty Years with Melatonin and the Stone of Madness* (New York [Cham, Switzerland]: Springer International [Springer Nature], 2016), 11; English title: *My Life in Black*. And "Herophilus apparently thought that the pineal was a valve regulating the flow of 'pneuma' or 'spiritus' in Latin from the 3rd to the 4th ventricle." Josephine Arendt, *Melatonin and the Mammalian Pineal Gland* (London: Chapman and Hall, 1995). Cf. uncited materials at **http://www.viewzone.com/pineal.html**, accessed December 17, 2018.

6. René Descartes, "To Meyssonnier, 29 January 1640," *The Philosophical Writings of Descartes*, Volume 3, The Correspondence, trans. John Cottingham, Robert Stoothoff, Dugald Murdoch, Anthony Kenny (Cambridge: Cambridge University Press, 1984), 143.

7. "To be conscious, then, you need to be a single, integrated entity [… such as a] brain, with its neurons and axons, dendrites and synapses[; …] the

extent to which this brain is integrated[, however … is measurably based on] the conscious repertoire associated with any network of causally interacting parts." Christof Koch, "A 'Complex' Theory of Consciousness," (originally entitled "Consciousness Redux: A Theory of Consciousness") in *Scientific American Mind*, Volume 20, No. 4 (New York: Nature Publishing Group, 1 July 2009), 16–19; doi:10.1038/scientificamericanmind0709-16. Furthermore, "transformed information [is relayed] to the pyramidal neurons in the CA3 region via their axons that form synapses on the[se same] neurons." Max R. Bennett, *The Idea of Consciousness: Synapses and the Mind* (Amsterdam: Harwood Academic Publishers, 1997), 17.

8. John R. Searle with Daniel C. Dennett and David J. Chalmers, *The Mystery of Consciousness* (New York: The New York Review of Books, 1997). "[T]hat we don't have a theory that explains how it is possible that brain processes could cause consciousness [remains] a challenge[, … b]ut it is by no means a challenge to the fact that brain processes do in fact cause consciousness." John R. Searle, "How to Study Consciousness Scientifically," *Brain Research Reviews*, Volume 26, No. 2–3 (Amsterdam: Elsevier Science B.V., May 1998), 382; doi:10.1016/S0165-0173(97)00047-7.

9. "When a property of a system cannot be traced back to any of the individual parts in the system, it is called an emergent property." Jurgen Appelo, *Management 3.0: Leading Agile Developers, Developing Agile Leaders* (Boston: Pearson Education [Addison-Wesley], 2011), 104. Cf. Paul Humphreys, *Emergence* (New York: Oxford University Press, 2016); and Paul Humphreys, "Aspects of Emergence," *Philosophical Topics*, Volume 24, No. 1 (Fayetteville, Arkansas: University of Arkansas Press, Spring 1996): 53–70.

10. Ibid.

11. "[A] property [thus] is metaphysically supervenient on [another property] if and only if there [is logically] no way in which an object could have had [the second property] but lacked [the first]." *The Oxford Companion to Consciousness*, ed. Tim Bayne, Axel Cleeremans, and Patrick Wilken (Oxford: Oxford University Press, 2009), 254. This is basically a restatement of the original definition of strong supervenience. Jaegwon Kim, *Supervenience and Mind: Selected Philosophical Essays* (Cambridge: Cambridge University Press, 1993), 65.

12. "[T]here is a correlative range of ways in which system properties might *not* be aggregative[, … achieving emergence by doing] more than simply aggregate the properties of [such a system's] parts." Richard Campbell, *The Metaphysics of Emergence* (New York: Palgrave Macmillan, 2015), 207; emphasis in the original.

13. "[D]ownward causality is the constraint on the behavior of component parts that enables systematic capacities (the whole exerts an influence on the parts that now have a reduced field of action)." John Protevi, *Political Affect: Connecting the Social and the Somatic* (Minneapolis, Minnesota: University of Minnesota Press, 2009), 9.

14. "The fallacy of division [...] consists of assuming that what is true of the whole is also true of the parts[, ... so t]he error inherent in the fallacy of division is obvious, since it is well known that groups can have emergent properties not shared by their constituent parts." James Lett, *Science, Reason, and Anthropology* (Lanham, Maryland: Rowman and Littlefield, 1997), 65. Thus, "attributing emergent properties to the physical parts and configuration of the object that bears them commits the fallacy of division." Soo Lam Wong, "Ontological Emergence Without Vertical Causation," *Axiomathes* (The Hague/Kluwer: Springer Netherlands, 6 January 2020), 1–14; doi:10.1007/s10516-019-09470-x.

15. Steven Johnson, *Emergence: The Connected Lives of Ants, Brains, Cities, and Software* (New York: Scribner [Simon and Schuster], 2001).

16. "[C]onsciousness [...] is an emergent property of the behaviour of the micro-elements of a system" like the human brain. John R. Searle, *Consciousness and Language* (New York: Cambridge University Press, 2002), 31. "Consciousness is an emergent property of the physical human brain." Michael T. Walker, *The Social Construction of Mental Illness and Its Implications for Neuroplasticity* (Lanham, Maryland: Lexington Books [Rowman and Littlefield], 2016), 72.

17. "Evidence from functional neuroimaging [fMRI] studies [... show the presence of multiple] distinct anticorrelated cortical systems that mediate conscious awareness." Audrey Vanhaudenhuyse, et al., "Two Distinct Neuronal Networks Mediate the Awareness of Environment and of Self," *Journal of Cognitive Neuroscience*, Volume 23, No. 3 (Cambridge, Massachusetts: MIT Press, March 2011), 570–78; doi:10.1162/jocn.2010.21488. "Specifically, the 'external awareness' network encompassing lateral fronto-temporo-parietal cortices bilaterally, and the 'internal awareness' network including midline anterior cingulate/mesiofrontal and posterior cingulate/precuneal cortices, are functionally disconnected." Athena Demertzi, Andrea Soddu, and Steven Laureys, "Consciousness Supporting Networks," *Current Opinion in Neurobiology*, Volume 23, No. 2 (Philadelphia, Pennsylvania: Lippincott Williams and Wilkins, April 2013), 239–44; doi:10.1016/j.conb.2012.12.003.

18. René Descartes, *The Method, Meditations, and selections from the Principles*, trans. John Veitch (Edinburgh: William Blackwood and Sons, 1880 [1637–41]), 164; Meditation 6: Of the Existence of Material Things, etc.

19. "[T]he purpose of […] psychic fracture is to disconnect from painful memories." Henry Kellerman, *The Psychoanalysis of Symptoms* (New York: Springer Science + Business Media, 2008), 123. "[T]here are many ways to fracture personality, through accidental trauma, through environmental and social trauma, [and] through intentional abuse or neglect." Margaret M. McAllister, "Dissociative Identity Disorder: A Literature Review," *Journal of Psychiatric and Mental Health Nursing*, Volume 7, No. 1 (Oxford/Boston: Blackwell Scientific Publications, January 2000), 30; doi:10.1046/j.1365-2850.2000.00259.x. "[I]ncluded in a list of trauma-induced disruptions [… is] dissociative identity disorder (multiple personality disorder)[, … which manifests as] the fracture of self into partial personality fragments." *Combat Stress Injury*, ed. Charles R. Figley and William P. Nash (London and New York: Routledge [Taylor and Francis], 2007), 56. "Trauma can fracture the person into various self-states[, … where] the clinical outcome is dissociative identity disorder (DID)." Elizabeth F. Howell, "'Good Girls,' Sexy 'Bad Girls,' and Warriors: The Role of Trauma and Dissociation in the Creation and Reproduction of Gender," *Trauma and Sexuality*, ed. James A. Chu and Elizabeth S. Bowman (Binghampton, New York: Hawthorn Medical Press [Hawthorn Press], 2002), 14.

20. René Descartes, *Meditations on First Philosophy*, trans. Donald A. Cress (Indianapolis, Indiana: Hackett Publishing, 1993 [1641]), 10.

21. "[W]e have four independent methods [cooling of white-dwarf stars, oldest globular star clusters, Hubble expansion rate, and cosmic microwave background radiation] for deriving an age for the universe, and all four yield a consistent answer[: … from] 13.5 to 14 billion years of age." David A. Weintraub, *How Old Is the Universe?* (Princeton, New Jersey: Princeton University Press, 2011), 363. And light from the explosion of "[o]ne of the most distant objects known[, …] GRB 090423 (gamma ray burst 2009 April 23)[, …] took 13 billion years to reach the Earth and, therefore, started its journey when the star exploded 13 billion years ago[, … meaning] that the Universe must be at least 13 billion years old." Peter Altman, *Life and the Universe: Answerable and Unanswerable Questions* (New York: Cavendish Square, 2017), 81.

22. According to NASA's Exoplanet Exploration Program (in association with the Jet Propulsion Laboratory), "[b]ased on the deepest images obtained so far, [… there are] about 2 trillion galaxies in the observable universe[; … with each] galaxy of hundreds of billions of stars, this pushes the number of planets potentially into the trillions." Pat Brennan, "Our Milky Way Galaxy: How Big is Space?" on *NASA.gov* (Washington, D.C.: NASA's Astrophysics Division, 2 April 2019) at **https://exoplanets.nasa.**

gov/blog/1563/our-milky-way-galaxy-how-big-is-space/, accessed April 27, 2020. Specifically, a "galaxy is a conglomeration of billions of stars of various sizes[, … and t]oday it is estimated that there exists at least hundreds of billions of, maybe several trillion, galaxies in the universe." Itzhak Bars and John Terning, *Extra Dimensions in Space and Time* (New York: Springer Science+Business Media, 2010), 11.

23. "[T]hree minutes after the bang the primordial neutrons and protons were processed into hydrogen, helium, and lithium[; …] later than a few minutes after the bang the temperature and density were too low for nuclear reactions to occur and Big-Bang nucleosynthesis came to an end." Wendy L. Friedman and Edward W. Kolb, "Cosmology," *The New Physics for the Twenty-First Century*, ed. Gordon Fraser (Cambridge: Cambridge University Press, 2006), 24. The "big bang model [… predicts] a phase of primordial nucleosynthesis in which helium and deuterium were synthesized in the universe […] when it was more than a few minutes old." T. Padmanabhan, *After the First Three Minutes: The Story of Our Universe* (Cambridge: Cambridge University Press, 1998), 192–93.

24. Sigmund Freud, *The Ego and the Id* (Vienna: Internationaler Psychoanalytischer Verlag, 1923).

25. "[M]indfulness is rooted in the fundamental activities of consciousness: attention and awareness[, … which] permit the individual to 'be present' to reality." Kirk Warren Brown, Richard M. Ryan, and J. David Creswell, "Mindfulness: Theoretical Foundations and Evidence for Its Salutary Effects," *Psychological Inquiry*, Volume 18, No. 4 (Mahwah, New Jersey: Lawrence Earlbaum Associates, 2007), 212.

26. "To breed an animal that is *permitted to promise*—isn't this precisely the paradoxical task nature has set for itself with regard to man?" Friedrich Nietzsche, *On the Genealogy of Morality*, trans. Maudemarie Clark and Alan J. Swensen (Indianapolis, Indiana: Hackett Publishing, 1998 [1887]), 35; emphasis in the original.

27. "Mental time travel refers to the ability to cast one's mind […] forward in time to pre-experience events that may occur in the future[, … which] the data suggest […] is present [… in a limited way as a mental ability in primates such as the] great apes." Damian Scarf, Christopher Smith, and Michael Stuart, "A Spoon Full of Studies Helps the Comparison Go Down: A Comparative Analysis of Tulving's Spoon Test," *Frontiers in Psychology*, Volume 5 (Pully, Switzerland: Frontiers Research Foundation, 12 August 2014), 893; doi:10.3389/fpsyg.2014.00893. "Even chimpanzees [… can] only think a few minutes into the future." Mark R. Leary, "A Functional, Evolutionary Analysis of the Impact of Interpersonal Events on Intrapersonal

Self-Processes," *Self and Relationships*, ed. Kathleen D. Vohs and Eli J. Finkel (New York: Guilford Press, 2006), 222; citing Wolfgang Köhler, *The Mentality of Apes*, trans. Ella Winter (London: Routledge, Trench, Trübner and Co., Ltd., 1925) and Wolfgang Köhler, "Intelligence of Apes," *Pedagogical Seminary and Journal of Genetic Psychology*, Volume 32 (Provincetown, Massachusetts: Taylor and Francis, January 1925), 674–90.

28. "*Mental time travel* is [...] the faculty that allows humans to mentally project themselves backwards in time to re-live, or forwards to pre-live, events." Thomas Suddendorf and Michael C. Corballis, "The Evolution of Foresight: What Is Mental Time Travel and Is It Unique to Humans?" in *Behavioral and Brain Sciences*, Volume 30, No. 3 (Cambridge: Cambridge University Press, June 2007), 299; doi:10.1017/S0140525X07001975, emphasis in the original. Specifically, "[h]umans need to understand this ability of the animal to live in the present for within it lays a tranquillity and mental ease which we rarely experience." Peter Ffitch, *Hands, the Achilles' Heel: The Undisclosed Logic of Human Behaviour* (Leicester, England: Matador [Troubador Publishing], 2018), 294. And "[i]f by eternity is understood not endless temporal duration but timelessness, then he lives eternally who lives in the present." Ludwig Wittgenstein, *Tractatus Logico-Philosophicus*, trans. C. K. Ogden (New York: Harcourt, Brace, and Company, 1922), 185; proposition 6.43.1.1.

29. "All intuitive activity is directed by ideas that are for the most part subconscious[, ... so o]nly the clearest, most intense ideas are perceived by consciousness, while the great mass of current, but weaker ideas remains unconscious." Sigmund Freud and Joseph Breuer, *Studies in Hysteria*, trans. Nicola Luckhurst (New York: Penguin Books, 2004 [1908]), 224.

30. "[That c]onsciousness of external events [... involves a measurable] delay suggests that conscious awareness requires many passes of signals back and forth between widespread cortical and lower brain regions[, ... so that the] pre-conscious processes from which consciousness emerges [...] remain forever hidden from awareness but still exert important influences on our conscious mind, affecting our choices to act [... and making o]ur unconscious actions occur significantly faster than our conscious actions." Paul L. Nunez, *The New Science of Consciousness* (Amherst, New York: Prometheus Books, 2016), 28. For an examination of how the conscious mind is "just the tip of the whole iceberg," while "the unconscious [... and] also the preconscious" aspects of the mind are the primary determinates of behavior, see A. Nurilia and A. H. Affendy, "The Influence of Subconscious Mind on Human Behavior," *Journal of Postgraduate Current Business Research*, Volume 2, No. 2 (Kuala Lumpur, Malaysia: Asian Borderlands Research Network [ABRN] Asia, 2017).

31. "Most of this [the brain's cortex] surface area has six layers of neurons and is sometimes called the *neocortex* to distinguish it from areas with fewer layers, as are found mainly in earlier evolving groups[; … a]ll the cells that make up the six layers of the cortex have their origin in the hollow nerve tube from which the brain grows." Raymond L. Neubauer, *Evolution and the Emergent Self: The Rise of Complexity and Behavioral Versatility in Nature* (New York: Columbia University Press, 2012), 64; emphasis in the original.

32. "In evolutionary terms, the brain stem is the oldest part of the brain[; … it represents the] subcortical structure that connects the spinal cord to the rest of the brain and houses many structures involved in autonomic functions." M. Hunter Manasco, *Introduction to Neurogenic Communication Disorders* (Burlington, Massachusetts: Jones and Bartlett Learning [Ascend Learning], 2014), 29.

33. "The most recently evolved limbic structures that surround the brain stem serve a number of functions central to emotion and cognition." Don M. Tucker, Douglas Derryberry, and Phan Luu, "Anatomy and Physiology of Human Emotion: Vertical Integration of Brain Stem, Limbic, and Cortical Systems," *The Neuropsychology of Emotion*, ed. Joan C. Borod (New York: Oxford University Press, 2000), 62. "The limbic system is involved in both memory and emotion." Bennett L. Schwartz, *Memory: Foundations and Applications* (Los Angeles [Thousand Oaks, California]: SAGE Publications, 2014), 54. "In addition to emotion, the limbic system is involved in olfaction, memory, and homeostasis." Matthew H. Rouse, *Neuroanatomy for Speech-Language Pathology and Audiology* (Burlington, Massachusetts: Jones and Bartlett Learning [Ascend Learning], 2020), 326. A mnemonic for the roles and functions of the limbic system is the acroymn HOME, referring to Homeostasis, Olfaction, Memory, and Emotion. Hal Blumenfeld, *Neuroanatomy through Clinical Cases* (Sunderland, Massachusetts: Sinauer Associates [Oxford University Press], 2010 [2002]), 761–820.

34. Leakey refers to "the origin of modern humans—the evolution of people like ourselves, fully equipped with language, consciousness, artistic imagination, and technological innovation unseen elsewhere in nature." Richard Leakey, *The Origin of Humankind* (New York: Basic Books [Perseus Books Group], 2008), xv.

35. "[T]he thalamus serves as a sensory gate or filter that directly and indirectly modulates the access of sensory information to the cortex, amygdala, and hippocampus." John H. Krystal, et al., "Recent Developments in the Neurobiology of Dissociation: Implications for Posttraumatic Stress Disorder," *Handbook of Dissociation: Theoretical, Empirical, and Clinical Perspectives*, ed.

Larry K. Michelson and William J. Ray (New York: Plenum Press [Plenum Publishing], 1996), 173; citing David A. McCormick and Marcus von Krosigk, "Corticothalamic Activation Modulates Thalamic Firing Through Glutamate 'Metabotropic' Receptors," *Proceedings of the National Academy of Sciences*, Volume 89, No. 7 (Washington, D.C.: National Academy of Sciences, 1 April 1992), 2774–78; doi:10.1073/pnas.89.7.2774. "The cerebellum is the portion of the brain through which the cerebral motor cortex achieves the synthesis and coordination of individual muscle contractions required for normal voluntary movements." William W. Campbell, *DeJong's the Neurologic Examination* (Hong Kong: Lippincott Williams and Wilkins, 2005), 511. "The cerebellum [...] coordinates the timing and execution of complex voluntary movements." Charles R. Goodlett, "The Cerebellum," *Neuroscience in Medicine*, ed. P. Michael Conn (Totowa, New Jersey: Humana Press [Springer Science+Business Media], 2008), 221. "[T]he limbic system's major focus of interest is the amygdala, which is linked to the production and regulation of emotions—especially aggression and fear." Karen Huffman and Catherine A. Sanderson, *Real World Psychology* (New York: John Wiley and Sons, 2013), 57. "The endocrine system and the nervous system are directly linked by the hypothalamus in the brain." Don H. Hockenbury and Sandra E. Hockenbury, *Psychology* (New York: Worth Publishers, 2008), 62. Magnesium-dependent "protein kinase M ζ [... or] PKMζ maintains long-term spatial memory storage in the hippocampus." Todd Charlton Sacktor, "PKMζ, LTP Maintenance, and the Dynamic Molecular Biology of Memory Storage," *Essence of Memory*, ed. Wayne S. Sossin, et al. (Amsterdam: Elsevier, 2008), 35.

36. "The cerebral cortex [... and its structures] make up about 80% of the brain's weight." Karen Huffman, Katherine Dowdell, and Catherine A. Sanderson, *Psychology in Action* (New York: John Wiley and Sons, 1994), 69. "The cerebrum is most highly developed in humans, where it constitutes about 80% of the total brain weight[, ... and where t]he outer layer of the cerebrum is the highly convoluted *cerebral cortex*." Lauralee Sherwood, *Fundamentals of Human Physiology* (Belmont, California: Brooks/Cole [CENGAGE Learning], 2011); emphasis in the original. "[T]he cerebral cortex[, ...] what really makes us human[, ... is a] 3-millimeter-thick sheet of some 20 billion nerve cells." Richard O. Straub, *Health Psychology* (New York: Worth Publishers, 2002), 63. "The cerebral cortex—that thin surface layer—contains some 20 to 23 billion nerve cells and 300 trillion synaptic connections[, ... and s]upporting these billions of nerve cells are nine times as many spidery glial cells ('glue cells')." David G. Myers, *Psychology in Modules* (New York: Worth Publishers, 2004), 67. "The folds of the cerebral cortex create a massive surface area for neural activity, with billions of neurons (nerve cells) and glial cells making up the substance of the brain[; ... n]eurons are electrically active brain cells

that process information, whereas glial cells, which outnumber neurons by ten to one, perform supporting functions." Cyndi Dale, *The Subtle Body: An Encyclopedia of Your Energetic Anatomy* (Boulder, Colorado: Sounds True Publishing, 2009), 56.

37. See "Figure 11-1" in Anthony J. M. Verberne, "Modulation of Autonomic Function by the Cerebral Cortex," *Central Regulation of Autonomic Functions*, ed. Ida J. Llewellyn-Smith and Anthony J. M. Verberne (New York: Oxford University Press, 1990), 203. One study looks for a "possible neurobiological substrate of imagery and imagination" in the brain's neuronal circuitry, best exemplified in the structures of the cerebral cortex. Luigi F. Agnati, et al., "The Neurobiology of Imagination: Possible Role of Interaction-Dominant Dynamics and Default Mode Network," *Frontiers in Psychology*, Volume 4 (Pully, Switzerland: Frontiers Research Foundation, 24 May 2013), 296; doi:10.3389/fpsyg.2013.00296. Cf. P. Taylor, et al., "The Global Landscape of Cognition: Hierarchical Aggregation As an Organizational Principle of Human Cortical Networks and Functions," *Scientific Reports*, Volume 5, No. 1 (London: Springer Nature, 2015), 1–18; and B. L. Strehler, "Where is the Self? A Neuroanatomical Theory of Consciousness," *Synapse*, Volume 7, No. 1 (New York: Alan R. Liss, January 1991), 44–91, doi:10.1002/syn.890070105. See also the following *Brain* journal articles by one aptly named author: W. Russell Brain, "The Cerebral Basis of Consciousness," *Brain*, Volume 73, No. 4, (Oxford: Oxford University Press, December 1950), 465–79, doi:10.1093/brain/73.4.465; and Russell Brain, "The Physiological Basis of Consciousness: A Critical Review," *Brain*, Volume 81, No. 3, (Oxford: Oxford University Press, September 1958), 426–55, doi:10.1093/brain/81.3.426.

38. "[T]he capacity for sentience spawned a superior brain[, … as] the connection between feelings and consciousness provides the basis for a model that explains why evolution followed this particular trajectory [… in which s]entience was sufficiently useful to provide certain survival skills." Bjørn Grinde, *The Evolution of Consciousness* (Cham, Switzerland: Springer International Publishing [Springer Nature], 2016 [2014]), 75. See also Nicholas Maxwell, *The Human World in the Physical Universe: Consciousness, Free Will, and Evolution* (Lanham, Maryland: Rowman and Littlefield, 2001).

39. "[E]ven if the same general pathways emerge, it might take twenty billion years to reach self-consciousness this time—except that the earth would be incinerated billion of years before." Stephen Jay Gould, *Wonderful Life: The Burgess Shale and the Nature of History* (New York: W. W. Norton and Company, 1989), 311.

40. Referencing a conversation in the summer of 1950 when, during a debate with Edward Teller and John von Neumann about extraterrestrial

life, Fermi asked, "Where is everybody?" Paul Davies, *The Eerie Silence: Renewing Our Search for Alien Intelligence* (New York: Houghton Mifflin Harcourt, 2010), 116.

41. The Search for Extra-Terrestrial Intelligence, "Drake Equation," *SETI* (Mountain View, California: SETI Institute, 2 October 2018) at **https://www.seti.org/drake-equation-index**, accessed April 27, 2020. One can "define a region in the parameter space of the Drake equation, where the Fermi paradox definitely holds." Nikos Prantzos, "A Joint Analysis of the Drake Equation and the Fermi Paradox," *International Journal of Astrobiology*, Volume 12, No. 3 (Cambridge: Cambridge University Press, July 2013), 246–53; doi:10.1017/S1473550413000037. "Drake made his first estimate with his equation in 1961[, … predicting] that there are 10 civilizations within our galaxy with which communication might be possible[; … in contrast, i]n 1966, Carl Sagan, a huge proponent of the equation, used much higher estimates of the values of the equation's variables to calculate the number communicating civilizations in the Milky Way to be around one million." John M. Henshaw, *An Equation for Every Occasion* (Baltimore, Maryland: Johns Hopkins University Press, 2014), 128. "[T]he product of all the variables on the right side of the equation, with the exception of L, can be reduced to P, interpreted as the production rate of communicating civilizations in the Milky Way[, … although one is never compelled to] provide an actual estimate of L." Garry Chick, "Length of Time Such Civilizations Release Detectable Signals, L, after 1961 to the Present," *The Drake Equation: Estimating the Prevalence of Extraterrestrial Life through the Ages*, ed. Douglas A. Vakoch and Matthew F. Dowd (Cambridge: Cambridge University Press, 2015), 284. "The Drake Equation's primary function is as a roadmap [… in that i]t identifies obstacles to our knowledge, and sheds light on our own ignorance." Duncan H. Forgan, *Solving Fermi's Paradox* (Cambridge: Cambridge University Press, 2019), 11; doi:10.1017/9781316681510. But more recently, "[f]or intelligence evolution, it is found that a rare-intelligence scenario is slightly favored at 3:2 betting odds." David Kipping, "An Objective Bayesian Analysis of Life's Early Start and Our Late Arrival," *Proceedings of the National Academy of Sciences* (Washington, D.C.: National Academy of Sciences, 18 May 2020); doi:10.1073/pnas.1921655117. Specifically, according to a new technique, "there should be around 36 active civilizations in our Galaxy." Tom Westby and Christopher J. Conselice, "The Astrobiological Copernican Weak and Strong Limits for Intelligent Life," *The Astrophysical Journal*, Volume 896, No. 1 (Bristol, England: Institute of Physics Publishing, June 2020), 58; doi:10.3847/1538-4357/ab8225. Some critics, however, have taken issue with "the Astrobiological Copernican Weak Condition: that an initially Earth-like planet will always develop intelligent life." Ethan Siegel, "36 Alien Civilizations

in The Milky Way? The Science behind a Ridiculous Headline," *Forbes.com* (Jersey City, New Jersey: Forbes Media, 16 June 2020) at **https://www.forbes. com/sites/startswithabang/2020/06/16/36-alien-civilizations-in-the-milky- way-the-science-behind-a-ridiculous-headline/**, accessed June 16, 2020.

42. Evan Solomonides and Yervant Terzian, "A Probabilistic Analysis of the Fermi Paradox," *American Astronomical Society Meeting Abstracts*, Volume 228, id.404.09 (Washington, D.C.: American Astronomical Society, June 2016).

43. "Clinical neuroplasticity may be defined as an active reorganization contrary to loss of activation or connectivity simply due to brain damage." R. Beisteiner and E. Matt, "Brain Plasticity in fMRI and DTI," *Clinical Functional MRI: Presurgical Functional Neuroimaging*, ed. Christoph Stippich (Berlin / Heidelberg, Germany: Springer-Verlag [Springer Science+Business Media], 2015), 289. "*Neuroplasticity* may be viewed as a fundamental property of neurons and the nervous system [… and] involves the changing properties of neural elements, either during development, due to natural or artificial alterations in input, or in cases of neural trauma." Christopher A. Shaw, "Is There a Theory of Neuroplasticity?" in *Toward a Theory of Neuroplasticity*, ed. Christopher A. Shaw and Jill McEachern (Philadelphia, Pennsylvania: Psychology Press [Taylor and Francis], 2013), 3; emphasis in the original.

44. "The brain's lifelong ability to reorganize and change its structure and function by forming new neural connections [… routinely occurs, and, taking the form of a] 'rewiring,' officially known as neuroplasticity, is what makes our brains so wonderfully adaptive." Huffman, et al., *Psychology in Action*, 56. "Neuroplasticity can be defined as the ability of the nervous system to respond to intrinsic or extrinsic stimuli by reorganizing its structure, function and connections." Steven C. Cramer, et al., "Harnessing Neuroplasticity for Clinical Applications," *Brain*, Volume 134, No. 6, (Oxford: Oxford University Press, June 2011), 1591–1609; doi:10.1093/brain/awr039.

45. "[P]hysical processes can be detected and measured by physical instruments via physical interactions between the detector and the detected[, … and a]ccordingly, various physical brain imaging methods are able to detect neural activity patterns and neural signals in the brain." Pentti O Haikonen, *Consciousness and Robot Sentience,* 2nd Edition (Singapore: World Scientific Publishing, 2012), 33. Yet, the same author observes that "brain imaging technologies […] can only detect and measure physical processes that are related to the brain activity[; accordingly, b]rain imaging methods do not detect qualia or mental content, [but] instead they detect physical processes that may or may not be related to conscious mental content." Ibid, 175. Adding to the analysis is the "dynamic-core hypothesis[: … a] group of neurons can contribute directly to conscious experience only if it is part of

a functional cluster[, … but t]o sustain conscious experience, it is essential that this functional cluster be highly differentiated [… and likewise] will be associated with conscious experience only if the reentrant interactions within the core are sufficiently differentiated." Gerald M. Edelman and Giulio Tononi, "Reentry and the Dynamic Core: Neural Correlates of Conscious Experience," *Neural Correlates of Consciousness*, ed. Thomas Metzinger (Cambridge, Massachusetts: MIT Press, 2000), 146. However, although "the neural pathways that instantiate the *process* of visual imagination may be identified by means of fMRI [… and b]rain imaging may detect that a specific locality in my visual cortex will light up when I imagine the Washington monument, [… nonetheless,] fMRI will not be able to differentiate whether I am visualizing the Washington monument or the Mona Lisa." Arnold H. Modell, *Imagination and the Meaningful Brain* (Cambridge, Massachusetts: MIT Press, 2003), 193–94; emphasis in the original. Moreover, while a "functional analysis of consciousness is possible, [...] the instruments of neuroscience—fMRI, EEG, MEG—will not uncover the constituent mechanisms of a particular feeling, image, thought or sense of being." Ibid. Efforts have nevertheless been underway "to develop a four-dimensional probabilistic atlas and reference system for the human brain." John Mazziotta, et al., "A Probabilistic Atlas and Reference System for the Human Brain: International Consortium for Brain Mapping (ICBM)." *Philosophical Transactions of the Royal Society of London B: Biological Sciences*, Volume 356, No. 1412 (London: The Royal Society, 29 August 2001), 1293–1322; doi:10.1098/rstb.2001.0915. "Magnetoencephalography (MEG) and electroencephalography (EEG) [… with some] temporal precision allows us to explore the timing of basic neural processes at the level of cell assemblies." Sylvain Baillet, John C. Mosher, and Richard M. Leahy, "Electromagnetic Brain Mapping." *IEEE Signal Processing Magazine*, Volume 18, No. 6 (New York: Institute of Electrical and Electronics Engineers [IEEE], November 2001), 14–30; doi:10.1109/79.962275.

46. "Mental states as dynamic emergent properties of brain states cause behavior [..., as] they are inextricably interfused with their generating brain processes [… and] cannot exist apart from the active brain." Roger W. Sperry, "The Impact and Promise of the Cognitive Revolution," *American Psychologist*, Volume 48, No. 8 (Washington, D.C.: American Psychological Association, August 1993), 880; doi:10.1037/0003-066X.48.8.878. "[P]henomenal consciousness is realized by a particular level of brain operational organization and that understanding human consciousness requires a description of the laws of the immediately underlying neural collective phenomena, the nested hierarchy of electromagnetic fields of brain activity—operational architectonics." Andrew A. Fingelkurts, Alexander A. Fingelkurts, and Carlos F. H. Neves, "Consciousness as a Phenomenon in the Operational

Architectonics of Brain Organization: Criticality and Self-organization Considerations," *Chaos, Solitons and Fractals*, Volume 55 (Amsterdam: Elsevier, October 2013), 13–31; doi:10.1016/j.chaos.2013.02.007.

47. *The Gateless Barrier: The Wu-Men Kuan (Mumonkan)*, trans. Robert Aitken (New York: North Point Press, 1990 [1228]), 186.

48. Duncan MacDougall, "Hypothesis Concerning Soul Substance Together with Experimental Evidence of the Existence of Such Substance," *Journal of the American Society for Psychical Research*, Volume 1, No. 5 (New York: American Society for Psychical Research, May 1907), 237–75; simultaneously published in *American Medicine* (Philadelphia, Pennsylvania: American Medical Publishing, April 1907), later correspondence established the "weighing" of the "soul" as resulting in an average of 21 grams over a small sample, with a negative result for dogs, suggesting only humans have "souls," or at least ones that may be crudely measurable.

49. "Life is impossible without a functioning brain, heart and liver, and at least one functioning lung and one kidney." John W. Harcup, *Human Anatomy in Full Color* (Mineola, New York: Dover Publications, 2013 [1996]), 23. Specifically, "[t]he human body has five vital organs […] essential for survival[, namely, the brain, the heart, the liver, the lungs, and the kidneys, a]lthough […] people can live with one lung and one kidney and only part of their liver." Rocky Termanini, *The Nano Age of Digital Immunity Infrastructure Fundamentals and Applications* (Boca Raton, Florida: CRC Press [Taylor and Francis], 2017), 291.

50. "Some have referred to the […] cessation of respiration and pulse as 'clinical death.'" David C. Parish, Hemant Goyal, and Francis C. Dane, "Mechanism of Death: There's More to It than Sudden Cardiac Arrest," *Journal of Thoracic Disease*, Volume 10, Number 5 (Hong Kong: AME Publishing Company, May 2018), 3081–87; doi:10.21037/jtd.2018.04.113.

51. "[Given that i]schemia means lack of blood supply, necrosis means death of cells or tissues, and infarct is an area of ischemic necrosis[, the] degeneration or deterioration of individual cells [that can be caused by] ischemia." Robert L. Bacon and Nelson R. Niles, *Medical Histology: A Text-Atlas with Introductory Pathology* (New York: Springer-Verlag, 1983), 456.

52. "Death [may be] induced by organ failure, which [can] happen[] when the total number of tissue cells reaches a fraction […] of 50%." Michael Meyer-Hermann, "Estimation of the Cancer Risk Induced by Therapies Targeting Stem Cell Replication and Treatment Recommendations," *Scientific Reports*, Volume 8, No. 11776 (Berlin: Nature Research [Springer Nature], 6 August

2018); doi:10.1038/s41598-018-29967-6. Specifically, "[o]nce the number of cells that are unable to function, due to lack of adequate energy supply, reaches a critical mass, organ failure ensues." Lane B. Scheiber II and Lane B. Scheiber, *Changing the Global Approach to Medicine*, Volume 2: Medical Vector Therapy (Bloomington, Illinois: iUniverse, 2011), 55. Nonetheless, a "large number of cells must die in order to induce organ failure." Beth A. Erickson-Wittmann, Jason Rownd, and Kevin Khater, "Biological and Physical Aspects of Radiation Oncology," *Principles and Practice of Gynecologic Oncology*, ed. Richard R. Barakat, Maurie Markman, and Marcus Randall (Hong Kong: Lippincott Williams and Wilkins [Wolters Kluwer], 2005), 332.

53. Eelco F. M. Wijdicks, "The Diagnosis of Brain Death," *New England Journal of Medicine*, Volume 344, No. 16 (Waltham, Massachusetts: Massachusetts Medical Society, 19 April 2001), 1215–21.

54. "'Brain death' is a colloquial term for human death determined by brain criteria [… and] is used when observable functions of the brain have ceased irreversibly even though other organs continue to function through technological support." James L. Bernat, *Ethical Issues in Neurology* (Oxford: Butterworth-Heinemann [Elsevier], 1994), 25. Historically, brain death was called "a state beyond coma," characterized by flat EEG activity in conjunction with loss of consciousness and autonomic functions like respiration. Pierre Mollaret and Maurice Goulon, "Le coma dépassé," *Revue Neurologique Société de Paris*, Volume 101, No. 1 (Paris: Société Française de Neurologie [Elsevier], 1959), 3–15. The currently accepted "definition of death [is one] that would permit the removal of organs before they deteriorated from lack of circulation." Henry K. Beecher, "A Definition of Irreversible Coma: Report of the Ad Hoc Committee of the Harvard Medical School to Examine the Definition of Brain Death," *JAMA: Journal of the American Medical Association*, Volume 205, No. 6 (Chicago: American Medical Association, 1968), 337–40. Some opponents of this definition contend that, "although death is properly understood as a biological phenomenon, 'brain death' is a social construct created for utilitarian purposes, primarily to permit organ transplantation." Robert M. Taylor, "Reexamining the Definition and Criteria of Death," *Seminars in Neurology*, Volume 17, No. 3 (New York: Thieme [Stratton] Medical Publishers, 1997), 265–70; doi:10.1055/s-2008-1040938. Even government physicians conclude that "the term 'brain death' implies that there is more than one kind of death[, … which] is a serious error[, … in that] 'brain death' implies that death is a state of the cells and tissues constituting the brain[, … when i]n fact, what is directly at issue is the living or dead status of the human individual, not the individual's brain[; …] the condition that warrants a determination of death using the neurological standard is *not* the 'death of the brain' in this sense." The President's Council

on Bioethics, "Controversies in the Determination of Death" (Washington, D.C.: U.S. Government Printing Office, December 2008), 17. Moving the focus from brain to brain stem brings the realization that "awareness is correlated with cortical activity." Philip Low, "Cambridge Declaration of Consciousness," ed. Jaak Panskeep, et al. (Cambridge: Churchill College [University of Cambridge], 7 July 2012), presented at the *Francis Crick Memorial Conference on Consciousness in Human and non-Human Animals.* Or, specifically, that "we can further reduce the critical structure of the brain itself to the cortico-cerebral-thalamoreticular complex." Julius Korein and Calixto Machado, "Brain Death: Updating a Valid Concept," *Brain Death and Disorders of Consciousness*, ed. Calixto Machado and D. Alan Shewmon (New York: Kluwer Academic / Plenum Publishers, 2004), 4. In saying that "although brain death is not sufficient for the biological death of a human organism, it is sufficient for the death or ceasing to exist of a person," those opposing the use of brain death as a determinant are basically contending that, so long as an artifical brainstem could conceivably regulate everything an unconscious brain could, brain death is not necessarily the end of an organism. Jeff[erson] McMahan, "An Alternative to Brain Death," *Journal of Law, Medicine and Ethics*, Volume 34, No. 1 (Boston: American Society of Law, Medicine and Ethics, Spring 2006), 44–48; doi:10.1111/j.1748-720X.2006.00007.x.

55. "Ischaemic damage can occur when the brain is deprived of oxygen for more than 3 minutes." Wolfgang Keil, et al., "Injuries Due to Asphyxiation and Drowning," *Handbook of Forensic Medicine*, ed. Burkhard Madea (Chichester, England: Wiley-Blackwell [John Wiley and Sons], 2014), 412. "Cerebral hypoxia causes loss of consciousness in less than a minute but, if the blood circulation and oxygenation are restored within about 3 minutes, recovery should be complete[; … conversely, h]ypoxia for longer than about 3 minutes causes brain damage and coma, with dilated pupils unresponsive to light, inert or rigid limbs, unresponsiveness to all stimuli, abolition of brainstem reflexes and, ultimately, no electrical activity on EEG (brain death)." Crispian Scully, *Scully's Medical Problems in Dentistry* (London: Churchill Livingston [Elsevier Health], 2014), 382. "Long lasting anoxia, caused by cessation of blood flow to the brain for more than 5–10 minutes, results in irreversible damage and extensive cell death in the brain." Pim Van Lommel, "About the Continuity of Our Consciousness," *Brain Death and Disorders of Consciousness*, ed. Calixto Machado and D. Alan Shewmon (New York: Springer Science+Business Media, 2004), 124. Cf. Lawrence M. Weinberger, Mary H. Gibbon, and John H. Gibbon Jr., "Temporary Arrest of the Circulation to the Central Nervous System," *Archives of Neurology and Psychiatry*, Volume 43, No. 4 (Chicago: American Medical Association, 1940), 615–34; doi:10.1001/archneurpsyc.1940.02280040002001.

56. A revived person who recounts an experience while clinically dead may have undergone a "dying brain" episode; "[f]or the dying-brain account, the central assumption does not revolve around the presence or absence of anoxia [lack of blood flow to the brain] per se, but of neural disinhibition[, … inasmuch as] the EEG principally measures surface cortical activity." Jason J. Braithwaite, "Towards a Cognitive Neuroscience of the Dying Brain," *Skeptic*, Volume 21, No. 2 (Altadena, California: The Skeptics Society, 2008), 8–16. "[Given] the 18% rate of NDE [or near-death experience, … s]urely, if an afterlife existence were real, […] why did only 18% glimpse it? [… Moreover, for a remembered NDE,] there must have been sufficient neural activity to encode the experience, to represent the experience, and to store the experience[, … yet with regard to the brain,] it is not at all clear how a memory of an experience can occur without the use of memory itself." Ibid. As "[d]eath is the cessation of all biological functions[, … b]rain death […] may be pronounced when it is judged that brain failure is irreversible, even if heart and lung function is maintained artificially[; … in addition, s]ome individuals who have been pronounced clinically dead and then revived, or who have undergone resuscitation after a cardiac arrest, [… are those whose experiences might] represent physiological changes in the dying brain." Alice Roberts, *The Complete Human Body: The Definitive Visual Guide* (New York: Dorling Kindersley [Penguin Random House], 2016), 426. Pointedly, "clinical death is different from actual death." H. K. Chopra and Navin C. Nanda, *Textbook of Cardiology* (New Delhi, India: Jaypee Brothers Medical Publishers, 2013), 390. Even from a religious perspective, brain death is understood to be "the irreversible cessation of all brain function, including the brain stem, due to the sustained lack of blood circulation[, … and i]n medical terms, no one has ever been revived after brain death[, … so p]eople who report near-death experiences are those who have been revived after clinical death[, … but] they have not suffered brain death or biological death." Joseph T. Kelley, *101 Questions and Answers on the Four Last Things* (Mahwah, New Jersey: Paulist Press, 2006), 15.

57. "Brain dead patients exist betwixt and between alive and dead[, … and] there are no documented cases of anyone recovering from this state." Margaret Lock, "On Dying Twice: Culture Technology and the Determination of Death," *Living and Working with the New Medical Technologies: Intersections of Inquiry*, ed. Margaret Lock, Allan Young, and Alberto Cambrosio (Cambridge: Cambridge University Press, 2000), 233. The same author later wrote more emphatically: "There is also unanimous agreement that the clinical criteria for whole-brain death is infallible, if the tests are performed correctly, and that whole-brain death is an irreversible state, from which no one […] has ever recovered." Margaret Lock, "Living Cadavers and the Calculation of Death,"

Death, Mourning, and Burial: A Cross-Cultural Reader, ed. Antonius C. G. M. Robben (Oxford: Blackwell Publishing, 2004), 93.

58. Clinical death "produces cessation of circulation, which in turn causes loss of consciousness [...] within seconds." Parish, et al., "Mechanism of Death," 3081–87. At this point, "the organs become deprived of oxygen and stop working within seconds, and we are then lifeless," yet awareness may persist for up to three minutes, according to the AWARE study. Sam Parnia and Josh Young, *Erasing Death: The Science That Is Rewriting the Boundaries Between Life and Death* (New York: HarperCollins, 2013), 19–20.

59. "Cardiac arrest results from anoxia (absence of oxygen to the tissue) or interruption of the electrical stimuli to the heart[, ... and w]ithin 1 to 2 minutes after cessation of cardiac activity, respiratory efforts will cease [... and a]t 4 to 6 minutes after the cessation of cardiac activity, brain cells will begin to die[; ... a]t 10 minutes after the cardiac activity has ceased with no intervention, the brain will die and death is inevitable." Margaret Schell Frazier and Jeanette Drzymkowski, *Essentials of Human Diseases and Conditions* (St. Louis, Missouri: Saunders [Elsevier], 1996), 486.

60. "Brain death now appears to be a well-established legal concept, but it remains quite controversial [... in that] some scholars [... think that] 'brain death' and, thus our concept of death generally, is a social and legal construct[, ... while o]thers maintain its biological basis[; ... furthermore, there] is recent, growing awareness that the medical standards for determining the cessation of brain function are not as certain and uniform as many people have believed." Janet Dolgin and Lois L. Shepherd, *Bioethics and the Law* (New York: Wolters Kluwer, 2019), 542. "Brain death is declared medically when a patient is in an irreversible coma due to brain injury[, ... a standard which] is accepted worldwide[: ...] What differs is the procedure for determining brain death[, a]nd these societal differences reveal how bioethical practices and laws can vary so wildly, for reasons that have nothing to do with the science." Michael S. Gazzaniga, *The Ethical Brain: The Science of Our Moral Dilemmas* (New York: Dana Press, 2005), 10; citing a survey of "brain death criteria throughout the world [...] through review of literature and legal standards and personal contacts with physicians[, ... which revealed] major differences in the procedures for diagnosing brain death" at Eelco F. M. Wijdicks, "Brain Death Worldwide: Accepted Fact but No Global Consensus in Diagnostic Criteria," *Neurology*, Volume 58, No. 1 (Hagerstown, Maryland: Lippincott Williams and Wilkins, 8 January 2002), 20–25, doi:10.1212/WNL.58.1.20. "What ethical and legal considerations should apply to the discontinuation of artificial support in the presence of still-functioning fragments of the brain [...] remains a topic of active medical, philosophical, and ethical

discussion." Fred Plum, "Clinical Standards and Technological Confirmatory Tests in Diagnosing Brain Death," *The Definition of Death: Contemporary Controversies*, ed. Stuart J. Youngner, Robert M. Arnold, and Renie Schapiro (Baltimore, Maryland: Johns Hopkins University Press, 2002), 35.

61. Mark T. Hughes, "Thinking about Medicine," *Oxford American Handbook of Clinical Medicine*, ed. John A. Flynn, Michael J. Choi, and L. Dwight Wooster (New York: Oxford University Press, 2013), 19–20.

62. "All 50 states have adopted by law the neurological criteria for determining death, whether by statute, regulation, or judicial decision [… through the] adoption of the Uniform Determination of Death Act[, … although a small number of states] require that a specialist in neuroscience or related field must confirm when brain death has occurred." Nikolas T. Nikas, Dorinda C. Bordlee, and Madeline Moreira, "Determination of Death and the Dead Donor Rule: A Survey of the Current Law on Brain Death," *The Journal of Medicine and Philosophy*, Volume 41, No. 3 (Cary, North Carolina: Oxford University Press, June 2016), 237–56; doi:10.1093/jmp/jhw002. "The President's Commission guidelines for the determination of brain death culminated in a proposal for a legal definition that led to the Uniform Determination of Death Act (UDDA) in 1981[; … a]ll states and the District of Columbia have statutes for determining brain death based on the UDDA, but certain statutes [… have a] requirement that determination of brain death should be done by two different physicians, the use of confirmatory testing, and the notification of next of kin before the declaration of brain death." Fred Rincon, "Neurological Criteria for Death in Adults," *Critical Care Medicine: Principles of Diagnosis and Management in the Adult*, ed. Joseph E. Parrillo and R. Phillip Dellinge (Philadelphia, Pennsylvania: Saunders [Elsevier], 2014 [Maryland Heights, Missouri: Mosby 1995]), 1099. Cf. Shivani Ghoshal and David M. Greer, "Why Is Diagnosing Brain Death So Confusing?" in *Current Opinion in Critical Care*, Volume 21, No. 2 (Hagerstown, Maryland: Lippincott Williams and Wilkins, February 2015), 107–12; doi:10.1097/MCC.0000000000000180.

63. "[A]n EEG showing electrocerebral inactivity (ECI) is usually not required to make the determination of brain death[; moreover, a]n ECI recording considered alone […] should not be considered synonymous with brain death." Mark H. Libenson, *Practical Approach to Electroencephalography* (Philadelphia, Pennsylvania: Saunders [Elsevier], 2010), 299. And an "EEG is desirable, but not required, only in those circumstances in which the diagnosis of brain death is suspected but not fully [established or determined]." Michael Jeffrey Aminoff, *Electrodiagnosis in Clinical Neurology* (London: Churchill-Livingstone [Elsevier], 2005), 764.

64. "Functional transcranial Doppler ultrasound (fTCD) is a relatively new and non-invasive technique that assesses cerebral lateralisation through measurements of blood flow velocity in the middle cerebral arteries." Sarah Illingworth and Dorothy V. M. Bishop, "Atypical Cerebral Lateralisation in Adults with Compensated Developmental Dyslexia Demonstrated Using Functional Transcranial Doppler Ultrasound," *Brain and Language*, Volume 111, No. 1 (San Diego, California: Academic Press [Elsevier Science], October 2009), 61–65; doi:10.1016/j.bandl.2009.05.002. Cf. Margaret F. Docker, "Doppler Ultrasound Monitoring Technology," *British Journal of Obstetrics and Gynaecology* Volume 100, No. S9 (London: Royal College of Obstetricians and Gynaecologists, March 1993), 18–20; doi:10.1111/j.1471-0528.1993. tb10630.x. "Transcranial Doppler US [… is] a non-invasive tool for evaluating the cerebral arteries[, …including] evaluation of cerebral blood flow velocities [… and] diagnosis and monitoring of acute cerebrovascular disorders[, … as well as] confirmation of a clinical diagnosis of brain death." Suzanne Verlhac, "Transcranial Doppler in Children," *Pediatric Radiology*, Volume 41 (Berlin: Springer-Verlag [European Society of Pediatric Radiology], May 2011), 153–65; doi:10.1007/s00247-011-2038-y. Still, "transcranial doppler ultrasonography (TCD) […] is the most important method to confirm brain death […] and represented half of the tests that confirmed brain death diagnosis[, …] performed at the bedside, non-invasive and low cost." Julio Mijangos-Mendez, et al., "Diagnosing Brain Death and the Role of Transcranial Doppler Ultrasound: A Four-Year Experience Study," *Critical Care Medicine*, Volume 48, No. 1 (Philadelphia, Pennsylvania: Elsevier, January 2020), 351; doi:10.1097/01.ccm.0000626704.68954.77. Even as it relates to non-Western medicine such as acupuncture, "[t]he usage of advanced exploratory tools such as multidirectional transcranial Doppler ultrasound sonography […] provides revealing insights." Gerhard Litscher, "Modernization of Traditional Acupuncture using Multimodal Computer-based High-Tech Methods—recent Results of Blue Laser and Teleacupuncture from the Medical University of Graz," *Journal of Acupuncture and Meridian Studies*, Volume 2, No. 3 (Seoul, South Korea: Elsevier, September 2009), 202–209; doi:10.1016/S2005-2901(09)60056-X.

65. "[T]he American Academy of Neurology's recently updated guidelines on the determination of brain death do not include SSEPs as an ancillary test." *Oxford Textbook of Neurocritical Care*, ed. Martin Smith, Giuseppe Citerio, and W. Andrew Kofke (Oxford: Oxford University Press, 2016), 174. "The somatosensory evoked potential (SSEP) is [, … however, almost exclusively used] to evaluate functional damage to the complete sensory pathway[, … while] using SSEP to predict mortality has yielded mixed results." *Textbook of Neuroanesthesia and Neurocritical Care*, Volume 2:

Neurocritical Care, ed. Hemanshu Prabhakar and Zulfiqar Ali (Singapore: Springer Nature, 2019), 184.

66. "Manner of death is in one of five classifications: natural, accident, suicide, homicide, or undetermined[, while also, s]ome states have an additional category[, most closely aligned with accident,] called therapeutic misadventure." Ann Bucholtz, *Death Investigation: An Introduction to Forensic Pathology for the Nonscientist* (New York: Routledge [Taylor and Francis], 2015), 50.

67. Patients who are "minimally conscious [...] with no cognitive impairments overhear doctors discussing them as if they were, quite literally, not there." Stephanie Pywell, "Potential Legal Implications of Advances in Neuroimaging Techniques for the Clinical Management of Patients with Disorders of Consciousness," *Jahrbuch für Wissenschaft und Ethik*, Volume 19, No. 1 (Berlin: Walter de Gruyter, July 2015), 115–46; doi:10.1515/jwiet-2015-0110, German edition of *Yearbook for Science and Ethics*. Cf. Eelco F. M. Wijdicks, "Who Improves from Coma, How Do They Improve, and Then What?" in *Nature Reviews Neurology*, Volume 14, No. 12 (London: Nature Publishing Group, December 2018), 694–96; doi:10.1038/s41582-018-0084-x.

68. "Complete blindness (occasionally dubbed NLP, or 'no light perception') is incredibly rare [... but h]appens when the connection between the eyes and brain is completely cut off[, ... perhaps when] there is brain damage, the optic nerve has been severed, or the eyes have been removed[, ... the result of which is that t]hey see nothing." See "What Do Blind People See?" on *The OrCam Blog* (Jerusalem, Israel: OrCam, 11 April 2018) at **https://www.orcam. com/en/blog/what-do-blind-people-see/**, accessed May 13, 2020. No mental state can overcome a physical deficiency. Moreover, "no light perception (NLP) [...] indicates an irreversible condition." Ferenc Kuhn and Robert Morris, "Management of Open Global Injuries," *Management of Complicated Vitreoretinal Diseases*, ed. Fabio Patelli and Stanislao Rizzo (Cham, Switzerland: Springer International Publishing [Springer Science+Business Media], 2015), 42. The permanently blind may see "nothing[, ... but] they use their other senses to encode spatial relationships." Jim Davies, "What Do Blind People Actually See?" on *Nautilus* (New York: NautilusNext, 13 August 2014) at **http://nautil.us/blog/what-do-blind-people-actually-see**, also accessed May 13, 2020.

69. "[T]he limbic system has been regarded to play a crucial role in memory processing—a finding that makes sense also from an evolutionary point of view." Hans J. Markowitsch, "Neuroanatomy of Memory," *The Oxford Handbook of Memory*, ed. Endel Tulving and Fergus I. M. Craik (New York: Oxford University Press, 2000), 468. "[R]egions of the limbic system

are primarily engaged in the encoding of autobiographical and semantic information, while cortical areas in the orbitofrontal and anterolateral temporo-polar regions are principally engaged in information retrieval." Hans J. Markowitsch, "Which Brain Regions Are Critically Involved in the Retrieval of Old Episodic Memory," *Brain Research Reviews*, Volume 21, No. 2 (Amsterdam: Elsevier Science, September 1995), 117–27; doi:10.1016/0165-0173(95)00007-0. According to others, however, "[o]nce encoded by the hippocampal formation, the memory trace is then transferred to other parts of the brain for shortand long-term storage[, … so t]he limbic system seems not to be involved in the storage and retrieval of long term memories." Walter Hendelman, *Atlas of Functional Neuroanatomy* (Boca Raton, Florida: CRC Press [Taylor and Francis], 2006), 203.

70. "[I]t takes time to form a lasting memory, a process called consolidation[; … t]he hippocampus acts as a sort of 'switching station' between short-term and long-term memory." Dennis Coon and John O. Mitterer, *Introduction to Psychology: Gateways to Mind and Behavior* (Belmont, California: Wadsworth [CENGAGE Learning], 2007), 270–71; citing Nicola J. Broadbent, Larry R. Squire, and Robert E. Clark, "Spatial Memory Recognition Memory and the Hippocampus," *Proceedings of the National Academy of Sciences*, Volume 101, No. 40 (Washington, D.C.: the United States National Academy of Sciences, 27 September 2004), 14515–20; doi:10.1073/pnas.0406344101. "The conversion from short-term to long-term memory is called memory consolidation[, … and t]he amygdaloid body and the hippocampus, two components of the limbic system […] are essential to memory consolidation." Frederic H. Martini, *Anatomy and Physiology* (Singapore: Pearson Education [Prentice Hall], 2005), 404. "[T]he human amygdala is a critical component of the neural substrates of emotional experience, involved particularly in the generation of fear, anxiety, and general negative affectivity." Adam K. Anderson and Elizabeth A. Phelps, "Is the Human Amygdala Critical for the Subjective Experience of Evidence of Intact Dispositional Affect in Patients with Amygdala Lesions," *Journal of Cognitive Neuroscience*, Volume 14, No. 5 (Cambridge, Massachusetts: MIT Press, 1 July 2002), 709–20. "[A] critical function of the human amygdala is to enhance the perception of stimuli that have emotional significance." Adam K. Anderson and Elizabeth A. Phelps, "Lesions of the Human Amygdala Impair Enhanced Perception of Emotionally Salient Events," *Nature*, Volume 411, No. 6835 (London: Nature Research [Springer Nature], 17 May 2001), 305–09; doi:10.1038/35077083. "[T]he amygdala is concerned to a great extent with olfactory stimuli and their interrelations with the limbic brain." John E. Hall, *Guyton and Hall Textbook of Medical Physiology* (St. Louis, Missouri: Saunders [Elsevier], 1956), 760. "The contribution of the amygdala to odor memory has received

scant attention until recently [… and] is probably concerned with associative learning between olfactory and visual signals." Christopher H. Hawkes and Richard L. Doty, *The Neurology of Olfaction* (New York: Cambridge University Press, 2009), 26; citing Tony W. Buchanan, Daniel Tranel, and Ralph Adolphs, "A Specific Role for the Human Amygdala in Olfactory Memory," *Learning and Memory*, Volume 10, No. 5 (Cold Spring Harbor, New York: Cold Spring Harbor Laboratory Press, September 2003), 319–25; doi:10.1101/lm.62303. "[M]ultiple converging lines of evidence for involvement of the anterior cingulate gyrus in pain sensation are of particular significance, because this cortical area is part of the so-called medial pain system." Rolf-Detlef Treede, "Pain and the Somatosensory Cortex," *Pain: Current Understanding, Emerging Therapies, and Novel Approaches to Drug Discovery*, ed. Chas Bountra, Rajesh Munglani, and William K. Schmidt (New York: Marcel Dekker [Taylor and Francis], 2003), 87. "[E]vidence from anatomical, lesion, and electrophysiological studies […] clearly implicate the mediodorsal thalamus [… as one of the] important neural elements of a system dedicated to working memory processing." Patricia S. Goldman-Rakic and Harriet R. Friedman, "The Circuitry of Working Memory Revealed by Anatomy and Metabolic Imaging," *Frontal Lobe Function and Dysfunction*, ed. Harvey S. Levin, Howard M. Eisenberg, and Arthur L. Benton (New York: Oxford University Press, 1991), 78. The "thalamus [… is integrally] associated with working memory." Anya Mazur-Mosiewicz and Chad A. Noggle, "Rehabilitative Psychopharmacology," *Neuropsychological Rehabilitation*, ed. Chad A. Noggle, Raymond S. Dean, and Mark T. Barisa (New York: Springer, 2013), 319. "The epithalamus occupies the dorsolateral part of the diencephalon and consists of the pineal body (epiphysis cerebri) [… or] pineal gland[, …] an endocrine gland, which […] secretes indolamines such as melatonin and associated enzymes […] that show sensitivity to the variations in diurnal light and circadian rhythms." Orhan E. Arslan, *Neuroanatomical Basis of Clinical Neurology* (New York: The Parthenon Publishing Group, 2001), 114. "Both experimental studies and analysis of human pathology have shown the important role played by the hippocampal formation in certain aspects of memory [… and how it,] the hypothalamus, exerts a powerful control over autonomic functions." Bruce M. Carlson, *The Human Body: Linking Structure and Function* (London: Academic Press [Elsevier], 2019), 15. "The hypothalamus is critical to the autonomic functions of the body." David M. Yousem and Robert I. Zimmerman, *Neuroradiology* (Philadelphia, Pennsylvania: Mosby [Elsevier], 2010), 23.

71. "While emotions are usually goal-directed and a reaction to environmental events, they may also be spontaneously evoked during electrical brain stimulation either through artificial means or during an epileptic seizure."

David Andrewes, *Neuropsychology: From Theory to Practice* (New York: Psychology Press [Taylor and Francis], 2013), 397.

72. "Memory is a brain function that allows us to remember past experiences." Eduard Vieta, Carla Torrent, and Anabel Martínez-Arán, *Functional Remediation for Bipolar Disorder* (Cambridge: Cambridge University Press, 2014), 56. "Memory is a brain function that comprises encoding, consolidation, persistence, maintenance, and retrieval." Jociane C. Myskiw and Iván Izquierdo, "Posterior Parietal Cortex and Long-Term Memory: Some Data from Laboratory Animals," *Frontiers in Integrative Neuroscience*, Volume 6, No. 8 (Lausanne, Switzerland: Frontiers Research Foundation, 27 February 2012); doi:10.3389/fnint.2012.00008. Yet from an entirely different perspective, "[m]emory is no good as a criterion of the self because, to establish that the memory is an accurate memory as opposed to an illusory one, one first has to establish the very identity that the memory was supposed to establish." John R. Searle, "The Self as a Problem in Philosophy and Neurobiology," *The Lost Self: Pathologies of the Brain and Identity*, ed. Todd E. Feinberg and Julian Paul Keenan (New York: Oxford University Press, 2005), 14. But see also Roland Puccetti, "Brain Bisection and Personal Identity," *The British Journal for the Philosophy of Science*, Volume 24, No. 4 (Oxford: The British Society for the Philosophy of Science [Oxford University Press], December 1973), 339–55. However, "what is the value of the assurance of continuation [of some form of your life] when it doesn't involve any recollections of your existing life?" Hywel D. Lewis, *Persons and Life after Death* (London: Macmillan Press, 1978), 63; quoting English philosopher (Lord Baron) Anthony Quinton (1925–2010) in the transcript of a radio interview with the author, Hywel D. Lewis (1910–92), and Sir Bernard Williams (1929–2003). "As our memory [… is] the basis of self-identity within the brain[, … t]he role of memory in developing the self has been a focus of research in psychology; self-identity is created by accessing information in memory." Lynn A. Watson and Barbara Dritschel, "The Role of Self during Autobiographical Remembering and Psychopathology: Evidence from Philosophical, Behavioral, Neural, and Cultural Investigations," *Clinical Perspectives on Autobiographical Memory*, ed. Lynn A. Watson and Dorthe Berntsen (Cambridge: Cambridge University Press, 2015), 335–37.

73. "Concussive brain injury is also referred to as mild traumatic brain injury (TBI) [… and] is characterized by the immediate and transient changes in brain function which include temporary loss of memory." Kedar N. Prasad, *Neurodegenerative Disease and Micronutrients: Prevention and Treatment* (Boca Raton, Florida: CRC Press [Taylor and Francis], 2014), 233. "Memory loss is a characteristic symptom of brain damage." Rolland S. Parker, *Concussive Brain Trauma: Neurobehavioral Impairment and Maladaptation*

(Boca Raton, Florida: CRC Press, 2000), 270. For examples of "procedures designed to help individuals with traumatic brain injury reconstruct an organised and positive sense of personal identity," see Mark Ylvisaker and Timothy Feeney, "Reconstruction of Identity after Brain Injury," *Brain Impairment*, Volume 1, No. 1 (Cambridge: Cambridge University Press, 1 May 2000), 12–28; doi:10.1375/brim.1.1.12. "A tap on the head, and anything can go wrong[: …] You may not remember how to swallow [o]r you may look at food and perspire instead of salivate and salivate when you hear your favorite song." Michael Paul Mason, *Head Cases: Stories of Brain Injury and Its Aftermath* (New York: Farrar, Straus, and Giroux, 2008), 6. However, in the view of others, "[i]If every small tap on the head did damage to our brain, we wouldn't survive past the age of 2." Unknown author, "Can Slapping The Head Affect The Brain[?]" (unmoderated website) at **http://bt09x2.25u.com/b242.php**, accessed May 14, 2020.

74. The initial speculation that led to the "Orch OR" (or Orchestrated Objective-Reduction) hypothesis appeared over twenty-five years ago. Stuart R. Hameroff, "Quantum Coherence in Microtubules: A Neural Basis for Emergent Consciousness?" in *Journal of Consciousness Studies*, Volume 1, No. 1 (Thorverton, England: Imprint Academic, 1994), 98–118. The hypothesis was further developed and refined with the help of a renowned physicist: Stuart R. Hameroff and Roger Penrose, "Conscious Events as Orchestrated Space-Time Selections," *Journal of Consciousness Studies*, Volume 3, No. 1 (Thorverton, England: Imprint Academic, 1 January 1996), 36–53, doi:10.14704/nq.2003.1.1.3; and Stuart Hameroff and Roger Penrose, "Consciousness in the Universe: A Review of the 'Orch OR' Theory," *Physics of Life Reviews*, Volume 11, No. 1 (Amsterdam: Elsevier, March 2014), 39–78, doi:10.1016/j.plrev.2013.08.002. "[Penrose] and his team have found evidence that 'protein-based microtubules—a structural component of human cells—carry quantum information—information stored at a sub-atomic level[, … meaning] it's possible that this quantum information can exist outside the body, perhaps indefinitely, as a soul.'" Robert Lanza, "Life After Death?—Physicists Says 'It's Quantum Information that Transcends from One World to Another,'" *TheDailyGalaxy.com* (Cambridge, Massachusetts: Harvard University's Astronomy department, 13 August 2017) at **https://dailygalaxy.com/2017/08/life-after-death-renowned-physicists-says-its-quantum-information-stored-at-a-sub-atomic-level-that/**, accessed May 14, 2020. Early critics pointed out flaws in the hypothesis and its reliance on "non-algorithmic quantum gravitational phenomena," the presence of "cytoplasmic ions […] in the microtubule pore [… normally barred by] quantum-mechanical effects," and the observation that "consciousness does not directly depend on microtubule properties." Rick Grush and Patricia S.

Churchland, "Gaps in Penrose's Toiling," *Journal of Consciousness Studies*, Volume 2, No. 1 (Thorverton, England: Imprint Academic, 1 January 1995), 10–29. The indirect proof, though, has to do with evidence confirming quantum effects taking place at surprisingly low, biological-level temperatures. Gregory S. Engel, et al., "Evidence for Wavelike Energy Transfer Through Quantum Coherence in Photosynthetic Systems," *Nature*, Volume 446, No. 7137 (London: Nature Research [Springer Nature], 12 April 2007), 782–86, doi:10.1038/nature05678; and Quanyong Y. Lu, et al., "Room-Temperature Continuous Wave Operation of Distributed Feedback Quantum Cascade Lasers with Watt-Level Power Output," *Applied Physics Letters*, Volume 97, No. 23 (New York: American Institute of Physics, December 2010), 231119, doi:10.1063/1.3525859. This was enough for one of the hypothesis's founders to declare that "Orch OR has been discounted because it differs so markedly from conventional approaches [… but t]en years after, known neurobiology has moved toward Orch OR." Stuart Hameroff, "Consciousness, Neurobiology, and Quantum Mechanics: The Case for a Connection," *The Emerging Physics of Consciousness*, ed. Jack A. Tuszynsk (Berlin / Heidelberg, Germany: Springer-Verlag [Springer Science+Business Media], 2006), 196. Critic Dutch-American researcher Bernard J. Baars (1946–) has said, "If somebody comes up with just one single experiment" demonstrating quantum consciousness, "I will drop all my skepticism." Tanya Lewis, "Could Quantum Brain Effects Explain Consciousness?" on *LiveScience.com* (New York: TechMedia Network [Purch Group], 27 June 2013) at **https://www.livescience.com/37807-brain-is-not-quantum-computer.html**, also accessed May 14, 2020; quoting Baars. "Orch OR theory cannot be treated seriously without a precise description of the quantum states of the qubits, how these states become entangled, and a means of achieving quantum coherence over the required time scale." Francisco R. Villatoro, "On the Quantum Theory of Consciousness," *MappingIgnorance.org* (Leioa, Spain: University of the Basque Country's Scientific Culture program, 17 June 2015) at **https://mappingignorance.org/2015/06/17/on-the-quantum-theory-of-consciousness/**, also accessed May 14, 2020; citing Jeffrey R. Reimers, et al., "The Revised Penrose-Hameroff Orchestrated Objective-Reduction Proposal for Human Consciousness Is Not Scientifically Justified: Comment on 'Consciousness in the Universe: a Review of the "Orch OR" Theory' by Hameroff and Penrose," *Physics of Life Reviews*, Volume 11, No. 1 (Amsterdam: Elsevier, March 2014), 101–103; doi:10.1016/j.plrev.2013.11.003. One critic asserts "there is no evidence I'm aware of that quantum-mechanical phenomena operate in the brain, much less that they play a role in consciousness and memory." Jerry Coyne, "I Have Landed… to Find Quantum Quackery," *WhyEvolutionIsTrue.WordPress.com* (Chicago: Jerry A. Coyne, 16 November 2017) at **https://whyevolutionistrue.wordpress.com/2017/11/16/i-have-landed-to-find-quantum-quackery/**, also accessed May 14, 2020.

"The supposed superposition maintained by Hameroff is a vibration with an amplitude of the order of an atomic nucleus[, … h]owever, at the temperature of the brain, simple brownian motion of the surrounding fluid would quickly dampen out such quantum effects." Internet reply by Mark John Fernee (https://www.quora.com/profile/Mark-John-Fernee) *Quora.com* (Mountain View, California: Quora Inc., 5 March 2018) at https://www.quora.com/As-of-yet-is-there-experimental-evidence-to-support-the-Orch-OR-theory-of-consciousness-as-proposed-by-Sir-Roger-Penrose-and-Stuart-Hameroff, also accessed May 14, 2020; responding to the question "As of yet, is there experimental evidence to support the Orch-OR theory of consciousness as proposed by Sir Roger Penrose and Stuart Hameroff?" at the same URL.

75. "[P]icture a person whose memories are inaccessible but, in some sense, still there[; … t]he information is extracted in a way that leaves the brain with all its memory dispositions in some way intact, although no longer capable of being triggered in the usual ways." John Perry, *Identity, Personal Identity and the Self* (Indianapolis, Indiana: Hackett Publishing, 2002), 114. "Such events have the potential to spark psychogenic amnesia, in which memories for the trauma become inaccessible." Alan Baddeley, et al., *Memory* (New York: Psychology Press [Taylor and Francis], 2015), 280. "Signs indicative of the presence of dissociative amnesia include possession of unfamiliar objects that cannot be accounted for[, … and] the memory for the event, although inaccessible, is nevertheless preserved." Andrew C. Papanicolaou, et al., *The Amnesias: A Clinical Textbook of Memory Disorders* (New York: Oxford University Press, 2006), 216. "Despite losing all autobiographical memory, semantic memory is intact[; … indeed, a]nother way to think about dissociative amnesia is that it is a psychological loss of memory where a specific memory has become inaccessible but may remain available." *Encyclopedia of Human Memory*, Volume 1: A - D, ed. Annette Kujawski Taylor (Santa Barbara, California: Greenwood [ABC-CLIO], 2013), 369; the "Dissociative Amnesia" definitional entry. For reference, "[a]nterograde amnesia [… is t]he inability to recall or recognize events and facts that were encountered after the onset of amnesia (postmorbidly)[, … whereas r]etrograde amnesia [… is the i]nability to recall or recognize experiences and information acquired before the onset of amnesia (premorbidly)." Mieke Verfaellie, "Amnesia," *Encyclopedia of Behavioral Neuroscience*, ed. George Koob, et al. (San Diego, California: Academic Press [Elsevier Science], 2010), 41; the "Amnesia" entry in the glossary.

76. As "aging is those things that go wrong when cells lose their ability to divide, if we could replace our cells as rapidly as they deteriorate, we could probably live very long, if not indefinitely." Alexander Bürkle, "In Memoriam Bernard Strehler—Genomic Instability in Ageing: A Persistent Challenge,"

Mechanisms of Ageing and Development, Volume 123, No. 8 (Amsterdam: Elsevier, 30 April 2002), 899–906; doi:10.1016/S0047-6374(02)00027-1. Moreover, "[a]s a person ages, one of two things happens to individual cells: A cell will either slow down and lose function [… or else it] can proliferate uncontrollably, or in other words, become cancerous." Samantha Mathewson, "Sorry, You Can't Stop Aging—Here's the Math to Prove It," *LiveScience.com* (New York: TechMedia Network [Purch Group], 31 October 2017) at **https:// www.livescience.com/60825-aging-is-inevitable-according-to-math.html**, accessed January 3, 2020, citing Paul Nelson and Joanna Masel, "Intercellular Competition and the Inevitability of Multicellular Aging," *Proceedings of the National Academy of Sciences*, Volume 114, No. 49 (Washington, D.C.: the United States National Academy of Sciences, 30 October 2017), 12982–87; doi:10.1073/pnas.1618854114.

77. "Thanatophobia (from *Thanatos*, the Greek god or daemon of nonviolent death, and *phobos* meaning fear) is an excessive and persistent fear of one's own death[, … but] is more commonly referred to as *death anxiety*." *Phobias: The Psychology of Irrational Fear*, ed. Irena Milosevic and Randi E. McCabe (Santa Barbara, California: Greenwood Press [American Bibliographical Center - Clio or ABC-CLIO], 2015), 371; emphasis in the original. Although, "the term thanatophobia means an irrational and sudden sense or conviction of being on the point of dying and not the inevitable human fear of death." Laura Sirri and Silvani Grandi, "Illness Behavior," *The Psychosomatic Assessment*, ed. G. A. Fava, N. Sonino, and T. N. Wise (Basel, Switzerland: Karger, 2012), 169. Thanatophobia was coined by J. A. Ryle, "Angor Animi, or The Sense of Dying," *Guy's Hospital Reports* (London: Guy's Hospital, 1928), Volume 78, 230–35.

78. The top ten phobias revealed in a large, random-sample survey does not even include "death," with heights, snakes, and closed spaces topping the list. Mats Fredrikson, et al., "Gender and Age Differences in the Prevalence of Specific Fears and Phobias," *Behaviour Research and Therapy*, Volume 34, No. 1 (Oxford: Elsevier Science, January 1996), 37; doi:10.1016/0005-7967(95)00048-3. A survey of 3,000 adults in the U.S. supposedly showed public speaking as the top fear of 41% of respondents versus death at 20%. R. H. Bruskin Associates, "What Are Americans Afraid of?" in *The Bruskin Report: A Market Research Newsletter*, Volume 53 (July 1973), appearing in the *London Times* and cited by David Wallechinsky, Irving Wallace, and Amy Wallace, *The People's Almanac Presents the Book of Lists* (New York: William Morrow and Company, 1977). But a later resurvey saw death as the topmost fear when respondents were asked about their own fears rather than phobias generally. Karen Kangas Dwyer and Marlina M. Davidson, "Is Public Speaking Really More Feared Than Death?" in *Communication Research Reports*, Volume 29, No. 2 (Morgantown, West Virginia: World Communication

Association [West Virginia University's Speech Communication Department], 30 April 2012), 99–107; doi:10.1080/08824096.2012.667772.

79. As one study puts it, "[f]indings [that correlate fear of death with virtually any parameter or demographic] have been anything but consistent, with reports of negative relationships, positive relationships, no relationship, and even curvilinear associations." Lee Ellis, Eshah A. Wahab, and Malini Ratnasingan, "Religiosity and Fear of Death: A Three-Nation Comparison," *Mental Health, Religion and Culture*, Volume 16, No. 2 (London: Routledge [Taylor and Francis], 1 February 2013), 179–99; doi:10.1080/13674676.2011 .652606. This same study finds "on average females were more religious and feared death more than did males, and Muslims expressed considerably greater fear than did members of any other major religion[; … moreover, the] death apprehension theory [...] specifically predicts that death apprehension will be positively related to most religious beliefs and practices." Ibid. A subsequent study claims "quantitative differences between persons characterized by varying degrees of religious commitment." Victor Florian and Shlomo Kravetz, "Fear of Personal Death: Attribution Structure and Relation to Religious Belief," *Journal of Personality and Social Psychology*, Volume 44, No. 3 (Washington, D.C.: American Psychological Association, March 1983), 600–607. In an early study, "[a]ge and religious self-rating were the only 2 predictor variables found to be consistently associated with personal fear [of death]." Herman Feifel and Allan B. Branscomb, "Who's Afraid of Death?" in *Journal of Abnormal Psychology*, Volume 81, No. 3 (Washington, D.C.: American Psychological Association, June 1973), 282; doi:10.1037/h0034519. A study that soon followed even more assertively states that "older persons were least likely to indicate fear of their own death." Richard A. Kalish and David K. Reynolds, "The Role of Age in Death Attitudes," *Death Education*, Volume 1, No. 2 (Washington, D.C.: Hemisphere Publishing [Taylor and Francis], Summer 1977), 205–30; doi:10.1080/07481187708252892. Another study sees different responses between young and old to what it calls mortality "reminders." Molly Maxfield, et al., "Age-Related Differences in Responses to Thoughts of One's Own Death: Mortality Salience and Judgments of Moral Transgressions," *Psychology and Aging*, Volume 22, No. 2 (Arlington, Virginia: American Psychological Association, June 2007), 341–53; doi:10.1037/0882-7974.22.2.341. One study seems to split the difference by mapping a bell-shaped curve, wherein "[m]iddle-age and late middle-age persons were significantly less anxious [...] than their younger and older counterparts." J. W. Keller, "Perspectives on Death: A Developmental Study," *The Journal of Psychology*, Volume 116, 1st Half (Provincetown, Massachusetts: Journal Press [Routledge], January 1984), 137; doi:10.1080/00223980.1984.9923628. A more recent study finds the "strongest determinant of Death Anxiety was

found to be gender[, … where f]emale participants showed a significant higher level[; … younger p]articipants […] tended to report a higher level of Death Anxiety, same as participants of an age ranging between 50 and 60 years[, … while n]o significant association was found between [religious or political] worldview and Death Anxiety as measured." Karin Robah, "Determinants of Existential Death Anxiety: A Cross-Sectional Survey Study on the Effect of Age, Gender and Religious Affiliation on Death Anxiety," Bachelor's thesis, (Enschede, Netherlands: University of Twente, 2017).

80. "[P]ersons with only a grade school education have a greater fear of death than do those with a college education." Michael R. Leming and George E. Dickinson, *Understanding Dying, Death, and Bereavement* (Belmont, California: Wadsworth [CENGAGE Learning], 2011), 111. And "the effects of courses for health care workers and medical students in care at the end of life [… saw a result in which o]verall fear of death scores were reduced." Katalin Hegedus, Ágnes Zana, and Györgyi Szabó, "Effect of End of Life Education on Medical Students' and Health Care Workers' Death Attitude," *Palliative Medicine*, Volume 22, No. 3 (London: SAGE Publications, April 2008), 264–69; doi:10.1177/0269216307086520. Moreover, a philosophical observation is that "[f]ear of death is universal[, … b]ut what lies beneath that fear is the terror of *insignificance*[, … o]f not being remembered." Erich Segal, *The Class* (New York: Bantam Books, 1985), 516–17; emphasis in the original.

81. A one-time chair of Harvard Medical School's Physiology Department observes that "the emotion of fear is associated with the instinct for flight, and the emotion of anger or rage with the instinct for fighting." Walter B. Cannon, *Bodily Changes in Pain, Hunger, Fear, and Rage* (New York: D. Appleton and Co., 1916), 187. Specifically, the "strongest instinct that all animals have is that of survival[; … a]nimals and humans will respond to dangerous threatening situations with the fight or flight response in order to protect themselves or run away from dangerous threatening situations in order to stay alive." John L. Rigg, "Traumatic Brain Injury and Post–traumatic Stress," *War Trauma and Its Wake*, ed. Raymond Monsour Scurfield and Katherine Theresa Platoni (London and New York: Routledge [Taylor and Francis], 2013), 117.

82. As an example, "[v]asovagal syncope [or fainting in the face of danger] may seem to be a disadvantageous evolutionary adaptation[, … but it] ultimately favours brain self-preservation in potentially threatening circumstances[; …] the everyday struggle for life has generated a self-preservation instinct[, …] defined as the behaviour that endeavors to ensure the survival of the organism[, … which is entirely] mediated by the autonomic nervous system." Jean-Jacques Blanc, Paolo Alboni, and David G. Benditt, "Vasovagal Syncope

in Humans and Protective Reactions in Animals," *Europace*, Volume 17, No. 3 (Oxford: Oxford University Press, March 2015), 345–49; doi:10.1093/europace/euu367. However, "the instinct of self-preservation subsumes all other biological drives since, in the self-aware animal, the violation of any primitive need signals a danger to the entire organism[; ... by contrast, i]n humans, [... it] may be bent away from biological and toward the psychosocial." Benjamin Kissin, *Conscious and Unconscious Programs in the Brain* (New York: Plenum Medical Book [Plenum Publishing], 1986), 24.

83. "[P]hobias generally refer to persistent, irrational fears of certain situations, activities, people or things." Hymie Anisman, *Stress and Your Health: From Vulnerability to Resilience* (Chichester, England: Wiley-Blackwell [John Wiley and Sons], 2015), 177. Even those "whose fears include [...] just about everything outside of their comfort zone [... may benefit from] behavioral therapy." Jennifer MacKay, *Phobias* (Farmington Hills, Michigan: Lucent Books [Gale CENGAGE Learning], 2009), 20. Interestingly, "[t]he latest research shows that only about 30% of phobias are caused by trauma." Gary L. Laundre and Lloyd E. Richmond, *How to Expand Your Comfort Zone* (Grand Rapids, Michigan: Richmond House Publishing, 2001), 20.

84. (Quoting Epicurus) "[W]hen we exist, death is not present to us; and when death is present, then we have no existence." Diogenes Laertius, *The Lives and Opinions of Eminent Philosophers*, trans. Charles Duke Yonge (London: J. Haddon and Son, 1853 [ca. 300 BCE]), 469.

85. Isaac Asimov, *Fantastic Voyage II: Destination Brain* (New York: Doubleday, 1987), 71; voiced by a fictional character. Cf. *Today in Science History website* (Louisville, Kentucky: Ian Ellis, ca. 20 November 2008) at https://todayinsci.com/A/Asimov_Isaac/AsimovIsaac-Quotations.htm, accessed September 30, 2019.

86. "[A]ll are of the dust, and all turn to dust again" (Eccles. 3:20).

87. There are "stories of elephants and ants burying their dead or dolphins assisting dead companions to the surface[, ... and l]ike non-human primates, elephants have been observed to surround a dead conspecific, interact directly with it, touch it with their feet or trunks, at times attempt to lift it with either foot or tusks, and vocalize in apparent distress[; ... generally, t]hanatological behaviour among cetaceans (whales, dolphins and porpoises) is also becoming increasingly well documented and shows many parallels with primate and proboscid data." André Gonçalves and Dora Biro, "Comparative Thanatology an Integrative Approach: Exploring Sensory/Cognitive Aspects of Death Recognition in Vertebrates and Invertebrates," *Philosophical Transactions of the Royal Society of London (Series B, Biological Sciences)*, Volume 373, No. 1754 (London: The Royal

Society, 5 Sep 2018), 20170263; doi:10.1098/rstb.2017.0263. Concerning "the biology and evolution of death-related behavior in nonhuman animals[, ...] biologist Joyce Poole writes [... of having] observed a[n elephant] mother, her facial expression one I could recognize as grief, stand beside her stillborn baby for 3 days." Jessica Pierce, "The Dying Animal," *Journal of Bioethical Inquiry*, Volume 10, No. 4 (Dordrecht, Netherlands: Springer Science+Business Media, December 2013), 469–78; doi:10.1007/s11673-013-9480-5; indirectly citing Joyce Poole, *Coming of Age With Elephants: A Memoir*, (Westport, Connecticut: Hyperion, 1996). Moreover, "dolphins reacted differently to the death of a pod member, depending on whether the animal had died suddenly or after a long period of illness." Rowan Hooper, "Dolphins Appear to Grieve in Different Ways," *New Scientist*, Volume 211, No. 2828 (London: New Science Publications, 3 September 2011), 10; doi:10.1016/S0262-4079(11)62128-3.

88. "[I]n the future, millions of cryogenically frozen human beings could spend centuries in a non-dead state [... awaiting] future technological breakthroughs." David Hershenov, "The Problematic Role of 'Irreversibility' in the Definition of Death," *Bioethics*, Volume 17, No. 1 (Oxford: Wiley-Blackwell, February 2003), 89–100; doi:10.1111/1467-8519.00323. Cf. The Cryogenic Society of America, Inc. (CSA) in Oak Park, Illinois at **http://www.cryogenicsociety.org** and the Alcor Life Extension Foundation in Scottsdale, Arizona at **https://alcor.org/**, where the severed head of the late Baseball Hall of Fame inductee Ted Williams is in frozen stasis at one of their facilities. "[C]ryogenic freezing [... is] when someone has an incurable illness, you can freeze their bodies and then thaw them out in the future when scientists have invented a cure." Scott Adams, *The Dilbert Future: Thriving on Business Stupidity in the 21st Century* (New York: HarperBusiness [HarperCollins], 1998), 10. "[C]ryogenic storage [i]s a way of traveling into the future[, ... in] that your body will be stored, preserved at extremely low temperatures, until the technology exists to defrost you, revive you, and cure you of any illness you were suffering from[, ... assuming] that by the time you are revived any aging will be reversible." Brian Clegg, *How to Build a Time Machine: The Real Science of Time Travel* (New York: St. Martin's Press, 2011), 79.

89. "[T]he whole of this earthly life is a [...] testing-ground for people in which they develop their moral characters and are given a free choice[; ... as an example,] Muslims believe that a person's earthly life is merely a preparation for the afterlife." Libby Ahluwalia, *Understanding Philosophy of Religion* (Dublin: Folens Publishers, 2008), 249 and 263. "We cannot tell from within it, during the brief period of observation afforded by a man's life on this earth, or indeed by scrutinizing the entire scroll of recorded history,

whether this earthly scene is a 'vale of soul making' or a 'fortuitous concourse of atoms.'" John Hick, *Faith and Knowledge: A Modern Introduction To the Problem of Religious Knowledge* (Eugene, Oregon: Wipf and Stock Publishers, 2009), 158. "In Judaism, the emphasis is on the current life rather than the next, [… whereas, i]n the Islamic worldview good and bad deeds done during earthly life determine the fate in the afterlife[; …] Hindus tend to distinguish 'good' deaths from 'bad' deaths, and see this as being significant for the fate of the soul." Michelle Sandhoff, "Religious Diversity in the US Armed Forces," *Inclusion in the American Military: A Force for Diversity*, ed. David E. Rohall, Morten G. Ender, and Michael D. Matthews (Lanham, Maryland: Lexington Books [Rowman and Littlefield], 2017), 182 and 184.

90. "Most Christians […] believe in an abstract sense of the hereafter as a place whose comforts or lack thereof depend upon one's behavior here on earth." Mary Roach, *Spook: Science Tackles the Afterlife* (New York: W. W. Norton and Company, 2005), 44. "Afterlife fates thus became determined by conditions and behavior on earth." Gregory Shushan, "The Afterlife in Early Civilizations," *The Palgrave Handbook of the Afterlife*, ed. Yujin Nagasawa and Benjamin Matheson (London: Palgrave Macmillan [Springer Nature], 2017), 35. In an explicit proving-ground thesis, one apologetic has said, "God instituted a two creation design—the first in which free will beings could make choices, and the second to reward those beings who choose to be with God in His second creation." Rich Deem, "Where is God When Bad Things Happen? Why Natural Evil *Must* Exist," *GodAndScience.org* (Pasadena, California: Richard Deem, 4 September 2008) at **https://web.archive.org/web/20220524145840/ https://www.godandscience.org/apologetics/natural_evil_theodicity.html**, accessed June 17, 2022. But perhaps of even greater concern than earthly behavior being a determinant of post-death fate is how a mistaken belief in an afterlife might affect the conduct of the living faithful.

91. "[T]he diameter of the part of the universe that we are able to observe is at least 93 billion light years." Kahane, "Our Cosmic Insignificance," 745. Consequently, its radius is roughly 14.25 billion parsecs, and since the volume of a sphere is the product of two-thirds of its circumference and its radius squared, the volume of the observable universe is thus approximately 10^{31} cubic parsecs.

92. "No brain, no pain[: …] Unlike vision, however, the pain system is not located in a simple neural cord running from a sensing device to a definable area of the brain." David G. Myers, *Psychology* (New York: Worth Publishers, 2001), 198. "All pain is produced by the brain—no brain, no pain." David Sheridan Butler and G. Lorimer Moseley, *Explain Pain* (Adelaide, Australia: Noigroup Publications [NOT Australasia], 2003), 70. "Given that [the]

brain is the final common site of the experience of pain ('no brain, no pain'), it is reasonable to hypothesize that interventions in addition to NF [or neurofeedback] that alter brain activity could also alter pain experience." Mark P. Jensen, et al., "New Insights into Neuromodulatory Approaches for the Treatment of Pain," *The Journal of Pain*, Volume 9, No. 3 (Philadelphia, Pennsylvania: Churchill Livingstone, March 2008), 193–99; doi:10.1016/j.jpain.2007.11.003. "[T]he brain is the final common pathway to the experience of pain ('no brain—no pain')." Mark P. Jensen, "The Neurophysiology of Pain Perception and Hypnotic Analgesia: Implications for Clinical Practice," *American Journal of Clinical Hypnosis*, Volume 51, No. 2 (New York: Routledge, October 2008), 123–48; doi:10.1080/00029157.2008.10401654.

93. "Nerve transmission relies on an elegant combination of chemistry and electricity [… where t]he brain has the task of interpreting all these electrical codes and presenting them to consciousness as a visual image or sound, a smell or a jolt of pain, depending on their nature and origin[, … b]ut a sensation like pain, whether originating in the fingertips or in the foot, does not really register until it completes the circuit and reaches the brain." Philip Yancey and Paul W. Brand, *The Gift of Pain: Why We Hurt and What We Can Do About It* (Grand Rapids, Michigan: Zondervan Publishing House [HarperCollins], 1997 [1993 as *Pain: The Gift Nobody Wants*]), 46–47. If the pain signal must reach the brain in order to "register," when the brain is dead and no longer functioning, there cannot logically then be any post-death sensation of pain.

94. The "melting point of sulfur [… is] 119 [degrees Celsius]" or 246.2 degrees Fahrenheit. Douglas J. Parker, Samantha T. Chong, and Tom Hasell, "Sustainable Inverse-Vulcanised Sulfur Polymers," *RSC Advances*, Volume 8, No. 49 (London: The Royal Society of Chemistry, 2018), 27892–99; doi:10.1039/C8RA04446E. Or more conservatively, "115.21 [… degrees Celsius is] the melting point of sulfur," which converts to 239.4 degrees Fahrenheit. Julia Burdge, *Chemistry* (New York: McGraw-Hill Education, 2009), 31. Brimstone burns at "444.6 [… degrees Celsius, which is] the boiling point of sulfur" or 832.28 degrees Fahrenheit. Paul A. Tiple, *Physics for Scientists and Engineers* (New York: Worth Publishers [Macmillan Learning], 1990), 562.

95. "[D]eath and hell delivered up the dead which were in them: and they were judged, every man according to their works[, … and] were cast into the lake of fire[, … which] is the second death[; … a]nd whosoever was not found written in the book of life was cast into the Lake of Fire" (Rev. 20:13–15). Other references include: "Depart from me, ye cursed, into everlasting fire" (Matt.25:41) and "it is better for thee to enter into life maimed, than having

two hands to go into hell, into the fire that never shall be quenched[, … and w]here their worm dieth not." (Mark 9:43–46).

96. "Most religious men I have met are politicians in disguise." Mohandas K. Gandhi, "The Daily Mail," *Indian Review*, Volume 22, No. 3 (Madras [Chennai], India: G. A. Natesan and Co., March 1921), 172; as quoted by D. P. in Section 5. The congruence of political and religious goals is based on the "underlying assumption […] that humans unchecked by social restraints tend toward violence, force, and selfishness and the institutions of family, community, and religion are needed to act as a curb on this." Dov Cohen, "Culture, Social Organization, and Patterns of Violence," *Journal of Personality and Social Psychology*, Volume 75, No. 2 (Washington D.C.: American Psychological Association, August 1998), 408–19; doi:10.1037/0022-3514.75.2.408. And "what is religious is, by its very nature, inherently political[, … so much so that f]undamentalisms and other conservative political uses of religion are structured on the acquisition or maintenance of power." Alison L. Boden, *Women's Rights and Religious Practice* (London: Palgrave Macmillan, 2007), 95 and 101.

97. "[T]he Standard Model […] describes in a unified framework three of the four fundamental forces in Nature[, … the fourth being gravity]: the electromagnetic, weak, and strong nuclear interactions." Abdelhak Djouadi, "The Higgs Mechanism and the Origin of Mass," *Mass and Motion in General Relativity*, ed. Luc Blanchet, Alessandro Spallicci, and Bernard Whiting (Dordrecht, Netherlands / New York: Springer Science+Business Media, 2011), 1. "[T]here are four fundamental forces in Nature; namely, electromagnetic, weak, strong and gravitational forces[: …] The Standard Model well represents the first three [… as] a gauge theory where all the fields mediating the interactions are represented by gauge potentials." Salvatore Capozziello and Mariafelicia De Laurentis, "Generating the Mass Particles from Extended Theories of Gravity," *Frontiers of Fundamental Physics and Physics Education Research*, ed. Burra G. Sidharth, Marisa Michelini, and Lorenzo Santi (Cham, Switzerland: Springer International Publishing [Springer Science+Business Media], 2014), 15.

98. "[I]n struggling to find a grand unification theory, or *GUT*[, … t]he aim of GUTs is to reduce all particles to one kind, interacting through one force—truly a *grand* unification." Michael Zeilik, *Astronomy: The Evolving Universe* (New York: Cambridge University Press, 2002), 477; emphasis in the original. "The unification of fundamental forces […] is high on the agenda of physics[; …] the road appears open for a *true* unification, in one gauge group with one universal gauge coupling, of the three forces […] within the paradigm of grand unification theories (GUTs)." R. G. E. Timmermans, "Low-Energy Precision Tests of

Electroweak Theory," *Trapped Charged Particles and Fundamental Interactions*, ed. Klaus Blaum and Frank Herfurth (Berlin / Heidelberg, Germany: Springer-Verlag, 2008), 2; emphasis in the original. Moreover, "[i]t is now believed that each of the fundamental forces can be described by a gauge theory, in which the interactions are mediated by gauge bosons[, … while] there is the hope that particle physics theories, GUTs in particular, might help to resolve some of the fundamental problems of classical (that is, non-quantum) cosmology." Edward W. Kolb and Michael S. Turner, "The Early Universe," *Nature*, Volume 294, No. 5841 (London: Nature Research [Springer Nature], 10 December 1981), 521–26; doi:10.1038/294521a0.

99. "GUTs predict proton decay, albeit at [a] tremendously low rate." Pierre van Baal, *A Course in Field Theory* (Boca Raton, Florida: CRC Press [Taylor and Francis], 2016), 143. "The instability of protons is a crucial prediction of supersymmetric GUTs[, … in contrast to] orbifold GUTs, where proton decay via dimension-five operators is absent." Sören Wiesenfeldt, "Proton Decay in Supersymmetric GUT Models," *Modern Physics Letters A*, Volume 19, No. 29 (Singapore: World Scientific, 2004), 2155–69; doi:10.1142/S021773230401545. "General consequences of GUTs [or Grand Unified Theories] and this phase transition ['in an expanding, cooling universe'] are the prediction of proton decay." James L. Stone, "Magnetic Monopole Search Experiments," *Inner Space/ Outer Space*, ed. Edward Kolb, et al. (Chicago: University of Chicago, 1986), 396.

100. "The Super-Kamiokande experiment has recently set a lower limit on the lifetime of a proton that decays [… at] longer than 10^{34} years." Ben Moore, *Elephants in Space: The Past, Present and Future of Life and the Universe* (Cham, Switzerland: Springer International Publishing [Springer Science+Business Media], 2014), 172; translated from *Elefanten im All—Unser Platz im Universum* (Zürich: Kein und Aber AG, 2012). "[F]or proton decay[, … l]ower limits on the proton lifetime are set at [… more than] 1.6×10^{34} years." K. Abe, et al., "Search for Proton Decay […] in 0.31 Megaton Years Exposure of the Super-Kamiokande Water Cherenkov Detector," *Physical Review Letters*, Volume 95, No. 1 (College Park, Maryland: American Physical Society, January 2017), 012004; doi:10.1103/PhysRevD.95.012004. "Scientists think that the proton may not be stable and estimate its half-life at more than 10^{32} years[, …] based on attempts to unify the electroweak and strong interactions." Jim Breithaupt, *New Understanding Physics for Advanced Level* (London: Hutchinson Education, 1987), 658.

101. One study measured the Universe's expansion rate 18% higher than conventional (raising the Hubble constant from 70 to 82.4), which revises the estimate of the age of the Universe from about 13.7 billion years down to 11.4 billion years. Inh Jee, et al., "A Measurement of the Hubble Constant

from Angular Diameter Distances to Two Gravitational Lenses," *Science*, Volume 365, No. 6458 (Washington, D.C.: American Association for the Advancement of Science, 13 September 2019), 1134–38; doi:10.1126/science.aat7371. "Their original estimates [based on measuring the Hubble constant using gravitational lensing] would have meant that the Universe was only 2 billion years old." Tamara Davis, "An Expanding Controversy," *Science*, Volume 365, No. 6458 (Washington, D.C.: American Association for the Advancement of Science, 13 September 2019), 1076–77; doi:10.1126/science.aay1331. Yet in an earlier conventional study, "results from Planck's all-sky survey [… puts] the 'best estimate' of the age [… of the Universe at] 13.798 [plus/minus] 0.037 billion years." John Gribbin, *13.8: The Quest to Find the True Age of the Universe and the Theory of Everything* (New Haven, Connecticut: Yale University Press, 2016 [2015]), 217.

102. Steven Wright in *Humorous Wit*, ed. Djamel Ouis (Trowbridge, England: Paragon Publishing, 2020). The quote also appears in Geoff Tibballs, *The Mammoth Book of Comic Quotes* (London: Constable and Robinson, 2004).

103. William James, *Human Immortality: Two Supposed Objections to the Doctrine* (Boston and New York: Houghton, Mifflin and Company, 1899), 17–18. According to James's theory, "there is a realm of consciousness [...] which breaks into the physical realm via our brains." Jim Spiegel, "William James on Human Immortality," *Wisdom and Folly blog* (Fairmount, Indiana: Jim and Amy Spiegel, 26 April 2016) at **https://wisdomandfollyblog.com/william-james-human-immortality/**, accessed December 31, 2019.

104. "The word 'heaven' is translated differently [...] as 'heavens' and is from the Hebrew[, … which] stems from [...] '*shamayim*,' which is 'heaven.'" Internet comment by Gina (**https://hermeneutics.stackexchange.com/users/19653/gina**), *Stack Overflow* (New York: Stack Exchange, 11 June 2018) at **https://hermeneutics.stackexchange.com/questions/33404/how-should-john-313-be-understood-in-view-of-the-ot-statements-about-enoch-and**, accessed April 9, 2020. In reconciling the passages "Enoch walked with God: and he was not; for God took him" (Gen. 5:24), "behold, there appeared a chariot of fire, and horses of fire, and parted them both asunder; and Elijah went up by a whirlwind into heaven" (2 Kings 2:11), and "[N]o man hath ascended up to heaven, but he that came down from heaven, even the Son of man which is in heaven" (John 3:13), some interpret that, specifically, "Jesus is referring to His authority to bring a message from heaven." J. Carl Laney, *Answers to Tough Questions: A Survey of Problem Passages and Issues from Every Book of the Bible* (Eugene, Oregon: Wipf and Stock Publishers, 2010 [1997]), 227.

105. For a clearly biased discussion about the experimental work on post-death consciousness and the near-death experiences of Gary Schwartz,

Raymond A. Moody, Kenneth Ring and Sharon Cooper, among others, see Joseph M. Higgins and Chuck Bergman, *The Everything Guide to Evidence of the Afterlife: A Scientific Approach to Proving the Existence of Life after Death* (Avon, Massachusetts: Adams Media [Simon and Schuster], 2011), 57–72. Recall one of the early flawed experiments involved weighing bodies just before and then after death, presupposing the difference constituted the weight (21 grams) of a "soul." MacDougall, "Hypothesis Concerning Soul Substance," 237–75.

106. Stephen Hawking, "Stephen Hawking: 'There Is No Heaven; It's a Fairy Story,'" *The Guardian*, Interview by Ian Sample (London: Guardian Media Group [Scott Trust Limited], 15 May 2011) at **https://www.theguardian. com/science/2011/may/15/stephen-hawking-interview-there-is-no-heaven**, accessed August 30, 2017.

107. Anton Pavlovich Chekhov, "Ward No. 6," *The Horse-Stealers: And Other Stories*, The Tales of Chekhov, Volume X, trans. Constance Garnett (New York: Macmillan, 1921 [1892]), 57.

108. Ira Rosofsky, "A Problem for Darwin: Why Do We Age and Die Rather Than Live Forever?" in *PsychologyToday.com* (New York: Sussex Publishers, 7 March 2009) at **https://www.psychologytoday.com/us/blog/ adventures-in-old-age/200903/problem-darwin-why-do-we-age-and-die- rather-live-forever**, accessed January 6, 2020; citing American ecologist Richard Levins (1930–2016) about human life expectancy as recently as the Middle Ages.

109. "Evolutionary theories of aging predict a trade-off between fertility and lifespan, where increased lifespan comes at the cost of reduced fertility." Maris Kuningas, et al., "The Relationship between Fertility and Lifespan in Humans," *Age*, Volume 33, No. 4 (Dordrecht, Netherlands: Springer Science+Business Media, December 2011), 615–22; doi:10.1007/s11357-010-9202-4.

110. The quote—which appears at Richard Dawkins, *The God Delusion* (London: Bantam Press, 2006), 396—is widely considered misattributed but based on the following excerpt from Twain's autobiography: "Annihilation has no terrors for me, because I have already tried it before I was born—a hundred million years—and I have suffered more in an hour, in this life, than I remember to have suffered in the whole hundred million years put together." Mark Twain (Samuel Clemens), *Autobiography of Mark Twain*, The Complete and Authoritative Edition, Volume 2, ed. Benjamin Griffin and Harriet Elinor Smith (Berkeley, California: University of California Press, 2013 [1924]), 69.

111. Arthur Schopenhauer, "On the Doctrine of the Indestructibility of Our True Nature by Death," in *Selected Essays of Arthur Schopenhauer:*

With Biographical Introduction and Sketch of His Philosophy, trans. E. B. Bax (London: G. Bell and sons, 1891), 241.

112. Irvin D. Yalom, *Staring at the Sun: Overcoming the Terror of Death* (San Francisco: Jossey-Bass, 2008), 81; quotation of Epicurus.

113. "The most important are the laws of conservation of matter and of energy[, … wherein t]he former states that matter can be neither created nor destroyed[, … and as to the latter, t]he total energy of a system also remains the same." *Science and Technology Encyclopedia* (London: George Phillips [Octopus Publishing], 1999), 120; the "conservation, laws of" entry (also published in a 2000 edition by the University of Chicago). "Matter / energy may be altered but not created (from nothingness) nor destroyed (reduced to nothingness)[, … in that] The First Law [of Thermodynamics] teaches that matter/energy cannot spring forth from nothing without cause, nor can it simply vanish[, … and] the Second Law states that entropy always increases or remains constant in a closed system." Ashley Leonard and Will Craig, *Mechanical Engineering* (Waltham, England: ED-Tech Press, 2019), 49. "[T]he law of conservation of energy, the energy of a closed system can be transformed from one form to another, [… or s]imply put, energy can be changed from one form to another, but it cannot be created, nor can it be destroyed." Henshaw, *Equation for Every Occasion*, 61. There are many "philosophies of nature which presuppose that the physical universe is a completely self-contained or self-sufficient system, that is to say a 'closed' system." G. J. Whitrow, "Is the Physical Universe a Self-Contained System?" in *The Monist*, Volume 47, No. 1 (La Salle, Illinois: Open Court [the Hegeler Institute], Fall 1962), 77–93; doi:10.5840/monist19624714.

114. "[T]he concept of entropy suggested [...] a physical means by which the universe would ultimately wind down[; … viewing] entropy as disorder [...] evolved into a narrative that could be stated: *the disorder and randomness of our world is only increasing.*" *The American Heritage Book of English Usage*, ed. Editors of the American Heritage Dictionaries (Boston: Houghton Mifflin, 1996), 158; the "Entropy" entry, emphasis in the original. Entropy is the "idea that the mechanical universe would inevitably 'wind down' as energy is dissipated to heat and heat is radiated at ever-lower temperatures." Steve Adams, *Frontiers: Twentieth Century Physics* (London and New York: Taylor and Francis, 2002), 411. "Increasing entropy is a measure of disorder in an aging system, where death is the ultimate or maximum disorder." Daniel Hershey and William E. Lee III, "Entropy, Aging and Death," *Systems Research*, Volume 4, No. 4 (Chichester, England: John Wiley and Sons, December 1987), 269–81; doi:10.1002/sres.3850040406.

115. "A shattered teacup *could*, in theory, spontaneously reassemble—it is not forbidden by Newton's laws—but it is astronomically improbable, thanks to the second law of thermodynamics[: … T]he arrow of time reveals itself as a change in the amount of disorder in a system, a change that always proceeds from lower to higher entropy." Dan Falk, *In Search of Time: The Science of a Curious Dimension* (New York: Thomas Dunne Books [St. Martin's Press], 2008), 141; emphasis in the original. Cf. Roger Highfield and Peter Coveney, *The Arrow of Time* (London: Ebury Publishing [Penguin Random House], 2015).

Chapter 12: Free Will

1. Voltaire (François-Marie Arouet), *A Philosophical Dictionary*, Volume 2, trans. Abner Kneeland (Boston: J. P. Mednum, 1852 [1764]), 275; the "Rights," Section 1, entry.

2. "[T]he outcome of a decision can be encoded in brain activity […] up to 10 s[econds] before it enters awareness." Chun Siong Soon, et al., "Unconscious Determinants of Free Decisions in the Human Brain," *Nature Neuroscience*, Volume 11, No. 5 (New York: Nature Publishing Group, May 2008), 543–45; doi:10.1038/nn.2112.

3. Benjamin Libet, "The Timing of Mental Events: Libet's Experimental Findings and Their Implications," *Consciousness and Cognition*, Volume 11, No. 2 (New York: Elsevier Science, June 2002), 291–99; doi:10.1006/ccog.2002.0568.

4. "[F]ree will is […] neither verifiable nor falsifiable by empirical evidence." Robert Northcott, "Free Will Is Not a Testable Hypothesis," *Erkenntnis*, Volume 84, No. 3 (Dordrecht, Netherlands: Springer, 2 February 2019), 617–31; doi:10.1007/s10670-018-9974-y.

5. "[T]he (pruned) branch tips no longer represent ultimate […] outcomes" and no longer attract the attention of the decision-maker. William S. Cooper, "Decision Theory as a Branch of Evolutionary Theory: A Biological Derivation of the Savage Axioms," *Psychological Review*, Volume 94, No. 4 (Washington, D.C.: American Psychological Association, October 1987), 395–411.

6. "According to cognitive neuroscientists, we are conscious of only about 5 percent of our cognitive activity, *so most of our decisions, actions, emotions, and behavior depends on the 95 percent of brain activity that goes beyond our conscious awareness.*" Marianne Szegedy-Maszak, "Mysteries of the Mind," *U.S. News and World Report*, Volume 138, No. 7 (Washington, D.C.: U.S. News and World Report, Inc., 28 February 2005), 52–54; emphasis in the original. "Some 95 per cent of thought happens below the radar." Emma Young, "Lifting the Lid on the Unconscious," *NewScientist.com* (London: New Scientist Ltd.,

25 July 2018) at **https://www.newscientist.com/article/mg23931880-400-lifting-the-lid-on-the-unconscious/**, accessed May 16, 2020. Cf. Steve Ayan, "There Is No Such Thing as Conscious Thought," *Scientific American*, Volume 30, No. 2 (New York: Nature Research [Springer Nature], March 2019).

7. "Decision-making is [...] one of the 'executive functions' [... and the subject of] research efforts [...] focused on the dorsolateral prefrontal cortex sector [... and] the ventromedial prefrontal cortex." Antoine Bechara and Martial Van Der Linden, "Decision-Making and Impulse Control after Frontal Lobe Injuries," *Current Opinion in Neurology*, Volume 18, No. 6 (London: Lippincott Williams and Wilkins, December 2005), 734–39; doi:10.1097/01. wco.0000194141.56429.3c. "Ventromedial prefrontal cortex (VMF) damage can lead to impaired decision-making," indicating that this lobe is the brain area involved in this faculty. Lesley K. Fellows and Martha J. Farah, "Different Underlying Impairments in Decision-Making Following Ventromedial and Dorsolateral Frontal Lobe Damage in Humans," *Cerebral Cortex*, Volume 15, No. 1 (New York: Oxford University Press, January 2005), 58–63; doi:10.1093/ cercor/bhh108. "[T]he part of the brain that is responsible for decision making and reasoning [... is] the frontal lobe." Karen Huffman, *Psychology in Action* (New York: John Wiley and Sons, 2008), 197.

8. See the image by historicair (public domain), "Diagram of Freud's psyche theory," *Wikimedia.org* (San Francisco, California: Wikimedia Foundation's Wikimedia Commons, 16 December 2006) at **https://commons.wikimedia. org/wiki/File:Structural-Iceberg.svg**, accessed February 19, 2019.

9. "We are aware only of the tip of the action iceberg [... regarding] conscious thought (ie my intention)." Patrick Haggard, "Conscious Intention and Motor Cognition," *Trends in Cognitive Sciences*, Volume 9, No. 6 (Oxford: Elsevier Science, June 2005), 290–95; doi:10.1016/j.tics.2005.04.012. "[T]he conscious Self (sometimes thought of as the 'conscious ego' or 'conscious mind') has often been likened to the tip of an iceberg that is supported by a vaster, unconscious base." Max Velmans, *Towards a Deeper Understanding of Consciousness* (London and New York: Routledge [Taylor and Francis], 2017), 170. Yet, in the view of others, "[t]he iceberg mind is an oversimplification [... because] conscious thinking probably controls many aspects of our unconscious thinking." Jan De Houwer, "An Iceberg Is Not a Good Metaphor for the Mind," *PsychologyToday.com* (New York: Sussex Publishers, 1 March 2020) at **https://www.psychologytoday.com/us/blog/ spontaneous-thoughts/202003/iceberg-is-not-good-metaphor-the-mind**, accessed May 16, 2020.

10. See "Figure 1: Electroencephalographic (EEG) Patterns during the Awake State, General Anesthesia, and Sleep," in Emery N. Brown, Ralph

Lydic, and Nicholas D. Schiff, "General Anesthesia, Sleep, and Coma," *New England Journal of Medicine*, Volume 363, No. 27 (Boston: Massachusetts Medical Society, 30 December 2010), 2638–50; doi:10.1056/NEJMra0808281. "[A]nesthesiologists assume that general anesthesia is associated with unconsciousness similar to a dreamless sleep." Robert D. Sanders, et al., "Unresponsiveness [is not equal to] Unconsciousness," *Anesthesiology*, Volume 116, No. 4 (Philadelphia, Pennsylvania: Lippincott Williams and Wilkins [American Society of Anesthesiologists], April 2012), 946–59; doi:10.1097/ALN.0b013e318249d0a7. Cf. Kannathal Natarajan, et al., "Nonlinear Analysis of EEG Signals at Different Mental States," *Biomedical Engineering Online*, Volume 3, No. 1 (London: BioMed Central, 16 March 2004), 7; doi:10.1186/1475-925X-3-7.

11. A "relevant aspect of brain physiology is that whereas the brain becomes very much less active during non-REM sleep compared with being awake, during REM sleep the brain becomes very active, including activation of areas of the parietal lobe related to visual imagery, and the amygdala and paralimbic cortex which are related to emotional processing." *The Oxford Companion to Consciousness*, ed. Tim Bayne, Axel Cleeremans, and Patrick Wilken (Oxford: Oxford University Press, 2009), 241; the "Dreaming, Scientific Perspectives" entry. "You are considered to be asleep when you are unconscious but can still be awakened by normal sensory stimuli[; … t]wo general levels of sleep are recognized, each typified by characteristic patterns of brain wave activity[: …] deep sleep, also called Mslow wave or non-REM (NREM) sleep [… and] rapid eye movement (REM) sleep." Frederic H. Martini, *Anatomy and Physiology* (Singapore: Pearson Education [Prentice Hall], 2005), 405. "When we are awake and alert, the brain generates beta waves[, … but a]s brain activity gears down and drowsiness sets in, alpha brain waves are generated." Don H. Hockenbury and Sandra E. Hockenbury, *Psychology* (New York: Worth Publishers, 2008), 191. Cf. Francis Crick and Graeme Mitchison, "The Function of Dream Sleep," *Nature*, Volume 304, No. 5922 (London: Nature Research [Springer Nature], 14–20 July 1983), 111–14; doi:10.1038/304111a0.

12. Ezequiel Morsella, et al., "Homing in on Consciousness in the Nervous System: An Action-Based Synthesis," *Behavioral and Brain Sciences*, Volume 39 (Cambridge: Cambridge University Press, 2016), e168; doi:10.1017/S0140525X15000643.

13. In the midst of the Age of Enlightenment period and referring to the discovery of Newton's Laws of Motion, English philosopher and clergyman Samuel Clarke (1675–1729) declares that the "notion of the world's being a great machine, [...] as a Clock continues to go without the Assistance of

a Clockmaker; is the notion of materialism and fate." *The Leibniz-Clarke Correspondence*, ed. H. G. Alexander (Manchester, United Kingdom: Manchester University Press, 1956 [1717]), 14. Cf. Edward Dolnick, *The Clockwork Universe: Isaac Newton, the Royal Society, and the Birth of the Modern World* (New York: Harper Collins, 2011).

14. Carlo Cercignani, *Ludwig Boltzmann, The Man Who Trusted Atoms* (Oxford: Oxford University Press, 1998), 55.

15. Graham P. Collins, "Within Any Possible Universe, No Intellect Can Ever Know It All," *Scientific American*, Volume 300, No. 3 (New York: Nature Research [Springer Nature], 1 March 2009), 19–20; doi:10.1038/scientificamerican0309-19, originally entitled "Impossible Inferences," paraphrasing David H. Wolpert, "Physical Limits of Inference," *Physica D: Nonlinear Phenomena*, Volume 237, No. 9 (Amsterdam: North-Holland [Elsevier], 1 July 2008), 1257–81; doi:10.1016/j.physd.2008.03.040.

16. In saying that "[t]here is at present in the material world a universal tendency to the dissipation of mechanical energy[, for which] perfect *restoration* is impossible[,]" Lord Kelvin is restating his second law of thermodynamics, in which entropy irreversibly increases. William Thomson (Baron Lord Kelvin), "On a Universal Tendency in Nature to the Dissipation of Mechanical Energy," *Mathematical and Physical Papers*, Volume 1, Collected from Different Scientific Periodicals from May, 1841 to the Present Time (Cambridge: University Press, 1882), 512–14; from *Proceedings of the Royal Society of Edinburgh*, April 19, 1852. The notion of equating entropy with loss of information appears in the statement that "[g]ain in entropy always means loss of information." Gilbert N. Lewis, "The Symmetry of Time in Physics," *Science*, Volume 71, No. 1849 (New York: American Association for the Advancement of Science, June 6, 1930), 573 at **https://science.sciencemag.org/content/71/1849/569**, accessed October 6, 2017; doi: 0.1126/science.71.1849.569.

17. "[E]ntropy, as it is normally defined, does increase[, … at least] within any region large enough to be considered a fair sample of the Universe[; … i]t doesn't follow, however, that the Universe was initially more orderly than it is now[, … as] order is the absence of disorder[: … O]rder is present whenever the maximum possible randomness consistent with given constraints exceeds the actual randomness." David Layzer, *Cosmogenesis: The Growth of Order in the Universe* (New York: Oxford University Press, 1990), 138.

18. "[In] quantum mechanics there *is* such a principle, namely the uncertainty principle (or from a more 'modern' standpoint, the no-cloning theorem)[, … although a]n event can be 'arbitrary,' in the sense of being undetermined by previous events, without being random in the narrower technical sense

of being generated by some known or knowable probabilistic process." Scott Aaronson, "The Ghost in the Quantum Turing Machine," *The Once and Future Turing*, ed. S. Barry Cooper and Andrew Hodges (Cambridge: Cambridge University Press, 2016), 227; emphasis in the original. "[The] position and time of the particle become in fact undetermined in a concrete point as they become functions of the traveling wave[; ... hence, t]he uncertainty principle is a direct consequence of the probabilistic approach to quantum phenomena." Volodymyr Krasnoholovets, "On the Origin and Conceptual Difficulties of Quantum Mechanics," *Developments in Quantum Physics*, ed. Frank H. Columbus and Volodymyr Krasnoholovets (New York: Nova Science Publishers, 2004), 100. "[E]xperiment[s] [...] reflect[...] the uncertainty relations and the probabilistic nature of our quantum predictions." Arkady Plotnitsky, *Epistemology and Probability: Bohr, Heisenberg, Schrödinger, and the Nature of Quantum Theoretical Thinking* (New York: Springer Science+Business Media, 2010), 45. "[Q]uantum mechanics [...] theory [... is a] probabilistic description of nature and the Heisenberg uncertainty principle[, ... but e]ven if electron condition is undetermined at the quantum level, collective electron behavior in the form of electric current—in electric motors, in television and computer circuits—is well determined and foreseen by the deterministic laws of electromagnetism." Gianfranco Spavieri, *Science and Myth* (Portland, Oregon: Conscious Publishing, 2000), 103. "[Although] quantum mechanics, based as it is on the probabilistic interpretation, on the uncertainty relations, [... has been experimentally confirmed,] Heisenberg's Uncertainty Principle cannot be a criterion of reality." A. H. Klotz, "On the Nature of Quantum Mechanics," *Synthese*, Volume 77, No. 2 (Dordrecht, Netherlands: Kluwer Academic Publishers, November 1988), 139–93.

19. "The limit on our accuracy of measurement is known as Heisenberg's Uncertainty Principle[, ... and says that, operating] in the quantum realm, where dimensions are sufficiently small, certain complementary pairs of concepts, like position and velocity, or energy and time, can coexist only with a limited sharpness that Planck's constant dictates." John D. Barrow, *Impossibility: The Limits of Science and the Science of Limits* (Oxford: Oxford University Press, 1998), 23.

20. "Most philosophers take it for granted that [...] an event can have more than one set of independently sufficient causes[, ... making] for a lot of work for theorists of causation." Martin Bunzl, "Causal Overdetermination," *The Journal of Philosophy*, Volume 76, No. 3, ed. The Columbia University Philosophy Department (New York: The Journal of Philosophy, Inc. [Columbia University], March 1979), 134–50; doi:10.2307/2025525.

21. "Bell's theorem may still be used in its original formulation to rule out local determinism." Daniele Tommasini, "Einstein-Podolsky-Rosen and Bell's Paradoxes in Quantum Field Theories," *Quantum Field Theory: New Research*, ed. O. Kovras (New York: Nova Science Publishers, 2005), 189.

22. Stephen Hawking and Leonard Mlodinow, *The Grand Design* (New York: Bantam Books, 2010), 72; emphasis in the original.

23. Yet, "this letter itself was denounced as a forgery by Mozart's most important nineteenth-century biographer, Otto Jahn, and has since been repeatedly denounced by other scholars." Neal Zaslaw, "Mozart as a Working Stiff," *On Mozart*, ed. James M. Morris (Cambridge: Cambridge University Press [The Woodrow Wilson Center], 1994), 109. Cf. Edward Holmes, *The Life of Mozart* (New York: Cosimo, 2005), 255.

24. The concept of "free will" is not directly mentioned here, but the mechanism for the conscious mind to act as observer can be deduced from the fact that "impairments of the components of internal representations […] can account for several disparate abnormalities in the awareness and control of action." Sarah-Jayne Blakemore, Daniel M. Wolpert, and Christopher D. Frith, "Abnormalities in the Awareness of Action," *Trends in Cognitive Sciences*, Volume 6, No. 6 (Oxford: Elsevier Science, June 2002), 237–42; doi:10.1016/s1364-6613(02)01907-1.

25. C. W. Rietdijk, "A Rigorous Proof of Determinism Derived from the Special Theory of Relativity," *Philosophy of Science*, Volume 33, No. 4 (Chicago: The University of Chicago Press, December 1966), 341–44.

26. "[A]ll events in spacetime are equally real, which implies the block-universe picture in which there is no ontological difference between past, present, and future." Roberto Mangabeira Unger and Lee Smolin, *The Singular Universe and the Reality of Time* (Cambridge: Cambridge University Press, 2015), 419. Cf. Hermann Minkowski, *Space and Time: Minkowski's Papers on Relativity*, ed. Vesselin Petkov (Montreal, Quebec, Canada: Minkowski Institute Press, 2012), 111–14; originally, Minkowski's "Space and Time" lecture given at the 80th Meeting of Natural Scientists in Cologne on September 21, 1908, later published as Hermann Minkowski, "Die Grundgleichungen für die Elektromagnetischen Vorgänge in bewegten Körpern," *Mathematische Annalen*, Volume 68, No. 4 (Berlin / Heidelberg, Germany: Springer, December 1910), 472–525, doi: 10.1007/BF01455871, English title: "The Fundamental Equations for Electromagnetic Processes in Moving Bodies" in *Mathematical Annals*.

27. "Quantum mechanics is indeterministic, in that the outcomes of measurements are chosen at random from the slate of possibilities[, … s]o, if

quantum effects help to shape our conscious choices, they sever the connection between us and the initial conditions of the universe." George Musser, "The Quantum Physics of Free Will," *Scientific American* (New York: Nature Research [Springer Nature], 6 February 2012) at **https://www.scientificamerican.com/article/quantum-physics-free-will/**, accessed February 25, 2019.

28. "King (Chinook) salmon are found in the ocean [...] and run upstream [...] to spawn[, as they] migrate into fresh water in the fall." California Coastal Commission, *California Coastal Access Guide* (Berkeley, California: University of California Press, 2003 [1981]), 64.

29. "[N]ot much, if any, space is left in human nature for constructive forces that might strive toward growth and development[, ... and the] denial of them must by necessity lead to a defeatist attitude toward the possibility of overcoming our resistances through our own efforts." Karen Horney, *Self-Analysis* (London: Routledge [Kegan Paul], 1999 [1942]), 269. However, "[a]n event is inevitable if, in addition to having been determined, it could not have been avoided[, ... so] to claim the occurrence of inevitable events is to allow the possibility of determined but avoidable events[, ... and hence,] the concepts of determination and avoidability are not mutually exclusive." Arthur C. Danto, "Determinism and Inevitability," *Philosophic Exchange*, Volume 2, No. 1, Article 2 (Brockport, New York: [State University of New York's] College of Arts and Science's Center for Philosophic Exchange, Summer 1971), 19.

30. "[E]very being who cannot act except *under the idea of freedom* is precisely because of that actually free in a practical sense." Immanuel Kant, *Groundwork for the Metaphysics of Morals*, trans. Christopher Bennett, Joe Saunders, and Robert Stern (Oxford: Oxford University Press, 2019 [1785]), 60; (Akademie ed.,) 448. "Because freedom entails the moral law, we must think of ourselves as bound by it." J. B. Schneewind, "Autonomy, Obligation, and Virtue: An Overview of Kant's Moral Philosophy," *The Cambridge Companion to Kant*, ed. Paul Guyer (New York: Cambridge University Press, 1992), 329; citing *Groundwork*, 4:447–8 / 115–16. "Kant accepts a strict form of causal determinism for the natural world, according to which every event follows necessarily from prior events according to empirical laws." Andrew Reath, "Kant's Critical Account of Freedom," *A Companion to Kant*, ed. Graham Bird (Oxford: Blackwell Publishing, 2005), 275.

31. Attributed variously (and thus, to all but one, misattributed) to Gautama Buddha ("Every wakeful step, every mindful act is the direct path to awakening[, so w]herever you go, there you are."); Confucius ("Wherever you go, go with all your heart"); Thomas à Kempis; Lord Buckley; and Earl Mac Rauch, screenwriter, "The Adventures of Buckaroo Banzai Across the 8th Dimension" on *IMDB.com* (Seattle, Washington: Amazon [Internet Movie

Database], 8 November 1984) at **https://www.imdb.com/title/tt0086856/ quotes**, accessed August 8, 2019; among many others.

32. Charles Darwin, *Metaphysics, Materialism and the Evolution of Mind: the Early Writings of Charles Darwin*, with commentary by Howard E. Gruber, transcribed and annotated by Paul H. Barrett (Chicago: University of Chicago Press, 1974 [ca. 1837]), 129.

33. "[C]ourts embracing free will have done so because they have deemed it a necessary assumption for an operable justice system, [… although] any scientific discoveries that undermine free will do not therefore undermine all the foundations on which the criminal legal system is based[; … with regard to deterrence specifically,] new discoveries in neuroscience can serve as a tool for reprioritizing our society's legal intuitions in a way that leads us to a more effective and humane system." Kelly Burns and Antoine Bechara, "Decision Making and Free Will: A Neuroscience Perspective," *Behavioral Sciences and the Law*, Volume 25, No. 2 (New York: John Wiley and Sons, 28 March 2007), 263–80; doi:10.1002/bsl.751. "[Even i]f we lack the kind of free will required for moral responsibility, [… however,] significant punishment can be justified on consequentialist grounds […] without betraying important concerns about justice." Kevin J. Murtagh, "Free Will Denial and Punishment," *Social Theory and Practice*, Volume 39, No. 2 (Tallahassee, Florida: Florida State University's Philosophy Department, April 2013), 223–40; doi:10.5840/soctheorpract201339213, cited in a later work, Kevin J. Murtaugh, "Free Will Skepticism, General Deterrence, and the 'Use' Objection," *Free Will Skepticism in Law and Society*, ed. Elizabeth Shaw, Derk Pereboom, and Gregg D. Caruso (Cambridge: Cambridge University Press, 2019), 139. Nonetheless, one "serious misgiving raised against utilitarian deterrence theory is […] that it sometimes requires people to be harmed severely, without their consent, in order to benefit others." Derk Pereboom, *Free Will, Agency, and Meaning in Life* (New York: Oxford University Press, 2014), 165.

34. Jesse Bering, "Scientists Say Free Will Probably Doesn't Exist but Urge: 'Don't Stop Believing!'," *Scientific American Mind*, weblog (New York: Nature Research [Springer Nature], 6 April 2010) at **https://blogs.scientificamerican. com/bering-in-mind/scientists-say-free-will-probably-doesnt-exist-but-urge-dont-stop-believing/**, accessed March 19, 2019; citing Roy F. Baumeister, E. J. Masicampo, and C. Nathan DeWall, "Prosocial Benefits of Feeling Free: Disbelief in Free Will Increases Aggression and Reduces Helpfulness," *Personality and Social Psychology Bulletin*, Volume 35, No. 2 (Los Angeles [Thousand Oaks, California]: SAGE Publications [Society for Personality and Social Psychology], February 2009), 260–68, doi:10.1177/0146167208327217;

and (by incorporation) Kathleen D. Vohs and Jonathan W. Schooler, "The Value of Believing in Free Will: Encouraging a Belief in Determinism Increases Cheating," *Psychological Science*, Volume 19, No. 1 (Los Angeles [Thousand Oaks, California]: SAGE Publications [American Psychological Society / Association for Psychological Science], January 2008), 49–54, doi:10.1111/j.1467-9280.2008.02045.x.

35. Ron R. Rickards, *Eternal Harmony*, Volume 1: the Unity of Truth in God (Bloomington, Indiana: WestBow Press, 2016), 438; characterizing David H. Wolpert's knowledge-limit proof.

36. See, for example, Massimiliano Sassoli de Bianchi, "The Observer Effect," *Foundations of Science*, Volume 18, No. 2 (New York: Springer Science+Business Media, June 2013), 213–43, doi:10.1007/s10699-012-9298-3; and Kenneth Baclawski, "The Observer Effect," *IEEE Conference on Cognitive and Computational Aspects of Situation Management (CogSIMA)*, (Boston/New York/Piscataway, New Jersey: Institute of Electrical and Electronics Engineers [IEEE], 11–14 June 2018), 83–89, doi:10.1109/COGSIMA.2018.8423983.

37. For a fictionalized account of the power of hypnosis, see the novel by Biff Dunnigan, *The Conceit of Memory* (Woodland, California: Phrase Bound Publications, 2015) at **https://www.phrasebound.com/books/ TheConceitOfMemory**.

38. As one anti-dualist notes, "[i]t is possible to imagine a limiting case in which [...] even my own body was no longer categorizable as mine or even a body." John R. Searle, *The Rediscovery of the Mind* (Cambridge, Massachusetts: MIT Press, 1992), 135. Another quote in a review of the book states that "[a]ccording to Searle, the main point in Rosenfield's book 'is that we have to think of the experience of our own body as the central reference point of all forms of consciousness.'" David Sosa, "Slouching towards Dualism," *Revue Internationale de Philosophie*, Volume 55, No. 216 (2) (Paris: De Boeck Supérieur [Association Revue Internationale de Philosophie], June 2001), 257–63.

39. Kenan Malik, *Man, Beast and Zombie: The New Science of Human Nature* (London: Weidenfeld and Nicolson, 327).

40. "Spontaneous fluctuations in activity in different parts of the brain can be used to study functional brain networks [... using] resting-state functional MRI (rfMRI) for the purpose of mapping the macroscopic functional connectome." Stephen M. Smith, et al., "Functional Connectomics from Resting-State fMRI," *Trends in Cognitive Sciences*, Volume 17, No. 12 (Oxford: Elsevier Science, December 2013), 666–82; doi:10.1016/j.tics.2013.09.016. See

also Nikos K. Logothetis, "What We Can Do and What We Cannot Do with fMRI," *Nature*, Volume 453, No. 7197 (London: Nature Research [Springer Nature], 12 June 2008), 869–78; doi:10.1038/nature06976.

41. "[A]ctivity in inferior temporal and inferior occipital regions showed a positive correlation to the self-rated vividness of the visual images[, … and the] visual imagery is selectively related to activity of inferior-temporal and occipital regions[, … meaning that] the cerebral correlate of visual imagery is different from that of non-imaginal thinking." Georg Goldenberg, et al., "Regional Cerebral Blood Flow Patterns in Visual Imagery," *Neuropsychologia*, Volume 27, No. 5 (Oxford: Pergamon Press, 1989), 641–64; doi:10.1016/0028-3932(89)90110-3. In addition, "mental imagery involves the efferent activation of visual areas in prestriate occipital cortex, parietal and temporal cortex, and that these areas represent the same kinds of specialized visual information in imagery as they do in perception." Martha J. Farah, "The Neural Basis of Mental Imagery," *Trends in Neurosciences*, Volume 12, No. 10 (Amsterdam: Elsevier [North-Holland Biomedical Press], October 1989), 395–99; doi:10.1016/0166-2236(89)90079-9. See also Allan M. Schrier and Roger W. Sperry, "Visuomotor Integration in Split-Brain Cats," *Science*, Volume 129, No. 3358 (Washington, D.C.: American Association for the Advancement of Science, 8 May 1959), 1275–76; doi:10.1126/science.129.3358.1275.

42. "Charles Darwin […] developed the concepts of the prodigality of nature and the struggle for existence, which led to the resultant concept of natural selection and survival of the fittest[, as well as the requirement that …] the environment be competitive, savage, brutal, [and thus] then the fittest will be the strongest physically and the most vicious." Emory S. Bogardu, *A History of Social Thought* (Los Angeles: University of Southern California Press, 1922), 258. Spencer originally coins the term "survival of the fittest, which I have here sought to express in mechanical terms, [and it] is that which Mr Darwin has called 'natural selection', or the preservation of favoured races in the struggle for life." Herbert Spencer, *The Principles of Biology*, Volume 1 (New York: D. Appleton and Co., 1866), 444–45; section 165.

43. Humans seem to be born with both of these cross-purposed instincts: selfishness and a (sometimes grudging) willingness to cooperate. Various social influences, however, can tap into and engage either of these instincts. The Spencerian "survival of the fittest" mechanism would tend to promote self-preservation via egocentric self-interest, although some competitors may come to find that coordination within the context of a social order actually better secures their ultimate survival than individualism. The umpire declares, "Play ball!" for all to hear; personal excellence and talent may emerge in individual statistics, but the effort of both participating teams shapes the game.

Then, "[l]et us try to *teach* generosity and altruism because we [humans] are born selfish." Richard Dawkins, *The Selfish Gene* (Oxford: Oxford University Press, 1976), 3; emphasis in the original. A plethora of studies purport to demonstrate that humans are inherently selfish, while seemingly just as many further (or counter) studies claim to debunk this Hobbesian view as a myth. Evolution is grounded in the adaptive, natural selection that results from random, genetic mutation; the next progression comes in the form of socializing behavior. Psychological egoism may be self-limiting; selfishness taken to an extreme could cause the eventual extinction of the human species. "It is even possible that ZD [zero-determinant] strategies win every single matchup against non-ZD strategies[, … while the strategizers themselves may] yet be evolutionarily unstable and be driven to extinction." Christoph Adami and Arend Hintze, "Evolutionary Instability of Zero-Determinant Strategies Demonstrates That Winning Is Not Everything," *Nature Communications*, Volume 4, No. 2193 (Berlin: Nature Research [Springer Science+Business Media], 1 August 2013); doi:10.1038/ncomms3193. And while "human nature supports both prosocial and selfish traits[, … studies involving twins (both identical and fraternal, as a way to separate out the effects of heredity and/ or environment) tend to reveal] overwhelming evidence for genetic effects on behaviors such as sharing and empathy." Matthew Robison, "Are People Naturally Inclined to Cooperate or Be Selfish?" in *Scientific American Mind*, Volume 25, No. 5 (New York: Nature Publishing Group, 1 September 1, 2014); doi:10.1038/scientificamericanmind0914-78a. In terms of fitting in, "a psychopath is a man who either suffers himself from the demands of society or else makes society suffer[, … so in a] sense we are all psychopaths, for each of us suffers from the necessity of self-imposed control for the good of the community." Konrad Lorenz, *On Aggression*, trans. Marjorie Kerr Wilson (New York: Harcourt, 1966 [Munich: Deutscher Taschenbuch Verlag GmbH and Co., 1963]), 246–47.

44. "The evolutionary principle of 'the survival of the fittest' seems to predispose individuals to selfishness." Francis Heylighen, "Evolution, Selfishness and Cooperation," *Journal of Ideas*, Volume 2, No. 4 (1992), 70. The wisdom of the collective ought to temper social misconduct. Instead, selfish Wall Street bankers, for example, with their greedy speculative investment strategies somehow feel empowered to threaten the solvency of the world's economic systems and are paradoxically rewarded by democratic governments with the gift of immunity from prosecution, sweeping deregulation over future misbehavior, and massive pecuniary breaks in taxation. The degree to which humans are inherently selfish is "characterized by the reward system of the brain-shaping behavior[, … and these] characterizations are partial truths based on the segments

of the selfish–selfless spectrum." James W. H. Sonne and Don M. Gash, "Psychopathy to Altruism: Neurobiology of the Selfish–Selfless Spectrum," *Frontiers in Psychology*, Volume 9 (Pully, Switzerland: Frontiers Research Foundation, 19 April 2018), 575; doi:10.3389/fpsyg.2018.00575. "[P]eople become selfish when placed in market environments[, ... and s]ome anthropologists argue that markets replace exchange based on reciprocity and, in doing so, change the nature of humanity[; ...] market outcomes may not change when agents are unselfish[, ... but] it takes only one selfish buyer to push the market price to the lowest competitive level." Joel Sobel, "Do Markets Make People Selfish," *(Working/Discussion) Paper* (San Diego, California: University of California, 2007). A study involving adults and children demonstrates that, as we age, whatever inherent selfishness we may have had can be overcome when we develop the ability to formulate judgments. Myrna Beth Shure, "Fairness, Generosity, and Selfishness: The Naive Psychology of Children and Young Adults," *Child Development*, Volume 39, No. 3 (Chicago: University of Chicago Press, September 1968), 875–886; doi:10.2307/1126990.

45. The "extinction trajectory would play out under conditions that resemble the 'perfect storm' that coincided with past mass extinctions [i.e., the so-called 'Big Five' during the Ordovician, Devonian, Permian, Triassic, and Cretaceous periods]: multiple, atypical high-intensity ecological stressors, including rapid, unusual *climate change* and highly elevated atmospheric CO_2[; ....] current extinction rates are higher than those that caused Big Five extinctions in geological time [... and] could be severe enough to carry extinction magnitudes to the Big Five benchmark in as little as three centuries." Anthony D. Barnosky, et al., "Has the Earth's Sixth Mass Extinction Already Arrived?" in *Nature*, Volume 471 (London: Nature Research [Springer Nature], 2 March 2011), 51–57; doi:10.1038/nature09678, emphasis in the original. But "[a]voiding a true sixth mass extinction will require rapid, greatly intensified efforts to conserve already threatened species and to alleviate pressures on their populations—notably habitat loss, overexploitation for economic gain, and climate change." Gerardo Ceballos, et al., "Accelerated Modern Human-Induced Species Losses: Entering the Sixth Mass Extinction," *Science Advances*, Volume 1, No. 5 (Washington, D.C.: American Association for the Advancement of Science, 19 June 2015): e1400253; doi:10.1126/sciadv.1400253. Yet, "misinformation by climate-change deniers has confused public understanding[, ... b]ut new studies have quantified the rate of the sixth extinction, and explained in unprecedented detail its causes." Tim Flannery, *Atmosphere of Hope: Searching for Solutions to the Climate Crisis* (Melbourne, Australia: Text Publishing, 2015), 64.

46. "[I]ndependent fMRI experiments revealed that overcoming biased empathic judgments is associated with increased activation in the right supramarginal gyrus (rSMG)." Giorgia Silani, et al., "Right Supramarginal Gyrus Is Crucial to Overcome Emotional Egocentricity Bias in Social Judgements," *The Journal of Neuroscience*, Volume 33, No. 39 (Washington, D.C.: Society for Neuroscience, 25 September 2013), 15466–76; doi:10.1523/jneurosci.1488-13.2013. Cf. Katrin Preckel, Philipp Kanske, and Tania Singer, "On the Interaction of Social Affect and Cognition: Empathy Compassion and Theory of Mind," *Current Opinion in Behavioral Sciences*, Volume 19 (Amsterdam: Elsevier, February 2018), 1–6; doi:10.1016/j.cobeha.2017.07.010.

47. "[S]ympathy [… is] an outpouring of our own identification with the other, showing pity and concern in a way which perhaps fails to understand the other because it comes from our own concern[; … whereas e]mpathy is the capacity to enter into the feelings and experiences of another […. and] to understand what the other is experiencing as if you were the other [… without trying to] simply project their personal experiences on to someone whose reaction is quite different from their own." Janet Seden, *Counselling Skills in Social Work Practice* (New York: Open University Press [McGraw-Hill Education], 2005 [1999]), 74. So, "[w]hereas empathy requires an understanding of another person's feelings, sympathy involves feeling sorrow or concern for another person." Jose B. Ashford and Craig Winston LeCroy, *Human Behavior in the Social Environment* (Belmont, California: Brooks/Cole [CENGAGE Learning], 2008), 314; citing N. Nancy Eisenberg, Michelle Wentzel, and Jerry D. Harris, "The Role of Emotionality and Regulation in Empathy-Related Responding," *School Psychology Review*, Volume 27, No. 4 (Bethesda, Maryland: National Association of School Psychologists, 1998), 506–21.

48. Simon Baron-Cohen, *Zero Degrees of Empathy* (London: Allen Lane [Penguin], 2011). For a study purporting to determine that psychopathy's lack-of-empathy is rooted in neurology, see Jean Decety, et al., "An fMRI Study of Affective Perspective Taking in Individuals with Psychopathy: Imagining Another in Pain Does Not Evoke Empathy," *Frontiers in Human Neuroscience*, Volume 7 (Lausanne, Switzerland: Frontiers Research Foundation, 24 September 2013), 489; doi:10.3389/fnhum.2013.00489.

49. "There was a significant negative correlation between fT [fetal testosterone exposure] and scores on [two empathy tests performed when subjects were aged 6 to 8]." Emma Chapman, at al., "Fetal Testosterone and Empathy: Evidence from the Empathy Quotient (EQ) and the 'Reading the Mind in the Eyes' Test," *Social Neuroscience*, Volume 1, No. 2 (Hove, England: Psychology Press [London: Taylor and Francis], 2006), 135–48; doi:10.1080/17470910600992239. Also, "it is not difficult to imagine that a

parent's failure to bond with an infant could produce the kinds of neurological and clinical changes associated with psychopathy." Kent A. Kiehl and Morris B. Hoffman, "The Criminal Psychopath: History, Neuroscience, Treatment, and Economics," *Jurimetrics*, Volume 51 (Chicago: American Bar Association's Section of Science and Technology, Summer 2011), 355–97. Yet, in other studies, there is "no evidence that cognitive empathy is impaired by testosterone." Amos Nadler, et al., "Does Testosterone Impair Men's Cognitive Empathy?" in *Proceedings: Biological Sciences*, Volume 286, No. 1910 (London: Royal Society of London, 11 September 2019), 20191062; doi:10.1098/rspb.2019.1062.

50. "[A] single administration of testosterone in [...] young women significantly altered [... their] cognitive empathic behavior." Peter A. Bos, et al., "Testosterone Reduces Functional Connectivity during the 'Reading the Mind in the Eyes' Test," *Psychoneuroendocrinology*, Volume 68 (Amsterdam: Elsevier, June 2016), 194–201; doi:10.1016/j.psyneuen.2016.03.006.

51. The study established an "egocentricity bias in the emotional domain (EEB) [... through a] visuo-tactile paradigm assessing the degree to which empathic judgments are biased by one's own emotions if they are incongruent to those of the person [with whom] we empathize." Silani, et al., "Right Supramarginal Gyrus."

52. "[R]esults demonstrate that while individuals with psychopathy exhibited a strong response in pain-affective brain regions when taking an imagine-self perspective, they failed to recruit the neural circuits that are [or] were activated in controls during an imagine-other perspective, and that may contribute to lack of empathic concern." Jean Decety, et al., "An fMRI Study of Affective Perspective Taking in Individuals with Psychopathy: Imagining Another in Pain Does Not Evoke Empathy," *Frontiers in Human Neuroscience*, Volume 7, No. 489 (Lausanne, Switzerland: Frontiers Research Foundation, 24 September 2013); doi:10.3389/fnhum.2013.00489.

53. "[R]educed functioning of certain regions of the brain may generate deficits in generating fear, guilt and empathy; on the other hand, increased activity in brain regions associated with pleasure and reward structure may result in psychopaths getting pleasure from harming others." John Douard and Pamela D. Schultz, *Monstrous Crimes and the Failure of Forensic Psychiatry* (Dordrecht, Netherlands: Springer Science+Business Media, 2013), 123. Moreover, psychopaths can make "rational deliberations about strong moral issues [...] without involving the emotions[, ... and i]n the imaging studies showing blood flow to the brain's pleasure center, when people witness the punishment of those who have harmed them, the punishment is proportional to the harm caused[, so that o]nly a callous sadist would take pleasure in seeing

grossly disproportionate punishment imposed." Anthony Walsh and Virginia L. Hatch, "Capital Punishment, Retribution, and Emotion: An Evolutionary Perspective," *New Criminal Law Review: An International and Interdisciplinary Journal*, Volume 21, No. 2 (Berkeley, California: University of California Press, Spring 2018), 272 and 280; doi:10.1525/nclr.2018.21.2.267. "The strange patterns of brain activation and connectivity in highly psychopathic individuals suggest they did not experience empathy when imagining the pain of others, and possibly took pleasure in it." Tanya Lewis, "Blame the Brain: Why Psychopaths Lack Empathy," *Live Science* (New York: Future US, 24 September 2013) at **https://www.livescience.com/39904-why-psychopaths-lack-empathy.html**, accessed March 21, 2020.

54. "The clinical diagnosis of psychopathy describes individuals who suffer from a profound affective deficit, including shallow emotion and inability to experience empathy, guilt or remorse[; …i]t is estimated that 1% of the general population meet criteria for the disorder, whereas psychopaths constitute 15–25% of the prison population." Scott M. Freeman, et al., "The Posteromedial Region of the Default Mode Network Shows Attenuated Task-Induced Deactivation in Psychopathic Prisoners," *Neuropsychology*, Volume 29, No. 3 (Washington, D.C.: American Psychological Association, May 2015), 493; doi:10.1037/neu0000118. Other studies put the percentage much higher; for example, of "prisons and forensic hospitals throughout California[, …f]orty percent [… of male inmates] were psychopaths." J. Reid Meloy and Carl B. Gacono, "The Internal World of the Psychopath," *Psychopathy: Antisocial, Criminal, and Violent Behavior*, ed. Theodore Millon, et al. (New York: The Guilford Press, 1998), 103.

55. "[U]nder instructions to empathize, […] psychopathic participants relied […] on deliberate mechanisms to boost the activation of their own actions, emotions and sensations[, … allowing them,] while deliberately empathizing with others, […] to recruit vicarious activations." Harma Meffert, et al., "Reduced Spontaneous but Relatively Normal Deliberate Vicarious Representations in Psychopathy," *Brain*, Volume 136, No. 8 (Oxford: Oxford University Press, August 2013), 2550–62; doi:10.1093/brain/awt190. "How to Spot Someone with Antisocial Personality Disorder[: …includes the individual's f]ailure to conform to social norms." Simon Baron-Cohen, *The Science of Evil: On Empathy and the Origins of Cruelty* (New York: Basic Books [Perseus Books Group], 2011), 198.

56. The notion of doing evil without being evil has been termed the "banality of evil" and is based on making motive the essential element of evil; to the extent the actor lacks a malicious intention or profound dogmatic attachment to the evil enterprise, the aim to fulfill a role within the enterprise as a "joiner"

perhaps ought not to be considered evil in itself with respect to the motivating force of leadership. Hannah Arendt, *Eichmann in Jerusalem: A Report on the Banality of Evil* (New York: Viking Press, 1963).

57. "Free will can't really mean that at any moment a person's behavior is totally unpredictable (and therefore entirely unconstrained)[; … s]uch a universe would be, from psychology's perspective at least, the same as one governed entirely by chance, which is just another way of saying it is not governed at all." John Baer, James C. Kaufman, and Roy F. Baumeister, "Introduction: Psychology and Free Will," *Are We Free? Psychology and Free Will*, ed. John Baer, James C. Kaufman, and Roy F. Baumeister (New York: Oxford University Press, 2008), 4. "[I]f undetermined quantum events *did* sometimes have nonnegligible effects on the brain or behavior, this would [… not by itself prove] free will[, … because] such undetermined events would be unpredictable and uncontrollable by the agent's themselves, like the unanticipated emergence of a thought or the uncontrolled jerking of an arm—just the opposite of what we think free and responsible actions would be like." Robert Kane, "Introduction: The Contours of Contemporary Free-Will Debates (Part 2)," *The Oxford Handbook of Free Will*, ed. Robert Kane (New York: Oxford University Press, 2011), 8. "[I]f chaos is a factor in generating human behavior, then it may be that what we are calling free will is simply a way of accounting for a certain level of longed-for indeterminacy in our behavior, of trying to fit it into a pattern that we can understand—and think we can control." William R. Clark and Michael Grunstein, *Are We Hardwired?: The Role of Genes in Human Behavior* (New York: Oxford University Press, 2000), 269. And yet, "[i]ronically, it is customary to assign our own unpredictable behavior and that of other humans to irrationality: were we to behave rationally, we reason, the world would be more predictable[, … when, i]n fact, it is just when we behave rationally, moving logically, like a computer, from step to step, that our behavior becomes provably *un*predictable[, … and thus, r]ationality combines with self-reference to make our actions intrinsically paradoxical and uncertain." Seth Lloyd, *Programming the Universe: A Quantum Computer Scientist Takes on the Cosmos* (New York: Alfred A. Knopf [Random House], 2006), 136.

58. Alejandro Jenkins and Gilad Perez, "Looking for Life in the Multiverse," *Scientific American*, Volume 302, No. 1 (New York: Nature Research [Springer Nature], January 2010), 42–51; doi:10.1038/scientificamerican0110-42.

59. Stephen Hawking, *Brief Answers to the Big Questions* (New York: Bantam Books, 2018), 52.

60. See Andrea Lavazza, "Free Will and Neuroscience: From Explaining Freedom Away to New Ways of Operationalizing and Measuring It," *Frontiers*

in Human Neuroscience, Volume 10, No. 262 (Lausanne, Switzerland: Frontiers Research Foundation, 1 June 2016); doi:10.3389/fnhum.2016.00262, citing Benjamin Libet, et al, "The Unconscious Initiation of a Free Voluntary Act," *Brain*, Volume 106, No. 3 (Oxford: Oxford University Press, September 1983): 623–42, doi:10.1093/brain/106.3.623.

61. See this animated video for an apt depiction of the "unfree victim" concept: Jon Matter (DarkMatter2525), "How God Favors Evil," *YouTube* video, 2:27 (New Haven, Connecticut: Yale University Press, 27 March 2012) at **https://www.youtube.com/watch?v=Z1BzP1wr234** (God favors evil), accessed April 14, 2019.

62. The biblical basis for this uncharitable view appears to originate with "Wherefore let them that suffer according to the will of God commit the keeping of their souls to [H]im" (1 Pet. 4:19). Others say, "Natural disasters are natural [… and] not the avenging spirit of your personal beliefs." C. Barnett, "Stop Saying Natural Disasters Are God's Will," *World Religion News* (San Francisco: Andromeda Edison, 1 October 2017) at **https://www. worldreligionnews.com/religion-news/stop-saying-natural-disasters-gods-will**, accessed April 10, 2020; the article (and its website generally) cites many examples, including Nick Duffy, "Pastor Claims Hurricane Harvey Was God's Punishment for Texas Failure to Pass Anti-LGBT Law," *PinkNews* (London: PinkNews Media Group, 31 August 2017) at **https://www.pinknews. co.uk/2017/08/31/pastor-claims-hurricane-harvey-was-gods-punishment-for-texas-failure-to-pass-anti-lgbt-law/**. As another opposing view states: "Suffering is not God's will, but contrary to it and when people suffer God suffers." David K. Chester, "The Theodicy of Natural Disasters," *Scottish Journal of Theology*, Volume 51, No. 4 (Edinburgh: T&T Clark, November 1998), 485–506; doi:10.1017/S0036930600056866. Among several instances cited, "[w]hen asked if the Asian tsunami was the hand of God, the Rev. Bernard Smith responded: 'You have to look at [… the fact that m]ost of the people who were killed were nonbelievers.'" Lane DeGregory, "The Hand of God?" in *Tampa Bay Times* (St. Petersburg, Florida: Times Publishing Company [the Poynter Institute], 24 August 2005) at **https://www.tampabay.com/ archive/2005/01/04/the-hand-of-god/**, also accessed April 10, 2020.

63. See this video for an animated depiction of the vengeful nature of the god of the Old Testament: Jon Matter (DarkMatter2525), "Is Christianity Moral?" on *YouTube* video, 5:25 (New Haven, Connecticut: Yale University Press, 16 May 2014) at **https://www.youtube.com/watch?v=35_JHx_OzA4**, accessed April 14, 2019.

64. "[D]isaster survivors combine both nature-based and human-based explanations of disasters." Alessandro Massazza, Chris R. Brewin, and

Helene Joffe, "The Nature of 'Natural Disasters': Survivors' Explanations of Earthquake Damage," *International Journal of Disaster Risk Science*, Volume 10, No. 3 (Beijing: Beijing Normal University Publishing Group, September 2019), 293–305; doi:10.1007/s13753-019-0223-z. "*The Rule of 7*: no [catastrophe] happens in isolation or as the result of a single event [… but] requires a minimum of 7 things to go wrong[, … a]nd one of those 7 is always human error." Bob Mayer, *Stuff Doesn't Just Happen I: The Gift of Failure: Titanic, Kegworth, Custer, Schoolhouse, Donner, Tulips, Apollo 13* (Knoxville, Tennessee: Cool Gus Publishing, 2018). Cf. Barry A. Turner, "The Organizational and Interorganizational Development of Disasters," *Administrative Science Quarterly*, Volume 21, No. 3 (Ithaca, New York: Cornell University's Johnson Graduate School of Management, September 1976), 378–97; doi:10.2307/2391850.

Chapter 13: Morality

1. Arthur Schopenhauer, *The Basis of Morality*, trans. Arthur Brodrick Bullock (New York: Macmillan, 1915), 213. Additional quotes by Schopenhauer from the same source include: "Compassion for animals is intimately connected with goodness of character, and it may be confidently asserted that he, who is cruel to living creatures, cannot be a good man," (Ibid., 223); and "Compassion [… is] the source of all genuine, that is, disinterested virtue, being, so to say, incarnate in every good deed," (Ibid., 275).

2. "[W]hatsoever ye would that men should do to you, do ye even so to them" (Matt. 7:12) and "[A]s ye would that men should do to you, do ye also to them likewise" (Luke 6:31). "None of you truly believes until he wishes for his brother what he wishes for himself" (Hadith #13, attributed to the Prophet Muhammad in Abu Zakariyya Yahya ibn Sharaf al-Nawawi's *Forty Hadith*). "[T]hou shalt love thy neighbour as thyself" (Lev. 19:18) and "[T]he stranger that dwelleth with you shall be unto you as one born among you, and thou shalt love him as thyself" (Lev. 19:34). "Let no man do to another that which would be repugnant to himself" (*Mahabharata*, 13:5571 [or Book 5, Chapter 49, Verse 57]). "[H]urt not others with what pains yourself" (*Udana-Varga* 1.5.18 [or Book 1, Chapter 5, Verse 18]). "[The] perfect virtue [...] is not to do to others as you would not wish done to yourself'" (Confucius, *Analects* 12.2 [or Book 12, Chapter 2]) and "What you do not want done to yourself, do not do to others" (Confucius, *Analects* 15.23 [or Book 15, Chapter 23]). "Regard your neighbor's gain as your own gain and you neighbor's loss as your own loss" (Lao Tzu, *T'ai-shang Kan-ying P'ien*, 213–228). "One going to take a pointed stick to pinch a baby bird should first try it on himself to feel how it hurts," or generally, "A man should journey treating all creatures

as he himself would be treated" (*Sutrakritanga* 1:11.33). "That nature alone is good which refrains from doing to another whatsoever is not good for itself" (*Dadisten-I-dinik*, 94:5). "[T]he best and most just way to live [… is when] we do not do what we blame others for doing." Diogenes Laertius, *The Lives and Opinions of Eminent Philosophers*, trans. Charles Duke Yonge (London: J. Haddon and Son, 1853 [ca. sixth century BCE]), 19; quoting Thales[, the Milesian]. "[T]he principle of doing to others what one wishes for oneself is found across many religions and cultures[; … s]ometimes called the 'Golden Rule', this principle is woven through Christianity, Islam, Buddhism, Hinduism, and native beliefs, even appearing in Scientology and other modern spiritual movements." Cornelia C. Walther, *Development, Humanitarian Aid, and Social Welfare: Social Change from the Inside Out* (Cham, Switzerland: Palgrave Pivot / Palgrave Macmillan [Springer Nature], 2020), 80; doi:10.1007/978-3-030-42610-1_5.

3. "The just in this case, then, is the proportional; the unjust is what is contrary to the proportion[: … T]here is first proportional equality and then reciprocal exchange." Aristotle, *Nicomachean Ethics*, trans. Robert C. Bartlett and Susan D. Collins (Chicago: University of Chicago Press, 2012 [ca. 340 BCE]), 96 and 100; V.5.1131b16 and V.5.1133a10–11. "[U]nequals do not receive unequal things in proportion to their inequality[, … for e]quality is twofold[: …] one sort is numerical[, … while] the other according to worth." Aristotle, *Politics*, Volume 3: Books V and VI, trans. David Keyt (Oxford: Clarendon Press [Oxford University Press], 1999 [ca. 350 BCE]), 2; V.1.1301b26–29.

4. Dave Kerpen, *The Art of People: 11 Simple People Skills That Will Get You Everything You Want* (New York: Crown Publishing [Penguin Random House], 2016), 96.

5. "[C]onsequentialism finds the locus of value in the outcome or consequences of the act." Gilbert Burgh, Terri Field, and Mark Freakley, *Ethics and the Community of Inquiry* (Melbourne: Thomson Social Science Press, 2006), 12. Yet, "[t]here is no one single idea which forms the core of consequentialism, none that is universally agreed upon to be an inescapable part of the consequentialist outlook." Joseph Raz, *The Morality of Freedom* (New York: Clarendon Press [Oxford University Press], 1986), 268.

6. "[A] deontological theory [is] one that either does not specify the good independently from the right, or does not interpret the right as maximizing the good[; … such theories] characterize the rightness of institutions or acts independently from their consequences." John Rawls, *A Theory of Justice* (New York: Oxford University Press, 1999 [1971]), 26. "[B]y a categorical imperative, Kant understands a principle of conduct that applies to a person in virtue of his nature as a free and equal rational being[, … while it] does not

presuppose that one has a particular desire or aim[, … although] it directs us to take certain steps as effective means to achieve a specific end." Ibid., 222–23.

7. Walter Sinnott-Armstrong, "Consequentialism," *The Stanford Encyclopedia of Philosophy*, Winter 2015 Edition, ed. Edward N. Zalta (Palo Alto, California: Metaphysics Research Lab, Stanford University, 20 May 2003) at **https://plato. stanford.edu/entries/consequentialism/**, accessed April 18, 2019.

8. See John Harris, *The Value of Life: An Introduction to Medical Ethics* (London: Routledge and Kegan Paul, 1985), 42–44. The consequentialist would further say that "if I am ever responsible for anything, then I must be just as much responsible for things that I allow or fail to prevent, as I am for things that I myself, in the more everyday restricted sense, bring about." J. J. C. Smart and Bernard Williams, *Utilitarianism: For and Against* (New York: Cambridge University Press, 1973), 95.

9. Judith Jarvis Thomson, "Killing, Letting Die, and the Trolley Problem," *The Monist*, Volume 59, No. 2 (La Salle, Illinois: Open Court for the Hegeler Institute, 1 April 1976), 204–17; doi:10.5840/monist197659224. Cf. Judith Jarvis Thomson, *Rights, Restitution, and Risk*, ed. William Parent (Cambridge, Massachusetts: Harvard University Press, 1986), 94, Chapter 7: The Trolley Problem; citing Philippa Foot, "The Problem of Abortion and the Doctrine of the Double Effect," *Oxford Review*, No. 5 (Oxford: Oxford University Press, 1967), 5–15.

10. Thomas M. Scanlon, *Moral Dimensions: Permissibility, Meaning, Blame* (Cambridge, Massachusetts: Belknap Press [Harvard University Press], 2008), 8–36; Chapter 1: The Illusory Appeal of Double Effect.

11. "[P]roponents of the doctrine of double effect always include an assessment of proportionality in their analysis […] because a proportionality test is necessary if the principle is to have any plausibility." Alasdair Cochrane, *Animal Rights without Liberation* (New York: Columbia University Press, 2012), 97. "The principle of double effect [has, as a] condition, proportionality, [which] must always be taken into account." Suzanne Uniacke, "(The Principle of) Double Effect," *Routledge Encyclopedia of Philosophy*, Volume 3: Descartes to Gender and science, ed. Edward Craig (London: Routledge [Taylor and Francis], 1998), 120. Specifically, the "theory of the double effect becomes controversial when it is applied to cases in which the action of causing the bad effect is held to be impermissible when taken by itself[, … as] Aquinas is taken by many commentators to have held th[e] killing [of] a human being [to be]." Alan Donagan, *The Theory of Morality* (Chicago: University of Chicago Press, 1977), 159. Moreover, "the Doctrine of Double Effect […] is taken as the paradigm case of justifiable homicide[, … although n]o matter how well-intentioned the use of defensive force and however legitimate the

cause, it cannot avoid facing the deeply problematic nature of harming or killing another human being." Whitley R. P. Kaufman, *Justified Killing: The Paradox of Self-defense* (Lanham, Maryland: Lexington Books [Rowman and Littlefield], 2009), 150.

12. Exceptions to the exceptions abound, like immoral altruism, as when we are asked to "[c]onsider the racist organ donor, for example, who wishes to donate their organs, but only to those of their own race." Niall Scott and Jonathan Seglow, *Altruism* (London: McGraw-Hill Education, 2007), 2. Nor is it "the case that empathizing with others generates [the kind of] altruism that is always moral." Julinna C. Oxley, *The Moral Dimensions of Empathy* (New York: Palgrave Macmillan, 2011), 60.

13. Socrates asks, "Is 'what is holy' holy because the gods approve it, or do they approve it because it is holy?" Plato, *The Collected Dialogues*, ed. Edith Hamilton and Huntington Cairns, trans. Lane Cooper (Princeton, New Jersey: Princeton University Press, 1961 [ca. 399 BCE]), 178; the "Euthyphro" dialogue.

14. "[P]rosocial religions with Big Gods [are] reliable builders of trust [… because] belief is easy to fake—opening the door to impostors who masquerade as believers who receive group benefits but do not contribute, and worse, exploit the system." Ara Norenzayan, *Big Gods: How Religion Transformed Cooperation and Conflict* (Princeton, New Jersey: Princeton University Press, 2013), 60.

15. "Religion with Big Gods is the key reason why there is prejudice toward atheists[, … so that] most people who share these cultural traditions distrust atheists." Ibid., 87. "[R]eligious people tend to believe in deities that punish people for misbehavior[, … and thus, i]f someone believes they will be punished for breaking a promise, they should be less likely to break that promise, all else being equal." Jesse Marczyk, "The Distrust of Atheists: What Makes the Non-religious Seem Less Trustworthy?" in *PsychologyToday.com* (New York: Sussex Publishers, 16 May 2018) at **https://www.psychologytoday. com/us/blog/pop-psych/201805/the-distrust-atheists**, accessed April 10, 2020.

16. Internet comment by Sven2547 (**https://disqus.com/by/Sven2547/**), *Patheos. com* (Virginia Beach, Virginia: BeliefNet [BN Media Associates], 17 February 2017) at **https://www.patheos.com/blogs/crossexamined/2017/02/bad-atheist-arguments-morality-doesnt-come-god/#comment-3160881455**, accessed April 30, 2019; in response to Bob Seidensticker, "Bad Atheist Arguments: 'Morality Doesn't Come From God,'" (16 February 2017) at the parent URL.

17. The quote is misattributed to American journalist H. L. Mencken (1880–1956), who did, however, write: [R]eligion, generally speaking, has been a

curse to mankind—that its modest and greatly overestimated services on the ethical side have been more than overcome by the damage it has done to clear and honest thinking." H. L. Mencken, "What I Believe," *Forum*, Volume 84, No. 3 (New York: Forum Publishing Company, September 1930), 139.

18. "Despite the commonsense belief that people do not confess to crimes they did not commit, 20 to 25% of all DNA exonerations involve innocent prisoners who confessed." Saul M. Kassin, "False Confessions: Causes, Consequences, and Implications for Reform," *Current Directions in Psychological Science*, Volume 17, No. 4 (Los Angeles [Thousand Oaks, California]: SAGE Publications [American Psychological Society / Association for Psychological Science], August 2008), 249–53; doi:10.1111/j.1467-8721.2008.00584.x. One "plausible reason for a voluntary false confession [would be] to protect someone else[, … and] it is not unheard of for an individual to accept blame and the punishment for something he did not do to protect another." David E. Zulawski and Douglas E. Wicklander, *Practical Aspects of Interview and Interrogation* (Boca Raton, Florida: CRC Press [Taylor and Francis], 2002), 78. Furthermore, "false confession may result from the individual's unconscious need to expiate guilt feelings through punishment[, … possibly involving] real or imagined past transgressions." Guy Norfolk and Margaret M. Stark, "Care of Detainees," *A Physician's Guide to Clinical Forensic Medicine*, ed. Margaret M. Stark (Totowa, New Jersey: Humana Press, 2000), 162. Also, "certain commonly used techniques lead suspects to confess to crimes they did not commit[, … while] police and others cannot distinguish between uncorroborated true and false confessions." Saul M. Kassin, "On the Psychology of Confessions: Does Innocence Put Innocents at Risk?" in *American Psychologist*, Volume 60, No. 3 (Washington, D.C.: American Psychological Association, April 2005), 215. See also Saul M. Kassin and Gisli H. Gudjonsson, "The Psychology of Confessions: A Review of the Literature and Issues," *Psychological Science in the Public Interest*, Volume 5, No. 2 (Los Angeles [Thousand Oaks, California]: SAGE Publications [Association for Psychological Science], November 2004), 33–67; Saul M. Kassin, "The Psychology of Confessions," *Annual Review of Law and Social Science*, Volume 4 (Palo Alto, California: Annual Reviews, 23 December 2008), 193–217; and Jennifer T. Perillo and Saul M. Kassin, "Inside Interrogation: The Lie, the Bluff, and False Confessions," *Law and Human Behavior*, Volume 35, No. 4 (New York: Springer [American Psychology–Law Society], August 2011), 327–37.

19. "If I owe a person money, and cannot pay him, and he threatens to put me in prison, another person can take the debt upon himself, and pay it for me; but if I have committed a crime, every circumstance of the case is changed; moral justice cannot take the innocent for the guilty even if the innocent would offer itself[; …] it is no longer justice; it is indiscriminate revenge."

Thomas Paine, *The Age of Reason* (New York: D. M. Bennett, 1877 [1795]), 22. "[M]y own guilt [...] is deemed 'original' and inescapable[, ... yet] I am still granted free will with which to reject the offer of vicarious redemption[; ... s]hould l exercise this choice, however, I face an eternity of torture much more awful than anything endured at Calvary, or anything threatened to those who first heard the Ten Commandments." Christopher Hitchens, *God Is Not Great: How Religion Poisons Everything* (Toronto, Ontario, Canada: McClelland and Stewart [Penguin Random House], 2008), 209. "I find something repulsive in the idea of vicarious redemption[, ... and] we rightly sneer at the barbaric societies that practice this unpleasantness in its literal form[, ... as t]here's no moral value in the vicarious gesture[; ... t]he whole apparatus of absolution and forgiveness strikes me as positively immoral." Christopher Hitchens, *Letters to a Young Contrarian* (New York: Basic Books [Perseus Books Group], 2009), 58.

20. Bernard J. Nebel and Richard T. Wright, *Environmental Science: The Way the World Works* (Englewood Cliffs, New Jersey: Prentice Hall, 1981), 98. Specifically, "individuals that possess favorable traits are more likely to reproduce and pass those traits to the next generation[, ... which] leads to a change in the genetic composition of the population[; ... n]atural selection works only on heritable variation, that is, traits having a genetic basis." Robert E. Ricklefs and Gary L. Miller, *Ecology* (New York: Chiron Press, 1973), 11.

21. "The theory of natural selection is a theory about the evolution of species[, ... and t]his claim seems beyond dispute." Alexander Rosenberg, *The Structure of Biological Science* (Cambridge: Cambridge University Press, 1985), 180. "[E]volution is a theory[, ... but i]t is also a fact[, ... or part of] the world's data[, ... and e]very cell in your body shows the evidence of evolution." Donald R. Prother, *Evolution: What the Fossils Say and Why It Matters* (New York: Columbia University Press, 2007), 103 and 105. Even the Unabomber realizes that "[t]he principle of natural selection is beyond dispute." Theodore J. Kaczynski, *Technological Slavery* (Port Townsend, Washington: Feral House, 2010), 281.

22. Pew Research Center, "The Evolution of Pew Research Center's Survey Questions About the Origins and Development of Life on Earth," *PewForum. org*, "Belief in Evolution Highest Among Atheists and Agnostics Lower Among Evangelicals" (Washington, D.C.: The Pew Charitable Trusts, 6 February 2019) at **https://www.pewforum.org/?attachment_id=31306**, accessed May 7, 2019.

23. "[T]he history of inequalities suffered by African Americans have led not only to lost opportunities in the competition for a piece of the American dream, but to a pervasive sense of meaninglessness and lack of self-respect within the the poorest African-American communities." Cornel West,

"Nihilism in Black America," *Moral Soundings*, ed. Dwight Furrow (Lanham, Maryland: Rowman and Littlefield, 2004), 51; paraphrasing himself from Cornel West, *Race Matters* (Boston: Beacon Press, 1993). "Discrimination is the behavioral consequence of stigma[, … with the result that s]ome people ultimately accept these negative beliefs and prejudices and lose self-esteem, which in turn may lead to feelings of shame and hopelessness." Vikram Patel, et al., "Global Mental Health," *Global Health: Diseases, Programs, Systems, and Policies*, ed. Michael H. Merson, Robert E. Black, and Anne J. Mills (Burlington, Massachusetts: Jones and Bartlett Learning, 2011), 468. Moreover, "prejudice and discrimination lower the self-esteem of people with stigmatized identities." Jennifer Crocker and Julie A. Garcia, "Internalized Devaluation and Situational Threat," *The SAGE Handbook of Prejudice, Stereotyping and Discrimination*, ed. John F Dovidio, et al. (London: SAGE Publications, 2010), 395; citing Daryl M. Scott, *Contempt and Pity: Social Policy and the Image of the Damaged Black Psyche 1880–1996* (Chapel Hill, North Carolina: The University of North Carolina Press, 1997). In the context of labor, "[d]iscrimination of any kind (e.g., on the basis of gender, race, religion, or age) is bad for worker health." David Haber, *Health Promotion and Aging* (New York: Springer Publishing, 2013), 404. "The patterns of racial disparities in health suggest that there are multiple ways by which racism can affect health[, … and] recent research continues to document an inverse association between discrimination and health." David R. Williams and Selina A. Mohammed, "Discrimination and Racial Disparities in Health: Evidence and Needed Research," *Journal of Behavioral Medicine*, Volume 32, No. 1 (New York: Springer Science + Business Media, February 2009), 20–47; doi:10.1007/s10865-008-9185-0. Cf. Nour Kteily, Gordon Hodson, and Emile Bruneau, "They See Us as Less Than Human: Metadehumanization Predicts Intergroup Conflict via Reciprocal Dehumanization," *Journal of Personality and Social Psychology*, Volume 110, No. 3 (Washington D.C.: American Psychological Association, March 2016), 343–70; doi:10.1037/pspa0000044.

24. Tanu Priya, "The Effects of Racial, Sexual or Religious Discrimination," *LawLex.org* (Mumbai, India: Sajid Sheikh, 28 November 2013) at https://lawlex.org/lex-bulletin/the-effects-of-racial-sexual-or-religious-discrimination/8682, accessed May 6, 2019. Also, Department of Economic and Social Affairs, "Prejudice and Discrimination: Barriers to Social Inclusion" (New York: the United Nations, 7 February 2018) at https://www.un.org/development/desa/dspd/2018/02/prejudice-and-discrimination/ (https://www.un.org/development/desa/dspd/wp-content/uploads/sites/22/2018/02/RWSS-Policy-Brief-Option-4_6Feb.pdf), also accessed May 6, 2019. Cf. "What Are the Effects of Prejudice and Discrimination?" on *BBC* (London: The British Broadcasting Corporation, ca. May 2019)

at **https://www.bbc.co.uk/bitesize/guides/zyfbwmn/revision/5**, accessed May 5, 2019. Although, alone, "prejudice does not necessarily translate into discrimination." *The SAGE Encyclopedia of Economics and Society*, ed. Frederick F. Wherry and Juliet Schor (Los Angeles [Thousand Oaks, California]: SAGE Publications, 2015), 1307.

25. The "vindictive person is one who desires to get even—to seek revenge—for wrongs sustained at the hands of others[, … until they pay] back full measure, pain for pain." Jeffrie G. Murphy, "Two Cheers for Vindictiveness," *Punishment and Society*, Volume 2, No. 2 (Los Angeles [Thousand Oaks, California]: SAGE Publications, April 2000), 131–43; doi:10.1177/14624740022227917. Vengeance is not necessarily an "automatic or pervasive response to injustice." Karina Schumann and Michael Ross, "The Benefits, Costs, and Paradox of Revenge," *Social and Personality Psychology Compass*, Volume 4, No. 12 (Hoboken, New Jersey: Wiley-Blackwell Publishing, December 2010), 1193–1205; doi:10.1111/j.1751-9004.2010.00322.x. Cf. Kyler Rasmussen, "Entitled Vengeance: A Meta-Analysis Relating Narcissism to Provoked Aggression," *Aggressive Behavior*, Volume 42, No. 4 (Hoboken, New Jersey: Wiley-Liss, July 2016 [1 November 2015]), 362–79; doi:10.1002/ab.21632.

26. "[T]here is thus an evolutionary benefit for helping [… and cooperating with tho]se partners" with whom we mate, forage for food, and form coalitions. Michael Tomasello and Ivan Gonzalez-Cabrera, "The Role of Ontogeny in the Evolution of Human Cooperation," *Human Nature*, Volume 28, No. 3 (New York: Springer Science+Business Media, 18 May 2017), 275; doi:10.1007/s12110-017-9291-1. Cf. David G. Rand, Samuel Arbesman, and Nicholas A. Christakis, "Dynamic Social Networks Promote Cooperation in Experiments with Humans," *Proceedings of the National Academy of Sciences of the United States of America*, Volume 108, No. 48 (Washington, D.C.: National Academy of Sciences, 29 November 2011), 19193–98; doi:10.1073/pnas.1108243108. Furthermore, "cooperation is widely recognized as a powerful evolutionary strategy." Telmo Pievani, "Born to Cooperate? Altruism as Exaptation and the Evolution of Human Sociality," *Origins of Altruism and Cooperation*, ed. Robert W. Sussman and C. Robert Cloninger (New York: Springer Science+Business Media, 2011), 42–43. And even "indirect reciprocity can have a sound evolutionary benefit over direct reciprocity." Joost C. M. Uitdehaag, "The Dependency Game: Multiperson Reciprocal Sharing Leads to Stable Cooperation Which Can Evolve into Group Formation," *Journal of Theoretical Biology*, Volume 260, No. 2 (Amsterdam: Elsevier, 21 September 2009), 253–60; doi:10.1016/j.jtbi.2009.06.009.

27. J. Maynard Smith, "Group Selection and Kin Selection," *Nature*, Volume 201, No. 4924 (London: Nature Research [Springer Nature], 14 March 1964),

1145–47; doi:10.1038/2011145a0, citing William D. Hamilton, "The Evolution of Altruistic Behavior." *The American Naturalist*, Volume 97, No. 896 (Chicago: University of Chicago Press [American Society of Naturalists], September/ October 1963), 354–56; and (indirectly) William D. Hamilton, "The Genetical Evolution of Social Behaviour," *Journal of Theoretical Biology*, Volume 7, No. 1 (Amsterdam: Elsevier, July 1964), 1–52; doi:10.1016/0022-5193(64)90038-4.

28. An "N-player prisoner's dilemma game['s … d]etailed simulation experiments show [… the ability] to promote higher levels of cooperation as compared with panmictic [or random mating] populations." Golriz Rezaei, Michael Kirley, and Jens Pfau, "Evolving Cooperation in the N-player Prisoner's Dilemma: A Social Network Model," *Artificial Life: Borrowing from Biology*, ed. Kevin Korb, Marcus Randall, and Tim Hendtlass (Berlin / Heidelberg, Germany: Springer-Verlag, 2009), 44. See also Daniel B. Neill, "Optimality under Noise: Higher Memory Strategies for the Alternating Prisoner's Dilemma," *Journal of Theoretical Biology*, Volume 211, No. 2 (Amsterdam: Elsevier, 19 April 2001), 159–80, doi:10.1006/jtbi.2001.2337; and Michael Doebeli and Christoph Hauert, "Models of Cooperation Based on the Prisoner's Dilemma and the Snowdrift Game," *Ecology Letters*, Volume 8, No. 7 (Oxford: Blackwell Publishing, 1 June 2005), 748–66, doi: 10.1111/j.1461-0248.2005.00773.x. But for a contrary view, see Carlos Gracia-Lázaro, et al., "Heterogeneous Networks Do Not Promote Cooperation When Humans Play a Prisoner's Dilemma," *Proceedings of the National Academy of Sciences*, Volume 109, No. 32 (Washington, D.C.: the United States National Academy of Sciences, 7 August 2012), 12922–26; doi:10.1073/pnas.1206681109.

29. Socrates, replying to Polus: "[As to whether I] would rather suffer than do injustice[, …] if I have to choose between them, I'd rather suffer than do." Plato, *Gorgias*, trans. Benjamin Jowett (Millis, Massachusetts: Agora Publications, 1994 [ca. 405 BCE]), 34.

30. "Moral evil is caused by human beings, whereas natural evil exists independently of human actions[; … in this context, a] theodicy is an attempt to justify God in the face of evil [… and in particular,] Augustine's theodicy [states the following:] Angels and humans brought moral evil into the world through abuse of free will[, … while n]atural evil results from the breakdown of the natural order following moral evil." Anne Jordan, Neil Lockyer, and Edwin Tate, *Philosophy of Religion* (Cheltenham, England: Stanley Thornes Publishers, 1999), 214. "Augustine, first of all, only refers to moral evil, whilst denying the existence of natural evil (Jolivet 1936, 63–72), and, second, he makes the human ability to perform the good to depend upon divine grace, thus making God responsible for the existence of moral evil." Paul Vermeer, *Learning Theodicy: The Problem of Evil and the Praxis of Religious Education*

(Leiden, Netherlands: Koninklijke Brill, 1999), 65. "[D]rawn in large measure from Pauline texts in the New Testament and the dominant context of neo-Platonism[,] Augustine's theodicy [… states that] both moral and natural evil are ultimately the result of free rational beings who sin: they willfully turn from God as the highest good toward a lesser good." Robert John Russell, "The Groaning of Creation," *The Evolution of Evil*, ed. Gaymon Bennett, et al. (Göttingen, Germany: Vandenhoeck and Ruprecht, 2008), 126.

31. "[I]f it is not the case that 'good' denotes something simple and indefinable[, … then] either it is [… disputably] complex […] or else it means nothing at all[; …] 'Good,' then, is indefinable [… and few] ethical writer[s … have] clearly recognised and stated this fact." G. E. Moore, *Principia Ethica*, ed. Thomas Baldwin (Cambridge: Cambridge University Press, 1993 [1903]), 66 and 68; Chapter 1, sections 13–14.

32. "There is the expectation or fear of failure and possibly rejection[, … whose effects via t]hese threatening consequences [serve to] inhibit venturesome behavior and result in cautiousness." Jack Botwinick, *Aging and Behavior* (New York: Springer Science+Business Media, 1984), 166; chapter 10, doi:10.1007/978-3-662-38517-3_10. And "[f]or individuals with healthy amygdala functioning and intact fear conditioning [i.e., non-psychopaths], caution and anticipatory fear serve to deter antisocial conduct." Matt DeLisi, *Psychopathy as Unified Theory of Crime* (Cham, Switzerland: Palgrave Macmillan [Springer Nature], 2016), 41.

33. "Language evolved to solve the crisis that began when our species acquired social learning[, … and it does so] by being the conduit that carries the information our species needs to reach agreements and share ideas[; … o]ur social complexity depends on language: without it we might still be living like the Neanderthals." Mark Pagel, *Wired for Culture: Origins of the Human Social Mind* (New York: W. W. Norton and Company, 2012), 277.

34. William L. Rowe, *William L. Rowe on Philosophy of Religion: Selected Writings*, ed. Nick Trakakis (Burlington, Vermont: Ashgate Publishing, 2007 [1979]), 61 et seq.

35. Ibid., 163 et seq. Cf. William L. Rowe, "The Problem of Evil and Some Varieties of Atheism," *American Philosophical Quarterly*, Volume 16, No. 4 (Champaign, Illinois: University of Illinois Press, October 1979), 335–41.

36. See Stephen J. Wykstra, "The Humean Obstacle to Evidential Arguments from Suffering: On Avoiding the Evils of 'Appearance,'" *International Journal for Philosophy of Religion*, Volume 16, No. 2 (The Hague/Kluwer: Martinus Nijhoff [Springer Netherlands], January 1984), 73–93, doi:10.1007/ BF00136567; William Alston, "The Inductive Argument from Evil and

the Human Cognitive Condition," *Philosophical Perspectives*, Volume 5 (Atascadero, California: Ridgeview Publishing Company, 1991), 29–67, doi:10.2307/2214090; Kirk Durston, "The Consequential Complexity of History and Gratuitous Evil," *Religious Studies*, Volume 36, No. 1 (Cambridge: Cambridge University Press, March 2000), 65–80, doi:10.1017/S0034412599005089; Michael Bergmann, "Skeptical Theism and Rowe's New Evidential Argument from Evil," *Nous*, Volume 35, No. 1 (Hoboken, New Jersey: [Wiley-]Blackwell Publishing, June 2001), 278–96, doi:10.1111/0029-4624.00297; and Justin P. McBrayer, "Skeptical Theism," *Philosophy Compass*, Volume 5, No. 7 (Hoboken, New Jersey: [Wiley-]Blackwell Publishing, 27 June 2010), 611–23, doi:10.1111/j.1747-9991.2010.00306.x.

37. "Be thou chaste as ice, as pure as snow, thou shalt not escape calumny." *Hamlet*, 3.1.147–48.

38. "[S]in […] is any feeling or thought or speech or action that comes from a heart that does not treasure God over all other things." John Piper, *Living in the Light: Money, Sex and Power* (Epsom, England: The Good Book Company, 2016), 24.

39. Eve Garrard, "The Nature of Evil," *Philosophical Explorations*, Volume 1, No. 1 (Assen, Netherlands: Van Gorcum, 1998), 43–60; doi:10.1080/10001998018538689.

40. "Epicurus's old questions [about God and evil] are yet unanswered. Is [H]e willing to prevent evil, but not able? then [H]e is impotent. Is [H]e able, but not willing? then [H]e is malevolent. Is [H]e both willing and able? whence then evil?" David Hume, "Dialogues concerning Natural Religion," *The Philosophical Works of David Hume [… containing] 'Dialogues concerning Natural Religion'* (London: G. Fenton, 1824 [1779]), 78; Part 10, dialog by Philo character, referencing a 300 BCE fragment from Epicurus. "'If,' saith he, 'there be a God, from whence proceed so many evils? And if there be no God, from whence cometh any good?'" Anicius Manlius Severinus Boethius, *The Theological Tractates: The Consolation of Philosophy*, trans. H. F. Stewart based on an earlier 1690 translation by I. T. (London: William Heinemann, 1918 [ca. 524]), 151. "The entire problem of evil may be thought of as part of the problem of the hiddenness of God, since the presence of evil in the world is a fact that makes for the hiddenness of God[; … in fact, i]f you consider any aspect of the world or of our human circumstances that seems difficult to reconcile with the existence of a deity who is omnipotent, omniscient, and benevolent, to be part of the problem of evil, then the hiddenness of God is part of the problem of evil." Robert McKim, *Religious Ambiguity and Religious Diversity* (New York: Oxford University Press, 2001), 6. "The problem of vindicating an omnipotent and omniscient God in the face of evil (this is

traditionally called the problem of theodicy) is insurmountable." Sam Harris, *The End of Faith: Religion, Terror, and the Future of Reason* (New York: W. W. Norton and Company, 2004), 173. "[To say that] evil doesn't exist in the world [… is] clearly the three-monkey argument about 'hear no evil …' and has been described […] as a gratuitous insult to mankind, a symptom of insensitivity and indifference to human suffering." Christopher Hitchens, *The Portable Atheist: Essential Readings for the Nonbeliever* (Boston: Da Capo Press [Perseus Books Group], 2007), 236. From the perspective of another religion, "[t]he Buddhist is under no compunction to deny or explain away the fact of evil[: … E]vil is real for the Buddhist and must be removed as far as possible at all levels of existence for the good and happiness of mankind." K. N. Jayatilleke, "The Buddhist Conception of Evil," *Facets of Buddhist Thought: Collected Essays* (Kandy, Sri Lanka: Buddhist Publication Society, 2009 [1974]), 207; posthumously from an essay by the author (Jayatilleke) in *The Message of the Buddha* (Boston: George Allen and Unwin, 1975), 252–53. "The strategies that deny the genuineness of evil avoid the problem without solving it." Mustafa Ruzgar, "An Islamic Perspective: Theological Development and the Problem of Evil," *Religions in the Making: Whitehead and the Wisdom Traditions of the World*, ed. John B. Cobb Jr. (Eugene, Oregon: Cascade Books [Wipf and Stock Publishers], 2012), 78. A theodicy that says "'God is omnipotent […] but does not] prevent all instances of evil […] because the evil actions of others are ingredients in the ultimate good' is free of any logical contradiction between 'God exists' and 'evil exists' [… simply] because it denies there is any *genuine* evil [… as opposed to] 'only apparent evil.'" David Ray Griffin, *Evil Revisited: Responses and Reconsiderations* (Albany, New York: State University of New York Press, 1991), 79, emphasis in the original; initial quote to which Griffin is responding he attributes to Nelson Pike.

41. "[T]he Free Will Defence and the problem of evil […] insists on the possibility that it is not within God's power to create a world containing moral good without creating one containing moral evil[; … Leibniz's Lapse thus falsely contends] that God, if omnipotent, could have actualized just any world [H]e pleased." Alvin Plantinga, *The Nature of Necessity* (Oxford: Clarendon Press [Oxford University Press], 1974), 184. "[Swinburne] claims that we cannot be genuinely free if God knows the future [… and] knowing the future of free human beings would be a logical impossibility." Atle Ottesen Søvik, *The Problem of Evil and the Power of God* (Leiden, Netherlands: Brill, 2011), 28; referring to Richard Swinburne, *Providence and the Problem of Evil* (Oxford: Clarendon Press [Oxford University Press], 1998). "A world containing free moral agents that misuse their freedom to do evil is a possibility that would make consistent God's perfection and evil existing[; … an advocate of such] a free will theodicy […] would try to show that free will

actually does provide an adequate reason why God does permit evil." Robert Arp and Benjamin W. McCraw, "(Editors') Introduction" for *The Problem of Evil: New Philosophical Directions* (Lanham, Maryland: Lexington Books [Rowman and Littlefield], 2016), 12. "Those who claim to have surmounted [... the insurmountable problem of theodicy] by recourse to notions of free will and other incoherencies, have merely heaped bad philosophy onto bad ethics." Harris, *End of Faith*, 173.

42. William Steig (1907–2003), best known as the author of the childrens' book *Shrek!*, in a never-published submission (his first) to *The New Yorker* magazine: a drawing of a man crouched in a box, captioned "People are no damn good." Sebastian Smee, "'Love and Laughter,' between the Lines," *The Boston Globe* (Boston: Globe Newspaper Company, 4 July 2010) at **http://archive.boston.com/ae/theater_arts/articles/2010/07/04/love_and_laughter_between_the_lines/?page=2**, accessed April 3, 2019. A copy of the image can be viewed on *LiveJournal.com* (Moscow: Rambler Media Group, 2 April 2015) at **https://pics.livejournal.com/larvatus/pic/003bkre7/s640x480**, or commercially on *Art.com* (Emeryville, California: Art.com, Inc., 2006) at **https://www.art.com/products/p20067223343-sa-i7243089/william-steig-people-are-no-damn-good-cartoon.htm**, both also accessed April 3, 2019.

43. Plato, *Gorgias and Timaeus*, trans. B. Jowett (Mineola, New York: Dover Publications, 2003 [1892; dialogues ca. 405 BCE and 360 BCE, respectively]), 198.

44. "[P]hilosophers, therefore, thought concerning the supreme God, that He [as the 'creative force'] is both the maker of all created things, the light by which things are known, and the good in reference to which things are to be done[; ... and] these philosophers may be more suitably called Platonists." Saint Augustine (of Hippo), *The Works of Aurelius Augustine: The City of God*, ed. and trans. Marcus Dods (Edinburgh: T. and T. Clark, 1871 [ca. 426]), 318–19; Book 8, Chapter 9.

45. Or per another translation, "There is therefore only a single categorical imperative, and it is this: *act only according to that maxim through which you can at the same time will that it become a universal law.*" Immanuel Kant, *Groundwork of the Metaphysics of Morals*, trans. Mary Gregor (1996), rev. Jens Timmerman (Cambridge: Cambridge University Press, 2011 [1785]), 71; emphasis in the original. "For all rational beings stand under the law that each of them is to treat itself and all others never merely as a means, but always at the same time as an end in itself." Ibid., 95.

46. "If (as utilitarians assert) there is nothing that is good in and of itself, then there is no external standard by which to validate any of our subjective valuations[; ... as a consequence, any] regime of shared responsibilities is

outcome-oriented [… and] does not let an agent off the hook until he has actually accomplished the prescribed ends, through some judicious [and likely subjective] choice among permissible means." Robert E. Goodin, *Utilitarianism as a Public Philosophy* (Cambridge: Cambridge University Press, 1995), 11 and 313. And "subjective criteria are *outcome-oriented.*" Yvonne Denier, *Efficiency, Justice and Care: Philosophical Reflections on Scarcity in Health Care* (Dordrecht, Netherlands: Springer, 2007), 62; emphasis in the original.

47. "[T]he three articles of moral faith, *God, freedom of the human will, and a moral world,* are the only articles in which it is permissible for us to transport ourselves in thought beyond all experience and out of the sensible world." Immanuel Kant, "God as Cause of the World," *Lectures on Philosophical Theology,* trans. Allen W. Wood and Gertrude M. Clark (Ithaca, New York: Cornel University Press, 1978 [1772–89]), 131. "Kant could not see how forms of intuition or categories grounded in the knowing subject could yield *a priori* cognition of items beyond sensory experience, such as God [or] the human soul." Gary Hatfield, et al., "Translator's Introduction" for *Theoretical Philosophy after 1781,* ed. Henry Allison and Peter Heath (Cambridge: Cambridge University Press, 2002), 31. "The final aim to which the speculation of reason as used transcendentally is ultimately directed concerns three objects: the freedom of the will, the immortality of the soul, and the existence of God[; … w]ith regard to all three the merely speculative interest of reason is only very slight." Immanuel Kant, *Critique of Pure Reason,* trans. Werner S. Pluhar (Indianapolis, Indiana: Hackett Publishing, 1966 [1781/1787]), 730; A798/B826.

48. "[T]he debt to strands of Lutheran piety can be detected in later works such as *Religion within the Boundaries of Mere Reason* and in Kant's later emphasis upon morality as the route to religious belief." Christopher J. Insole, *The Intolerable God: Kant's Theological Journey* (Grand Rapids, Michigan: William B. Eerdmans Publishing, 2016), 14. "Though Kant was raised by parents who were Pietistic Christians, he reacted strongly against any suggestion that religious experiences were helpful or even possible." Keith Ward, *Religion in the Modern World* (Cambridge: Cambridge University Press, 2019), 80. "Religion, therefore, is fueled by Kant's Lutheran upbringing, as many of Kant's critics have argued." Chris L. Firestone and Nathan Jacobs, *In Defense of Kant's Religion* (Bloomington, Indiana: Indiana University Press, 2008), 72. "We are required by reason to become morally perfect, but Kant (perhaps reflecting his Lutheran upbringing) holds that no human can achieve that goal in a finite lifetime." C. Stephen Evans, *A History of Western Philosophy: From the Pre-Socratics to Postmodernism* (Downers Grove, Illinois: IVP Academic [InterVarsity Press], 2018), 438. "[As for the] difficulties [that] are deeply

embedded in some versions of the Christian tradition[, ...] Kant simply makes them acute by giving them an explicit philosophical formulation." John Hare, "The Place of Kant's Theism in his Moral Philosophy," *Kant on Practical Justification: Interpretive Essays*, ed. Mark Timmons and Sorin Baiasu (New York: Oxford University Press, 2013), 316. But "Kant found something like that notion [of a tyrannical or egoistic deity] in the Pietistic faith of his parents and in his early education, and he rejected it vehemently." Keith Ward, *Morality, Autonomy, and God* (London: OneWorld Publications, 2013), 134. "Both (the slumber of imaginary conviction and this skepticism or dogmatism) are the death of a sound philosophy, although the 'slumber' might at least still be called pure reason's euthanasia." Kant, *Critique of Pure Reason*, 443; A407/B434.

49. Re the Thirteenth Amendment: Claudine L. Ferrell, "Fourteenth Amendment (1868)," *Reconstruction: A Historical Encyclopedia of the American Mosaic*, ed. Richard Zuczek (Santa Barbara, California: ABC-CLIO, 2016), 124–25. Re the Nineteenth Amendment: Eric Lane and Michael Oreskes, *The Genius of America: How the Constitution Saved Our Country— and Why It Can Again* (New York: Bloomsbury USA, 2007), 142; and Michael Anthony Lawrence, *Radicals in their Own Time: Four Hundred Years of Struggle for Liberty and Equal Justice in America* (New York: Cambridge University Press, 2011), 179.

50. "History and Etymology for sentient: Latin *sentient-*, *sentiens*, present participle of sentire to perceive, feel." *The Merriam-Webster.com Dictionary*, s.v. "sentient (*adj.*)" (Springfield, Massachusetts: Encyclopædia Britannica, Inc., ca. 22 April 2009) at **https://www.merriam-webster.com/dictionary/ sentient**, accessed January 8, 2020.

51. "Sentience is the capacity to perceive or feel things[, ... and as it] refers to the response of the central nervous system to activation of the peripheral sensory system[,] is sometimes termed 'phenomenal consciousness and awareness of (the quality of) sensory input[,' ... inasmuch as t]he mainstream view in Western society is that at least vertebrate animals are sentient." *The Encyclopedia of Applied Animal Behaviour and Welfare*, ed. D. S. Mills, et al. (Wallingford, England: Centre for Agriculture and Bioscience International [The Association of International Research and Development Centers for Agriculture], 2010), 540; the "Sentience" entry. Furthermore, "[s]entience and consciousness usually coexist, but [... perhaps mistakenly,] are often regarded as interchangeable." Peter McCullagh, *Conscious in a Vegetative State? A Critique of the PVS Concept* (Dordrecht, Netherlands: Kluwer Academic Publishers [Springer Science+Business Media], 2004), 85. And "[t]here is general agreement among neuro-scientists that consciousness arises on the

basis of sentience." Errol E. Harris, *Reflections on the Problem of Consciousness* (Dordrecht, Netherlands: Springer, 2006), 111.

52. The sentiment has entered the popular culture with such sayings as "No food with a face" from "The One with Two Parts: Part 2," Season 1, Episode 17, *Friends*, dir. Michael Lembeck; transcript available on *Tripod.com* (Waltham, Massachusetts: Lycos [Carnegie Mellon University], ca. 8 November 2002) at **http://uncutfriendsepisodes.tripod.com/season1/117uncut.htm**, accessed January 8, 2020; originally broadcast for television by NBC (New York: the National Broadcasting Company [then owned by GE, or the General Electric Company], 23 February 1995). And, other sayings like "[M]eat[: … I]t's murder" from "The One with the Fake Party," Season 4, Episode 16, *Friends*, dir. Michael Lembeck; transcript available on *Tripod.com* (ca. 9 May 2006) at **http://uncutfriendsepisodes.tripod.com/season4/416uncut.htm**, also accessed January 8, 2020; originally broadcast for television by NBC on March 19, 1998.

53. Steve Wells, "Cruelty and Violence in the Bible," *SkepticsAnnotatedBible.com* (Moscow, Idaho: SAB Books, 10 May 2004) at **http://skepticsannotatedbible. com/cruelty/long.html**, accessed June 4, 2019.

54. World Water Assessment Programme, "Water for People, Water for Life," *World Water Development Report* (Paris: the United Nations Educational, Scientific and Cultural Organization [UNESCO], 2003); cited as "(World) water uses … Agricultural use 70%" in "Facts and Trends: Water," version 2 (Geneva, Switzerland: World Business Council for Sustainable Development, 25 Aug 2005), 5; it should be noted that the agricultural use is only 30% among "[h]igh-income countries" but 82% among "[l]ow-and middle income countries" in the same report. More recently, it has been identified that "[a] griculture is the largest consumer of freshwater by far and accounts for 70% of freshwater withdrawals from rivers, lakes and aquifers—up to more than 90% in some developing countries." World Water Assessment Programme, "Facts and Figures: Agriculture Is the Largest Consumer of Freshwater" (Paris: the United Nations Educational, Scientific and Cultural Organization [UNESCO], 16 July 2013) at **https://web.archive.org/web/20220401211133/http://www. unesco.org/new/en/natural-sciences/environment/water/wwap/facts-and-figures/all-facts-wwdr3/fact2-agricultural-use**, accessed June 17, 2022.

55. "[T]he most widespread anthropocentric consequences of the contemporary industrialized animal husbandry paradigm is the significant set of contributions made by APIs [animal processing industries] to global climate change[, … raising] global-level concerns about land degradation and deforestation, air and water pollution, and subsequent biodiversity instability." A. G. Holdier, "Speciesistic Veganism: An Anthropocentric Argument," *Critical Perspectives on*

Veganism, ed. Jodey Castricano and Rasmus R. Simonsen (Cham, Switzerland: Palgrave Macmillan [Springer Nature], 2016), 52. "Total emissions from global livestock: 7.1 Gigatonnes of Co2-equiv per year, representing 14.5 percent of all anthropogenic GHG [greenhouse gas] emissions." The Food and Agriculture Organization, "Major Cuts of Greenhouse Gas Emissions from Livestock Within Reach" (Rome: the United Nations, 26 September 2013) at **http:// www.fao.org/news/story/en/item/197623/icode/**, accessed February 18, 2020. See also "Veggie-Based Diets Could Save 8 Million Lives by 2050 and Cut Global Warming," *University of Oxford News and Events* (Oxford: University of Oxford, 22 March 2016) at **http://www.ox.ac.uk/news/2016-03-22-veggie-based-diets-could-save-8-million-lives-2050-and-cut-global-warming**, also accessed February 18, 2020. And Marco Springmann, et al., "Analysis and Valuation of the Health and Climate Change Cobenefits of Dietary Change," *Proceedings of the National Academy of Sciences*, Volume 113, No. 15 (Washington, D.C.: the United States National Academy of Sciences, 12 April 2016), 4146–51; doi:10.1073/pnas.1523119113. For a contrary view involving the advocacy of sustainable farming practices, see Simon Fairlie, *Meat: A Benign Extravagance* (White River Junction, Vermont: Chelsea Green Publishing, 2010). Furthermore, had everyone been vegan in 2019, there would not have been a so-called "wet," live-animal market in Wuhan, China, where some poor bat, raised for human consumption, ended up zoonotically launching the CoViD-19 global pandemic.

Chapter 14: The Purpose of Life

1. Sometimes misattributed to Mark Twain, but a quotation of Sarah Frances Brown, cited by her son, in H. Jackson Brown Jr., *P.S. I Love You* (Nashville, Tennessee: Rutledge Hill Press, 1990), 13.

2. Eleanor Roosevelt, *You Learn by Living: Eleven Keys for a More Fulfilling Life* (New York: HarperCollins, 1960), Foreword.

3. Ivan Goncharov, *Oblomov*, trans. Marian Schwartz (New York: Seven Stories Press, 2008 [1859]), 254.

4. Sartre's primary Existentialist thesis can be expressed as follows: "Existence is inherently meaningless and pointless but brutally and oppressively present[; … it] is contingent[, … as t]here might as easily have been nothing as something and, in particular, one's own existence is inherently meaningless and contingent." *Jean-Paul Sartre: Basic Writings*, ed. Stephen Priest (London and New York: Routledge [Taylor and Francis], 2002), 24; referencing such translations as Jean-Paul Sartre, *Nausea*, trans. Lloyd Alexander (New York: New Directions Publishing, 1964 [1938]). Cf. Albert

Camus, *The Stranger*, trans. Matthew Ward (New York: Vintage International [Random House], 1989 [1942]).

5. Albert Camus, *The Myth of Sisyphus and Other Essays* (New York: Alfred A. Knopf [Random House], 1955 [1942]).

6. "[T]he purpose of our life is to be happy." Dalai Lama XIV Bstan-'dzin-rgya-mtsho, *Mind in Comfort and Ease: The Vision of Enlightenment in the Great Perfection*, trans. Matthieu Ricard, Richard Barron, and Adam Pearcey, ed. Patrick Gaffney (Boston: Wisdom Publications, 2007), 193. Cf. Todd B. Kashdan, Robert Biswas-Diener, and Laura A. King, "Reconsidering Happiness: the Costs of Distinguishing Between Hedonics and Eudaimonia," *The Journal of Positive Psychology* Volume 3, No. 4 (London: Routledge [Taylor and Francis], 2008), 219–33; doi:10.1080/17439760802303044.

7. "We think Earth formed as a solid object about 4.5 billion years ago[, … while c]arbon-isotope evidence suggests that life in a primitive form has evolved about 3.85 billion years ago, and the fossil record suggests life was abundant 3.5 billion years ago." Peter Coles, *From Cosmos to Chaos: The Science of Unpredictability* (New York: Oxford University Press, 2006), 184. "Although the Earth formed some 4.56 billion years ago, […] it was effectively uninhabitable [… until after at least another 760 million years, when] the late heavy bombardment and its planet-sterilizing impacts came to an end." Kevin W. Plaxco and Michael Gross, *Astrobiology: A Brief Introduction* (Baltimore, Maryland: Johns Hopkins University Press, 2011), 174.

8. Tal Kachman, Jeremy A. Owen, and Jeremy L. England, "Self-Organized Resonance during Search of a Diverse Chemical Space," *Physical Review Letters*, Volume 119, No. 3 (New York: American Physical Society, July 2017), 38001–5; doi:10.1103/PhysRevLett.119.038001.

9. Jordan M. Horowitz and Jeremy L. England, "Spontaneous Fine-Tuning to Environment in Many-Species Chemical Reaction Networks," *Proceedings of the National Academy of Sciences*, Volume 114, No. 29 (Washington, D.C.: the United States National Academy of Sciences, July 2017), 7565–70; doi:10.1073/pnas.1700617114. For more efficient absorption and emission of energy, atoms will rearrange themselves in a "thermodynamic mechanism for far-from-equilibrium self-organization." Kachman, et al., "Self-Organized Resonance." Thus, "physics guarantees that atoms rearrange themselves to be able to deal with the chaotic flow of energy[, … and t]hese atomic structures just happen to resemble what we refer to as 'life.'" Robin Andrews, "Life Is Inevitable Consequence of Physics, according to New Research" *IFLScience. com* (London: Elise Andrew, 31 July 2017) at **https://www.iflscience. com/physics/life-inevitable-consequence-physics/all/**, accessed June 3, 2019. Furthermore, experimental "results provide a chemical connection

between RNA and DNA in a prebiotic context." Jianfeng Xu, et al., "Prebiotic Phosphorylation of 2-Thiouridine Provides either Nucleotides or DNA Building Blocks via Photoreduction," *Nature Chemistry*, Volume 11, No. 5 (New York: Nature Research [Springer Nature], May 2019), 457–62; doi:10.1038/s41557-019-0225-x.

10. "[T]he Milky Way is scheduled to experience a galactic collision—and lose its separate identity—in the relatively near future[, … as t]he neighboring Andromeda galaxy, also known as M31, is presently directed on a collision course with the Milky Way." Fred C. Adams and Greg Laughlin, *The Five Ages of the Universe: Inside the Physics of Eternity* (New York: Touchstone [Simon and Schuster], 1999), 84. Cf. John Dubinski, "The Great Milky Way Andromeda Collision," *Sky and Telescope*, Volume 112, No. 4 (Cambridge, Massachusetts: Sky Publishing [New Track Media], October 2006), 30–36; and T. J. Cox and Abraham Loeb, "The Collision between the Milky Way and Andromeda," *Monthly Notices of the Royal Astronomical Society*, Volume 386, No. 1 (Oxford: Oxford University Press, May 2008), 461–74, doi:10.1111/j.1365-2966.2008.13048.x. As for the death of our sun, "[i]n about five billion years, the Sun will expand to the orbit of Venus […] for several hundred million years[, … and a]fter that, the Sun will expand again[, … but t]his time, it will engulf the Earth and its surface will approach the orbit of Mars." Sun Kwok, *Stardust: The Cosmic Seeds of Life* (Berlin / Heidelberg, Germany: Springer-Verlag [Springer Science+Business Media], 2013), 63. Cf. I. Juliana Sackmann, Arnold I. Boothroyd, and Kathleen E. Kraemer, "Our Sun. III. Present and Future," *The Astrophysical Journal*, Volume 418 (Philadelphia, Pennsylvania: IOP Publishing [Institute of Physics], November 1993), 457; doi:10.1086/173407.

11. "[A] supernova has to be within 10 parsecs (30 light years) or so to be dangerous to life on Earth […] because the atmosphere shields us from most dangerous radiations[; … fortunately, n]o stars currently within 20 parsecs will go supernova within the next few million years." Koji Mukai and Eric Christian, "Answer to: Could the Earth be Destroyed by a Nearby Supernova?" on *Ask an Astrophysicist* (Greenbelt, Maryland: NASA's Goddard Space Flight Center, in response to a question submitted 21 May 1998) at **https://imagine.gsfc.nasa.gov/ask_astro/snr.html**, accessed May 7, 2020; citing Michael Richmond, "Will a Nearby Supernova Endanger Life on Earth?" on *RIT.edu* (Rochester, New York: Rochester Institute of Technology, revised 5 December 2009) at **http://spiff.rit.edu/richmond/answers/snrisks.txt** [originally, **http://stupendous.rit.edu/richmond/answers/snrisks.txt**]. Also, the European Southern Observatory (ESO) has recently discovered a black hole in the HR 6819 system (*aka* HD 167128 or QV Telescopii in the constellation Telescopium) just 1,000 light years from Earth. Thomas

Rivinius, et al., "A Naked-Eye Triple System with a Nonaccreting Black Hole in the Inner Binary," *Astronomy and Astrophysics*, Volume 637, No. L3 (Les Ulis, France: EDP Sciences [Édition Diffusion Presse Sciences], May 2020); doi:10.1051/0004-6361/202038020.

12. "[W]e shouldn't be surprised that earth fits life because, in fact, life has adapted to fit earth." David Waltham, *Lucky Planet: Why Earth is Exceptional—and What That Means for Life in the Universe* (New York: Basic Books, 2014), 162–63.

13. George B. Berkeley, *Three Dialogues between Hylas and Philonous*, ed. Michael B. Mathias (New York: Routledge, 2016 [1714]), 114–15.

14. George Berkeley, *A Treatise Concerning the Principles of Human Knowledge*, ed. Charles Porterfield Krauth (Philadelphia, Pennsylvania: J. B. Lippincott and Company, 1874 [1710]), 195.

About the Author

Sherman O'Brien earned a bachelor's degree in Philosophy at age seventeen from the University of California. He spent most of his life in Santa Monica, California and is now retired after a career in the fields of computers and education. Visit http://www.ShermanOBrien.com for more information.

Index

Euler's number (or identity)
131
Eve, serpent speaks directly
to (see: Adam and Eve)
Everett interpretation [see:
quantum (mechanics)
– many-worlds
interpretation of]
evil, banality of (see: Arendt,
Hannah)
existence exists (axiom) 15,
32, 41–43, 106–7, 116
existentialism 266

F

fallacy of…
composition 36, 61
division 164
part-to-whole 258
post hoc ergo propter hoc
40
the "stolen concept" 17
falsifiability 26, 80, 106, 126–
28, 144
faster than the speed of light
24
fecundity, principle of 63, 107
Fermat's Last Theorem 155
Fermi, Enrico (Fermi
paradox) 169
fermions 25, 42, 58, 68
Fibonacci spirals (see:
fractals)
fine-tuned universe 39–40,
117

Fitch, Frederic (1908–87)
[knowability, paradox
of] 49
Flood, the (biblical) 79, 153
fMRI 165, 212, 214
Fogelin, Robert 146
forgiveness 233–35, 239, 255,
280
four-dimensional 59, 133
fractals 132
free lunch hypothesis 37
Fregoli syndrome 135–36
Freud, Sigmund 167
frontal lobe 52, 196
frozen universe (see:
McTaggart, John – …)
fundamentalism 229
fusiform gyrus 135
futurity [see: McTaggart,
John – A-series (of
time)]

G

galaxies 38, 42, 64, 72, 77, 92,
94, 119, 154, 166, 181,
203–4, 220, 269, 281
Andromeda 269, 281
Milky Way, the 72, 94, 269,
281
Galilei, Galileo 101, 156
Garden of Eden, the 230, 242,
255
genetic mutation 53, 111
Gerhardt, Paul 248
Gervais, Ricky 151
Gettier, Edmund 146

J

James, William 158, 159, 187
Jeans, James 77
Je pense, donc je suis (see: *cogito, ergo sum*)
Jesus (Christ) 155, 160, 189, 191, 233, 235, 238, 242, 256
John the Baptist 238
Judaism 8, 150, 156, 181
"just there" universe 34, 84
justified true belief (JTB) 145

K

Kaluza-Klein Theory 339n8.6
Kant , Immanuel 13, 15, 26–31, 40, 48, 51, 55, 105, 117, 138, 143, 205, 226, 258–60, 276
  categorical imperative, the 205, 226, 258–59
  categories (of thought), the 27–28, 82
  practical reason 260
  pure reason 30, 260
  thing-in-itself 27, 29–31, 48, 55, 84, 108
  transcendental idealism 28, 48, 272
Kelvin, Lord 198
  Thomson, Sir William 198
knowledge
  acquired 72, 87, 90–91, 209
  analytic 27, 28
  a posteriori 14, 17–18, 28
  a priori 29–30
  as a cure for ignorance 124, 162
  basis for 13–14
  factual 152
  lack of 49, 79
  limitations on 12, 27, 49, 95, 112
  moral 219
  nature of 92, 200, 278
  of good and evil 219, 230, 255
  perfect 227
  revealed 154
  scientific 151
  secular 247
  specific 144, 237
  synthetic 27
Koenraadt, Mathijs 157
Kundera, Milan 95

L

Lake of Fire, the 183
Laplace, Pierre-Simon de 198, 200
  Laplace's demon 198–200
lateral postcentral gyrus 53
lateral sulcus 52
Latin phrases (translated) 3, 16, 31, 36, 40, 98, 156, 260–61, 272
law of non-contradiction (LNC) 21, 22, 51, 68, 77, 104
laws of physics, the 36, 40, 64, 93, 102, 117, 201, 279
laws of thermodynamics 65, 198, 268